797,885 Books

are available to read at

Forgotten Books

www.ForgottenBooks.com

Forgotten Books' App
Available for mobile, tablet & eReader

ISBN 978-1-332-04681-2
PIBN 10275474

This book is a reproduction of an important historical work. Forgotten Books uses state-of-the-art technology to digitally reconstruct the work, preserving the original format whilst repairing imperfections present in the aged copy. In rare cases, an imperfection in the original, such as a blemish or missing page, may be replicated in our edition. We do, however, repair the vast majority of imperfections successfully; any imperfections that remain are intentionally left to preserve the state of such historical works.

Forgotten Books is a registered trademark of FB &c Ltd.
Copyright © 2015 FB &c Ltd.
FB &c Ltd, Dalton House, 60 Windsor Avenue, London, SW19 2RR.
Company number 08720141. Registered in England and Wales.

For support please visit www.forgottenbooks.com

1 MONTH OF FREE READING

at

www.ForgottenBooks.com

By purchasing this book you are eligible for one month membership to ForgottenBooks.com, giving you unlimited access to our entire collection of over 700,000 titles via our web site and mobile apps.

To claim your free month visit:
www.forgottenbooks.com/free275474

* Offer is valid for 45 days from date of purchase. Terms and conditions apply.

English
Français
Deutsche
Italiano
Español
Português

www.forgottenbooks.com

Mythology Photography **Fiction**
Fishing Christianity **Art** Cooking
Essays Buddhism Freemasonry
Medicine **Biology** Music **Ancient Egypt** Evolution Carpentry Physics
Dance Geology **Mathematics** Fitness
Shakespeare **Folklore** Yoga Marketing
Confidence Immortality Biographies
Poetry **Psychology** Witchcraft
Electronics Chemistry History **Law**
Accounting **Philosophy** Anthropology
Alchemy Drama Quantum Mechanics
Atheism Sexual Health **Ancient History**
Entrepreneurship Languages Sport
Paleontology Needlework Islam
Metaphysics Investment Archaeology
Parenting Statistics Criminology
Motivational

A GENEALOGICAL HISTORY

OF THE

FELTON FAMILY;

DESCENDANTS OF

LIEUTENANT NATHANIEL FELTON,

Who came to Salem, Mass., in 1633;

WITH

FEW SUPPLEMENTS AND APPENDICES,

Of the Names of some of the Ancestors of the Families that have Intermarried with them.

AN INDEX

ALPHABETICALLY ARRANGED,

OF THE

FELTON FAMILIES,

ALSO

An Index of other names than Felton.

By CYRUS FELTON,

The Compiler of "A Brief Account of some of the Descendants of Nathaniel and Mary Felton, of Salem, Mass." Published August, 1877.

MARLBOROUGH:
PRATT BROTHERS, PRINTERS AND PUBLISHERS.

Astor, Lenox and Tilden
Foundations.
1896

2838

PREFACE.

A Compiler of a Genealogy sometimes gives a few reasons why he engaged in such an undertaking. Not having as good eyesight as people in general, we participate in but few of the parties for pleasure, but have occupied some of our leisure hours in historical and genealogical researches. We had heard persons remark that they wished for a record of their ancestors, in a continuous line to their first settling in the country. We had a desire for some knowledge of our ancestors, and felt that the information now collected would gratify, not only those now upon the stage but generations yet to come.

Many years ago we commenced to note down facts, such as marriages, deaths, and other items relating to this family, as we found them in newspapers and books.

Some 30 years ago we visited Salem, Marblehead and Danvers, where the Feltons first settled on arriving in America, and where most of the first three generations lived and were buried.

In 1876, being in failing health, we partly gave up farming, and extended our researches to other parts of the state (even to Philadelphia, at the time of the centennial exhibition,) and the next year, 1877, we brought out the Felton Family pamphlet of 19 pages, giving some account of 40 to 50 families that lived before this century. Had 70 copies printed and disposed of them in nine months, and not enough to supply the demand. This new and enlarged edition gives some account of upwards of 300 families, and is brought down nearly to the present time, 1886. CYRUS FELTON.

INTRODUCTION.

NATHANIEL FELTON was the venerable patriarch of the family in Massachusetts, whose descendants are compiled in this genealogy.

Nathaniel Felton came to Salem in 1633, when 17 years of age; he made a voyage to England in 1634, and returned to Salem in 1635; the next year, 1636, had 20 acres given to him.

In 1643, he sold to William Brown Sen., "the Lott southeast of Rev. Mr. Skelton's Lott, with an old house upon it." About 1645, he settled near Felton Hill, Salem, the part afterwards called Danvers,—now Peabody. He said in 1700, he had lived there 55 years. Nathaniel Felton was a juryman in 1655, grand juryman in 1676, 1679 and 1683; a constable in 1657. He was chosen Ensign in 1679, and Lieut. 1681. He became a member of the church in 1648, and his oldest two children were baptized that year.

He was a witness to many wills, deeds, agreements, etc. Rev. Dr. Felt, author of annals of Salem, says, "He was a man of good faith and judgment. He was frequently called to give his testimony about litigated estates." In 1674, he was overseer of the estate of his deceased brother-in-law, John Marsh. In 1676, he was overseer and appraiser of the estate of his brother-in-law, Christopher Waller. In 1684, he was overseer and appraiser of Dr. Zerubbabel Endicott's estate, son of the then Gov. John Endicott.

Nathaniel Felton was overseer of several other estates. Beside those named above, he was an appraiser of the following estates: Rebecca Bacon in 1655; Ann Fuller in 1662; Wm. Cantlebury in 1663; Henry Bullock in 1664; Thos. James in 1666; Ralph Tompkins in 1666; Richard Bishop in 1675; Henry Coleborne in 1676; Isaac Goodale in 1679; Isaac Gould in 1679; John Tompkins Sen. in 1681; Edward Bridges in 1682; Thomas Goldthwaite in 1683; John Bowden in 1683; Edward Beacham in 1684; Thomas Rix in 1685; Wm. Babb in 1691; probably this list is not complete.

At the pretended trial of John Proctor, who was executed in the year of the witchcraft delusion, 1692, Nathaniel Felton and the neighbors living near the bounds of Salem Village presented the following paper, written by Nathaniel Felton the first signer. "We, whose names are underwritten, having several years known John Proctor and his wife, do testify that we never heard or understood that they were ever suspected to be guilty of the crime now charged upon them: and several of us, being their near neighbors, do testify that, to our apprehension, they lived Christian-like in their family, and were ever ready to help such as stood in need of their help."

In the original paper, there were some, perhaps many names cut off by scissors, says C. W. Upham's History of Witchcraft. Below are the twenty names found on the paper.

Nathaniel Felton Sen., and Mary Felton, his wife.
Samuel Marsh, and Priscilla Marsh, his wife.
James Houlton, and Ruth Houlton, his wife.
John Felton, and Nathaniel Felton Jr.
Samuel Frayll, and Ann Frayll, his wife.
Zachariah Marsh, and Mary Marsh, his wife.
Samuel Endicott, and Hannah Endicott, his wife.
Samuel Stone, and George Locker.
Samuel Gaskill, and Revidal Gaskill, his wife.
George Smith, and Edward Gaskill.

Lieut. Nathaniel Felton was a prominent, worthy and highly respected citizen.

His deposition of April 6th, 1705, signed by his own hand, before John Higginson, Justice of the Peace, said he had been in Salem about 72 years. The same time he testified that North River in Salem was called Naumkeag by the Indians; also, concerning the site of the old Indian settlement at Naumkeag.

Nathaniel Felton married Mary Skelton, daughter of Rev. Samuel Skelton, the first minister of Salem, Mass. Mr. Skelton was a preacher in Lincolnshire, England, and being persecuted for his non-conformity, came to this country in June 1629, and was ordained as pastor, with Francis Higginson as teacher, at Salem, Mass., on the sixth of August 1629.

In August 1879, 250 years afterwards, the two hundred and fiftieth anniversary of the First Church in Salem, Mass., the oldest church in America, was celebrated in that ancient town, incorporated, in 1836, a city. Mr. Higginson died the next year after he arrived in America, in August 1630, in the 43d year of his age.

The Colonial authorities granted to Rev. Mr. Skelton, for his sacrifice in leaving Old England, about 200 acres then in Salem, and it was called "Skelton Neck," then New Mills, now Danversport.

Rev. Samuel Skelton's wife died Mar. 15th, 1631, leaving one son and three daughters; two of them were born in England, and two in America. Winthrop's History of Massachusetts, says, Mrs. Skelton "was a goodly and helpful woman; she lived desired and died lamented, and well deserves to be honorably remembered." Rev. Mr. Skelton died three years afterwards, August 2d, 1634.

·Their children were Mary Skelton, who married Nathaniel Felton Sen.; she died May, 8th 1701, aged 75 or more years. They lived husband and wife 56 or more years. Lieut. Nathaniel Felton died 4 years afterwards, July 30th, 1705, aged 90 years.

Susannah Skelton, a daughter of Rev. Mr. Skelton, was the second wife of John Marsh. They had several children. Mr. Marsh's estate was settled in 1674; the widow Susannah Marsh married second, Thomas Rix, whose estate was settled in 1685.

Elizabeth Skelton, another daughter of Mr. Skelton, married Robert Sanford of Boston, where they lived and had several children.

Samuel Skelton Jr., in 1649, supposed then of age, sold his part of "Skelton Neck" to John Porter. A few years afterwards, his three sisters sold their shares, 60 acres, to the same person.

Rev. Mr. Skelton's two immediate successors were famous preachers; Rev. Roger Williams and Rev. Hugh Peters were born in Wales in 1599, and were educated at Oxford, Eng.

The name "Skelton" was preserved in the Felton family, as a Christian name, for several generations.

BENJAMIN FELTON, a brother of Nathaniel, came to America in 1635, when he was 22 years of age. He soon afterwards took the oath of a freeman. In 1636, he had 20 acres of land granted him. In 1637, Benjamin Felton had ten acres south side of Derby's Fort. The following is found on record, dated October 1636: "Whereas Benjamin Felton enioned (enjoined) to send away Robert Scarlett for his misdemeanors etc.; but having hope of amendment he is admitted to stay." Benjamin Felton was called a farmer and turner by trade. He lived in Salem near the meeting-house, and in 1651, was chosen to take care of it. He probably had care of the house many years, for we find in "March 1673, Benjamin Felton was chosen to ring the bell and to take care of the Meeting-house."

In 1659, he purchased a dwelling-house and one quarter of an acre of land in Salem, for £12, of Charles Gott of Wenham, who was agent and attorney for the Rev. and famous Hugh Peters, a former pastor of the Salem Church. He afterwards purchased more land in Salem of the same person.

June 29th 1669, Benjamin Felton was appointed to keep the Salem prison. "He accepted the trust for one year, having as much as Mr. Wilson, the keeper of the Ipswich prison." June 19th, 1676, "Agreed with John Marston to move the prison into Benjamin Felton's Garden." He kept the prison till 1684, when Jeremiah Rogers took charge of it. Mr. Rogers purchased some land of Mr. Felton, near the meeting-house, that Mr. F. bought of Mr. Gott. Benjamin Felton was grand juryman in 1668; he was frequently called upon to witness deeds etc.

Mr. Savage (author of Early Settlers in New England) says Benjamin Felton's wife, Mary Felton, was a sad burden to her husband. He died in 1688 aged about 75 years. March 25th 1689, John Bly received for digging graves for Goodman Felton and others; 1£ and 1 shilling.

Benjamin and Mary Felton's children were:

(1.) JOHN FELTON, baptised Dec. 26th 1639; he lived in Salem, part of the time, up to about 1685. Among the arrivals in Salem in 1680, from Barbadoes, were John Felton and wife, and one child and several servants. When John Felton resided in Salem, his cousin of the same name and about six years younger, was called John Felton Jr. In few cases they were witnesses together. He probably left Salem in 1685.

(2.) EXERCISE FELTON was probably their daughter, and perhaps their oldest child. The following from Roxbury records; "The 22d of 3d month (May) 1659, Exercise Felton, a maid of Salem," was living in that place. In 1661, Joseph Miles was married Mary Whelan; she died in 1663, all of Salem. Joseph Miles married 2d, the 7th of 9th month, (December 7th) 1664, probably 1663, by Major Hathorne, Exercise Felton all of Salem: Children were:

 i. KATHERINE, b. Nov. 5th, 1664.
 ii. MARY, b. April 1st, 1666; probably died young.
 iii. SUSANNAH, b. Oct. 7th, 1667.
 iv. ABIGAIL, b. July 5th, 1669.
 v. MARY, again, b. March 27th, 1671.

(3.) REMEMBER FELTON, bapt. May 28, 1643; m. Oct. 1664, George Samon; he died in Salem, Feb. 12th, 1672. Children:
 i. ELIZABETH.
 ii. MARY, b. March 16, 1668-9.
 iii. SUSANNAH, b. May 30, 1670.
 iv. GEORGE JR. b. March 1st, 1672.

(4.) BENJAMIN FELTON JR. bapt. Feb. 18th, 1645-6; he died in 1668. Probably he married and had one or two children. In 1668, a widow Felton was living in Salem. In 1673 Wm. Lord Sen. of Salem left Mrs. Felton, a widow, a small legacy. His will, dated March 1668, proved in 1673, mentions wife Abigail Lord; gave his property to the children of his kinsmen, Wm. Lord, viz., Wm. Lord, Jr., Abigail Lord, Mrs. Felton, widow Joseph Grafton and Richard Prince. We suppose the Mrs. Felton named was widow of Benjamin Felton Jr., who died in 1668. Probably this widow Felton was living in Salem in 1711, when a deed of land was given, bounded westerly by land of widow Felton. In 1720, Benjamin

Felton served by signing and sealing a deed, as one, or in place of one of the selectmen of Salem, with Jonathan Putnam, James Houlton, Jacob Manning, and J. Barton. We suppose the last named Benjamin Felton was son of the above named widow Felton, and grandson of Benjamin Felton Sen. of Salem.

(5.) NATHANIEL FELTON, baptised in 1648, was son of Benjamin Felton Sen. December 2d, 1714, William Felton of Salem, married Amy Dennis of Marblehead. Probably a descendant of Benjamin Felton Sen. of Salem.

JUDITH FELTON, born in England, a daughter of Nathaniel Felton, says Salem records, married about 1644, John Ingersoll who was born in England about 1625. He was son of Richard Ingersoll, and brother of Dea. Nathaniel Ingersoll of Salem Village. Judith (Felton) Ingersoll was sister to Benjamin and Nathaniel Felton of Salem. John Ingersoll died in Salem in 1683 aged 58 years. His will dated November 20th, 1683, names his son John Jr., executor. Nathaniel Felton, his brother-in-law, appointed overseer, with the widow Judith Ingersoll. Their children were 8 in number.

    i. JOHN JR. b. 12 of 7 month, (Sept.) 1644: m. March 1670, Mary Cooms; had 5 children.
    ii. NATHANIEL, b. 2d of 10 month, (Dec.) 1647; m. in 1670 Mary Preston; had 2 children.
    iii. RUTH b. 20 of 4 month, (June) 1649; m. Richard Ropes, (or Rose); he deceased in 1684; left 2 sons and 2 daughters.
    iv. RICHARD, b. 1st of 7 month, (Sept.) 1651; m. Sarah—; had 1 child.
    v. SARAH, b. 28 of 6 month, (August) 1655; m. David Ropes; had 6 children.
    vi. CAPT. SAMUEL, b. 6 of 8 month, (Oct.) 1658; m. Sarah —; had 5 children; their daughters were: Sarah, Margaret and Susannah Ingersoll. Capt. Samuel Ingersoll died about 1695, and his widow Sarah Ingersoll, became the second wife of Philip English. Mr. English and his first wife were imprisoned in witchcraft times, 1692, but broke out of Boston prison and ran away; but returned soon after the delusion was over, and he was one of the selectmen of Salem in 1700.

John and Judith Ingersoll's children occupied a series of houses on the west side of Daniels street, Salem, leading from Essex street to the harbor. John Ingersoll, sr., was a mariner.

MARGARET FELTON, another sister of Benjamin and Nathaniel Felton, m. Christopher Waller. Her brothers were witnesses to several of Mr. Waller's deeds given between 1660 and 1670.

In 1676, Nathaniel Felton was overseer of Mr. Waller's estate, who left to Joseph Woodrow property when 21 years of age. Mr. Woodrow was taxed in Salem Village (now Danvers), in 1682. Mrs. Margaret Waller married before 1687, Robert Fuller, who was dismissed from Rehoboth church, to Salem first church in 1679. At Salem March 12th, 1691, at a meeting of the committee appointed by the town, for ordering, disposing, and building of seats in the meeting-house, Lieut. Nathaniel Felton, Mr. Robert Fuller, and Jeremiah Meacham, sen., were assigned the seat behind the minister. Mr. Fuller and wife were living in 1697. An agreement was made before marriage, if she survives her husband, her house lot, which was near Nathaniel Felton's, to go to Mary Salmon, supposed Mary Samon, who was born in 1669, a granddaughter of her brother, Benjamin Felton, sen.

MRS. ELEANOR FELTON, the mother of Benjamin, Nathaniel, Judith and Margaret Felton, probably arrived in Salem in 1635. She was a member of the Salem church before 1637. That year she had twenty acres granted her, and as much more in 1639. In 1652, the 28th of the 11th month, " Eleanor Felton sold to William Marston, one dwelling-house and 20 rods of land in Salem, near North River."

The same year, 1652, the town of Salem granted Mrs. Felton and Christopher Waller four acres of meadow north side of Ipswich River. Probably Mrs. Felton's husband, Nathaniel? Felton, had deceased before she came to America.

The name Nathaniel Felton has been quite common in few families. We have counted, including children, 20 Nathaniel Feltons and 8 Nathan Feltons.

Three of Lieut. Nathaniel Felton's great-grandson were named Nathaniel Felton, and each of them had a son Nathaniel, and a grandson Nathaniel Felton. All three of the great-grandson were born in Salem in 1714, 1723 and 1730, and in the part afterwards called Danvers, now Peabody. The one born in 1714, settled at Roxbury, Mass., and lived 92 years, 9 months. The one born in 1723, settled on Felton Hill, now Peabody, Mass. The one born in 1730, moved with his father and brothers to New Salem, Mass.

The descendants of Lt. Nathaniel Felton continued to reside in Salem, that part called Danvers then South Danvers, now, 1885, Peabody, about 100 years after he settled in America. Most of them lived within a square mile, at places called Felton Hill or Mount Pleasant, and at Felton Corner, sometimes called Feltonville. The "Felton School" is in Feltonville, town of Peabody. Between 1709 and 1725 John Felton and Daniel Felton, brothers, sons of Nathaniel Felton, jr., settled at Marblehead. About 1740 a few Felton families moved into the interior and western part of the state, and built for themselves new homes, which were afterwards centres of family interest. Nathaniel Felton, the fourth of Salem, settled in Roxbury. His son, Dea. Joshua Felton, was a prominent man in the place. Jacob Felton settled in Marlborough in 1738, and afterwards his brother, David Felton, and their relative, Archelaus Felton. In 1762 David Felton removed to Petersham.

In 1740 Ebenezer Felton of Salem, a carpenter, or housewright he was called, went into the wilderness to Salem Plantation, afterwards called New Salem, when he was 55 years of age, and was the most prominent person in the place. Deacon Felton was accompanied by his five sons. His eldest son, David Felton, also a housewright, had married a daughter of James Houlton, sen., of Salem. Many of the descendants are scattered over what was old Hampshire County, now Hampshire, Franklin and Hampden Counties, Mass.

In 1745 Skelton Felton and his son Joseph Felton settled in Rutland, Mass., the part afterwards called Oakham. Joseph Felton's son, Capt. Benjamin Felton, who was an officer during the revolutionary war and in several battles, settled in Brookfield, Mass.

The descendants of Lieut. Nathaniel Felton, the New England progenitor and patriarch, are widely scattered in New England, New York, Ohio, and many of the Western States, and few in California.

In regard to health and longevity in the Felton family race, there has been a large number of old people; we have a list of nearly 100 octogenarians, and about as many between 70 and 80 years of age. There are few cases of remarkable longevity. About one dozen Feltons have lived to the age of our first ancestor in this country, 90 years. The oldest person I have found in my researches was living in 1884, then aged 97 years. Mrs. Lydia Felton, widow of George W. Felton, of Petersham, Mass.

---

† Signifies family continues.

FELTON FAMILY.

FIRST GENERATION.

(1.) i. NATHANIEL FELTON, b. about 1615, came from England to Salem, Mass., in 1633, where he lived about 72 years. He married Mary Skelton, daughter of Rev. Samuel Skelton, the first minister of Salem. Mrs. Mary Felton died May 8, 1701, aged about 75 years. He died about 4 years afterwards, July 30, 1705, aged 90 years. His will dated October, 1703, proved May, 1706, mentions sons John and Nathaniel, daughters, Elizabeth, a widow, Ruth and Hannah. Their children were:

    2†. i. JOHN, b. about 1645; m. in 1670 Mary Tompkins.
    3†. ii. RUTH, bapt, Oct. 29, 1648; m. James Houlton, of Salem.
    4. iii. MARY, bapt. April 6, 1651; died young.
    5†. iv. ELIZABETH, b. Mar. 18, 1652; m. Thomas Watkins.
    6. v. NATHANIEL, bapt. Oct. 28, 1654; died young.
    7†. vi. NATHANIEL², b. Aug. 15, 1655; m. Anne Horn.
    8. vii. MARY, b. Jan. 15, 1657; bapt. May 30, 1658.
    9†. viii. HANNAH, bapt. June 20, 1663; m. in 1684, Samuel Endicott.
    10. ix. SUSANNA, bapt. Mar. 29, 1665.

SECOND GENERATION.

2. i. JOHN FELTON² (*Nathaniel¹*), b. about 1645; m. in 1670, Mary Tompkins, bapt. April 29, 1649, daughter of John Tompkins, sen., of Salem. She d. Dec. 12, 1688, aged 40 years. He m. 2d Hannah —— (Appendix A). They lived near Felton Hill, in Salem. He was sometimes called John Felton, jr., when his cousin John Felton resided in Salem. He was called Jr., in 1678, 1681, 1684. He was a constable in 1685 and 1687; grand juryman, and on jury trials in 1693 and 1694; a surveyor of highways 1693 to 1695. June 25, 1713, John Felton, Hannah Felton, with 38 others, were dismissed from the first church in Salem, to form a church in the Middle

Precinct, afterwards called South Danvers, now Peabody. John Felton was called a cooper in 1706. He d. Feb. 19, 1717–18, in his 73d year. His will dated Oct., 1715. proved March, 1718, names three sons and four daughters. Son John, the executor, to have the home place.

   11†.   i. NATHANIEL, b. June 8, 1672; m. Elizabeth Foot.
   12†.   ii. MARY, b. March 31, 1674; m. Freeborn Reeves.
   13.   iii. JOHN, b. March 22, 1676; d. April 6, same year.
   14†.   iv. HANNAH, b. April 18, 1677; m. Arthur Chamnes.
   15†.   v. ELIZABETH, b. Feb. 28, 1678–9; lived 86 years.
   16†.   vi. SAMUEL, b. Jan. 1, 1681–2; m. Sarah Goodale.
   17†.   vii. JOHN, b. Aug. 22, 1686; m. Mary Waters.
   18.   viii. RUTH, b. Sept. 14, 1693, bapt. 1694; was living in 1715.
   19.   ix. SUSANNA, b. Sept. 15, 1696; a school teacher in the Danvers part of Salem in 1742–3; suppose living in 1765.

(3.) ii. JAMES HOULTON, son of Joseph Houlton, of Salem, m. before 1685, Ruth Felton, bapt. Oct., 1648, daughter of Nathaniel Felton, who gave her 10 acres of land in 1684. James Houlton was one of the selectmen of Salem for a num ber of years. In 1708, Mrs. Catharine Dealand kept school in James Houlton's house. A school-house was erected in the Danvers part of Salem a few years afterwards. Mrs. Ruth Houlton died about 1706, aged 58 years. Probably left no children. James Houlton, m. 2d, Nov. 4, 1706, Mrs. Mary Lindsey, a widow with two children; one daughter that afterwards m. John Reas; the son was Ralph Lindsey.

    i. MARY, b Sept. 11, 1707; m. Ebenezer Proctor (No. 35).
    ii. JAMES, jr., b. Jan. 12, 1708–9; m. Hannah ——. He died about 1733, and the widow m. Joseph Cressey of Beverly in March, 1734.
    iii. JOSEPH, b. Jan. 13, 1710–11; m. Rebecca Felton. (No. 75).
    iv. RUTH, b. Jan. 24, 1712–13; m. Samuel Johnson.
    v. SARAH, b. April 10, 1715; m. 1736, David Felton (No. 84).
    vi. JOHN, b. May 7, 1717; sup. d. young. (See Houlton, Appendix B.)

James Houlton died in 1729; his estate settled that year.

5. iv. THOMAS WATKINS, m. in 1678, Elizabeth Felton, b. March 18, 1652; bapt. May 1st, 1653, daughter of Lieut. Nathaniel Felton. She was a widow at the date of her father's will in 1703; Mrs. Watkins d. March, 1730–1, aged 78 years. Her estate settled the next year.

2C. i. THOMAS WATKINS, JR., b. Dec. 15, 1678; sup. d. before his mother.

(7.) vi. NATHANIEL FELTON² (*Nathaniel¹*), b. Aug. 15, 1655; m. Ann Horn, daughter of Dea. John Horn, of Salem. (Appendix C.)

Part, if not all, of Dea. John Horn's descendants took the surname of Orne, by dropping the H. There have been several prominent persons in the Orne family.

Nathaniel Felton, jr., lived near Felton Hill, Salem. He was one of the 8 constables in 1721. He d. about January, 1733-4; aged 78 years. His will dated July 6, 1731, proved Feb., 1733-4; his eldest son, Skelton, executor; mentions wife Ann, sister Elizabeth Watkins, sons Skelton, Jonathan, Ebenezer, John and Daniel; daughters Margaret Sheldon, Sarah Marsh and Mary Felton, who had 40£. The six oldest children were baptized in 1691. Lived husband and wife upwards of 50 years. Perhaps the children not all in this order:

- 21†. i. SKELTON, m. May, 1712; Hepsibah Sheldon.
- 22†. ii. JOHN, m. Jan., 1709, Mary Pitman, of Marblehead.
- 23†. iii. EBENEZER, b. in 1685; m. Mehitable ——, about 1710.
- 24†. iv. JONATHAN, m. Jan., 1718-19, Rebecca Needham.
- 25†. v. DANIEL, b. about Oct., 1687; m. Sarah ——.
- 26. vi. MARGARET, bapt. in 1691; m. —— Sheldon.
- 27. vii. SARAH, m. in 1720, David Marsh.
- 28. viii. MARY, had by will £40.

(9.) viii. SAMUEL ENDICOTT, b. about 1659, son of Dr. Zerubbabel Endicott, and grandson of Gov. John Endicott, who was Governor of Massachusetts Colony 16 years. Samuel Endicott m. in 1684, Hannah Felton, bapt. June 20, 1663, dau. of Nathaniel Felton, sen., of Salem. The Endicott Farm was on Cowhouse River, sometimes called Ipswich River, Endicott River, now Waters River. The farm on the north side now in Danvers. Samuel Endicott d. in 1694, aged 35 years. In September, 1697, Mrs. Endicott was appointed guardian to the three children.

- 29. i. JOHN, b. Oct. 18, 1685; died before his father.
- 30†. ii. SAMUEL, JR., b. Aug. 30, 1687; m. Anne Endicott, his cousin.
- 31†. iii. RUTH, b. 1689; m. 1710, Martin Herrick.
- 32†. iv. HANNAH, b. 1691; m. 1712, Benjamin Porter.

Mrs. Hannah (Felton) Endicott, m. 2d, December, 1697, Thorndike Proctor, b. July 15, 1672, the youngest child by the first wife of John Proctor who was executed for witchcraft in Salem, Aug. 19, 1692. (For Proctor, see Appendix B.)

In 1736, Thorndike Proctor was one "of a committee of four to erect a school in ʸᵉ quarter of ʸᵉ Parish." He d. about 1759, aged 87 years.

- 33†.   v. NATHAN, b. Oct. 18, 1698; m. 1723, Mary Reed.
- 34†.   vi. THORNDIKE, JR., b. June 2, 1700; m. 1720, Abigail Wilson.
- 35†.   vii. EBENEZER, b. Aug. 16, 1702; m. Mary Houlton, dau. of James Houlton, of Salem.
- 36†.   viii. JONATHAN, b. Aug. 2, 1705; m. Desire Jacobs.

THIRD GENERATION.

(11.) i. NATHANIEL FELTON³, the third (*John²*, *Nathaniel¹*), b. June 8, 1672; m. June 29, 1698, Elizabeth Foot, who was b. April, 1675, dau. of Isaac Foot, and sister of Malachi Foot, all of Salem. (See Appendix E.)

Nathaniel Felton³, was a weaver and had his father's loom. Was a tythingman in 1721. He was called Nathaniel Felton tertiary, until his grandfather died in 1705. We suppose he was the first settler on Felton Hill, now in Peabody. He d. about 1732, aged 60 years. His son, Malachi Felton, was appointed administrator. Feb. 26, 1733, guardianship of his two youngest children, viz., Isaac, minor, upwards 14 years, and Samuel, minor, about 13 years, was granted to John Felton. The estate inventoried June 1733.

- 37.   i. ABIGAIL, b. May 12, 1699; bapt. in September; m. Aug. 25, 1737, James Taylor.
- 38.   ii. SAMUEL, b. Aug. 7, 1701; d. Feb. 2, 1717–18, aged 16 years.
- 39†.   iii. MALACHI, b. May 14, 1705; m. Feb., 1735, Abigail Jacobs.
- 40.   iv. MARY, b. Mar. 16, 1707; m. Nov. 20, 1753, Caleb Balch, of Danvers.
- 41.   v. ELIZABETH, b. May 17, 1709; was living in 1765, when her brother Benjamin died.
- 42.   vi. NATHANIEL, JR., b. Dec. 29, 1710; d. April 3, 1712, aged 15 months.
- 43†.   vii. BENJAMIN, b. Sept. 9, 1712; m. Joanna ——.
- 44†.   viii. NATHANIEL, b. May 9, 1714; m. in 1741, Anna Jacobs.
- 45.   ix. ISAAC, b. Mar. 6, 1716; d. Feb. 2, 1717–18, aged 11 months.
- 45½.   x. ISAAC, again, b. in 1719; aged 14 years in 1733; was taxed in Danvers, part of Salem, in 1748
- 46.   xi. SAMUEL, again, b. May 21, 1720; was living in 1733.

(12.) ii. FREEBORN REEVES, b. the 10th day of 5th month (July), 1658, son of Jonathan and Elizabeth Reeves, of Salem; m. November, 1715, Mary Felton, b. March 31, 1674, dau. of John Felton (No. 2). They had one son; Mrs. Mary Reeves was living March, 1721.

47. i. FREEBORN REEVES, JR., his uncle Samuel Felton was his guardian, and in 1733, John Felton took him for 4½ years, sup. till he was of age.

(14.) iv. ARTHUR CHAMNESE, of Marblehead, m. Oct., 1701, Hannah Felton, of Salem, b. April 18, 1677; dau. of John Felton (No. 2). Had one child or more. In December, 25th day, 1722, their dau., Mary Chamnese (No. 48), received of her uncle Samuel Felton, the sum of " £6 in bills of credit."

48. i. MARY CHAMNESE, sup. b. about 1702.

June 20, 1712, Mrs. Hannah Chamnese, m. 2d, William Webber, of Marblehead, and had one son; we sup. Mr. Webber was a merchant. Probably Mrs. Webber deceased before the date of her father's will, Oct., 1715.

49. ii. WILLIAM WEBBER, JR., b. Nov. 18, 1713.

(15.) v. ELIZABETH FELTON, b. Feb. 28, 1678–9; dau. of John Felton (No. 2). Miss Felton d. about 1765, aged 86 years. In April, 1765, her estate settled by Dea. Malachi Felton; the appraisers were John Porter, Nathaniel Felton, Jonathan Proctor and Dea. Malachi Felton; sureties were Samuel Felton and Jonathan Proctor.

(16†.) vi. SAMUEL FELTON^3 ($John^2$, $Nathaniel^1$), b. Jan. 1, 1681–2; m. in 1709, Sarah Goodale, b. about 1685, dau. of Zachariah Goodale, sen., of Salem. (See Goodale, App. F.) Samuel Felton was a weaver by trade, and lived on Felton Hill, in Salem, now in Peabody.

The compiler of this family has seen Samuel Felton's account book; it is 5¼ by 3⅔ inches, and bound with leather, and about ⅜ of an inch thick; about a dozen or more leaves had been cut away; it then contained 64 leaves. In 1703, Samuel Felton was warned to train under Capt. Samuel Brown, of Salem. Mr. Felton died in Danvers, Oct. 5, 1772, aged 90 years, 9 months. His will dated June 10, 1754, then in the new town of Danvers, proved Nov. 2, 1772, mentions wife Sarah, sons Jacob, David, Samuel, Zachariah, his son Stephen's two children, Stephen and Sarah Felton, and three daughters, Sarah Webber, Hannah Howe and Elizabeth Dealand. Samuel and Zachariah, the two executors, had the home place. After Mr. Felton's death in 1772, there were four Felton families living on Felton Hill in Danvers: Samuel and Zachariah named above, Dea. Malachi Felton, their cousin, and Nathaniel Felton, their second cousin.

50†. i. STEPHEN, b. April 19, 1710; m. Dorcas Upton.
51.   ii. AMOS, b. Jan. 7, 1711–12; d. March 13, 1712.
52†. iii. JACOB, b. March 2 (O. S.), 13th (N. S.), 1712–13; m. Sarah Barrett.
53†. iv. SARAH, b. Feb. 2, 1714–15; m. John Webber, of Marblehead.
54†. v. HANNAH, b. Oct. 24, 1716; m. Moses Howe, of Marlborough.
55†. vi. SAMUEL, JR, b. Feb. 17, 1718–19; m. Mary Smith.
56†. vii. DAVID, b. Nov. 6, 1720; m. Zerviah Howe, of Marlborough.
57.   viii. ELIZABETH, b. Aug. 2, 1722; died young.
58†. ix. ELIZABETH, again, b. Nov. 19, 1723; m. Benjamin Dealand, jr.
59†. x. ZACHARIAH, b. Feb. 20, 1725–6; m. Tamison Upton.

(17.) vii. JOHN FELTON^3 ($John^2$, $Nathaniel^1$), b. Aug. 22, 1686; m. April, 1721, Mary Waters, dau. of John, Jr., and Mary Waters, of Salem. (App. G.) John Felton lived upon his father's place, near Felton Hill, Salem. He was a fence-viewer and juryman in 1721–22. He d. in Danvers in 1777, aged 90 years. His will, dated Danvers, May, 1765, proved April, 1777, mentions wife Mary, sons Ebenezer (who d. before his father), Timothy (the executor), John, Elisha, William; daughters Abigail Mackintire, Hannah Upton, Eunice and Lydia. Elisha and William had land given them in Amherst, N. H. John and Mary Felton had 14 children.

60.   i. MARY, b. March 9, bapt. same month, 1721–2.
61†. ii. JOHN, JR., b. July 23, 1723; m. Elizabeth Smith.
62.   iii. EUNICE, bapt. Jan. 31, 1724–5; was living in 1765.
63.   iv. NATHAN, bapt. 1725–6; his estate settled by his father in 1760.
64.   v. LYDIA, bapt. Jan. 14, 1727–8; living in 1765.
65.   vi. ABIGAIL, bapt. Feb. 23, 1728–9; m. Archelaus Mackintire, Feb., 1761.
66.   vii. MEHITABLE, bapt. Dec. 6, 1730; d. young.
67.   viii. HANNAH, bapt. July 15, 1732; m. Wm. Upton, of Reading, Dec., 1755.
68†. ix. ELISHA, bapt. Dec. 30, 1733; m. Rachael Holt.
69.   x. MEHITABLE, bapt. Mar. 30, 1735.
70†. xi. WILLIAM, bapt. Nov. 7, 1736; m. Rebecca ——.
71.   xii. THOMAS, bapt. July 16, 1738; not named in the will.
72†. xiii. EBENEZER, bapt. Sept. 28, 1740; a soldier in 1775.
73†. xiv. TIMOTHY, bapt. Dec. 19, 1742; m. Hannah Proctor.

(21.) i. SKELTON FELTON³ (*Nathaniel²*, *Nathaniel¹*), b. about 1680; m. May, 1712, Hepsibah Sheldon, dau. of William Sheldon, of Salem. She was an adult when baptized, May 12, 1706. Skelton Felton's grandmother, Mary (Skelton) Felton, lived 20 years after the birth of her grandson. Skelton Felton was a juryman in 1719.

July 16, 1716, Samuel Endicott (only son of Samuel, deceased), and Robert Endicott (only son of Dr. John, deceased), conveyed land to Skelton, in right of his wife, Hepsibah Felton: it was conveyed to William Sheldon, of Salem, in 1689; it was near Nathaniel Felton's land. Wm. Sheldon died about 1694. Skelton Felton lived in Salem about 65 years. In April, 1744, he bought of James and Patience Wright, of Rutland, Mass., 150 acres of land in that town. The deed was signed in Salem before Daniel Epes, Justice of the Peace. The witnesses were Daniel Epes, Jr., and Samuel Epes, Jr.

Mr. Felton moved to Rutland with his son Joseph, and died in 1749, aged nearly 70 years. His will, dated Rutland, Jan. 5, 1745, proved May, 1749, mentions wife Hepsibah, son Joseph, daughters Lydia Foster, Rebecca Houghton (sup. Houlton), Anna, Hepsibah and Ruth. Had 7 or more children.

74†. i. LYDIA, b. Dec. 28, 1712; m. Ebenezer Foster.
75†. ii. REBECCA, bapt. Feb. 7, 1714; m. Joseph Houlton.
76†. iii. JOSEPH, bapt. Aug. 14, 1715; m. Mary Trask, of Salem.
77†. iv. ANNA, bapt. 1717; m. Jacob Shaw, of Leicester.
78. v. BENJAMIN, bapt. May 8, 1720; not named in the will, 1745.
79†.' vi. HEPSIBAH, bapt. Jan. 20, 1722–23; m. Samuel Haywood, of Holden.
80. vii. RUTH, bapt. May 1725; m. March 8, 1747–8, John Grout, of Rutland.

(22.) ii. JOHN FELTON³ (*Nathaniel²*, *Nathaniel¹*); he was baptized with his brothers in 1691. He m. Jan. 18, 1709, Mary Pitman, of Marblehead; probably she was baptized when an adult, in Salem, Oct. 21, 1705. She was granddaughter of Thomas Pitman, sen., of Marblehead. John Felton was a cooper, and bought land in Marblehead in 1709. In 1720, he purchased with Joshua Orne, an island near Marblehead, called "Charles Island," of Mary Brattle, widow of Edward Brattle, Esq., of Marblehead. His wife, Mary, was living in 1718. Mr. Felton m. 2d, Nov., 1719, Sarah Foot, b. about 1685. She d. in Marblehead Feb. 18, 1749, aged 63 years, 6 months. He died about 1771, sup. between 85 and 90 years. His will, dated Oct., 1761, proved January, 1772, mentions son Francis, the executor; dau. Mary, who m. Isaac Williams, and three grandchildren, Sarah, Lydia and Hannah Felton. Had 3 chil. by his last wife.

81.†   i. JOHN, JR., who m. April, 1743, Hannah Kimball.
82.   ii. MARY, who m. June, 1746, Isaac Williams.
83.† iii. FRANCIS, b. Aug. 15, 1726; m. Mehitable Kimball.

(23.) iii. EBENEZER FELTON[3] (*Nathaniel*[2], *Nathaniel*[1]), b. in 1685, was a housewright by trade. He m. 1st, Mehitable ———, and had a son, David, b. about 1711; was bapt. with his mother Feb. 21, 1713. Mr. Felton m. 2d, Oct. 1716, Jehoadan Ward, b. March, 1690-91, daughter of John and Jeboadan Ward, of Salem. (See Appendix H.) Ebenezer Felton was one of the first settlers in New Salem, Mass. He went there with his 5 sons in 1740. The first minister in New Salem Plantation, Rev. Samuel Kendall, was ordained Dec. 15, 1742, at a church organized that year. In November, 1742, Mr. Felton and wife were dismissed from Salem church to New Salem. Ebenezer Felton was the first deacon of the church, chosen in July, 1744, the church then voted to have communion once in two months. Dea. Felton was the first Town Clerk of New Salem, and one of the Selectmen the year it was incorporated, 1753. He was probably the patriarch and father of the new township. He was called of New Salem Plantation in 1740, when 55 years of age. He died in 1776, aged 90 years. Mrs. Felton probably lived several years after her husband's decease. It is said the women of the first settlement were fit companions of the hardy men who settled New Salem. A gentleman reports a story, which is given in Holland's "History of Western Massachusetts," which he heard from the lips of the wife of the first deacon of the church in New Salem, of the following purport:

"On some occasion, all the men of the settlement were called twenty or thirty miles from home, into the valley of the Connecticut, and were obliged to be absent over night. At an early hour, all the women, with the few children of the settlement, assembled in the fort for the night. With military strictness, they kept a watch, and about midnight, one of them discovered the enemy stealthily approaching the fort from different directions, and in considerable numbers. The "Commander-in-chief" immediately called the roll of the men of the settlement, in a hoarse, masculine voice, and named some who had never existed. An answer was given to each name, in a corresponding tone. She then commanded them to load and prepare to fire. Then followed a noise like the ramming down of cartridges, at which the Indians retired with all convenient speed. Their presence was verified the next day by the discovery of their tracks near the fort. There were many Indians in the vicinity, but the settlers effectually guarded themselves against their depredations."

Dea. Felton's will, dated Nov. 24, 1762, proved Sept., 1776, mentions wife Jehoadan, sons David, Ebenezer, Amos, Benjamin, Nathaniel, the executor; and grandchildren Benjamin, Mehitable, and Sarah Southwick. The 10 children were all b. in Old Salem, Mass.

84†.	i.	DAVID, b. 1711; m. 1736, Sarah Houlton, of Salem.
85†.	ii.	ESTHER, bapt., with others, 1727; m. Isaac Southwick.
86†.	iii.	EBENEZER, JR., b. about 1720; m. 1753, Lydia Stacy.
87†.	iv.	AMOS, b. in Salem, June 5, 1724; m. Hannah Neal.
88†.	v.	BENJAMIN, b. in 1727; bapt. Dec. 5th, that year; m. 1st, Miss Rich.
89.	vi.	NATHANIEL, bapt. June 23, 1728; died young.
90.	vii.	JOHN, twin, bapt. June 23, 1728; died young.
91†.	viii.	NATHANIEL, bapt. May 31, 1730; m. Mary Whiting.
92.	ix.	JOHN, bapt. Nov. 12, 1732.
93.	x.	MEHITABLE, bapt. Feb. 15, 1735–6.

(24.) JONATHAN FELTON³ (*Nathaniel²*, *Nathaniel¹*), bapt. in 1691, with his brothers; m. Jan. 1718–19, in Salem, Rebecca Needham, a grandchild of Anthony Needham, and sup. dau. of Anthony Needham, jr., who m. in 1695. (See Appendix I for Needham.)

Jonathan Felton was living in 1761, when his son of the same name was Jonathan Felton, jr. Sup. he deceased before July, 1773.

94†.	i.	MARY, bapt. July 29, 1721; m. Jonathan Tarbell.
95†.	ii.	NATHANIEL, bapt. May 5, 1723; m. Mrs. Dorcas Felton.
96.	iii.	JONATHAN, JR., bapt. in 1725; died young.
97†.	iv.	ANTHONY, bapt. before 1736; m. Elizabeth Prichard.
98†.	v.	JONATHAN, bapt. Feb. 6, 1736–7; m. Anne Whittemore.

The church records have it, that John and Rebecca Felton had Ruth, Archelaus and Daniel baptized; probably a mistake for Jonathan and Rebecca Felton. It is said that Nathaniel Felton, jr., born in 1759 (son of Nathaniel above, No. 95), was nephew to Archelans Felton, of Marlborough, and Daniel Felton, of Needham, Mass.

99†.	vi.	RUTH, bapt. May 25, 1740; m. Stephen Whittemore.
100†.	vii.	ARCHELAUS, bapt. May, 1740; m. Elizabeth Hunter.
101†.	viii.	DANIEL, bapt. March 11, 1743; m. Abigail Cook.

(25.) v. DANIEL FELTON[3] (*Nathaniel*[2], *Nathaniel*[1]) b. about October, 1687; m. Sarah ———, and settled at Marblehead. Mr. Felton and his two sons were blacksmiths by trade, and all living in that town in 1756, and afterwards. Daniel Felton died May 8, 1760, aged 72 years, 7 months.

In 1760, Mrs. Sarah Felton sold her son Thomas some land in Marblehead. Mrs. Felton died May 4, 1763, aged 75 years.

102†.   i. Daniel, Jr., m. in 1750, Sarah Martin.
103†.   ii. Thomas, m. in 1754, Hannah Halfpenny.
104†.   iii. One daughter, m. ——— Nutt, sup. John Nutt.

(30.) ii. SAMUEL ENDICOTT, b. Aug. 30, 1687, son of Samuel and Hannah (Felton) Endicott, m. in Salem, Dec. 20, 1711, Anne Endicott, his cousin, b. in 1693, dau. of Dr. John Endicott. In 1694, after the death of his father, the name of Endicott, in Salem and vicinity, was borne by a single descendant only, a lad of 7 years of age. In 1736, Capt. Samuel Endicott was one of a committee of four, the others, Mr. Thorndike Proctor, John Felton, and Daniel Marble, " to erect a school in ye quarter of ye parish." Capt. Samuel Endicott died in Danvers, May, 1766, aged 79 years. His great-grandfather, Gov. John Endicott, died 101 years before this date, aged 77 years. Mrs. Anne Endicott died May 1723, aged 30 years. Capt. Endicott m. 2d, Feb. 1724, Mrs. Margaret Foster, a widow, whose maiden name was Pratt.

105†.   i. John, b. April 29, 1713; m. Elizabeth Jacobs.
106.   ii. Sarah, b. Sept. 19, 1715; died young.
107.   iii. Samuel, Jr., b. March 12, 1717; m. in 1752, Mary Putnam; had 6 children; he died in 1773, aged 56 years.
108.   iv. Sarah, b. Jan. 13, 1720; m. Dr. Benjamin Jones, b. in 1716.
109.   v. Robert, b. in 1721; deceased when a boy.
110.   vi. Margaret, b. Dec., 1724; m. June, 1743, Hebert Clark.
111.   vii. Hannah, b. Dec., 1724, twin; m. Sept., 1769 Francis Nourse.
112.   viii. Ann, b. Nov. 1727; m. Dec., 1761, Thomas Andrew.
113.   ix. Elias, b. Dec., 1729; m. Eunice Andrew. Had five children.
114.   x. Joseph, b. Feb., 1731; m. 1st, Miss Putnam, 2d, Sarah Hathorne.
115.   xi. Lydia, b. in 1734; m. Peter Putnam.
116.   xii. Ruth, b. in 1739; m. Joseph Dole. Mrs. Ruth Dole died in 1828, aged 89 years.

(31.) iii. MARTIN HERRICK, b. or bapt. Jan. 26, 1679-80, son of Joseph and Mary Herrick, who was son of Henry

Herrick, the emigrant. Martin Herrick m. July 17, 1710, Ruth Endicott, b. in 1689, dau. of Samuel and Hannah (Felton) Endicott. He settled in Lynn, now Lynnfield, on a farm, and died in 1739, aged 59 years. Martin and Ruth Herrick had 4 or more children.

117. i. BENJAMIN, b. in 1711, m. Sarah Potter, and had Martin, b. May 30, 1747, and graduated at Harvard College in 1772; was a school teacher and physician in Reading, Mass., where he died July 4, 1820, aged 73 years; he m. and had 4 daughters.

118. ii. SAMUEL, b. about 1713; m. Elizabeth Jones, of Wilmington, in 1742; had 9 children; he m. 2d, widow Sarah Whipple, and had 4 children. Mr. Samuel Herrick's 7th child, Jacob Herrick, graduated at Harvard College in 1777, and died in 1832.

119. iii. RUTH, m. in 1733, Nathaniel Flint.
120. iv. EDITH, the 4th child.

Samuel Herrick, named above, died at Reading in 1792, aged 79 years. Was one of the Selectmen of Reading in 1771.

(32.) iv. BENJAMIN PORTER, m. April 3, 1712, Hannah Endicott, b. in 1691, dau. of Samuel and Hannah (Felton) Endicott. Benjamin Porter was son of Israel Porter, who was son of John Porter, who purchased "Skelton Neck" of the children of Rev. Samuel Skelton, the first minister of Salem, Mass. They had 5 children. Benjamin Porter's will, dated Dec. 15, 1726, proved Jan. 18, 1726-7, names his father-in-law, Thorndike Proctor, and brother-in-law, Samuel Endicott.

121. i. JOHN, b. about 1713.
122. ii. HANNAH, b. about 1715; m. about 1733, Joseph Fowle or Fowles, written both ways. Mrs. Fowles died in 1746.
123. iii. BENJAMIN, JR., b. about 1717-18.
124. iv. SAMUEL, b. about 1721.
125. v. BARTHOLOMEW, b. about 1724.

(33.) v. NATHAN PROCTOR, b. Oct. 18, 1698, son of Thorndike and Hannah (Felton) Proctor, m. May, 1723, Mary Reed, b. March 9, 1697, dau. of Jacob Reed, of Salem. They had 9 children.

126†. i. STEPHEN, b. March, 1724; m. Elizabeth ——, had 6 children.
127. ii. JACOB, b. Feb. 12, 1726-7; died Nov. 16, 1728.
128. iii. MARY, b. Dec. 20, 1728.
129. iv. HANNAH, b. Oct. 22, 1730.
130. v. RUTH, b. Jan. 21, 1732-3.

131†. vi. NATHAN, JR, b. Nov. 25, 1735; m. Abigail ———, had 6 children.
132.   vii. JACOB, b. Oct. 12, 1737; m. and had children.
133.   viii. SARAH, b. April 11, 1741.

(34.) vi. THORNDIKE PROCTOR, JR., b. June 2, 1700, son of Thorndike and Hannah (Felton) Proctor, m. April 1721, Abigail Wilson. When the proprietors of New Salem Plantation held their meetings in Old Salem, before New Salem was incorporated, Thorndike Proctor, Jr., was their clerk. They had 4 or more children.

134.   i. HANNAH, b. Nov. 9, 1723; died in 1727.
135.   ii. THORNDIKE, JR., b. Nov. 26, 1725.
136†. iii. ABIGAIL, b. Aug. 27, 1727; m. Geo. Dealand, Jr.
137.   iv. HANNAH, b. Sept. 3, 1729.

(35.) vii. EBENEZER PROCTOR, b. Aug. 16, 1702; son of Thorndike and Hannah (Felton) Proctor; he was a shoemaker in 1725; m. Mary Houlton, b. Sept. 11, 1707, dau. of James Houlton, of Salem. Mr. Proctor m. Miss Houlton before the decease of her father in 1729.

(36.) viii. JONATHAN PROCTOR, b. Aug. 2, 1705; son of Thorndike and Hannah (Felton) Proctor; m. about 1736, Desire Jacobs, sup. dau. of John and Abigail Jacobs, of Salem. Jonathan Proctor d. in March, 1751, aged 45 years. Mrs. Proctor and three children died the next September, September, 1751. They had 7 children. Nathan Proctor, uncle to the children, was appointed their guardian; he also settled his brother's estate. Mrs. Desire Proctor's age was 35 years.

138.   i. DESIRE, b. about 1737; died in the Autumn of 1751, aged about 15 years.
139†. ii. JONATHAN, JR., b. in 1739; he was at the capture of Louisburg.
140.   iii. THORNDIKE, b. about 1741; was lost at sea; sup. he was m. in 1771, to Sarah Aborne, of Salem.
141†. iv. HANNAH, b. in 1743; m. Timothy Felton, sen. (No. 73.)
142.   v. SARAH, b. about 1745; died same month as her mother, in the fall of 1751, aged 6 years.
143.   vi. EBENEZER, b. about 1747; died same month as his mother, aged 4 years.
144.   vii. ELIZABETH, b. in 1750; a distinguished schoolteacher; taught 50 years. She died Nov. 2d. 1824, aged 74 years.

(39.) iii. MALACHI FELTON[4] (*Nathaniel*[3], *John*[2], *Nathaniel*[1]), b. May 14, 1705; m. Feb., 1735, Abigail Jacobs, baptized in 1706, dau. of John Jacobs, and great-granddaughter of George Jacobs, who was hung for witchcraft, Aug. 19, 1692, on a branch of one of his own oak trees, and was buried on his own land, near the Iron Factory, now in Danvers. John Jacob's mother, and sister Margaret, were put in prison in the awful delusion time, 1692. George Jacobs, jr., the grandfather of Mrs. Felton, saved his life by running away; afterwards returned. (For Jacobs, see Appendix J.)

Malachi Felton was a school-teacher in 1736 and 1737. In 1751, one of a committee of six that reported about incorporating the town of Danvers. In 1764, the moderator at the annual meeting in Danvers. In 1743, he was chosen Deacon of the Church in Middle Precinct, and held the office 36 years, till his demise in 1779 or 1780, aged 74 years. His will was dated March 11, 1779. Mrs. Felton was living in 1768. They had 5 children. Lea. Felton lived on his father's place, on Felton Hill, Danvers, now Peabody.

145†.   i. ABIGAIL, bapt. April 30, 1738; m. Joseph Richardson.
146.   ii. ELIZABETH, bapt. June 16, 1741.
147†.   iii. MARY, bapt. Jan. 1742-3; m. Dea. Benjamin Kent.
148.   iv. MALACHI, JR., bapt. June 16 1745.
149†.   v. SARAH, bapt. Feb. 10, 1750; m. Robert Wilson.

It was said at the Danvers centennial celebration, June, 1852, that Dea. Malachi Felton was one of these good men who lived long and well, and were content so to do, without any proclamation made of it.

FOURTH GENERATION.

(43.)   viii. BENJAMIN FELTON[4] (*Nathaniel*[3], *John*[2], *Nathaniel*[1]), b. Sept. 9, 1712; m. Joanna (sup. Foster, dau. of Jonathan, and granddaughter of Dea. David Foster, of Danvers). He settled in Watertown, where he was living in 1753. He had a scythe mill in the adjoining town of Newton. He was constable in Watertown in 1762. He was guardian for Jonas Coolidge. Benjamin Felton died Aug. 15, 1765, agep 53 years. His will, dated Dec. 27, 1764, mentions wife Joanna, dau. Lucy, and brothers and sisters.

Ebenezer Stetson m. in Watertown July 1st, 1765, Lucy Ruggles, and named their first child, b. May 22, 1766, Benjamin Felton, suppose in memory of the above Benjamin Felton. There is a Felton street in Watertown, and one in Waltham. Mrs. Joanna Felton, m. May 7, 1767, Samuel Livermore, Esq., of Waltham; his third wife. Mrs. Livermore died the same year, Sept. 5, 1767, aged 46 years. Mr. Livermore m. the fourth time in 1770, and d. Aug. 7, 1773, aged 71 years. He had for a long time the greatest share of the municipal busines the town; was Selectman 22 years, representative 17 years. Capt. Samuel Livermore's son, Elijah Livermore, settled in Livermore, Me. Anna Livermore, daughter of the last-named Mr. Livermore, m. Cyrus Hamlin, Esq., and were the parents of Hon. Hannibal Hamlin, Vice-President of the United State, and Rev. Dr. Cyrus Hamlin. Benjamin and Joanna Felton had 2 children.

150. i. BENJAMIN, JR., bapt. Nov. 22, 1752; died July 15, 1754, aged 2 years.
151. ii. LUCY, bapt. May 29, 1756; died July 26, 1766, aged 10 years.

(44.) viii. NATHANIEL FELTON⁴, (*Nathaniel³, John², Nathaniel¹*), b. May 9, 1714; m. July, 1741, Anna Jacobs, of Salem. They moved to Roxbury, where the births of their children are recorded. He was called a scythe-maker in 1746, and a blacksmith in 1785. He purchased and sold land in Mendon, and in Northborough. In 1773, Nathaniel Felton was one of the committee of correspondence in Roxbury. Capt William Heath, who was a general during the revolution, was chairman of the committee. Mr. Felton and family resided at Marlborough, Mass., several years during the revolutionary war. Nathaniel Felton died in Roxbury, Feb. 24, 1807, aged 92 years, 9 months. His estate was settled the same year by Dea. Joshua Felton and Jesse Daggett: children named Joshua, William, Edward Jackson, Abigail Richardson, and Mary Pond. Mrs. Felton's name is written Hannah Felton on the Roxbury records. Had 8 children.

152†. i. NATHANIEL JR., b. 1st or 4th, 1742; m. Mary Williams.
153†. ii. JOSHUA, b. March 21st, 1743; m. Mary Wardell.
154†. iii. WILLIAM, b. March 18th, 1745; m. Eunice Williams.
155†. iv. HANNAH, b. May 9th, 1749; lived 58 years.
156. v. SAMUEL, bapt. June 9th, 1751; died young.
157†. vi. ABIGAIL, b. Nov. 17th, 1753; m. Joseph Richardson.
158†. vii. MARY, bapt. June 27, 1756; m. Nathaniel Wardell.
159†. viii. EDWARD JACKSON, b. Sept. 4th, 1758; m. Tamison Baker.

(50.) i. STEPHEN FELTON⁴, (*Samuel,³ John², Nathaniel¹*), b, April 19th, 1710; m. Nov. 1742, Dorcas Upton b. Sept. 4th, 1718, dr. of William Upton: (For Upton, Appc. K.) Mrs. Felton was twin to Timothy Upton. Stephen Felton lived on Felton Hill, but a few rods from Dea. Malachi Felton's place. Mr. Felton died in 1751, aged 41 years, leaving two minor children; the guardianship of each was granted to Samuel Felton, their grandfather. The widow Dorcas Feltod m. March 28, 1754, Nathaniel Felton, (No. 95). They settlen the estate of the late Stephen Felton of Danvers. Mrs. Dorcas Felton, d. a widow, March 23rd, 1803, aged 84 years.

160†. i. STEPHEN, JR., b. about 1744; bapt. 1746-7; m. Elizabeth Baker.
161†. ii. SARAH, bapt. in 1746-7 ; m. Dea. Joseph Ross of Salem.

(52.) iii. JACOB FELTON^4, ($Samuel^3$, $John^2$, $Nathaniel^1$), b. March 13th, 1712-13, in Salem, that part afterwards Danvers, now Peabody. He was cordwainer by trade, now called shoemaker. He settled in Marlborough about 1738, where he had two uncles, John and Benjamin Goodale. He was a sealer of leather between 20 and 30 years; the last time chosen in 1787. He m. about 1740, Sarah Barrett, b. Jan. 15, 1715, dau. of Thomas and Elizabeth (Stow) Barrett of Marlborough; had one son. She d. March 26, 1742, aged 27 years. Mr. Felton m. 2d, in 1749, Hasadiah Howe, b. March 26, 1725, dau. of Ephraim Howe, and granddau. of Capt. Eleazer Howe all of Marlborough (App. L.) In 1761, Jacob Felton was one of the six wardens in town; also one of the committee of nine, for 5 years, to seat the meeting-house so called. In 1762, was constable and collector of taxes. In 1766, was chosen a committee to provide a school master for the year; he was grand juryman for the year 1773. He was sergeant of a company in 1757 ; and commissioned lieutenant July 1, 1762, in the second military company of Marlborough, whereof Jesse Rice was captain and Artemas Ward of Shrewsbury was colonel of the regiment.

In 1770, the town of Marlborough chose two committees, one for the East part, the other for the West part; they were to sell town lands, formerly town ways. The West part committee was Gershom Rice, Lieut. Jacob Felton and Col. Edward Barnes. Jacob Felton served till his demise in 1789. Lt. Felton was chosen in 1777 (the year after the Declaration of Independence) a selectman of the town. Jacob Felton bought several hundred acres in Cheshire county, N. H. In 1761, the 28 proprietors of Township Monadnock numbers 4 and 5 in Cheshire county, met at the house of Col. Abraham Williams in Marlborough, Mass., and chose three assessors for the New Hampshire lands, viz.: Noah Church, Lt. Jacob Felton and Dr. Ebenezer Dexter. Mr. Felton served several years. The places were afterwards called Fitzwilliam and New Marlborough or Marlborough in New Hampshire. Two of his sons settled in Cheshire county, N. H. Jacob Felton's house erected in 1752 was within two furlongs northwest of

Marlborough Lake. It is now, 1886, standing about two furlongs westerly of where it was built, one of the oldest houses in town. Mr. Felton purchased his house spot of Zerubbabel Rice, who married a sister of Mr. Felton's first wife, and Mr. Rice was uncle to Mr. Felton's second wife. Mrs. Felton's father, Ephraim Howe, gave them 8 acres adjoining their home place. Lieut. Jacob Felton died Nov. 20, 1789, in his 77th year, and on the day his eldest son was 48 years of age, and just 26 years before the compiler of this Felton Family was born. Mrs. Felton died Feb. 25, 1819, aged almost 94 years. She died just 68 years after the birth of her oldest daughter. The compiler was present at her funeral. The last few years she could read without spectacles. She did not want her descendants to have her first or christian name. In 1762, a school house was built near Jacob Felton's where it stood upwards of 30 years. Lt. Felton had 6 children by his last wife.

162†. i. JOHN, b. Nov. 9, (O. S.) 20 (N. S.) 1741; m. Persis Rogers.
163†. ii. SARAH, b. Feb. 14, or 25, 1750-1; m. Capt. Dudley Hardy.
164†. iii. STEPHEN, b. Sept. 14 (O. S.) 25 (N. S.) 1752; m. Levinah Stowe.
165. iv. SILAS, b. Nov. 15, 1754; d. Sept. 4, 1775, aged almost 21 years.
166†. v. MATTHIAS, b. March 28, 1756; m. Sarah Maynard.
167†. vi. LUCY, b. July 23, 1760; m. Theophilas Hardy.
168†. vii. JOEL, b. May 14, 1762; m. Susanna Hunt.

(54.) v. MOSES HOWE, b. March 6, 1724-5, son of Gershom, and grandson of Capt. Eleazer Howe, all of Marlborough; m. about 1746, Hannah Felton, b. Oct. 24, 1716, dau. of Samuel Felton of Felton Hill, Salem. Moses Howe resided at Marlborough, where he died July 8, 1771, aged 46 years; his death caused by falling from the roof of a building, about 11 days before June 27, 1771. Mrs. Howe died Nov. 22, 1789, aged 73 years; her brother, Jacob Felton, died two days before, Nov. 20, 1789; they were both buried in one day, in the two oldest cemeteries in the town. They had 5 children.

169. i. GERSHOM, b. Sept. 26, 1747; d. May 20, 1752, aged 4 years.
170†. ii. SAMUEL, b. Jan. 12, 1748-9; m. Hannah Burnap.
171†. iii. JONATHAN, b. Aug. 15, 1751; m. Elizabeth Robinson.
172†. iv. SARAH, b. Aug. 20, 1753; m. John Gassett.
173†. v. GERSHOM again, b. Jan. 13, 1746; m. Lovinah Bartlett.

(55.) vi. SAMUEL FELTON[4] (*Samuel*[3], *John*[2], *Nathaniel*[1]) b. Feb. 17th, 1718-19; m. in 1756, Mary Smith, it is said dau. of James Smith. He lived in Danvers, on Felton Hill, where he died Feb., 1782, aged 63 years. His will, dated Nov. 29th, 1781, proved March 5th, 1782, mentions wife and six children. Their mother appointed guardian for the three youngest children. Mrs. Felton died Feb. 12th, 1810. Their two oldest sons were soldiers in the revolutionary war.

174.†   i. DAVID, b. April 20th, 1757; m. Hannah Swinton.
175.†   ii. ASA, b. Jan. 10, 1759; m. Mary Eppes.
176.   iii. RUTH, b. Nov. 17th, 1761; died Aug. 29th, 1766, aged almost 5 years.
177.   iv. RUTH, b. Aug. 29th, 1766, the day her sister Ruth died.
178.†   v. SARAH, b. Sept. 6th, 1768; m. Capt. Jonathan Landers.
179.†   vi. SAMUEL, Jr., b. Nov. 24th, 1772; m. Jane Doke, or Doak.
180.†   vii. MARY, bapt. June 15th, 1777; m. Thomas Dodge.

(56.) vii. DAVID FELTON[4], (*Samuel*[3], *John*[2], *Nathaniel*[1],) b. Nov. 6th, 1720; m., Oct., 1747, Zerviah Howe, b. Oct. 9th, 1729, dau. of Gershom, and grand-dau. of Capt. Eleazer Howe, all of Marlborough. David Felton was a tanner, and settled in Marlborough, north side of Marlborough Lake, and about half a mile eastward of his brother, Jacob Felton place. In 1762, David Felton moved to Petersham, Mass., where his wife died June 28th, 1773, aged 43 years. He m. 2d in 1774, Elizabeth Wilder of that town. David Felton was highway surveyor two years in Marlborough and two years in Petersham. He was collector of taxes in 1775. He d. about Feb., 1777, aged 56 years. His will, dated June 29th, 1776, proved April, 1777, mentions wife, Elizabeth, and 9 children. The first-named 7 children were born in Marlborough. David Felton owned the land now used for an engine house north side of Marlborough Lake, sometimes called Howe's Pond and Williams Pond.

181.   i. ZERVIAH, b. Nov. 24th, 1748; d. Oct. 22d, 1755, aged 7 years.
182.†   ii. NANNE, b. Nov. 28th, 1750; m. David Stone.
183.†   iii. DANIEL, b. Sept. 19, (o. s.), 30, (n. s.), 1752; m. Lois Wilder.
184.†   iv. RACHEL, b. Sept. 23d, 1754; m. Jonathan Johnson.
185.   v. ZERVIAH, again, b. Nov. 15th, 1756; not named in the will 1776.
186.†   vi. TAMISON, b. Nov. 28th, 1758; m. Daniel Benjamin.

187.† vii. GEORGE WEBBER, b. April 20th, 1761 ; m. Hannah Oliver.
188.† viii. PHEBE, b. in Petersham, Sept. 12th, 1763 ; m. Lemuel Stimson.
189.† ix. AMOS, b. Sept. 18th, 1765; m. Sarah Putnam.
190.† x. NABBY, or Abigail, b. July 26th, 1767; m. Caleb Pierce.
191.† xi. LYDIA, b. Feb. 10th, 1770; m. Jedediah Howe.
192. xii. DAVID, Jr., b. Sept., 1772; not named in the will of 1776.

(58.) ix. BENJAMIN DEALAND, Jr., son of Benjamin and Mary Dealand of Salem, m., Sept. 27th, 1744, Elizabeth Felton, b. Nov. 19, 1723, dau. of Samuel Felton, of Felton Hill, Salem. (See App. M for Dealand.) Some Benj. Dealand collector of taxes in Danvers, 1756. He died about 1804. In January, 1805, Capt Nathan Felton, of Danvers, was administrator of the late Benjamin Dealand's estate, the widow Dealand was living. They had 4 or more children.

193.† i. BENJAMIN, Jr., b. Aug., 1745 ; m. Mary Haywood.
194.† ii. ELIZABETH, b. about Oct.,1748; m. Ebenezer Howe.
195.† iii. HANNAH, bapt. June 8, 1754 ; Samuel Beaves.
196. iv. MARY, b. Nov. 20, 1773; m. John Mackintire. Mrs. M. was living in 1804.

Widow Katherine Dealand (Deland, Daland, written 3 ways) taught a school in James Houlton's house before there was a school-house in that part of Salem afterwards Danvers. She taught from 1709 to 1713, and the latter year received £5 for teaching school She was the mother of Benjamin Dealand, Sen., named above.

(59.) x. ZACHARIAH[4] FELTON, (*Samuel*[3], *John*[2], *Nathaniel*[1],) b. Feb. 20, 1725-6 ; m. Dec., 1754, Tamison Upton, b. Sept. 1st, 1733, dau. of James Upton, who was brother of Dorcas Upton, that married Stephen Felton above named, No. 50. Zachariah Felton lived on Felton Hill, now called Mt. Pleasant, in Peabody, where he died March 23d, 1780, aged (on gravestone 64 years) 54 years. His will, dated Danvers, Aug. 19th, 1776, proved May 2d, 1780 ; his widow, Tamison, the executrix; she had the Negro servant, Fortune. He gave his homestead to his nephew, Amos Felton. He gave some property to three more of his nephews, viz: Stephen, John and Asa Felton. He gave £13 6s. to his cousin, Mary Sprague, daughter of Ebenezer Sprague. The guardianship of Amos Felton, his nephew, 14 years of age, was granted May 1780, to Mrs. Tamison Felton. Mrs. Tamison Felton married May, 1788, John Dodge.

(61.) ii. JOHN FELTON[4] (*John[3], John[2], Nathaniel[1],*) b. July 23d, 1723; m. Nov., 1744, Elizabeth Smith. They lived in Danvers, at Felton Corner; it was then near the centre of the town of Danvers. In May, 1770, Mr. Felton, with his brother Ebenezer Felton, sold some land to John Felt of Salem. In 1787, his brother, Timothy Felton, was appointed his guardian. He died in 1801, aged about 78 years. Suppose they had one daughter. John Felton's estate was settled by Timothy Felton. Mrs. Felton was living in 1770.

197. i. Elizabeth, died Aug. 2d, 1805; supposed age about 60 years.

(65.) vi. ARCHELAUS MACKINTIRE m. Abigail Felton, bapt. Feb. 23d, 1728-9, dau. of John and Mary Felton— No. 17. In 1785, they lived in Reading, Mass., and in 1794, then of Reading, sold land in Danvers, near Timothy Felton's place, to William Goodale, of Danvers. Mr. Mackintire m. Miss Felton Feb. 5, 1761. Suppose they had three or more children.

(67. viii. WILLIAM UPTON, b. July, 1703, (son of Wm. and grandson of John Upton, who came from England to America about 1650); m. Dec. 9, 1755, for his second wife, Hannah Felton, bapt. July 15, 1732, dau. of John and Mary Felton, (No. 17.) Had 10 children. Mr. Upton was the eldest brother of Dorcas Upton, who m., first, Stephen Felton, (No. 50); m., second, Nathaniel Felton, (No. 95).

(68.) ix. ELISHA FELTON[4], (*John[3], John[2], Nathaniel[1],*) bapt. in Salem, Dec. 30, 1733. He learned the tanners trade in Marlborough, Mass., where he was living in 1752 and 1757. He moved to Amherst, N. H., where he and his brother William had land given them by their father. He was a tanner and farmer in Amherst. He m. Rachel Holt and had six children. Elisha Felton d. Sept. 2, 1805, aged 72 years. Mrs. Rachel Felton d. Oct. 27, 1807, aged 67 years.

197¼. i. JOHN, b. May 29, 1769; d. young.
197½. ii. SAMUEL, b. Sept. 14, 1771; d. young.
197¾. iii. MARY, b. July 10, 1774; d. Nov. 17, 1774, aged 4 months.
198.† iv. JOHN, again, b. Dec. 15, 1777; m. Lydia Muzzey, or Mussey.
199.† v. RACHEL, b. Oct. 10, 1779; m. Joseph Robertson.
200.† vi. ELISHA, b. Oct. 8, 1781; m. Lydia Wilkins.

(70.) xi. WILLIAM FELTON[4], (*John[3], John[2], Nathaniel[1],*) bapt. in Salem, Nov. 7, 1736; m. Rebecca ———, and settled at Amherst, N. H. He had land in Temple, N. H., and probably d. there in 1775, aged 39 years. The administrators of his estate were his brother, Elisha Felton of Amherst, and widow Rebecca Felton of Temple. The estate settled in Oct. 1775. There were 145 different articles named in the inventory. In 1775 widow Felton and one son, under 16 years of age, were living in Temple, N. H.

201. We have not the son's name.

(73.) xiv. TIMOTHY FELTON[4], (*John*[3], *John*[2], *Nathaniel*[1]) bapt. Dec. 19, 1742; m. in 1765, Hannah Proctor, a sister of Capt. Jonathan Proctor, late of Danvers, and grand-dau. of Thorndike Proctor, Sen., of Salem. Timothy Felton lived between one and two furlongs from Felton's Corner, Danvers. In 1796 he sold land for a school-house at Felton's Corner. It stood but a few rods from the one now (1885) standing in Feltonville, Peabody, Mass. Timothy Felton d. Oct. 12, 1811, aged 69 years. He was a soldier in the revolutionary war. His estate settled by his son, Nathan Felton, Esq., of Danvers. Mrs. Hannah Felton d. Sept. 19, 1815, (4 days before the great New England gale,) aged 72 yrs. They had 8 children.

202.† i. TIMOTHY, JR., b. Dec. 8, 1765; m. Polly Putnam.
203.† ii. HANNAH, b. Aug. 4, 1766; m. Nathaniel Felton, (No. 288.)
204.† iii. NATHAN, b. June 15, 1770; m. Lydia Proctor.
205.† iv. DESIRE, b. June 9, 1773; m. Amos Putnam.
206.† v. EBENEZER, b. Nov. 25, 1775; bapt. next day; he lived 74 years.
207.† vi. JOHN, b. April 25, 1779, bapt. same day; m. Phebe Goodale.
208.† vii. MARY, b. Dec. 17, 1781; m. Stephen Proctor.
209† viii. BETSEY, b. Oct. 17, 1789; m. Capt. Moses Preston.

(74.) i. EBENEZER FOSTER, (we have found one born May 10, 1713, and one born Aug. 28, 1710, and one born Nov. 21, 1715); m. Lydia Felton, bapt. Dec. 28, 1712, in Salem, dau. of Skelton Felton (No. 21.) Supposed Mr. Foster resided in Worcester county, and had three or more children. Probably these names below were their children: (Taken from Oakham records.)

210. i. Lieut. EBENEZER, JR., b. about 1732; m. Hannah ———. and had 11 children in Oakham. He was a town officer many years, and d. March 10, 1811, aged 79 years. Mrs. Hannah Foster d. Feb. 21 or 22, 1808, aged 68 years. They had 7 sons and 4 daughters. Mr. Foster was an innholder in 1763.

211. ii. SKELTON, published Oct., 1766, to Hannah Hinds of Rutland, Mass. He was constable, assessor and selectman several years in Oakham. Without doubt he was grand-son of Skelton Felton (No. 21.)
212. iii. BENJAMIN, pub. Feb., 1779, to Deborah Fitts, both of Oakham. He was a town officer several years. Selectman, 1782; assessor, 1784, 1785. He had two or more sons. His will dated March, 1808; set up June, 1811.
213. iv. SAMUEL, pub. Dec., 1786, to Patty Williams, both of Oakham. They had 6 children.

Ebenezer, Jr., b. in 1769, (son of Lieut. Ebenezer); a selectman in Oakham, 1802 to 1805.

(75.) ii. JOSEPH HOULTON, b. in Salem, Jan. 30, 1710–11; son of James Houlton, Sen., of Salem, (No. 3). He m. Rebecca ——, doubtless Rebecca Felton, who was bapt. in Salem, Feb. 7, 1714; dau. of Skelton Felton (No. 21) In 1732, Skelton Felton sold land in Salem to Joseph Houlton, Jr. He was about 30 years younger than his cousin of the same name. Joseph and Rebecca Houlton resided in Hopkinton, Mass., in 1735, 1736, where they had the births of 4 children recorded. He probably went back to Salem and settled his brother's, James Houlton, estate. He soon afterwards moved to New Salem plantation, with his brother-in-law, David Felton, (No. 84.) He was the Joseph Houlton called one of the first settlers in that place, where he was one of New Salem assessors, after the place was incorporated in 1753. His grandson, Joseph Houlton, was the founder of Houlton, Me. Joseph and Rebecca Houlton, we suppose, had seven or more children, and probably born in three towns, Salem, Hopkinton and New Salem.

214. i. MARY, b. May 1, 1731; m. James Cragin of New Salem.
215.† ii. SARAH, b. Aug. 13, 1732; m. James Felton of New Salem (No. 256.)
216. iii. RUTH, b. March 2, 1734–5; m. —— Ballard of New Salem.
217.† iv. JAMES, b. in Hopkinton July 1, 1736; m. Lois ——; settled in New Salem.
218. v. ELIZABETH, m. William Willson.
219. vi. HANNAH, m. Job Smith.
220. vii. NANCY, m. William Kellogg.

(76.) iii. JOSEPH FELTON[4], (*Skelton*[3], *Nathaniel*[2], *Nathaniel*[1],) bapt. Aug. 14, 1715; m. in 1736, Mary Trask of Salem.

Had 11 or more children; the 4 oldest were bapt. in Salem. He moved to Rutland in 1744. where he was a fence viewer in 1752 and 1755. In June, 1762, the part of Rutland called "Rutland West Wing" was incorporated a town and called Oakham. Mr. Felton was a fence viewer several years in Oakman. He was surveyor and collector of taxes in 1784. Mrs. Mary Felton d. in Oakham, Jan. 16, 1801, in her 85th year. They lived husband and wife 64 years. Joseph Felton d. in the same town Feb. 14, 1803, in his 88th year.

 221.† i. HANNAH. b. Aug. 18, 1737; m. Moses Hamilton.
 222.† ii. BENJAMIN, b. March 12, 1739; bapt. April, 1739; m. Jennie Dority.
 223. iii. SARAH, b. Oct. 21, 1741; m. ——— Curtis, of Hartford, Ct.
 224.† iv. HEPHSIBAH, b. Aug. 21, 1743; m. Capt. Wyman Hoyt.
 225.† v. DESIRE, b. Aug. 21, 1746; m. Joshua Slayton.
 226. vi. BETSEY, b. Aug. 29, 1748.
 227.† vii. SKELTON, b. Dec. 21, (n. s.) 1750; m. Silence Hale.
 228.† viii. MARY, b. Jan. 17, 1753; m. Joseph Ayres.
 229.† ix. LYDIA, b. July 3, 1755; m. Lt. Sampson Wetherell.
 230. x. ISABEL, b. March 23, 1759.
 231. xi. JOHN, b. Oct. 21, 1761; d. of canker-rash Nov. 7, 1775, age 14 years.
 231½. xii. A dau., said to have been a twin, d. of canker-rash Nov. 13, 1775.
 232.† xiii. ABIGAIL; m. Montgomery Bartlett.

(77.) iv. JACOB SHAW, of Leicester, m., March 16, 1753, Anna Felton of Rutland, Mass., bap. in 1717, dau. of Skelton Felton, (No. 21). They were living in Rutland in 1757. In 1761, Joseph Felton, of Rutland, was appointed by the Judge administrator of the estate of the late Jacob Shaw of Rutland.

(79.) vi. SAMUEL HAYWOOD, of Holden, m., March 1, 1744-5, Hephsibeth Felton of Rutland, bapt. Jan. 22, 1722-3, dau. of Skelton Felton, (No. 21). Mr. Haywood was a prominent and influential citizen of Holden, Mass. He was selectman many years. They had 11 children.

 233. i. ELIZABETH, b. April 18, 1746; d. young.
 234. ii. REBECCA, b. Oct. 21, 1747; d. young.
 235. iii. ELIZABETH, b. March 10, 1748-9; m., Oct. 11, 1770, Willoughby Prescott, of Concord, Mass.
 236. iv. REBECCA, b. Oct. 21, 1750.

237. v. HEPHSIBAH, b. July 25, 1752.
238. vi. HANNAH, b. April 23, 1754; m., June 13, 1779, James Lamb, of Paxton, Mass.
239. vii. RUTH, b. May 9, 1756.
240. viii. LUCINDA, born Dec. 17, 1757; m., July, 1782, Abel Jones, of Holden, Mass.
241. ix. SAMUEL, b. Nov. 26, 1759; died young.
242. x. SAMUEL, again, b. March 10, 1762; m., April 22, 1784, Ruth Melvin, of Holden. Samuel Haywood, a revolutionary pensioner, died in Rutland, Feb. 27, 1841.
243. xi. ROLAND, b. June 12, 1766.

(80.) vii. JOHN GROUT of Rutland, m. March 8, 1747–8, Ruth Felton of Rutland, bapt., May 1725, dau. of Skelton Felton; (No. 21.)

(81.) JOHN FELTON^4, (*John^3, Nathaniel^2, Nathaniel^1*), m. April 13th, 1743, Hannah Kimball, both of Marblehead. He d. in 1757. Mrs. Felton, administered on his estate. The estate inventorial in 1758. They had 3 daughters. Dec. 21, 1758, Hannah Felton, sup. the mother m. Thomas Skinner.

244. i. SARAH, supposed m. July 1765, Benjamin Bowdon.
245. ii. LYDIA, supposed m. Dec. 1768, Wm. Richardson.
246. iii. HANNAH, supposed m. Dec. 1773, Samuel Ashton.
The above marriages all in Marblehead, Mass.

(82.) ii. ISAAC WILLIAMS, m. June 1746, Mary Felton, dau. of John and Sarah Felton of Marblehead. They were living in 1761.

(83.) iii. FRANCIS FELTON^4, (*John^3, Nathaniel^2, Nathaniel^1*), b. Aug.15,1726; m. in 1750, Mehitable Kimball, b. Dec. 22, 1726, dau. of Thomas and Mehitable Kimball of Marblehead. Mrs. Felton d. Aug. 6, 1766, age 39 years. He m. 2 in 1768, Hannah Turner, b. Jan. 23, 1734, dau. of Isaac and Mary Turner. Francis Felton was town clerk of Marblehead several years, and a prominent man in the town. "July 18, 1774, Capt. Francis Felton of Marblehead gave two quintals of Fish to the poor of Boston." In 1775, two of his sons, John and Samuel were in the army in Col. John Glovers Marblehead regiment consisting of 584 persons, soldiers, mostly fishermen. Capt. Felton d. about 1794, aged 68 years. His estate was settled that year by Joshua Prentiss, the administrator. His widow was then living. Capt. Felton had 15 children.

247. i. MEHITABLE, b. Feb. 9, 1751; d. Nov. 3, the same year.

248. ii. MEHITABLE, b. in 1752, d. May 23, 1759, aged 7 years.
249†. iii. JOHN, b. Mar. 19, 1753, m. Rebecca Larkin.
250. iv. FRANCIS Jr., b. Aug 13, 1754; d. May 24, 1774, aged 19 years, 9 months.
251†. v. SAMUEL, b. Dec. 14. 1755; m. Esther Porter.
252. vi. MARY, b. Mar. 4, 1757; d. same month, aged 1 week.
253. vii. DANIEL, b, June 27, 1758; d. Dec. 8, 1816, aged 58 years. It is supposed by persons that he m. and had a son, Francis, who lived in Salem.
254. viii. MEHITABLE, b. Dec. 23, 1761.
255. ix. THOMAS, b. Mar. 14, 1764; lost suddenly at sea, Jan. 7, 1782, aged 18 years.
256. x. SARAH, b. Oct. 29, 1765.
257. xi.
258. xii. } Two sons, b. June 20, 1769; both d. same day.
259†. xiii. JAMES, b. July 22, 1770; m. Ruth Smith.
260. xiv. ELIAS TURNER, b. Apr. 9, 1772; d. May 17, 1774, the same month his brother Francis, aged 2 years.
261. xv. MARY, b. June 21, 1776.

(84.) DAVID FELTON[4] (*Ebenezer[3], Nathaniel[2], Nathaniel[1]*), b. in 1711; bapt. Feb. 21, 1713; m. Nov. 1736, Sarah Houlton, b. Apr. 10, 1715, dau. of James Houlton Sr. of Salem, No. 3 in the genealogy. David Felton was joiner, a house carpenter, and moved about 1740, to plantation of New Salem, now in Franklin County Mass. He sold some land in Salem in Feb. in 1739-40, and soon afterwards bought land in New Salem. Mrs. Sarah Felton d. Dec. 15, 1790, aged 75 years. Husband and wife 54 years. David Felton d. Mar. 20, 1792, aged 81 years. (Gravestones in New Salem.)

262†. i. JAMES, bapt. in Salem, Oct. 8, 1738; m. Sarah Houlton.
263†. ii. EBENEZER, supposed b. in 1741; bapt. in New Salem, Sept. 1743; m. Hannah Page.
264. iii. DAVID, JR., bapt. May 1745.

(85.) ii. ISAAC SOUTHWICK, sup. b. in 1720, son of Benjamin and Sarah (Southwick) Southwick of Reading, Mass.; m. Esther Felton, dau. of Dea. Ebenezer and Jehoadan Felton of New Salem, Mass. Mrs. Sarah Southwick named above was dau. of Isaac Southwick of Reading Mass. We suppose Isaac and Esther Southwick lived in Danvers, afterward New Salem. Isaac Southwick was a soldier in 1756, in Capt. John Burk's Co., in Col. Williams Regiment in the expedition against Canada. He d. soon after his return home near the close of the year of 1756. They had 3 children.

In January, 1757, Benjamin Felton of New Salem, uncle to the children, was their guardian and administrator of the estate. He rented the place 15 years, supposed till the son was of age in 1772.

265. i. BENJAMIN, supposed was bapt. in Danvers, July 16 1751; in 1772, he was called of Northampton, Mass.
266. ii. MEHITABLE, lived many years in New Salem and vicinity.
267. iii. SARAH, was living in Hatfield, Mass., in 1772.

(86.) iii. EBENEZER FELTON[4], (*Ebenezer*[3], *Nathaniel*[2], *Nathaniel*[1],) b. about 1721, bapt. Dec. 3, 1727 in Salem, he went with his parents to New Salem, where he m. June 24, 1753 Lydia Stacy. Had 4 or more children. Mr. Felton was living in 1792, for his nephew was called Ebenezer Felton Jr. of New Salem.

268. i. LYDIA, bapt. May, 1755.
269†. ii. STEPHEN, b. Oct. 22, 1756; m. Sally Daland.
270. iii. DANIEL, b. in 1759; d. Sept. 4, 1777, aged 19 years.
271†. vi. LYDIA, again, bapt. March, 1765; m. Jacob Harwood.

(87.) iv. AMOS FELTON[4], (*Ebenezer*[3], *Nathaniel*[2], *Nathaniel*[1],) b. June 5, 1724, and went to New Salem with his father's family, where he m. in 1776, Hannah Neal, b. Aug. 25, 1742. This family lived in Shutesbury, in the part set off to New Salem in Feb. 1824.

Amos Felton d. Jan. 20, 1806, aged 81 years. His will dated June 2, 1800, proved April 1806, mentions 4 children. Widow Hannah Felton d. in New Salem Oct. 21, 1836, aged 94 years, 2 months.

272†. . AMOS, JR., b. Dec. 5, 1779; m. Lydia King.
273. ii. HANNAH, living in 1800.
274. iii. CATHERINE, b. Aug. 26, 1784; m. Charles Felton.
275. iv. JOHN, had land in New Salem in 1806.

(88.) v. BENJAMIN FELTON[4], (*Ebenezer*[3], *Nathaniel*[2], *Nathaniel*[1],) b. in 1727, and bapt. same year. He lived in New Salem and settled the estate of his brother-in law, Isaac Southwick, and was guardian to their children. Probably had been one of the selectmen of the town; many of the town accounts were destroyed by fire some 30 years ago. Benjamin Felton m. 1st, Miss —— Rich, who lived only a few months: m. 2d.

widow Mary (Pierce) Conkey, widow of Dr. Alexander Conkey of New Salem, who d. Feb. 8, 1773 aged 35 years. Benjamin Felton d. March 21, 1813 aged 87 years. Mrs. Mary Felton, April 5, 1829, aged 80 years. They had 5 children, and lived on the western side of New Salem near Shutesbury.

276†. i. ELIZABETH, sup. b. about 1777; m. Dr. Zaccheus Richardson.
277.   ii. MARY, b. in 1780. d. Oct. 26, 1812 aged 32 years.
278†. iii. BENJAMIN JR., b. in 1782; m. Hephsibah Orcutt.
279†. iv. ABRAHAM, b. May 1784; m. Bethiah Pierce.
280†. v. EBENEZER, b. Feb. 3, 1788; d. in 1864 aged 76 years.

(91.) viii. NATHANIEL FELTON⁴, (*Ebenezer³*, *Nathaniel²*, *Nathaniel¹*,) bapt. May 31, 1730, in Old Salem and at age of 10 years went with his parents to New Salem. He m. Mary Whiting Nov. 1766. He d. in 1800 or 1801 aged 70 years. His will dated June 9, 1800, proved March 3, 1801. Names 3 children.

281†. i. MARY, m. Isaac Page.
282.   ii. HANNAH, d. unm. aged between 60 and 70 years.
283†. iii. NATHANIEL JR., m. Lucinda Reynolds.

(94.) i. JONATHAN TARBELL, b. Feb. 14, 1719-20; (s. of Dea. Cornelius Tarbell of Salem Village, now in Danvers, and first representative to the General Court from that town,) m. Nov. 1741, Mary Felton bapt. July 29, 1721, dau. of Jonathan Felton, Sr. April 19, 1775, Jonathan Tarbell lost a gun at or near Lexington. In February, 1776, the General Court voted to pay Jonathan Tarbell, £2 and 11 shillings for a lost gun on the 19th of April, 1775. Jonathan Tarbell (or perhaps his son) was a soldier and in Capt. Samuel Eppes Co. in 1775.

284. i. JONATHAN TARBELL, JR., perhaps a soldier in the Revolution.

(95.) ii. NATHANIEL FELTON⁴ (*Jonathan³*, *Nathaniel²*, *Nathaniel¹*,) bapt May 5, 1723; m. March 28, 1754, Mrs. Dorcas Felton, widow of Stephen Felton(No. 50). He settled on Mt. Pleasant, near Dea. Malachi Felton's place. He d. Feb. 8, 1776, aged 53 years. His will, dated Dec. 30, 1775, proved April 1776, mentions wife, Dorcas, the executrix, and the 4 children. The widow, Dorcas Felton, d. March 23, 1803, aged 84 years.

285†. i. ANNA, b. Nov. 5, 1754; m Daniel Prince.
286†. ii. MARY, b. March 28, 1756; m. John Eppes, Jr.

287.   iv. DORCAS, b. Jan. 26, 1758; d. a very aged person.
288†. iv. NATHANIEL JR., b. Aug. 5, 1759; m. Mary Prince.

(97.) iv. ANTHONY FELTON[4], (*Jonathan[3], Nathaniel[2], Nathaniel[1],*) bapt. before the year 1736; m. in 1763, Elizabeth Prichard of Boxford, Mass. They settled in Danvers, where Mrs. Felton d. Aug. 2, 1781. The birth of one child on the Danvers records. Mr. Felton m. 2d, about 1782, Elizabeth Nichols, who d. Aug. 2 (the same day of the month as his first wife), 1808. Anthony Felton d. April 26, 1789, sup. aged about 60 years.

289†.   i. JEDEDIAH, b. May 15, (bapt. 22), 1768; m. Mary Proctor.

(99.) vi. STEPHEN WHITTEMORE of Salem, m. March 18, 1762, Ruth Felton, bapt., May 25, 1740; dau. of Jonathan and Rebecca Felton of Salem. Mr. Whittemore was a mariner. His estate was settled in 1773, by his widow, Ruth Whittemore, with Jonathan Tarbell and Nathaniel Felton, sureties.

(100.) vii. ARCHELAUS FELTON[4], (*Jonathan[3], Nathaniel[2], Nathaniel[1]*), bapt. May 1740; he was in Marlboro in 1756; that year, when 16 years of age, was in Capt. William Williams Company in the service of No. 4, also in his company in 1760. A large number of troops of the Colony were called into service between 1756 and 1760. In 1757 were two large companies organized in Marlboro, Mass.; the following Feltons were in Col. Abraham Williams Company; Jacob Felton sergeant, David Felton, Elisha Felton and Archelaus Felton. Archelaus Felton m. Elizabeth Hunter, b. April, 1745, dau. of Edw. Hunter Sr., of Marlboro; was the mother of his children; she d. Feb. 9, 1774, aged 29 years. He m. 2d, Sept. 1774, Lydia Newton, b. in Marlboro Nov. 27, 1749, dau. of Micah Newton. Mr. Felton settled in the north-east part of Marlboro, and was a tanner by trade. His bark mill stone is now a house door stone for his grandson, Edward Felton.

Mr. Wm. Newton, now of Shrewsbury and aged 76 years, was born and brought up in Marlboro near Archelaus Felton's place, informed me lately that Mr. Felton said he never attended school but three evenings, and then to learn to cipher.

In 1787 Archelaus Felton was a fence viewer, a tythingman, and one of a committee of 7 to seat the meeting house for 5 years. He was an assessor in Marlboro 16 years, 1783 to 1799, and selectman in 1790. He died Mar. 30, 1825, aged 85 years; lived with his second wife 50 years. She died Dec. 29, 1834, aged 85 years.

Among the baptisms in the Middle Parish, Salem, now

Peabody, Archelaus Felton is recorded as son of John and Rebecca Felton; probably a mistake for Jonathan and Rebecca Felton. He was uncle to Nathaniel Felton, who was born in 1759, and died in Danvers in 1836. Archelaus Felton was a large man, but not corpulent.

> 291.† i. BETSEY, b. Nov. 11, 1766; m. John Weeks.
> 292.† ii. WILLIAM, b. Oct. 4, 1768; m. Catherine Hunt.
> 293.† iii. SARAH, b. Sept. 8, 1770; m. Aaron Morse.
> 294.† iv. JOHN, b. April 27, 1772; m. Olive Piper.

(101.) viii. DANIEL FELTON⁴, (*Jonathan³, Nathaniel², Nathaniel¹*), bapt. March 11, 1743; m., Dec., 1765, Abigail Cook of Danvers. Mr. Felton was a potter by trade, and settled in Needham, supposed at a place called Connecticut Corner near Dedham line. His will, dated Aug. 4, 1815, proved Feb. 3, 1829, mentions wife Abigail, son Isaac, the executor, and dau. Rebecca Guild. Daniel Felton d. Dec., 1828, (Needham records 83 years), 85 years.

> 295. i. ABIGAIL, b. about 1767; d. Feb. 25, 1813, aged 46 years.
> 296.† ii. REBECCA, b. about 1770; m. Joseph Guild.
> 297.† iii. ISAAC, b. about 1777; m. Anna Richards.

(102.) i. DANIEL FELTON⁴, (*Daniel³, Nathaniel², Nathaniel¹*). m. Aug. 5, 1750, Sarah Martin, dau. of John Martin and grand dau. of Robert Martin, all of Marblehead. He was a blacksmith. After the death of his mother, in 1763, they moved into the western part of the State. In 1764, when living at Rutland, Mass., had 6 children with them, all born in Marblehead. Soon afterwards they settled at Greenwich, Mass., where they resided 30 or more years. Mrs. Sarah Felton was living in 1797. Sup. by some of their descendants that Daniel Felton lived about 90 years.

Their children were probably not all in this order. Three oldest sons were soldiers in 1775, and afterwards.

> 298†. i. JAMES, b. about 1752; m. twice, Miss Ramsdell and Miss Olive Samson.
> 299. ii. RUTH, living in Rutland, Mass., in 1764.
> 300. iii. SARAH, b. before 1764; it is said m. six times, all sea captains.
> 301.† iv. DANIEL, JR., sup. b. about 1759; m. Polly Darling.
> 302.† v. ROBERT, b. Dec. 27, 1760; m. Sylvia Darling.
> 303. vi. THOMAS, living in 1764.
> 304. vii. HANNAH, living in 1764.

305†.	viii.	MARTIN, was a blacksmith; m. Mehitable Bancroft.
306.	ix.	POLLY, d. unmarried.
307.	x.	BETHIAH, m. —— Kemfield.
308.	xi.	REBECCA.

(103.) ii. THOMAS FELTON^4, (Daniel^3, Nathaniel^2, Nathaniel^1,) m. July 1754, Hannah Halfpenny, b. Oct. 28, 1733, both of Marblehead. In 1766, they bought land of Robert Hooper of Marblehead. Thomas Felton, like his father, was a blacksmith. He used to visit on Felton Hill, near the begining of this century, said the late Moses Preston of Peabody. Mr. Felton d. Dec. 20 or 22, 1804, or in 1805, aged 73 years, 6 months. Widow Hannah Felton, Feb. 4, 1822, aged 88 years, 3 months. Margaret Halfpenny, b. 1711-12; d. April 28, 1794, aged 82 years; supposed mother of Mrs. Hannah Felton. Thomas and Hannah Felton had 11 children.

309.	i.	HANNAH, b. May 8, 1756, Saturday; d. Sept. 3, 1747, aged 1 year 4 months.
310.	ii.	SARAH, b. August 22, 1757, Monday; m. Thomas Gale.
311.	iii.	THOMAS, JR., b. April 13, 1859, Friday; m. Martha Conway.
312.	iv.	HANNAH, b. Feb. 15, 1761, Sunday; d. August 29, 1765, aged 4½ years.
313	v.	JOHN, b. June 17, 1763, Saturday; lost at sea in 1778, aged 15 years.
314.	vi.	MARGARET, b. August 15. 1765, Thursday; m. Joseph Pratt.
315.	vii.	DANIEL, b. Oct. 7, 1767, Wednesday; d. Nov, 13, 1781, aged 14 years.
316.	viii.	JAMES, b. Nov. 9, 1769, Thursday; d. August 31, 1770, aged 9 months.
317.	ix.	JAMES, again, Dec. 27, 1771, Friday; m. Mary Brooks.
318.	x.	A son b. Nov. 9, 1775, Thursday; d. same day, aged 2 hours.
319.	xi.	HANNAH, b. April 7, 1777, Tuesday; d. same year, aged 1½ months.

(104.) iii. A sister of the above Thomas Felton, Sen., m. —— Nutt, supposed John Nutt, Capt. John Nutt. In 1763 her brother, Daniel Felton, sold their place in Marblehead to John Nutt, before they moved to Rutland and Greenwich. Her brother, Thomas Felton, says his sister Nutt, died in 1781 In 1772-73, Capt. John Nutt of Marblehead was chosen one of a committee on grievances, and in 1774 one of committee of correspondence. The first-named committee were: Azor Orne, Elbridge Gerry, Thomas Gerry, Jr., Joshua Orne and Capt. John Nutt. Capt. Nutt died before April, 1783. In April, 1783 there was a great fire in Marblehead, 17 buildings being burned; one of which was a barn on the estate of Capt. John Nutt.

(105.) i. JOHN ENDICOTT, b. April 29, 1713; (son of Capt. Samuel Endicott,) m. Elizabeth Jacobs, May 18, 1738. They had 3 sons and 1 daughter. He owned and lived upon the "Old Orchard Farm," the farm with the Endicott pear-tree.

320.† i. JOHN, JR., b. in 1739; m. Martha Putnam; had 12 children.
321. ii. ELIZABETH, b. 1741; d. young.
322. iii. WILLIAM, b. in 1742; m., Nov., 1767, Damaris Osborn; had one son, William, Jr., born in 1769, upon the "Old Orchard Farm."
323. iv. ROBERT, b. Oct. 29, 1756, (or 1746); m. Mary Holt, dau. of Rev. Nathan Holt of Danvers; had 5 children.

(113.) ix. ELIAS ENDICOTT, b. December, 1729, (son of Capt. Samuel, and grandson of Samuel and Hannah (Felton) Endicott of Salem—Danvers,) m. Eunice Andrews and had 5 or 6 children, viz..

323⅛.† i. ANNA, m. Israel Putnam of Danvers.
323¼. ii. EUNICE, m. Peter Putnam; she was a remarkably interesting and lovely woman.
323⅓. iii. ELIAS, b. Sept. 1, 1767; m., Aug., 1791, Nancy Creuzy of Beverly; had 3 children. Res. Danvers.
323½. iv. ISRAEL, b. Dec. 8, 1763; m. —— Ray of Topsfield; had 3 children. Res. Danvers.
323⅔. v. MARY, m. Zerubbabel Porter, July 17, 1738; he was no ordinary man; was called the first shoe manufacturer of Danvers; he died in 1845 "on his native spot," aged 86 years; he was father of Col. Warren Porter and Alfred Porter.
323¾. vi. MARGARET, lived to be old and was familiarly known as "Aunt Peggie."

(126.) i. STEPHEN PROCTOR, b. March 22, 1724-5, son of Nathan and Mary Proctor,—No. 33; m. Elizabeth ——, and had 6 children. He was highway surveyor in Danvers

FELTON FAMILY. 41

in 1761. He died September 13, 1807, aged 83 years. Mrs. Elizabeth Proctor died June 28, 1819.

 324. i. MARY, b. Nov. 30, 1760; d. Nov. 18, 1836, aged 76 years.
 325. ii. DANIEL, b. Jan. 2, 1762; m. Nabby Waters, 1791.
 326. iii. ELIZABETH, b. Oct. 2, 1765.
 327. iv. HANNAH, b. Dec. 17, 1767; died Oct. 24, 1851, aged 84 years.
 328. v. REBECCA, b. May 2, 1773.
 329†. vi. STEPHEN, JR., b. Sept. 23, 1775; m. Mary Felton, (No. 208.)

(131.) vi. NATHAN PROCTOR, JR., b. Nov. 25, 1735, son of Nathan Proctor, (No. 33); m. Oct. 1761, Abigail Waters daughter of John Waters, Jr.; suppose he lived a few years in Marlborough, Mass., before he married. He was chosen deacon of the South Danvers, (now Peabody) church in 1775. Had 6 children.

 330. i. NATHAN, JR., b. Sept. 18, 1764; m. in 1788, Abigail Proctor.
 331. ii. JACOB, b. Feb. 23, 1767; died in Ohio.
 332. iii. ABIGAIL, b. June 13, 1769; died young.
 333. iv. SARAH, b. Dec. 24, 1771.
 334. v. ABIGAIL, b. Dec. 23, 1774.
 335. vi. BETSEY, b. July 25, 1777.

(136.) i. GEORGE DEALAND, JR., b. June, 1721, son of George, and grandson of Mrs. Katherine Dealand, a school teacher in 1708 to 1713; m. Abigail Proctor, b. Aug. 27, 1727, daughter of Thorndike Proctor, Jr., of Salem. Had 2 or more children.

 335⅓. i. THORNDIKE, b. in 1752; m. and had Thorndike Dealand, Jr.
 335⅔†. ii. SARAH, b. May 1762; m. Stephen Felton. (No. 269.)

(139.) ii. JONATHAN PROCTOR, b. March 2, 1739; son of Jonathan and Desire, (No. 36.) In 1759, Jonathan Proctor, when 20 years of age, enlisted in Col. Bailey's regiment, and was in the war at Louisburg, from May 1759 till Nov. 30, 1760. He kept a diary during the 19 months. Capt. Proctor m. Judith ———, and had 8 children. He died in Danvers, Aug 4, 1808, aged 69 years. Mrs. Judith Proctor died Nov. 3, 1821, aged 76 years. Capt. Proctor's grandfather, Thorndike Proctor, Sr., gave him some land about 1752.

336†.   i. JONATHAN, JR., b. March 19, 1770; m. Phebe Gould.
337.   ii. JUDITH, b. Sept. 12, 1773.
338†. iii. MARY, b. Nov. 1, 1775; m. Jedediah Felton, (No. 278.)
339.   iv. BETTY, b. Jan. 6, 1778; died April 20, 1806, aged 28 years.
340.   v. HANNAH, b. June 1, 1780; died May 1, 1862, aged 82 years.
341.   vi. AMOS, b. July 5, 1782.
342†. vii. THORNDIKE, b. July 21, 1786; m. Eliza Wilson, (No. 365.)
343. viii. GEORGE, b. Dec. 23, 1789; m. Rebecca Kenney in 1820.

(144.) vii. ELIZABETH PROCTOR, b. in 1749, or 1750, daughter of Jonathan and Desire Proctor, (No. 36.) Her parents died when she was under 2 years of age. Her uncle Nathan Proctor was appointed her guardian. Miss Proctor was a distinguished school teacher; she taught upwards of 50 years. Miss Elizabeth Proctor deceased in Danvers, Nov. 2, 1824, aged 74 years.

FIFTH GENERATION.

(145.) i. JOSEPH RICHARDSON, b. Feb. 9, 1727; son of Reuben and Esther Richardson, (says Richardson's Genealogy); m. Feb. 11, 1761, Abigail Felton, bapt. April 30, 1738, daughter of Dea. Malachi Felton, of Danvers. Mr. Richardson when m. was of Stoneham. He was a miller in Danvers, and afterwards in Woburn, Mass., where he died in 1823, aged 96 years. Mrs. Abigail Richardson died in Woburn Feb. 16, 1795, aged 57 years. They had 8 children.

349.   i. JOSEPH, JR., b. in 1762; m. Anne Knights, Sept. 1795. Had 3 children.
350†. ii. ELIZABETH, b. Feb. 23, 1763; m. Abijah Richardson.
351. iii. MALACHI, b. April 16, 1766; m. March 22, 1792, Sarah Brown. He died Sept. 24, 1846, aged 80 years; residence, Stoneham, Mass. Had 4 children.
352.   iv. REUEL, b. 176–; m. Abigail Proctor, daughter of Jacob Proctor of South Danvers. He died about 1814; residence, Mason, N. H.
353.   v. ABIGAIL, b. 1773; m. Nathan Buckman, June 1795.
354.   vi. MARY, b. 1775; m. Samuel Symmons, April 1807.

355. vii. CALEB, b. May 20, 1777; m. Mary Eaton Parker, June, 1807.
356. viii. JOHN, b May 20, 1777, twin; killed by falling from a house, July 1807, aged 30 years.

(147.) iii. BENJAMIN KENT, b. in Newburyport, July 26, 1743; m. July 24, 1766, Mary Felton, bapt. Jan. 1742-3, daughter of Dea. Malachi Felton. It is said that Mr. Kent was a deacon, sup. in Danvers North Parish. Dea. Kent died Oct. 27, 1800, aged 57 years. Mrs. Kent, Aug. 12, 1786, aged 43 years.

357. i. BENJAMIN, JR., b. April 8, 1768; m. Elizabeth Fuller.
358. ii. JOSEPH, b. March 18, 1770, sup. m. twice, Lucy Thurston and Dorcas Felton, daughter of Stephen and Elizabeth Felton, (No. 160.)
359. iii. JOSHUA, b. Feb. 23, 1774.
360. iv. MARY, b. April 11, 1776.

(149.) v. ROBERT WILSON of Danvers, called the third in 1775, and m. that year Sarah Felton, who was bapt. Feb. 10, 1750, daughter of Dea. Malachi Felton. Mr. Wilson lived in Danvers and died June 4, 1797, aged 51 years. Mrs. Sarah Wilson died Nov. 20, 1836, aged 85 years. The Wilson cemetery near the centre of old Danvers, now in Peabody, not far from Felton's Corner. Had 9 children.

361†. i. ROBERT, JR., b. Sept. 5, 1776; m. Mary Southwick.
362†. ii. JOHN, b. Jan. 18, 1778; m. Clarissa Waldo.
363†. iii. SARAH, b. Jan. 6, 1780; m. Jonathan Batchelder.
364. iv. ABIGAIL, b. Nov. 5, 1781; died July 28, 1811, aged 30 years.
365†. v. ELIZABETH, b. Aug. 17, 1783; m. Dea. Thorndike Proctor, (No. 342.)
366†. vi. MALACHI, b. July 25, 1785; m. Sarah G. Tate.
367. vii. MERCY, b. Oct. 13, 1787; died on her birthday, 1796, aged 9 years.
368. viii. SAMUEL, b. in 1790; died same year, aged 3 months.
369†. ix. PHEBE, b. Jan. 25, 1793; m. Newhall Wilson.

(152.) i. NATHANIEL FELTON[5], (*Nathaniel[4], Nathaniel[3], John[2], Nathaniel[1],*) b. March 4, 1742; m. Dec. 1769, Mary Williams, b. April 14, 1747, daughter of Col. Joseph Williams of Roxbury. They had one son.

370. i. NATHANIEL, JR., bapt. Jan. 13, 1771; died young.

Mr. Felton died, and widow Mary Felton m. May 7, 1786, Samuel Waite, (not Nathaniel Waite as stated in Williams' Genealogy.) Mr. Waite's child died Oct. 9, 1795, aged 7 years. Mrs. Mary Waite died Oct. 12, 1835. aged 88 years. Mrs. Waite's sister, Martha Williams, m. William Williams, Jr., and their youngest child, b. Dec. 30, 1779, was named for his uncle, Nathaniel Felton. Nathaniel Felton Williams, Esq., was a distinguished merchant in Baltimore, Md.; many years. In 1841, he was appointed Collector of the Port of Baltimore, and was living there in January 1856, then aged 76 years. Mr. Williams said in a letter, "I have often heard from those that knew my Uncle Felton that he was an excellent man and greatly beloved by all that knew him."

Martha Elizabeth Williams, b. July 1815, daughter of N. F. Williams, Esq., of Baltimore, m. her cousin, Nathaniel Felton Williams, b. Aug. 6, 1800, son of Howell Williams, who was the seventh child of William and Martha Williams named above. This Nathaniel Felton Williams was in 1847, a very distinguished and noted man in Texas.

(153.) ii. JOSHUA FELTON[5], (*Nathaniel*[4], *Nathaniel*[3], *John*[2], *Nathaniel*[1],) b. March 21, 1743; m. Jan. 28, 1766, Mary Wardell. Mr. Felton was a blacksmith by trade, and resided in Roxbury, sup. at Felton Place now in Boston. He was chosen, June 1787, a deacon of Rev. Dr. Porter's church in Roxbury. It is said he attended church every Sunday, except one-half day, for 37 years. He kept a diary of every event that transpired in Roxbury for a great number of years. He was one of the standing committee of the Roxbury Charitable Society many years. He resided in Marlborough a few years during the revolutionary war, where he had a son baptized July, 1777. Dea. Felton m. 2d, Oct. 31, 1780, Mrs. Lois Pattee, who had one daughter by her first husband. Dea. Felton died Dec. 1816, aged 74 years. His will dated Dec. 14, 1816, proved Jan. 7, 1817, mentions wife Lois the executrix, daughters Mary Felton and Lucy Lincoln. Mrs. Lois Felton died Aug. 15, 1824, aged 74 years. Dea. Felton had 7 children by his first wife. After Dea Felton's decease two of his manuscripts were sold at public auction and one of them was presented by Elkanah Tabor in 1848, to Roxbury Public Athenæum.

371. i. MARY, b. Nov. 10, 1766; died unm. in Hingham.
372. ii. HANNAH, b. Feb. 2, 1768; died unm. about 1806.
373. iii. JOSHUA, JR., bapt. July 15, 1769; died young.
374†. iv. LUCY, b. July 31, 1770; m. Dea. David Lincoln of Hingham.
375. v. NATHANIEL. bapt. Aug. 29, 1773.

376. vi. LUCRETIA, bapt. Feb. 5, 1775.
377. vii. JOSHUA, JR., bapt. in Marlborough, July 1777.

(154.) iii. WILLIAM FELTON[5], (*Nathaniel*[4], *Nathaniel*[3], *John*[2], *Nathaniel*[1],) b. March 18, 1745; m. Nov. 24, 1773, Eunice Williams, b. Dec. 17 1740, daughter of Maj. Elijah Williams, and grand-daughter of Rev. John Williams, the first minister of Deerfield, Mass., who was taken captive by Indians in 1704, and redeemed in 1706. Maj. Elijah Williams was born Nov. 1712, was a prominent man, represented Deerfield many years in the General Court; m. Margaret Pynchon of Springfield, Mass., and died July 10, 1771, aged 59 years. Wm. Felton was a hatter by trade and lived in Roxbury till the beginning of the revolutionary war, then moved to Deerfield, Mass. In 1791 he was living at Northfield, Mass., where he was taxed for three polls. Mrs. Eunice Felton died about 1798, aged 58 years. Wm. Felton died at Dighton, Mass., about 1820, aged about 75 years. One of their daughters m. a Mr. —— Barrett. Polly Felton, perhaps their daughter, m. at Northfield, Mass., Sept. 28, 1802, Josiah Fisher both of Northfield.

378. i. HERIOT, (Harriet) bapt. in Roxbury, Nov. 13, 1774.
379. ii. EUNICE, bapt. at Deerfield in 1776.
380. iii. ELIJAH, bapt. in 1778, sup. died young.
381†. iv. WILLIAM, JR., b. June 12, 1779; m. Caroline Connable.
382†. v. ELIJAH WILLIAMS, b. about 1781; m. Almy Eliot.
383†. vi. CHARLES, b. Dec. 10, 1783; m. Catherine Felton, (No.   .)

(157.) vi JOSEPH RICHARDSON, b. Dec. 12, 1748; m. Jan. 27, 1774, Abigail Felton, b. Nov. 17, 1753, daughter of Nathaniel Felton of Roxbury, (No. 44.) (She was 15 years younger than her cousin, Abigail Felton, who m. in 1761, Joseph Richardson.) Joseph and Abigail Richardson of Roxbury had one daughter and two sons.

384. i. ABIGAIL, bapt. Dec. 1774; m. Thomas Ramswell and had 6 children.

Mrs. Ramswell died in the year 1800, leaving her 6th child about 2 weeks old; her name was Matilda Ramswell and b. in 1800, and m. Nathaniel Lawrence. In 1885, Mrs. Matilda Lawrence was living in Roxbury Highlands, aged 85 years. Mr. Ramswell afterwards m. a second time and had 6 more children.

385. ii. JOHN, m. Mary Trumbull.
386. iii. NATHANIEL, m. Nabby Pond of Ashford, Ct.

(158.) vii. NATHANIEL WARDELL, m. in Marlboro, Mass., Sept. 16, 1777, Mary Felton, b. June 22, 1756, daughter of Nathaniel Felton, then residing in that town, (No. 44.) They had one daughter. Probably Mr. Wardell was a relative of Jonathan Wardell, who established in 1712, the first public coach ever used in Boston. " It was to be found at the sign of the Orange Tree opposite Hanover Street."

Mrs. Mary Wardell after 1800, was the second wife of Rev. Enoch Pond, b. in Wrentham, April 27, 1756. Rev. Mr. Pond m. first Nov. 20, 1777, Peggy Smith of Wrentham and had 12 children. Mrs. Peggy Pond died Jan. 26, 1800. Rev. Enoch Pond died at Ashford, Ct., Aug. 8, 1807, aged 51 years. Rev. Mr. Pond was uncle to Rev. Dr. Enoch Pond of Bangor, Me., who died Jan. 21, 1882, aged 90 years, 6 months. Rev. Dr. Pond lived in Ashford, Ct., one year in a family with his Aunt Pond, and visited her after he commenced preaching. Mrs. Mary Pond lived many years after her husband's demise.

387.   i. Mary Wardell, Jr.

(159.) viii. EDWARD JACKSON FELTON[5], (*Nathaniel*[4], *Nathaniel*[3], *John*[2], *Nathaniel*[1],) b. Sept. 1758; (sup. the first Felton in New England with a double name.) He lived in Marlboro few years during the revolutionary war. He m. Tamison Baker and settled in Roxbury, and was a hatter by trade. They had 3 children.

In Roxbury, April 4, 1794, Widow Tammy Felton, (says Dea. Joshua Felton's diary,) m. George Wesson. Mrs. Wesson m. third, a Mr. Crane, and died aged about 82 years. Mr. E. J. Felton died April 14, 1790, aged 31 years.

388.   i. Nathaniel, b. Nov. 7, 1784.
389†.   ii. Joshua, b. April 15, 1787; m. Hepsy Skinner.
390.   iii. Sally, b. Aug. 31, 1789.

(160.) i. STEPHEN FELTON[5], (*Stephen*[4], *Samuel*[3], *John*[2], *Nathaniel*[1],) b. April 23, 1743; bapt. in 1746-7; m. Feb. 8, 1767, Elizabeth Baker of Danvers. He was a tanner, and resided at Beverly; afterwards lived in Wenham, where he was taxed in 1781 till 1798. Soon after 1798, went to Biddeford, Me. It is said he lived about 77 years. Had 4 children.

391†.   i. Stephen, Jr., b. about 1769; taxed in Wenham, 1791 to 1798.
392†.   ii. Phebe, b. May 28, 1771; m. Richard Skidmore, Jr.
393†.   iii. Sarah, b. March 2, 1773; m. Capt. John Derby.
394†.   iv. Dorcas, m. Joseph Kent; sup. his second wife.

(161.) ii. DEA. JOSEPH ROSS, of Salem, m. Sarah

Felton, bapt. with her brother Stephen in 1746-47; daughter of Stephen and Dorcas Felton, (No. 50.)

Mrs. Sarah Ross died Aug. 18, 1809, aged 64 years. Dea. Ross, March 25, 1818, aged 76 years. They had two or more children.

395†. i. JOSEPH, JR., m. Elsie Poor.
396. ii. NATHANIEL, died unm., aged about 28 years.

(162.) i. JOHN FELTON⁵, (*Jacob⁴, Samuel³, John², Nathaniel¹*) b. Nov. 9, (O. S.) 20, (N. S.) 1741; m. in Marlboro, Mass., Persis Rogers, and moved to Monadnock No. 5, afterwards called New Marlborough, or Marlborough in New Hampshire. His wife was a sister of John Rogers of that place. John Felton, like his father, was a shoe-maker. He was highway surveyor in 1773; a sexton 6 or 8 years from 1778; a corporal and soldier in the revolutionary war in 1777. In 1786, he sold part of his lot to Nathaniel and Thomas Kendall, and moved into N. Y. State. In 1881, Mr. Felton's place in Marlboro was owned by Hon. Rufus S. Frost, ex-Mayor of Chelsea, Mass. In Sept. 1797, John Felton and family were living at Suffrage, N. Y., soon afterwards settled at Milford, N. Y., not far from Coopertown. Soon after the war of 1812 to 1815, it is said they moved to Clarence in the western part of the State, where they died about 1820, of an epidemic disease, within a week of each other. Probably aged from 78 to 80 years. After Mr. Felton went to N. Y. State, he visited the Felton homestead in Marlboro, Mass., in Jan. 1789, (before his father's decease,) in Oct. 1790, and Nov. 20 (his birthday), 1792, aged 51 years. Their 9 children were born in Marlboro, N. H.

397†. i. JOHN, JR., b. Sept. 17, 1766; m. —— A civil engineer.
398. ii. SARAH, b. Aug. 10, 1768; m. —— Cole; had 4 or 5 children.
399. iii. ELIZABETH, b. May 20, 1770.
400†. iv. JEDEDIAH, b. Feb. 2, 1773; m. twice.
401. v. JACOB, b. Dec. 6, 1774; died Nov. 23. 1776, aged 2 years.
402†. vi. LEVI, b. July 22, 1776; m. —— Had 3 children.
403. vii. PERSIS, b. Jan. 16. 1779; m. John Haynes; settled in Mich. Had 3 children.
404†.viii. ANN SOPHIA, b. April 5, 1782; m. Bartholomew Johnson.
405†. ix. SYLVANUS, b. Aug. 22, 1785; m. Lydia Powers.

(163.) ii. CAPT. DUDLEY HARDY, who was a soldier from Marlboro in the revolutionary army, m. in 1776, Sarah Felton, b.

Feb. 25, 1751, daughter of Lieut. Jacob Felton, (No. 52.) After the war, they went to Rutland, Mass. His name was in Rutland jury box in 1788.

Mrs. Sarah Hardy was living in 1790; no issue. Capt. Hardy m. second about Dec. 1795, Mrs. Charity Sanderson of Cambridge, where he soon afterwards settled, in that part called Little Cambridge, now Brighton. Had one son, Charles, b. about 1797, who married a Miss Perkins, and had a son, Charles, Jr., born about 1825. Mrs. Charity Hardy died about 1812. Capt. Hardy about 1825.

(164.) iii. STEPHEN FELTON[5], (*Jacob*[4], *Samuel*[3], *John*[2], *Nathaniel*[1],) b. Sept. 14 (O. S.) Sept. 25, (N. S.) 1752, the same year and month too (a month of only 19 days) that the new style of reckoning was adopted in Great Britain and her colonies in America, when the third day of Sept. was called the fourteenth of Sept. Stephen Felton served one term in the army in 1775. He m. in 1775, Lovinah Stowe, b. May 17. 1755, daughter of David Stowe. (See appendix Q for Stowe.) He was constable and collector of taxes in 1789; he was chosen the year before, but declined serving. Marlboro had four rates made yearly. April 25, 1794, Dea. Samuel Howe, Stephen Felton and Capt. Aaron Brigham were a committee to build a new school-house in the west squadron in Marlboro, 20x25 feet, with a porch. Stephen Felton was a farmer and resided on his father's homestead about two furlongs northwest of Marlboro Lake, where he died Nov. 3, 1827, aged 75 years. He was buried Nov. 6, the day before the Nov. snow storm of Nov. 7, that was remembered many years afterwards, and to the present time. Lived husband and wife 52 years. Mrs. Lovinah Felton died March 6, 1842, aged nearly 87 years.

406†. i. SILAS, b. Feb. 24, 1776; m. Lucretia Fay.
407. ii. ELIJAH, b. Feb. 15, 1778, died March 22, same year.
408. iii. SALLY, b. June 18, 1779; died Feb. 21, 1780, aged 8 months.
409†. iv. WILLIAM, b. April 15, 1781; m. Lois Bartlett.
410†. v. LYDIA, b. Oct. 4, 1783; m. Luther Wood.
411†. vi. AARON, b. May 16, 1786; m. Lydia Bigelow.
412†. vii. JACOB, b. Nov. 16. 1790; m. Lucinda Wilkins.
413†. viii. STEPHEN, JR., b. July 10, 1795; m. Sally Weeks.

(166.) v. MATTHIAS FELTON[5], (*Jacob*[4], *Samuel*[3], *John*[2], *Nathaniel*[1],) b. March 28, 1756, named for his mother's uncle, Dea. Matthias Rice. Mr. Felton was in single life at the commencement of the revolutionary war, and was called out on the Concord and Lexington Alarm, 19th of April 1775, and served one term of six weeks. In 1776 was in the service three or more months. In 1777, he was drafted from a Marlboro company to serve two months. He served several years afterwards. He was married Oct. 18, 1781, (the day before the surrender of Cornwallis at Yorktown,) to Sarah Maynard of Framingham, Mass., b. March 28, 1757, just one year younger than her husband. She was sister to Hon. Needham Maynard, b Aug. 15, 1755, who was an aid to Gen. Warren at Bunker Hill. Hon. Mr. Maynard lived 89 years; he was cousin to Hon. Jonathan Maynard of Framingham, Mass. Lieut. Matthias Felton was a shoe maker, and soon after he was married went to Fitzwilliam, N. H., where his wife died. He m. second, Feb. 1785, Relief Kendall of Lancaster, Mass. She died Oct. 2, 1826, aged 71 years. He m. third, Nov. 22, 1827, Mrs. Eunice Brigham, widow of Levi Brigham late of Fitzwilliam. Mr. Felton was elected several years a sealer of leather. About 1795, be commenced keeping a public house in that town, which he continued about 30 years. A great deal of travel through Fitzwilliam in his day. He was elected a selectman in 1792, 1793, 1800, 1801, and in 1815. He used to visit the Felton homestead in Marlboro, Mass., every year until the last three years of his life; he rode to Newton one year to see the locomotive engine and cars. Lieut. Matthias Felton died Dec. 28, 1842, aged 86 years, 9 months. He had seven children.

414.   i. HANNAH. b. July 13, 1782; died Sept. 27, 1782.
415.   ii. SALLY, b. June 17, 1783; died June 1, 1785, aged 2 years.
416.   iii. RELIEF, b. Dec. 9, 1785; died Oct. 2, 1786, aged 10 months.
417†.   iv. JACOB, b. July 16, 1787; m. Elizabeth Morse.
418†.   v. ARTEMUS, b. April 2, 1789; m. Elizabeth Van Doom.
419†.   vi. MATTHIAS, JR., b. March 12, 1792; went to Ala.
420†.   vii. LYMAN, b. Jan. 8, or Feb. 8, 1794; m. Sarah Scott.

(167.) vi. THEOPHILAS HARDY, a brother of Capt. Dudley Hardy, m. June 11, 1778, Lucy Felton, b. July 23, 1760; daughter of Lieut. Jacob Felton, (No. 52.) Mr. Hardy was a tanner by trade and was living at Pittstown, Albany County, N. Y., in 1790. In 1797, at Norway on the Mohawk river, and in 1820, at Dryden, Tompkins County, N. Y. They had several children.

(168.) vii. JOEL FELTON^5, (*Jacob^4, Samuel^3, John^2, Nathaniel^1,*) b. May 14, 1762. He was a soldier in the revolutionary war, and in 1780, received from 11 to 12 £. for serving that year. He was a farmer and settled in Marlboro, about half a mile northwest from the Felton homestead, on a farm given him by his father. Mr. Felton was collector of taxes in 1793; served several years as highway surveyor. He m. Nov. 19, 1787, Susanna Hunt of Sudbury, b. Nov 9, 1766, daughter of Samuel Hunt. (See appendix R.)

Joel Felton died Jan. 2, 1829, aged 67 years. His widow, Susanna Felton, Oct. 16, 1841, aged 75 years. They had 9 children.

421†. i. SUSANNA, b. Oct. 29, 1788; m. Edward Rice.
422†. ii. LUTHER, b. April 28, 1790; m. Lydia Russell.
423†. iii. JOEL, JR., b. April 17, 1792; m. twice.
424†. iv. GEORGE, b. May 3, 1796; m. Betsey Hunting.
425†. v. LEVI, b. Jan. 17, 1799; m. Judith Abbott.
426. vi. SALLY, b. Oct. 18, 1800; died Sept. 27, 1804, aged 4 years.
427†. vii. NEWELL, b. March 3, 1803; a wheelwright by trade.
428†. viii. MATTHIAS, b. Oct 25, 1805; m. Lucy Hall.
429†. ix. JOHN, b. July 22, 1808; m. Lydia Jenkins.

(170.) ii. DEA. SAMUEL HOWE, b. Jan. 12, 1749, son of Moses and Hannah (Felton) Howe, (No. 54,) grandson of Ensign Gershom Howe and great-grandson of Capt. Eleazer Howe, all of Marlborough, Mass. Dea. Howe m. Oct. 24, 1771, soon after the death of his father, Hannah Burnap, b. Jan. 16, 1745, daughter of David and Hannah Burnap of Southboro, Mass. He resided in the west part of the town on his father's and grandfather's place. In 1794 was chosen deacon of the church, then the only church in town. In 1789 and 1800 was one of the selectmen of the town. Dea. Howe died July 31, 1820, aged 71 years. Widow Hannah Howe died Nov. 5, 1835, aged 90 years, 9 months. No issue. Dea. Samuel Howe's wife, his mother, grandmother, great-grandmother, and great-great-grandmother, were all Hannahs. Hannah Burnap, Hannah Felton, Hannah Bowker, Hannah Howe and Hannah Ward.

(171.) iii. JONATHAN HOWE, b. Aug. 15, 1751, son of Moses and Hannah (Felton) Howe of Marlboro, (No. 54;) m. Sept. 1773, Elizabeth Robinson of Northboro, Mass., and settled at Holden, Mass. Had 8 children.

430†. i. MOSES, b. Oct. 13, 1774; m. Betsey Temple.
431†. ii. HANNAH, b. Jan. 23, 1777; m. Amos Newell.
432. iii. BETSEY, b. Oct. 10, 1778; m. Elisha Smith.
433†. iv. LUCY, b. Sept. 25, 1780; m. Elias Blake.

434†. v. SAMUEL, b. Aug. 13, 1785; m. Persis Knights.
435.   vi. SALLY, b. March 14, 1788; sup. died young.
436†. vii. POLLY, b. Feb. 18, 1793; m. Joel Blake.
437†.viii. SARAH, b. June 17, 1796; m. John Read Bowls.

(172.) iv. JOHN GASCHET, (now written Gassett,) m. Dec. 3, 1772, Sarah Howe, b. Aug. 20, 1753, daughter of Moses and Hannah (Felton) Howe, (No. 54.) He was a housewright·by trade, and a soldier of the Revolution of 1776. They were living at Rutland in 1782, and in Holden in 1789. They removed from ·Holden back to Marlboro in 1796. Mrs. Gassett died in Marlboro, Mass., July 23, 1829, aged 76 years. John Gassett, died in Northboro, July 1834, aged 88 years. He walked very stooping the last 10 years of his life. Mr. Gassett was uncle to the late Henry Gassett, Esq., of Boston. Their ancestors were French Huguenots.

(173.) v. GERSHOM HOWE, b. Jan. 13, 1756, son of Moses and Hannah (Felton) Howe of Marlboro; (No. 54.) m. Sept. 24, 1783, Lovinah Bartlett of Holden. Mr. Howe was a blacksmith, and in 1789, resided at Keene, N. H. He died Feb. 16, 1801, aged 45 years.

(174.) i. DAVID FELTON^5, (Samuel^4, Samuel^3, John^2, Nathaniel^1,) b. April 20, 1757. He was a soldier from Danvers in the Revolution. He m. in 1784, Hannah Swinton of Danvers. In Sept. 1790, he bought of Ebenezer ·and Hannah Sprague, buildings and land in Danvers. He was a tailor by trade, and made George Peabody's first suit of clothes he had made by a tailor. Sup. Mr. Felton died in Marblehead, Oct. 15, 1818, aged 61 years. His widow, Hannah Felton, died Feb. 25, 1825, aged 66 years. Her will dated Danvers, April, 1820, proved March 4, 1825, mentions son John S., and dau. Hannah Felton. They had 4 children.

438†.   i. JOHN SWINTON, b. Oct. 2, 1787; m. Sally Wood.
439.   ii. DAVID, JR., b. Feb. 3, 1794; died Nov. 5, 1796.
440. iii. ANDREW, b. Dec. 17. 1797; died July 9, 1798.
441†. iv. HANNAH, b. Oct. 30, 1800; m. James Sleeper.

(175.) ii. ASA FELTON^5, (Samuel^4, Samuel^3, John^2, Nathaniel^1,) b. Jan. 10, 1759. He was a soldier in Capt. Samuel Eppes's company in 1775. He m. in 1781, Mary Eppes, who died Sept. 12, 1789. Mr. Felton m. second, Aug. 31, 1790, Sarah Gould, bapt. Nov. 2, 1766, daughter of Thomas Gould of Middleton, Mass. Asa Felton died July 16, 1800, aged 41 years. His death was caused· by a bite of a mad dog. His estate was settled by Andrew Gould; the appraisers were

Eleazer Putnam. Nathan Felton and Moses Preston. Son, James, chose Nathan Felton for guardian. Mrs. Sarah Felton, the mother, guardian to the four youngest children. Mrs. Felton died of dropsy, Aug. 9, 1848, aged 84 years. Had 7 children.

442†. i. POLLY, b. June 1, 1782; m. Rufus Putnam.
443†. ii. JAMES, b. Sept. 10, 1786; m. Sophronia Webb.
444. iii. FANNY, b. Aug. 17, 1791; died unm. June 14, 1855, aged 64 years.
445†. iv. PHEBE, b. March 9, 1793; m. Daniel Nickerson.
446. v. EZRA, b. May 5, 1795; died Oct. 29, 1797.
447†. vi. PATTY, b. Oct. 23, 1797; m. Moses Wilson.
448†. vii. ZACHARIAH, b. Feb. 4, 1800; m. Abigail H. Town.

(178.) v. CAPT. JONATHAN LANDER, of Salem; m. Sept. 24, 1786, Sarah Felton, b. Sept. 6, 1768, daughter of Samuel and Mary Felton of Danvers, (No. 55.) It is said they had several children. Have the birth of one daughter.

449†. i. SALLY, b. June 8, 1788; m. Samuel MacIntire.

(179.) vi. SAMUEL FELTON[5], (Samuel[4], Samuel[3], John[2], Nathaniel[1],) b. Nov. 24, 1772; (a few weeks after his grandfather, Samuel Felton's, death;) m. March. 1805, Jane Doke, or Doak, both of Salem. Mr. Felton was a shoe-maker, and kept the toll gate on the Andover turnpike several years. He kept first between Felton's Corner and Putnam's Lane, afterwards at the crossing of the Andover and Newburyport turnpikes in Danvers. He m. second in 1813, Eunice Porter, and again in 1817, Sarah Arabel Holt of Andover, Mass. It is said he died in Epping, N. H. He had several children.

450. i. SAMUEL, JR., b. July 3, 1813, in Danvers.
451. ii. ELIZA.
452. iii. ANDREW, sup. b. in 1822; m.; was a soldier; enlisted in 1861, aged 39 years.

(180.) vii. THOMAS DODGE of Beverly, m. July 16, 1797, Mary Felton, bapt. June 15, 1777, daughter of Samuel Felton of Danvers, (No. 55.) They had two or more children.

453. i. THOMAS, JR.
454. ii. MARY DODGE.

(182.) ii. DAVID STONE, b. Feb. 1751, in Petersboro, (son of David and Sarah Stone, nonagenarians.) He m. April 1774, Nane Felton, b. Nov. 28, 1750, daughter of David Felton of Petersham, (No. 56.) Sup. David and Nane Stone lived several years in Windsor and Woodstock, towns in Vermont. Mrs. Nancy (Felton) Stone died in Petersham, Jan. 25, 1820, aged 69 years. David Stone died before 1820. Had 8 children.

455. i. ASHBEL, b. April 21, 1776.
456. ii. JOEL, b. Oct. 29, 1777.
457. iii. ZERVIAH, b. July 18, 1779; living in P., Sept. 1832.
458. iv. DAVID, JR., b. July 14, 1782; (some David Stone had 5 children in Fitzwilliam, N. H., between 1813 and 1823.)
459. v. POLLY, b. May 16, 1784.
460. vi. BETSEY, b. June 7, 1786.
461. vii. JOSIAH, b. June 15, 1788; sup. m. Maria ———, and had at Gardner, Mass., a daughter Amelia Z. Stone, b. Jan. 26, 1819.
461½. viii. SALLY, b. June 14, 1791.

(183.) iii. DANIEL FELTON[5], (*David*[4], *Samuel*[3], *John*[2], *Nathaniel*[1],) b. in Marlboro, Mass., Sept. 19, (O. S.) 30, (N. S.) 1752, a month with only 19 days, and was just five days younger than his cousin, Stephen Felton, (No. 164.) They were born within half a mile of each other. Daniel Felton was m. May 5, 1774 by John Chandler, Esq., of Petersham, to Lois Wilder of that town. Their children were b. in Athol, Mass., where he was an assessor in 1779, and 1786. He was a tanner like his father. About 1793, he moved to Sudbury, Vt., where he died about Sept. 1823, aged 71 years. Mrs. Lois Felton died about April 1824, aged 72 years. Their daughters deceased before March 1856.

462†. i. WILLIAM WEBBER, b. July 4, 1775; m. Sally Gary.
463. ii. LUCY, b. June 22, 1776; m. Silas Canfield.
464. iii. DAVID, b. Sept. 5, 1777; died Aug. 17, 1779.
465. iv. LLOYD, b. May 5, 1779; died June 25, 1779.
466. v. ZERVIAH, b. April 19, 1780; m. Moses Hickock.
467. vi. LOIS, b. Aug. 15, 1781; m. Abram Ferrin.
468. vii. LYDIA, b. July 5, 1783; m. A. Fowler.
469†.viii. POLLY, b. March 9, 1785; m. Russell Shules.
470†. ix. SALLY, b. Jan. 21, 1787; m. Jonathan Bennett.
471†. x. LYMAN, b. Nov. 5, 1788; m. Dolly Young.
472†. xi. LLOYD, b. Feb. 2, 1790; m. Polly Woodard.
473†.xii. DANIEL, JR., b. Aug. 5, 1791; m. twice.

(184.) iv. JONATHAN JOHNSON, b. at Worcester, Mass., Jan. 27, 1749–50; (son of John and Susanna Johnson of that place;) m. in 1773, Rachel Felton, b. Sept. 23, 1754, daughter of David Felton of Petersham, (No. 56.) They had 9 sons at Petersham. Mrs. Johnson died June 14, 1799, aged 44 years. Mr. Johnson m. second, Dec. 1801, Margaret Wheeler, and had one son. Jonathan Johnson was a tailor by trade, and died Dec. 4, 1815, aged 66 years.

- 474. i. JOHN, b. Jan. 27, 1774; m. Betsey Stone.
- 475†. ii. AARON, b. Oct. 21, 1775; m. Betsey Crossit.
- 476. iii. JONATHAN, JR., b. Nov. 14, 1777; m. Melissa Wheeler.
- 477. iv. GEORGE, b. Feb. 9, 1780; m. Azubah Puffer.
- 478†. v. AMOS, b. March 13, 1782; m. Mary Knapp.
- 479†. vi. HENRY, b. March 23, 1785; m. Lucy Clement.
- 480. vii. WILLIAM. b. Oct. 4, 1787; m. Nancy Rogers.
- 481. viii. LEVI, b. May 9, 1790; m. Betsey Weeks.
- 482. ix. DANIEL, b. July 27, 1792; died Nov. 7, 1815, aged 23 years.
- 483. x. RUFUS, b. Oct. 31, 1802; died Feb. 13, 1805.

(186.) vi. DANIEL BENJAMIN, b. in Weston, Mass., Oct. 14, 1757, (son of Jonathan Benjamin;) m. Nov. 10, 1779, Tamison Felton, b. Nov. 28, 1758, daughter of David Felton, (No. 56.) They settled at Ashburnham, Mass. In 1721, what is now Waltham, then West Precinct, a Daniel Benjamin, probably a relative of the above, was elected one of the Precinct committee; was elected the first representative in Waltham in 1738, but declined the office; he was elected the first assessor, and one of the selectmen that year. Daniel Benjamin of Ashburnham, died May 10, 1819, aged 62 years, Mrs. Benjamin, March 21, 1843, aged 84 years.

- 484†. i. EUNICE, b. Dec. 5, 1780; m. Aaron Kemp.
- 485†. ii. DANIEL, JR., b. March 6, 1783; m. Rachel Witherell.
- 486. iii. NAHUM, b. Feb. 20, 1785; m. Judith Reed.
- 487. iv. TAMISON, b. May 16, 1787; died unm. in Ashburnham in 1860, aged 73 years.
- 488†. v. NABBY, b. June 17, 1789; m. Samuel Keyes.
- 489†. vi. SALLY, b. March 14, 1792; m. John Hunt.
- 490†. vii. LYDIA, b. May 11, 1794; m. Charles Damon.
- 491. viii. SAMUEL HOWE, b. May 27, 1796; died May 1, 1801, aged 5 years.
- 492†. ix. LOVICE, b. April 8, 1801; m. John Cramm.
- 493†. x. IRENE, b. Feb. 20, 1805; m. Emery Willard.

(187.) vii. GEORGE WEBBER FELTON[5], (*David[4], Samuel[3], John[2], Nathaniel[1],*) b. April 20, 1761, (was the fourth or fifth person born in Marlboro, Mass., given a double name;) m. in 1785, Hannah Oliver, b. March 2, 1758, daughter of John and Mary (Beaman) Oliver of Athol, Mass. They settled in Petersham, where Mr. Felton was one of the school committee in 1807. He died July 5, or 15, 1817, aged 56 years. Widow Hannah Felton was administratrix. She died June 6, 1844, aged 86 years.

 494†. i. HANNAH, b. April 2, 1786; m. Joseph Peconey.
 495†. ii. AURELIA, b. Dec. 30, 1787; died in 1819.
 496†. iii. GEORGE WEBBER, JR., b. May 17, 1789; m. Lydia Baker.
 497†. iv. ELIZABETH ALDEN, b. March 19, 1791; m. Nathaniel Farrow.
 498†. v. DAVID HOWE, b. Dec. 12, 1792; m. Nancy Fish.
 499†. vi. MOSES OLIVER, b. March 14, 1794; m. Susan Cummings.
 500†. vii. ALEXANDER, b. April 8, 1795; m. Fanny Wells.

(188.) viii. LEMUEL STIMSON, b. July 11, 1758, in Weston, Mass. He m. in 1780, Phebe Felton, b. Sept. 12, 1763, daughter of David Felton, (No. 56.) Mr. Stimson settled in Ashburnham, where he was a merchant several years. Mrs. Phebe Stimson died Sept. 17, 1830, aged 67 years. Husband and wife 50 years. Mr. Stimson m. second, May 1833, Catherine Goodale; she died Oct. 25, 1860; Mr. Stimson died 20 years before, Sept. 22, 1840, aged 82 years. Had 13 children.

 501. i. POLLY, b. Nov. 6, 1780; m. Artemus Jackson.
 502. ii. LYDIA, b. July 26, 1782; died Sept. 17, same year.
 503†. iii. PHEBE, b. Sept. 18, 1783; m. James Whitmore.
 504. iv. AMOS, b. Dec. 1785; died Nov. 14, 1795.
 505†. v. ROYAL, b. March 6, 1786; m. Relief Walker.
 506. vi. LEMUEL, JR., b. Aug. 1790; died Dec. 26, 1791.
 507†. vii. EDWARD, b. Oct. 3, 1792; m. Sarah Foster.
 508†. viii. CHARLES, b. May 9, 1795; m. Beulah Whitmore.
 509†. ix. ABIGAIL, b. May 25, 1797; m. Isaac Keyes.
 510†. x. LUCY, b. Aug. 20, 1799; m. John Cushing Davis.
 511†. xi. ELMIRA, b. Dec. 4, 1802; m. Benj. Whitney.
 512†. xii. ELBRIDGE, b. April 6, 1806; m. Elizabeth Caldwell.
 513†. xiii. MIRICK, b. Aug. 15, 1808; m. twice.

(189.) ix. AMOS FELTON^5, (*David^4, Samuel^3, John^2, Nathaniel^1,*) b. Sept. 18, 1765. He lived with his uncle Zachariah Felton on Mt. Pleasant, now in Peabody, Mass., and with his

FELTON FAMILY.

Aunt Tamison Felton, 10 years, at the same place till about 1790. An elm tree is now standing on Mt. Pleasant, set out by Amos Felton; and he is reported as saying at the time, when said tree was large enough to make him a coffin, he would be ready to fill it. In 1790, he m. Sarah Putnam, bapt. Oct. 29, 1769, daughter of William Putnam of Danvers, and moved to an adjoining town, Middleton, where 8 of their children were born. Mrs. Felton was sister to Dea. Ebenezer Putnam of Danvers. In 1798, Amos Felton was an assessor, and selectman, and constable in 1799. In 1805, he sold his farm in Middleton and went to Tunbridge, Vt. A few years before his decease he visited Marlboro and other towns in Mass. He died Oct. 29, 1829, aged 64 years; Mrs. Sarah Felton, Aug. 1848, aged 79 years.

514.   i. SALLY, b. Dec. 18, 1790; died Aug. 5, 1796.
515.† ii. NANCY, b. April 7, 1792; m. George Camp.
516. iii. ZACHARIAH, b. April 20. 1794; died July 29, 1796.
517†. iv. AMOS, JR., b. Sept. 24, 1795; m. Elsea Roberts.
518.   v. SALLY, b. Dec. 11, 1797; died Oct. 7, 1801.
519. vi. ZACHARIAH, b. April 30, 1800.
520†. vii. LUCY b. Feb. 20, 1802; m. Osman P. Farnham.
521†.viii. WILLIAM PUTNAM, b. April 26, 1804; m. Betsey Swain.
522†. ix. ABIJAH, b. May 27, 1806; m. Phebe Baldwin.
523.   x. ANSON, b. April 18, 1809; died in Tunbridge; July 22, 1822, aged 13 years.
524. ix. An infant, b. in July, died in Aug. 1811.
525†. x. DAVID, b. Aug. 30, 1812; m. Lucinda Baldwin.

(190.) x. CALEB PIERCE, m. Abigail Felton b. July 26, 1767 daughter of David Felton, (No. 56.) They lived in Shrewsbury, Vt., and Weathersfield, same state. They had one son and 6 or more daughters. The children probably not in this order.

526.   i. ROYAL, died a young man.
527. ii. ABIGAIL, m. Caleb Smith of Vt.
528. iii. SALLY, m. Mr. Johnson of Shoreham Vt.
529. iv. LUCY.
530.   v. LYDIA.
531. vi. LAURA.
532. vii. SOPHRONIA.
533. viii. ALMIRA, m. Abijah Smith, brother of Caleb Smith.

(191.) xi. JEDEDIAH HOWE, b. in Marlboro, Mass., June 28, 1770, (son of Phineas Howe of that town, who lived 93 years;) m. Sept. 28, 1795, Lydia Felton then of Marlboro,

b. Feb. 10, 1770; daughter of David Felton, (No. 56.) They had one son in Marlboro, then moved to Lunenburg, Vt., where he was killed by the falling of a tree in the woods, about the year 1817, aged 47 years. The widow returned, and lived in Marlboro several years; afterwards went to Lunenburg and died about the year 1831, aged about 61 years. They had 4 children.

534. i. EDWARD, b. July 4, 1796; died July 25, 1814, aged 18 years.
535†. ii. LYDIA, b. Sept. 1800; m. Eli Brigham.
536†. iii. LUCRETIA, b. June 1806; m. Lee Amsden.
537†. iv. REUEL, b. Sept. 1808; m. Mary S. Rice.

(193.) i. BENJAMIN DALAND, JR., bapt. Aug. 25, 1745; was son of Benjamin and Elizabeth (Felton) Daland of Danvers. Mr. Daland m. Feb. 1772, Mary Hayward, and had one son. April 19, 1775, the town of Danvers lost seven young men and their names are on a monument erected in Danvers in 1835; Benjamin Daland's age on the monument is 25 years; a mistake for 29 years. In Feb. 1776, the General Court voted to Capt. Eppes, about 20 £ for the use of 8 persons from Danvers, who had lost guns and so forth on the 19th of April last (April 1775;) the heirs of Benjamin Daland received 2£ 4s. The widow, Mary Daland, died July 1788.

538†. i. JOSEPH, b. Feb. 7, 1774; m. Phebe Guilford.

(194.) ii. EBENEZER HOWE, b. Nov. 4, 1746; (son of Ezekiel and Elizabeth (Rice) Howe;) m. Elizabeth Daland, b. about Oct. 1748, daughter of Benjamin and Elizabeth (Felton) Daland of Danvers, Mass. Ebenezer Howe was a cousin to Rev. Perley Howe, who was b. in Marlboro, and settled at Surry, N. H. Ebenezer Howe lived in Templeton, Mass., and afterwards in Gardner, Mass., where he was a prominent citizen. He was several years moderator at annual town meetings; also several years selectman, assessor, and 10 years from 1789, town treasurer. His wife, Elizabeth Howe, died Feb. 15, 1795, aged 46 years, 4 months. Mr. Howe m. second, Mary Hill. He died Dec. 1808, aged 62 years.

539†. i. TAMISON, b. Aug. 31, 1770; m. Joel Brooks.
540†. ii. PERLEY, b. Nov. 7, 1772; m. Jane T. Belcher.
541†. iii. EZEKIEL, b. March 20, 1775; m. Susanna Payson.
542. iv. SARAH, b. Dec. 11, 1777; m. Silas Wood.
543. v. BETSEY, b. April 12, 1781; m. John Miller.
544†. vi. BENJAMIN, b. Feb. 16, 1783; m. Keziah Hill.

545. vii. AMOS, b. June 17, 1785; the first birth in Gardner after its incorporation; he died in 1805, aged 20 years.

(195.) iii. SAMUEL REEVES, b. or bapt. June 6, 1754; m. May 31, 1771, Hannah Daland, bapt. in 1754, daughter of Benjamin and Elizabeth (Felton) Daland, (No. 58.) In 1775, Mr. Reeves was a soldier in the army from Danvers. Had 4 children.

546. i. BETSEY, b. Nov. 5, 1771; bapt. March, 1772.
547. ii. HANNAH, b. March, 1774.
548. iii. SUSANNA, b. April 8, 1777.
549. iv. BENJAMIN, b. Oct. 19, 1779.

(196.) iv. JOHN MACKINTIRE, (sup. son of John and Mehitable Mackintire, who lived in Danvers when the town was incorporated;) m. Nov. 20, 1777, Mary Daland, daughter of Benjamin and Elizabeth (Felton) Daland, (No. 58.) Mrs. Mary Mackintire was living when her father's estate was settled in 1805.

(198.) iv. JOHN FELTON[5], (*Elisha*[4], *John*[3], *John*[2], *Nathaniel*[1],) b. Dec. 15, 1777; m. Lydia Muzzey, or Mussey, b. Aug. 9, 1782, daughter of Dr. John and Beulah (Butler) Mussey of Pelham, Amherst and Peterborough, N. H. She was sister to Prof. R. D. Mussey of Dartmouth College, and Dr. Mussey of Salem, Mass. They were m. Feb. 26, 1807, and soon afterwards moved to Landgrove, Vt. Mrs. Felton died Oct. 6, 1812, aged 30 years. Mr. Felton m. second, Dec. 15, 1813, Mrs. Mary Pierce. She died Nov. 30, 1870. John Felton died Nov. 20, 1865, aged almost 88 years. John Felton had five daughters and one son.

550. i. MIRANDA, b. April 18, 1808; died Oct. 23, 1817.
551†. ii. HANNAH, b. Oct. 9, 1809; m. Eben. H. Tuttle.
552†. iii. LYDIA M., b. Sept. 26, 1812; m. Joel B. Fiske.
553†. iv. JOHN, JR., b. July 15, 1815; m. Sally Hall.
554. v. MARY, b. June 24, 1817; m. Hiram Farnum.
555†. vi. MIRANDA, b. Sept. 24, 1819; m. Wm. H. Adams.

(199.) v. JOSEPH ROBERTSON, m. about 1799, Rachel Felton, b. Oct. 10, 1779, daughter of Elisha Felton of Amherst, N. H., (No. 68.) They had one son. Mr. Robertson died and the Widow Robertson m. second, Dec. 1, 1814, Thomas Goodhue, who died about 6 months afterwards, in 1815, at Mount Vernon, N. H. Mrs. Rachel Goodhue died at Goffstown, N. H., Jan. 20, 1865, aged 85 years.

556†. i. GILMAN, b. May 1800; m. Relief Wyman.

FELTON FAMILY. 59

(200.) vi. ELISHA FELTON[5], (*Elisha*[4], *John*[3], *John*[2], *Nathaniel*[1],) b. Oct. 8, 1781; m. Dec. 30, 1806, Lydia Wilkins, daughter of Aaron Wilkins of Amherst, N. H. They lived at Amherst, where he died May 29, 1822, aged 41 years. Elijah Putnam was guardian to the two children. Widow Lydia Felton died July 30, 1839, aged 54 years.

 557†. i. HARRIET, b. July 5, 1808; m. Ezra D. Clarke.
 558†. ii. HIRAM GRANVILLE, b. Feb. 4, 1814; m. Jane Austin.
 559. iii. ORINDA, died young.

(202.) i. TIMOTHY FELTON[5], (*Timothy*[4], *John*[3], *John*[2], *Nathaniel*[1],) b. Dec. 8, 1765; m. in 1788, Mary Putnam, bapt. Jan. 26, 1767; daughter of Dea. Joseph Putnam of Danvers, who was a nephew of Gen. Israel Putnam of the revolutionary war. Mr. Felton was a tanner, and in 1793, and 1794, was living in Litchfield, N. H. He afterwards settled at Warner in the same state. He was a selectman in Warner in 1800, and 1801, and Justice of the Peace. History of Warner says, Mr. Felton was remarkable for extensive reading and general information. Hon. Levi Bartlett of Warner, says he was a man of sound judgment, correct morals, of superior intelligence, and well posted in history. In April 1787, Timothy Felton, then 21 years of age, transplanted an elm tree, at the junction of Andover and Prospect streets, at Felton's Corner, now in Peabody. The dimensions of the "Big Elm" in 1883, were— circumference, 26 feet, height, 80 feet; estimated to contain ten cords of wood. Timothy Felton, Esq., died Jan. 15, 1856, aged 90 years, 1 month. They had 3 children; the birth of only one recorded on Danvers' records.

 560. i. THORNDIKE, b. in Danvers, July 31, 1788; died in Warner in the winter of 1829, aged 41 years.
 561†. ii. CLARISSA, b. Feb. 16, 1791; m. Daniel Currier.
 562. iii. ASENATH, living in 1818.

(204.) iii. NATHAN FELTON[5], (*Timothy*[4], *John*[3], *John*[2], *Nathaniel*[1],) b. June 15, 1770; m. Jan. 24, 1796, Lydia Proctor, b. July 31, 1771, daughter of Benjamin Proctor of Danvers. Capt. Nathan Felton was a merchant at Felton's Corner, in Danvers, before and after 1803. He took a prominent part in the concerns of the town; was Justice of the Peace; Town Clerk 28 years; a selectman several years, and representative 15 years, first in 1805, last time in 1822. The following item taken from an Essex County newspaper in 1883: Nathan Felton's house was near the "Big Elm"; the L or ell of his house was standing in 1883, supposed to be about 175 years old; and in it was where "Old Square Felton" (as he was familiarly called,) performed the duties of town clerk for the old town of Danvers for twenty-seven years. Until within a few years Mr. Felton's house was owned by his grandson, Nathan A. Felton. In 1883, T. J. Osborn of Peabody owned the building. John Felton, an uncle of Nathan Felton, Esq., owned and lived at the place, before 1800. Nathan Felton, Esq., died Feb. 26, 1829, aged 58 years. Mrs. Lydia Felton died Nov. 28, 1832, aged 61 years.

At the centennial celebration of Danvers, June 16, 1852, Dr. Andrew Nichols of that town, read a lengthy poem. The following is from Dr. Nichols' poem:

> The name of Felton, too, by many here,
> In reminiscence must be held most dear.
> One, our Town Clerk for twenty-eight full years,
>   A selectman as long,— and for fifteen,
> A representative,—among compeers
>   Highly respected, must have been, I ween,
> Worthy a place in our centennial song,
>   Worthy a place in hearts, that well him knew,
> For friends ne'er met him, but he kept them long,
>   For his was humor, wit and wisdom too;
> His manners gentle, his affections strong,
>   In Nature's quiet gifts surpassed by few.

Capt. Nathan and Lydia Felton had 5 children.

563. i. MEHITABLE, b. May 15, 1797; died April 14, 1813, aged 16 years.
564. ii. NATHAN, JR., b. June 14, 1799; died in Gardiner, Me., Aug. 10, 1818, aged 19 years.
565.† iii. HANNAH PROCTOR, b. Feb. 25, 1802; m. Capt. Daniel Felton, (No. 694.)
566†. iv. LYDIA, b. Sept. 25, 1804; m. William Price.
567†. v. ELIZA MATILDA, b. Feb. 28, 1809; m. William Price.

(205.) iv. AMOS PUTNAM, b. Feb. 4, 1772; (son of Dr. James P. Putnam, and grandson of Dr. Amos Putnam, who was a prominent man in Danvers;) m. in 1798, Desire Felton, b. June 9, 1773; daughter of Timothy Felton (No. 73.) Amos and Desire Putnam lived in Hopkinton N. H., Lynnfield and Danvers, Mass. Mrs. Putnam died Dec. 11, 1834, aged 61 years. Amos Putnam died Oct. 24, 1848, aged 76 years. (Appendix S for Putnam.)

568. i. SALOME, b. Oct. 7, 1799; died unm. June 17, 1868, aged 68 years.

569. ii. ALFRED, b. in Hopkinton, N. H., Jan. 10, 1801; m. Mary Merrill, residence, Andover, Mass., had 4 sons, 1 daughter.
570. iii. JULIA ANN, b. Jan. 26, 1803; died unm. Sept. 24, 1868, aged 65 years.
571. iv. AMOS, JR., b. Feb. 11, 1806; died unm. March 13, 1867, aged 61 years.
572. v. MARY, b. in Danvers, Dec. 18, 1810; died March 30, 1834, aged 23 years.
573. vi. TIMOTHY FELTON, b. Feb. 14, 1815; died May 24, 1832, aged 17 years.
574. vii. BETSEY, b. March 7, 1817; died April 23, 1823.

(206.) v. EBENEZER FELTON[5], (*Timothy*[4], *John*[3], *John*[2], *Nathaniel*[1],) b. Nov. 25, 1775; was named for his uncle, Ebenezer Felton, who was a soldier and died that year. He lived in Salisbury, Mass., and was agent for the "Amesbury Iron Factory Company," incorporated March 1805, which made great improvements in the manufacture of nails.

In March 1810, Ebenezer Felton and his associates were made a corporation, by the name of "The Danvers Cotton Factory Company," for the purpose of manufacturing cotton in that town. The factory was at Brookdale, now (1886,) in West Peabody, Mass. The factory with many of the buildings was burned about 1876.

In 1812, Ebenezer Felton was captain of a military company in Danvers. Capt. Felton settled at Meadville, Pa., where he was a Justice of the Peace, and died unm. Aug. 5, 1849, aged 74 years.

(207.) vi. JOHN FELTON[5], (*Timothy*[4], *John*[3], *John*[2], *Nathaniel*[1],) b. 24, 1779; m. in 1802, Phebe Goodale, dau. of Capt. William and Phebe Goodale of Danvers. He settled on Mount Pleasant, on the then late Zachariah Felton's place. Capt. John Felton died Oct. 1852, aged 73 years, Mrs. Phebe Felton died April, 1861. They were husband and wife 50 years. Had 5 children.

575†. i. SERENA, b. Oct. 16, 1803; m. Warren Sheldon.
576†. ii. PHEBE, b. April 17, 1805; m. Joseph Merrill.
577†. iii. TIMOTHY PROCTOR, b. Jan. 14, 1807; m. Lydia Ann Haskell.
578†. iv. ELIZABETH CLARINDA, b. Oct. 25, 1811; m George W. Pousland.
579†. v. WILLIAM TAPLEY, b. Feb. 21, 1818; m. Harriet Stevens.

(208.) vii. STEPHEN PROCTOR, b. Sept. 23, 1775; (son of Stephen, of Nathan., of Thorndike, of John, of John of Ipswich, the emigrant;) m. in 1817, Mary Felton, b. Dec. 17, 1781, daughter of Timothy Felton, (No. 73.) They lived in Danvers, where they both died in 1853; Mrs. Proctor, Sept. 7, aged 71 years; Mr. Proctor, two months afterwards, Nov. 3, aged 78 years. Had two children.

 580†. i. NATHAN STEPHEN, b. Dec. 3, 1818; m. Martha A. Proctor.
 581. ii. EBENEZER WARREN. b. March 8, 1822; died Feb. 4, 1827, aged 5 years.

(209.) viii. MOSES PRESTON, b. July 6, 1789, son of Moses Preston, Senior, who purchased the Dea. Malachi Felton place on Mount Pleasant. (App. T.) Moses Preston, Sen., was thrown from a wagon, Dec. 27, 1823, and died Feb. 26, 1824, aged 65 years. His widow, Sarah Preston, died Jan. 28, 1855, aged 92 years.

Moses Preston, Jr., m. in 1817, Betsey Felton, b. Oct. 17, 1789, daughter of Timothy Felton, (No. 73.) He taught school several winters, was Justice of the Peace 14 years. He was captain of the militia; was b., lived and died on Mount Pleasant, now in Peabody, Mass. Capt. Preston was one of those good-men who lived long and well, and were content so to do without any proclamation made of it, as John W. Proctor, Esq., said at the Danvers' centennial celebration in June, 1852. Mrs. Betsey Preston died Nov. 2, 1854, aged 65 years. Capt. Preston, March 13, 1878, aged 88 years, 8 months. They had one daughter.

 582. i. ELIZA ANN, b. in 1829; died June 5, or 7, 1851, aged 22 years.

(210.) i. EBENEZER FOSTER, JR., b. about 1732; son of Ebenezer and Lydia (Felton) Foster; m. Hannah ———, and lived in Oakham, Mass., where he was an innholder in 1763, and constable, assessor and selectman several years. He also lived in New Braintree, Mass. Mrs. Hannah Foster died Feb. 1808, aged 68 years. Lieut. Ebenezer Foster died March 1811, aged 79 years. An inventory of Ebenezer Foster, late of New Braintree, was made the same year. Had 11 children.

 583. i. HANNAH, b. Aug., 1759; sup. 1758; died in 1761.
 584. ii. LYDIA, b. Feb. 1760; m. Stephen Lincoln.
 585. iii. JOSEPH, b. March, 1762.
 586. iv. ALPHEUS, b. May 1764, or 1765.
 587. v. ZADOCK, b. Feb. 1767; pub. to Sally Porter, Jan. 1789.
 588. vi. EBENEZER, JR., b. Feb. or Aug. 1769; m. and was one of the selectmen of Oakham, 1802 to 1805.

589. vii. HANNAH, b. May 18, 1772.
590. viii. WILLIAM, b. March 8, 1774; pub. to Betsey Nichols, Aug. 1799.
591. ix. BENJAMIN, b. Aug. 14, 1776; m. Mrs. Lydia Long, had 7 children.
592. x. MOLLY, b. Jan. 4, 1779; called Polly Foster in the will.
593. xi. SPENCER, b. May 26, 1781.

(214.) iv. JAMES HOULTON, b. in Hopkinton, Mass., July 1, 1736; son of Joseph and Rebecca (Felton) Houlton, (No. 75;) m. in New Salem, Mass., Lois ———, and had several children baptized in that town. He was called Capt. James Houlton.

594. i. MOLLY, or MARY, bapt. June 1760; sup. m. May 1773, John Ganson.
595†. ii. JOSEPH, bapt. June 1760; m. Sarah Putnam.
596. iii. EUNICE, bapt. June, 1760; m. Nov. 1778, Joel Dickinson.
597. iv. SUSANNA, bapt. May 1763.
597½. v. LUCINDA, sup. their dau.; m. Jan. 1781, Nahum Fairbanks.

(221.) i. MOSES HAMILTON, b. July 2, 1744; son of Nathan and Ruth Hamilton of Brookfield, Mass.; m. Jan. 15, 1767, Hannah Felton, b. Aug. 18, 1737, daughter of Joseph Felton, (No. 76.) They settled in New Braintree, Mass., and had 4 or more children, and all deceased before 1805. About 1805, Moses Hamilton Felton, (No. 605,) moved into the town and lived with them. Mrs. Hannah Hamilton died Dec. 11, 1822, aged 85 years. Moses Hamilton deceased in Feb. 1825, aged 80 years. He was a prominent man. Mr. Felton had his Uncle Hamilton's place.

(222.) ii. BENJAMIN FELTON[5], (*Joseph*[4], *Skelton*[3], *Nathaniel*[2], *Nathaniel*[1],) b. in Salem, March 12, 1739; bapt. April 11, 1739; in 1745, his parents went to Rutland, Mass. During the French and Indian wars, from 1756 to 1760, a large number of men were called into service. It is said that Benjamin Felton at the age of 16 years, was aroused from sleep in the night, to march with others to Canada, to repel the French and Indians, and did not succeed in returning home for four or five years. His name is found in a company of that date, 1756, commanded by Capt. Samuel Howe of Marlboro, Mass., that marched to the relief of Fort William Henry.

Benjamin Felton m. Dec. 24, 1767, Jennie Dorrity, and had two daughters. He m. second in Jan. 1771, Ruth Hamilton,

b. Dec. 3, 1752, daughter of Nathan and Ruth Hamilton of Brookfield, Mass., and had 11 children. Part of their children were b. in Sturbridge, Mass., the others in Brookfield, Mass.

Benjamin Felton served as a soldier through the revolutionary war, was at first an Orderly Sergeant, and at last a Lieutenant. He was at the battle of Bunker Hill; at the battle on, and the retreat from Long Island; in the battles at White Plains, at Trenton, Monmouth, etc. After the war he was captain of the militia, and commanded a body of cavalry under Gen. Shepard in the Shay's Insurrection in Mass., in the winter of 1786-87. In 1782, Capt. Felton was living in Brookfield, Mass. He sold his farm in 1818, to his son, Skelton Felton. In 1819, Capt. Felton received a pension of 94 dollars, 66 cents. Mrs. Ruth Felton died Feb. 20, 1819, aged 66 years, Capt. Felton the next year, Jan. 26, 1820, aged almost 81 years.

598†.   i. MARY, b. April 12, 1768; m. William Perry.
599†.   ii. JANE, b. April 25, 1769; m. Samuel Mower.
600†. iii. BENJAMIN, JR., b. July 20, 1771; m. Nancy Ellis.
601†.   iv. JOSEPH, twin, b. July 20, 1771; m. Sally Bartlett.
602†.   v. NATHAN, b. Jan. 25, 1775; m. Mary Hinds.
603†.   vi. RUTH, b. Aug. 15, 1778; m. Calvin Perry.
604†. vii. JOHN, b. Dec. 3, 1780; m. Mary Calhoun.
605†. viii. MOSES HAMILTON, b. Nov. 19, 1782; m. Persis Thompson.
606†.   ix. SKELTON, b. Nov. 13, 1784; m. Lucinda Adams.
607†.   x. SALLY, b. Feb. 27, 1787; m. Andrew Batchelder.
608†.   xi. AMORY, b. April 10, 1789; m. Mary S. Osborn.
609†. xii. HANNAH, b. Oct. 1, 1791; m. Jacil Kendrick.
610†. xiii. OLIVER CROSBY, b. Sept. 15, 1795; m. Eliza Upton.

(223.) iii. MR. CURTIS, of Hartford, Conn., a publisher of books, m. Sarah Felton. b. Oct. 21, 1741; daughter of Joseph and Mary (Trask) Felton, (No. 76.)

(224.) iv. CAPT. WYMAN HOYT, b. about 1745; m. about 1770, Hepsibah Felton, b. Aug. 21, 1743, daughter of Joseph Felton, (No. 76.) They settled in New Braintree. Capt. Hoyt died March 22, 1816, aged 71 years. Mrs. Hoyt died Feb. 3, 1831, aged 87 years. They had one son.

611†.   i. JOHN FRINK, b. in 1771; m. Anna Bowman.

(225.) v. JOSHUA SLAYTON, b. Dec. 16, 1744, in Brookfield, son of Thomas and Abiah Slayton; m. May 1770, Desire Felton, b. Aug. 21, 1746; daughter of Joseph Felton,

(No. 76.) Had one or more children. After the decease of Joshua Slayton, Mrs. Desire Slayton m. Rev. Mr. Bugbee of Paxton, Mass., and sup. they afterwards lived in the State of Vt. Joshua Slayton's son was:

612.   i. JAMES CALDWELL SLAYTON, b. in Brookfield, Mass., April 3, 1771.

(227.) vii. SKELTON FELTON[5], (*Joseph*[4], *Skelton*[3], *Nathaniel*[2], *Nathaniel*[1],) b. Dec. 21, 1750; m. Aug. 25, 1775, Silence Hale, b. in Bolton, Mass., Feb. 2, 1756, daughter of Experience Hale, who m. about 1755, Miss Rachel Pratt, daughter of Ephraim Pratt, who died at Shutesbury, Mass., in May 1804, aged 99 years, 6 months. Mrs. Rachel Hale died March 6, 1829, aged 92 years, 10 months. A few years after Mr. Felton m., settled in Barre, Mass., where he died July 9, 1822, aged 71 years; Mrs. Silence Felton, Sept. 27, 1830, aged 74 years, 7 months. Their son, Capt. Benjamin Felton, administered on the estate. They had 10 children.

613.   i. JOHN b. in Westhampton, Mass., Nov. 24, 1776; died Oct. 19, 1779.
614†.   ii. HANNAH, b. Sept. 2, 1778; m. Bartholomew Green.
615†.   iii. LYDIA, b. in Barre, July 20, 1781; m. John Smead.
616†.   iv. HEPSIBAH, b. June 2, 1783; m. Jeremiah Robinson.
617†.   v. SKELTON, b. June 15, 1785; m. Tryphosa Bullard.
618†.   vi. JOSIAH, b. March 13, 1788; m. Relief Smith.
619†.   vii. JONATHAN WALES, b. June 17, 1790; m. Lydia Bullard.
620†. viii. BENJAMIN, b. Sept. 6, 1792; m. Lucretia S. Nye.
621†.   ix. JOSEPH, b. Aug. 5, 1796; m. Deborah Foster.
622†.   x. OCTAVIA, b. March 18, 1799; m. Samuel Cone.

(228.) viii. JOSEPH AYRES, of Brookfield, Mass., m. Oct. 27, 1774, Mary Felton, b. Jan. 17, 1753; daughter of Joseph Felton of Oakham, Mass., (No. 76.) They had one son. Mr. Ayres was frozen to death while lumbering near Machias, Me. Mrs. Mary Ayres m. second, Jonathan Nye.

623.   i. ADIN AYRES, b. July 16, 1775.

(229.) ix. LIEUT. SAMPSON WETHERELL, b. April 29, 1753; (son of Sampson Wetherell, whose estate was settled in 1804,) of New Braintree; m. second, April 10, 1788, Lydia Felton, b. July 3, 1755, daughter of Joseph Felton, (No. 76.) Mr. Wetherell m. first in 1777, Grace Fisher, who died in 1786. Mrs. Lydia Wetherell died May 27, 1798, aged 43 years. Lieut.

Sampson and Lydia Wetherell had three children. Sampson Wetherell died, (father or son,) Oct. 28, 1803; if son, aged 50 years.

>624. i. JOHN, b. Jan. 3, 1789.
>625†. ii. ISABELLE, b. Dec. 1, 1791; m. Pemberton Ward.
>626†. iii. SAMPSON, JR., b. Aug. 5, 1795; sup. m. Lucy Kendall.

(232.) xiii. MONTGOMERY BARTLETT, m. Abigail Felton, daughter of Joseph Felton, (No. 76.) The name Abigail was not recorded with the other children. A daughter, Isabel, b. March 1759; and daughter, Betsey, b Aug. 1748. Perhaps one of these daughters m. Montgomery Bartlett. Mr. Bartlett's sister, or Mr. and Mrs. Bartlett's daughter, Sally Bartlett, m. in 1794, Joseph Felton, (No. 601.) It is said Mrs. Bartlett lived 80 years and upwards. Joseph and Sally (Bartlett) Felton had a son named Montgomery Bartlett Felton.

(249.) iii. JOHN FELTON^5, (*Francis^4, John^3, Nathaniel^2, Nathaniel^1,*) b. March 19, 1753; m. Jan. 19, 1775, Rebecca Larkin; who was a widow in 1801, when she conveyed property to her son, Samuel Felton, and daughter, Hannah Felton. Mrs. Rebecca Felton died about Jan. 1805. Jan. 14, 1805, administratorship was granted to John Drury upon the estate of Widow Rebecca Felton of Marblehead. Samuel Felton's account was 59 dollars. Part, if not all those named below were their children.

>627. i. JOHN H., who m. in Boston, Oct. 30, 1800, Elizabeth Gerrill.
>628. ii. SAMUEL, who m., July 1, 1802, Elizabeth Lilley.
>629. iii. HANNAH, who m. first, —— Spencer; had 3 children.
>630†. iv. FRANCIS, who m. Sally Graves.
>631†. v. THOMAS K., who m. Mrs. Mary Tucker.

(251.) v. SAMUEL FELTON^5, (*Francis^4, John^3, Nathaniel^2, Nathaniel^1,*) b. Dec. 14, 1755; m. Dec. 11, 1788, Esther Porter, both of Marblehead. They had one or more children.

>632. i. THOMAS, b. Sept. 6, 1800; sup. m. in Salem, April 25, 1827, Sarah Gould.

(259.) xiii. JAMES FELTON^5, (*Francis^4, John^3, Nathaniel^2, Nathaniel^1,*) b. July 22, 1770; m. Feb. 21, 1790, Ruth Smith, and settled in Salem, Mass., where she died, March 31, 1806, aged 45 years. He m. second, Oct. 1806, Sally Allen, she died April 8, 1813, aged 43 years. Sup. James Felton m. third in Boston, May 1816, Sarah Hudson. He m. again in 1822, Sally Gray Walls. Had 2 daughters by his last wife. James Felton died Oct. 20, 1833, aged 63 years. His children were:

 633†. i. JAMES, JR., b. June 8, 1790; m. Sarah Hunt.
 634†. ii. JOHN SMITH, b. July, 1792; m. Nancy Crandall.
 635. iii. RUTH, b. about 1798; died in Salem, unm., April 10, 1758, aged 60 years.
 636†. iv. MARY, b. about 1801; m. Harding P. Smith.
 637†. v. SARAH FRANCES, b. March 12, 1826; m. Howard Brown.
 638†. vi. ELIZABETH, b. July 12, 1828; m. Samuel Adams.

(262.) i. JAMES FELTON[5], (*David[4], Ebenezer[3], Nathaniel[2], Nathaniel[1]*,) bapt. in Salem, Oct. 8, 1738; m. in New Salem, Nov. 24, 1760, Sarah Houlton, b. April 13, 1732; daughter of Joseph and Rebecca (Felton) Houlton of New Salem. In 1801, James Felton represented New Salem in the General Court. His will dated June 3, 1792, proved Sept. 25, 1804. His age in 1804,—66 years. Widow Sarah Felton was living in 1805, then aged 73 years. Had 8 children. The daughters in this order in the will. The son under 21 years in 1792.

 639†. i. SARAH, m. sup. April 24, 1783, Jacob Amsden.
 640†. ii. LOIS, m. Jan. 1788, Asa Powers of Shutesbury, Mass.
 641†. iii. RUTH, m. Dec. 1785, Simeon Southwick.
 642. iv. ANNE, m. July 2. 1789, Joshua Wyatt.
 643. v. SUSANNA, m. July 28, 1791, Samuel Kellogg, Jr.
 644. vi. BOADICE, m. Ebenezer Reynolds.
 645. vii. LUCRETIA, m. ——— Shaw.
 646†. viii. JAMES, JR., m. Eunice Wheeler.

(263.) ii. EBENEZER FELTON[5], (*David[1], Ebenezer[3], Nathaniel[2], Nathaniel[1]*,) sup. b. about 1741; bapt. 1743; m. Jan. 1762, Hannah Page; had 2 sons, and 2 daughters. Mrs. Hannah Felton died July 8, 1773, aged 32 years. Ebenezer Felton, then Jr., was living in New Salem in 1792.

 647. i. HANNAH, bapt. in 1763; died in 1767.
 648†. ii. DAVID HOLTON, b. Oct. 25, 1767; m. Rebecca Hodskin.
 649†. iii. ROBERT, bapt. Jan. 30, 1771; m. and had children.
 650†. iv. HANNAH, bapt. April 11, 1773; m. John Powers.

.(269.) ii. STEPHEN FELTON⁵, (*Ebenezer⁴, Ebenezer³, Nathaniel², Nathaniel¹,*) b. Oct. 22, 1756; m. in New Salem Oct. 24, 1777, Sarah Daland, or Deland, b. May 22, 1762, daughter of George and Abigail Dealand, and great-grand-daughter of Thorndike Proctor, Sen., of Salem, Mass. Mrs. Sarah Felton was brought up in the family of Rev. Samuel Kendall, the first minister of New Salem, Mass. Stephen Felton was an early shoe-maker and farmer. They had 12 children; lived husband and wife 63 years. Mr. Felton died at Wendell, Mass., April 8, 1841, aged 84 years, Mrs. Sally Felton, March 18, 1848, aged almost 86 years.

651†. i. ABIGAIL, b. July 12, 1778; m. Samuel Foster.
652†. ii. RACHEL, b. May 24, 1780; m. Ezekiel Leonard.
653†. iii. STEPHEN, JR., b. May 18, 1782; m. Rhoda Ayers.
654. iv. LYDIA, b. June 10, 1784; died July 8, 1803, aged 19 years.
655†. v. DANIEL, b. March 9, 1787; m. Fanny Holden.
656†. vi. THORNDIKE, b. April 26, 1789; m. Joanna Chamberlain.
657†. vii. SALLY, b. June 26, 1791; m. Ebenezer Hooper.
658†.viii. PROCTOR, b. May 17, 1794; m. Mrs. Elizabeth Prescott.
659. ix. GEORGE, b. Jan. 25, 1797; died Sept. 30, 1802.
660†. x. EBENEZER, b. May 21, 1800; m. Phebe R. Drury.
661†. xi. ABIGAIL, b. March 1803; m. Dr. Levi Chamberlain.
662†.xii. GEORGE DELAND, b. Dec. 12, 1805; m. Emily Hurlbert.

(271.) iv. JACOB HARWOOD, m. June 23, 1782, Lydia Felton, bapt. March 1765; daughter of Ebenezer and Lydia Felton of New Salem, Mass. Sup. had two or more children.

663. i. JACOB, JR., sup. went with Capt. Joseph Houlton to Houlton, Me., where he was living in 1821.
664. ii. DANIEL HARWOOD, who lived in Franklin County Mass.

(272.) i. AMOS FELTON⁵, (*Amos⁴, Ebenezer³, Nathaniel², Nathaniel¹,*) b. Dec. 5, 1779; m. Lydia King, b. Jan. 27, 1779; daughter of Samuel King of New Salem. Mr. Felton resided in the east part of Shutesbury; in 1815, he headed a petition, with other names, to be set off from Shutesbury to New Salem; they were set off in 1824. Mrs. Lydia Felton died July 21, 1839, aged 60 years. Amos Felton m. second, Mrs. Eunice Thomas; she died in 1874. Mr. Felton died April 24, 1850, aged 70 years. Amos and Lydia Felton had 9 children.

FELTON FAMILY.   69

665.   i. BETSEY, b. July 19, 1801; died July 10, 1803.
666†.   ii. LYDIA, b. April 9, 1803; m. David Burnett.
667†.   iii. BETSEY, b. March 28, 1805; m. Eli Grout.
668.   iv. JEHOADAN WARD, b. July 29, 1807; died Dec. 22, 1824, aged 17 years.
669.   v. ESTHER M., b. Nov. 11, 1809; died May 19, 1833, aged 24 years.
670†.   vi. AMOS, JR., b. Feb. 17, 1812; m. Harriet Howard.
671†.   vii. DANIEL B., b. Aug. 31, 1814; m. Lydia Felton, (No.   .)
672†.viii. JOHN, b. May 4, 1817; m. Margaret Kellogg.
673.   ix. HANNAH NEAL, b. Oct. 13, 1819.

(276.) i. DR. ZACCHEUS RICHARDSON, m. Elizabeth Felton, daughter of Benjamin Felton, Sen., of New Salem, Mass. They had 3 children. He resided at Taunton, Mass., and died when the children were young. Mrs. Richardson also died about the same time as her husband. The children were brought up in their Grandmother Felton's family in New Salem. Some person named Zaccheus Richardson was in the war of 1812 to 1815, who drew for his services, 160 acres of land.

674.   i. BENJAMIN, b. Oct. 4, 1800; died unm. Sept. 3, 1828, aged 28 years.
675†.   ii. WILLARD, b. June 23, 1802; m. Louisa Merell.
676†.   iii. ELIZABETH, b. Oct. 23, 1804; m. Samuel Putnam.

(278.) iii. BENJAMIN FELTON^5, ($Benjamin^4$, $Ebenezer^3$, $Nathaniel^2$, $Nathaniel^1$,) b. in 1782; m. Hephsibah Orcutt; had no children. He lived and died in New Salem, May 9, 1854, aged 72 years. His will dated 1851, gave to Benjamin F. Leak; to Susan Coolidge, wife of N. B. Coolidge; to Patty Holden, wife of Simeon Holden; to Ebenezer Felton; to Betsey, wife of Samuel Putnam; to the heirs of Abraham Felton; to Samuel and Daniel Varnum Putnam.

(279.) iv. ABRAHAM FELTON^5, ($Benjamin^4$, $Ebenezer^3$, $Nathaniel^2$, $Nathaniel^1$,) b. May 1784; m Jan. 9, 1825, Bethiah Pierce, or Pearce, his cousin. Sup. their great-grandfather Abram Pearce died in New Salem, March 22, 1799, aged 77 years. Abram and Bethiah Felton's children were b. in New Salem. About 1832, they moved to Warwick, Mass., where he died May 12, 1844, aged 60 years. Mrs. Felton b. Dec. 31, 1792; died April 1876, aged 83 years, 3 months.

677.   i. MARY P., b. Jan. 1827; died Oct. 1827, aged 9 months.

678†.   ii. ALEXANDER CONKEY, b. April 1828; m. Maria B. Warren.
679†.   iii. BENJAMIN R., b. Nov. 20, 1830; resides at Warwick, Mass.

(280.) v. EBENEZER FELTON[5], (*Benjamin*[4], *Ebenezer*[3], *Nathaniel*[2], *Nathaniel*[1],) b. Feb. 3, 1788. He was the fourth Ebenezer Felton that had lived in New Salem. He died July 3, 1864, aged 76 years. He never married. It is supposed by few of his relatives that Mr. Felton and his brother had been town officers.

(281.) i. ISAAC PAGE, m. Mary Felton, daughter of Nathaniel Felton, Sen., of New Salem. They lived in or near New Salem and had five or more children.

680.   i. ISAAC, JR., b. in April 1792; m. Mabel Upton; he was living in 1884, aged 92 years.
681.   ii. JAMES, m.
682.   iii. CHARLOTTE, m.
683.   iv. WILLIAM CROUP, m.
684.   v. JANE, m.

(283.) iii. NATHANIEL FELTON[5], (*Nathaniel*[4], *Ebenezer*[3], *Nathaniel*[2], *Nathaniel*[1].) He m. first, Lucinda Reynolds, and had 5 children. He m. second, Mrs. Sally Frye, widow of John Frye; m. third, Patty Trask. It is said Mr. Felton died in Shutesbury, Mass., aged about 80 years.

685†.   i. NATHANIEL, JR., b. Aug. 20, 1802; m. Abigail Bowker.
686†.   ii. EVOLINE, m. William Frye.
687†.   iii. CLARISSA, m. Jacob Vaughan.
688†.   iv. LUCINDA, m. Jacob Vaughan.
689†.   v. JAMES SHEPARD, m. Mary E. Rawson.
690†.   vi. CYRUS WHITMAN, b. Feb. 15, 1819; m. twice.
691.   vii. WILLIAM, and others by his third wife.

(285.) i. DANIEL PRINCE, of Danvers, m. Aug. 1777, Anna Felton, b. Nov. 5, 1754, daughter of Nathaniel and Dorcas Felton of Danvers, (No. 95.) Mr. Prince m. first, Miss —————— Rae; his children by his last wife. It is said they settled at Bow, N. H.

691⅓.   i. DANIEL, JR.
691⅔.   ii. BETSEY, m. Mr. —————— Cheever.

(286.) ii. JOHN EPPES, JR., m. June 27, 1776, Mary Felton b. March 28, 1756; daughter of Nathaniel and Dorcas Felton of Danvers, (No. 95.) John Eppes was a soldier in

Samuel Eppes' company of Danvers in 1775. There were four Eppeses and four Feltons in Capt. Eppes' company. It is said John and Mary Eppes settled in Dunstable, now Nashua, N. H.

(288.) iv. NATHANIEL FELTON⁵, (*Nathaniel⁴, Jonathan³, Nathaniel², Nathaniel¹,*) b. in Danvers, Aug. 5. 1759; m. March 18, 1781, Mary Prince, said to have been a grand-daughter of Dr. Jonathan Prince of Danvers. Mrs. Felton died, and he m. second, Dec. 4, 1788, Hannah Felton, b. Aug. 4, 1768, dau. of Timothy Felton of Danvers, (No. 203.) Had 7 children by last wife. Mrs. Hannah Felton died Sept. 6, 1825, aged 57 years, Mr. Felton, May 20, 1836, aged 77 years. Nathaniel Felton was born, lived and died on Felton Hill. now called Mount Pleasant, Peabody, Mass. Their son, Col. Nathaniel Felton, was executor of the estate.

692†. i. REBECCA, b. March 20, 1789; m. Levi Preston, Jr.
693†. ii. NATHANIEL, b. Oct. 6, 1791; m. Polly Preston.
694†. iii. DANIEL, b. May 13, 1794; m. Hannah P. Felton, (No. 301.)
695. iv. HANNAH, b. Nov. 13, 1795; died Nov. 10, 1798.
696†. v. MARY PRINCE, b. June 30, 1799; m. James Marsh.
697†. vi. HARRIET, b. Sept. 19, 1803; m. Jasper Pope.
698†. vii. SARAH, b. Jan. 4, 1807; m. Jasper Pope.

(289.) i. JEDEDIAH FELTON⁵, (*Anthony⁴, Jonathan³, Nathaniel², Nathaniel¹,*) b. May 15, 1768; m. in 1796, Mary Proctor, b. Nov. 1, 1775, daughter of Capt. Jonathan Proctor of Danvers, (No. 139.) Mr. Felton was a potter by trade, and moved into New Hampshire. The History of Dublin, N. H., says the first workman in Pottersville, (a village near the northwest corner of Dublin,) was Felton, who came from Danvers. Probably it was Jedediah Felton. The manufacture of pottery was commenced at Pottersville about 1795, by Daniel Thurston. Mr. Felton settled at Mason, N. H. where he died Jan. 9, 1845, aged 76 years. Mrs. Mary Felton died five days before, Jan. 4, 1845, aged 69 years. They had several children. His will dated March 19, 1844; his son-in law, Amos Eliot, executor. His son, Daniel Felton, was in Ohio.

699†. i. DANIEL, m. Mary Gilman.
700†. ii. BETSEY, m. Amos Eliot.
701†. iii. MARY, m. Ira Hadley.

(290.) i. JONATHAN FELTON⁵, (*Jonathan⁴, Jonathan³, Nathaniel², Nathaniel¹,*) b. Nov. 17, 1779; m. Sept. 1801, Betsey Wood of Rowley, Mass., a sister of Rev. Jacob Wood, a Universalist minister. **Mr. Felton was a shoe-maker in Danvers,** and afterwards resided in Rowley a few years. They went to Salem in 1816, and he died in Sept. 1824, aged 45 years, His widow, Elizabeth Felton, died in Salem, Jan. 13, 1851, aged 71 years. Jonathan and Betsey Felton had 4 or more children.

702†. i. GEORGE W., b. Jan. 3, 1803 ; m. Mary Beals
703†. ii. SOPHIA JANE, b. July 10, 1805 ; m. John Burnham, Jr.
704. iii. WILLIAM, b. May 27, 1810; died Aug. 21, 1827, aged 17 years.
705. iv. SALLY, sup. their daughter; m. May 1840, John Crandall, Jr., of Salem.
706†. v. JONATHAN NEEDHAM, b. Nov. 3, 1817 ; m. Hannah Grant.

(291.) i. JOHN WEEKS, b. Oct. 1, 1768, (the oldest son of Capt. Jonathan Weeks, who was son of Col. John Weeks, all of Marlboro, Mass.;) m. in 1787, Betsey Felton, b. Nov. 11, 1766, daughter of Archelaus Felton of Marlboro, (No 100.) John Weeks was elected an assessor in 1799, and in 1803, but declined serving. He was one of the selectmen of Marlboro in 1808-9 and '10. He died Nov. 3, 1826, aged 58 years. Mrs. Betsey Weeks, May 4, 1838, aged 71 years. John and Betsey Weeks had 9 children. (For Weeks see App. V.)

707†. i. BETSEY, b. Aug. 21, 1789 ; m. John P. Maynard.
708†. ii. SALLY, b. July 22, 1792 ; m. Stephen Felton, Jr., (No. 201.)
709†. iii. THANKFUL, b. Jan. 22, 1795 ; m. Jabez S. Walcott.
710†. iv. MARY, b. Feb. 26, 1798 ; m. John Griswold.
711. v. WILLIAM, b. July 27, 1800 ; died Sept. 29, 1805.
712†. vi. HANNAH ADAMS, b. Jan. 6, 1803 ; m. Daniel Parmenter.
713†. vii. LYDIA, b. Dec. 4, 1804 ; m. Wm. Patch.
714†.viii. LUCY, b. Sept. 8, 1807 ; m. Wm. R. Wheeler.
715†. ix. JOHN, JR., b. April 12, 1810 ; m. Nancy Hager.

(292.) ii. WILLIAM FELTON[5], (Archelaus[4], Jonathan[3], Nathaniel[2], Nathaniel[1],) b. Oct. 4, 1768 ; m. in 1791, Catherine Hunt of Sudbury, b. May 7, 1772, daughter of Samuel Hunt, who died in Marlboro in 1812, aged 67 years. Mr. Felton was a farmer and resided about one-half mile southeast of Marlboro Lake. His name was in the jury box several years. In 1816, the town had a school house built, 22 feet square, in a new school district, and Wm. Gates, Wm. Felton and Abraham Gates were chosen to build said house. In 1836, Wm. Felton was one of a committee of ten appointed by the moderator to report to the town about the surplus revenue received from the United States treasury. Mrs. Catherine Felton died Feb. 3, 1833, aged 60 years. William Felton died Sept. 27, 1849, aged 81 years. They had 6 children.

716†. i. DANIEL, b. April 23, 1792; lived 23 years.
717†. ii. CATHERINE, b. Dec. 16, 1794; m. Isaac Temple Stevens.
718†. iii. WILLIAM, JR., b. Feb. 17, 1796; m. Mary Ann Stowe.
719†. iv. ELIZABETH, b. Feb. 19, 1805; m. James Potter.
720†. v. EDWARD, b. July 6, 1807; m. Lydia A. Stone.
721†. vi. SUSAN ANN, b. Feb. 1817; m. Wm. Giles.

(293.) iii. AARON MORSE, b. July 27, 1769; son of Capt. Wm. Morse, (who was a captain in the revolutionary war, and afterwards represented Marlborough in the General Court;) m. in 1787, Sarah Felton, b. Sept. 8, 1770, daughter of Archelaus Felton, (No. 100.) •After having two children in Marlboro, they moved to Cherry Valley, N. Y. It is said he died while on business at New Orleans, La. Mr. Morse was a merchant. Mrs. Sarah Morse was living in Dec. 1837, then aged 67 years. They had 3 or more children.

722†. i. JAMES OTIS, b. in Marlboro, Feb. 13, 1788; m. Mrs Mary G. Phillips.
723. ii. A child b. in Marlboro, Dec. 13, 1789; died Feb. 24, 1790.
724. iii. SARAH, died in infancy in Cherry Valley.

(294.) iv. JOHN FELTON[5], (*Archelaus*[4], *Jonathan*[3], *Nathaniel*[2], *Nathaniel*[1],) b. in Marlboro, April 27, 1772; m. April 1794, Olive Piper of Marlboro, Mass. Mrs. Felton came to Marlboro from Acton, Nov. 1785, and was taken into Josiah Howe's family. Mr. Felton and family were in Gerry, Mass., (now called Phillipston,) in 1795; in Royalston, Mass., in 1802; in Princeton, Mass., in 1805–6; afterwards in Cavendish, Vt., they moved from Vermont to Massena, St. Lawrence County, N. Y.; he was accidentally drowned in Grass River, March 5, 1822, aged 50 years. Mrs. Olive Felton died about 1842, in Ohio State.

725. i. BETSEY, b. in Gerry, Mass., April 9, 1795; died Sept. 26, 1805, aged 10 years.
726†. ii. JOHN, JR., b. July 23, 1797; m. Lucinda Ward.
727†. iii. LYDIA, b. July 17, 1799; m. William Ward.
728†. iv. NANCY, b. May 22, 1801; m. Joshua Paine.
729†. v. LYMAN, b. March 5, 1804; m. Eliza Sampson.
730†. vi. ELIZA, b. Sept. 28, 1806; m. Abel Spaulding.

(296.) ii. JOSEPH GUILD, b. in Dedham, Mass., March 14, 1760; m. Feb. 10, 1789, Rebecca Felton, daughter of Daniel Felton of Needham, (No. 101.) Soon after marriage they moved to Francistown, N. H., where their children were born. Mr. Guild died about 1802, aged about 42 years. Mr. Guild was uncle to Calvin Guild, who was living at Dedham, Mass., in 1882, and the author of the Guild Genealogy of 21 pages, published in 1873. Mrs. Rebecca Guild died March 14, 1853, aged sup. about 80 years.

 731.' i. DANIEL, b. April 29, 1792; m. Betsey Whipple; he died Dec. 23, 1828, aged 36 years.
 732. ii. ISAAC, b. May 16, 1794; m. Betsey Tracy; he died Aug. 16, 1854, aged 60 years.
 733. iii. CHARLES, b. June 19, 1799; m. Achsah Allerton.
 734†. iv. JOSEPHA, b. Dec. 28, 1801; m. Mark Fisher.

(297.) iii. ISAAC FELTON^5, (*Daniel^4, Jonathan^3, Nathaniel^2, Nathaniel^1*,) b. in Needham about 1777; m. Anna Richards of Dedham, Mass., b. about 1781. They settled at Needham, Mass., where Mr. Felton died July 1842, aged 63 years. Mrs. Anna Felton died at Dedham, Nov. 26, 1857, aged 76 years. Had 5 children.

 735†. i. JULIA, b. Oct. 22, 1802; m. Francis McIntosh.
 736. ii. DANIEL RICHARDS, b. Sept. 28, 1807.
 737†. iii. CHARLES COOK, b. Dec. 16, 1808; m. Mary C. Smith.
 738†. iv. MARY ANN, b. March 2, 1813; m. James P. Tolman.
 739†. v. HORACE, m. Charlotte ——.

(298.) i. JAMES FELTON^5, (*Daniel^4, Daniel^3, Nathaniel^2, Nathaniel^1*,) b. in Marblehead, Mass., about 1752; was a blacksmith, and when a young man moved into Hampshire County, Mass. James Felton was a soldier at Bunker Hill in June 1775; then of Greenwich, Mass. He m. first, —— Ramsdell; he m. second about 1783, Olive Sampson, daughter of Isaac Sampson, who lived in or near Williamstown, Mass. They had 7 sons and 7 daughters. James and Olive Felton's two oldest children were born in New Salem, Mass. He resided in several towns in Mass., and N. Y. In Pittstown, N. Y. a few years. James Felton died June 27, 1836, aged 84 years. Mrs. Olive Felton died at Coshocton, Ohio, and was buried in Ellery, Chautauqua County, N. Y. Mr. Felton died March 27, 1845, aged probably 80 years. Their children were: (probably not all in this order.)

 740‡. i. SAMPSON, b. Feb. 26, 1784; m. and had 8 children.

741†. ii. LYDIA, b. in New Salem; m. Andrew Weatherwax.
742†. iii. JAMES, JR., b. about 1788; m. and had 7 children.
743. iv. OLIVE, m. Samuel Ellis; living a widow in Ohio in 1856.
744†. v. EZRA, b. March 7, 1791; m. Hannah Sherman.
745†. vi. DAVID, a blacksmith; died in 1882.
746. vii. BETSEY, m. Adam Weatherwax.
747†.viii. DANIEL, b. May 7, 1802; m. twice; died in 1880.
748†. ix. ALEXANDER, b. June 19, 1804; m. Rachel ———.
749. x. MARTIN, living in Ohio in 1880.
750. xi. MERCY, m. Andrew Strope; living a widow at West Sand Lake, N. Y., in 1856.
751. xii. NANCY, m. Jonathan Maxon.
752 and 753. xiii and xiv. Were twins; both died young.

(299.) ii. DANIEL FELTON[5], (*Daniel[4], Daniel[3], Nathaniel[2], Nathaniel[1]*,) was a soldier in the Revolution. He m. Polly Darling and lived in old Hampshire County, Mass., and Western New York. They had two or more children.

754†. i. SUSAN FELTON, m. Sylvanus Goodenough.
754½. ii. JOHN FELTON.

(300.) iv. ROBERT FELTON[5], (*Daniel[4], Daniel[3], Nathaniel[2], Nathaniel[1]*,) b. Dec. 27, 1760; was a soldier in the revolutionary war. He m. Sylvia Darling, b. Feb. 3, 1772, and had 9 children.

755. i. POLLY, b. Feb. 7, 1790.
756. ii. LORINDA, b. Jan. 10, 1793; died young.
757†. iii. DARLING, b. Sept. 6, 1795; m. Sarah ———.
758. iv. BETSEY, b. Sept. 9, 1797.
759. v. AMANDA, b. May 25, 1800.
760. vi. LORINDA, b. June 14, 1803.
761. vii. HARRIET, b. March 27, 1806.
762†.viii. ROBERT, JR., b. Jan. 31, 1810; m. Caroline ———.
763†. ix. NELSON, b. July 17, 1812; m. Emily Raymond.

(305.) v. MARTIN FELTON[5], (*Daniel[4], Daniel[3], Nathaniel[2], Nathaniel[1]*,) b. since 1764; m. Mehitable Bancroft before 1792; he was a blacksmith, and living in Greenwich, Mass., that year. They were living in New Salem in 1797.

[The next four families are children of Thomas Felton, Sr., on page 39, and should have had the mark [†] for continuation.]

(310.) ii. THOMAS GALE, m. in Marblehead, April 5,

1778, Sarah Felton, b. Aug. 22, 1757, daughter of Thomas Felton, Sen., of that town, (No. 103.) They had 3 children. Mr. Gale died Nov. 18, 1790, aged 36 years. Mrs. Sally Gale, or Gail, died Dec. 22, 1806, aged 49 years.

 764. i. Hannah, b. Sept. 29, 1778; m. Sept. 14, 1797, —— Doak, and had i. Hannah, Jr., b. Aug. 29, 1798; ii. Mary, b. Dec. 18, 1800; iii. Francis, b. June 22, 1803.
 765. ii. Thomas, Jr., b. March 22, 1780.
 766. iii. Elizabeth, b. Nov. 19, 1781; m. —— Perkins, and had Mary, b. Oct. 4, 1801.

(311.) iii. THOMAS FELTON[5], (*Thomas*[4], *Daniel*[3], *Nathaniel*[2], *Nathaniel*[1],) b. April 13, 1759; m. July 20, 1780, Martha Conway, daughter of Cornelius Conway of Marblehead. Before May 1812, Mr. Conway's widow, Mary Conway, had m. John Bartlett of Newburyport, Mass. Thomas Felton, Jr., died Aug. 12, 1795, aged 36 years. In June 1804, Martha Felton, a widow of Marblehead, gave Widow Mary Beal, widow of Samuel Beal, part of a dwelling house of the late Neal Conway of that town. In March 1806, Mrs. Felton, then of Newbury, Mass., sold, probably the other part of the house to the same person. Mrs. Martha Felton died in Newbury in 1807. Six children.

 767. i. Hannah, b. Aug. 6, 1781; died Nov. 2, 1782.
 768. ii. Thomas, Jr., b. Sept. 17, 1782; died June 2, 1786.
 769†. iii. Cornelius Conway, b. June 27, 1784; m. Anna Morse.
 770. iv. Martha, b. Nov. 5, 1786; died Aug. 23, 1790.
 771. v. Hannah, b. Sept. 2, 1789; sup. died in Boston, May 1826, aged 36 years.
 772†. vi. Thomas, Jr., b. Sept. 2, 1791; m. Hannah Morse.

(314.) vi. JOSEPH PRATT, m., Sept. 20, 1792, Margaret Felton, b. Aug. 15, 1765, daughter of Thomas Felton, Sen., of Marblehead, (No. 103.) Mr. Pratt died Sept. 2, 1795, aged 27 years. Mrs. Margaret Pratt m. second, Jan. 20, 1803, —— Millet; he was lost at sea about two years afterwards. Mrs. Millet m. third, Feb. 5, 1809, Thomas Powers.

Joseph and Margaret (Felton) Pratt had two children.

 773. i. Joseph, Jr., b. Feb. 19, 1793.
 774. ii. Thomas Felton, b. Feb. 5, 1795.

(317.) ix. JAMES FELTON[5], (*Thomas*[4], *Daniel*[3], *Nathaniel*[2], *Nathaniel*[1],) b. Dec. 27, 1771; m. Dec. 20, 1795, Mary Brooks. He was a fisherman and lost at sea near Marblehead harbor, Jan. 14, 1805, aged 33 years. His widow, Mary Felton, settled the estate before Feb. 1807. She m. second, Feb. 15, 1807, Richard Parker of Marblehead, and had two more children.

James and Mary Felton had four children.

775. i. HANNAH, b. March 7, 1796; died Nov. 12, 1796.
776. ii. JAMES, JR., b. Aug. 21, 1798; lost at sea in a heavy squall, Sept. 23, 1815, called the great September gale in New England, and the great blow in 1815. James Felton was 17 years of age and one month.
777. iii. MARY, b. Feb. 2, 1801.
778. iv. MARGARET, b. June 3, 1803.

Richard and Mary Parker had: Richard, Jr., b. Dec. 1, 1807; Joseph Pratt, b. about 1809.

(320.) i. JOHN ENDICOTT^5, JR., b. in 1739; son of John^4, b. in 1713; of Samuel^3, b. in 1687, who was son of Samuel^2 and Hannah Felton Endicott of Salem.

John Endicott, b. in 1739, m. Martha Putnam, daughter of Samuel Putnam of Salem. They had 12 children, 7 of them were sons. Mr. Endicott owned and lived on the Endicott Orchard Farm, then in Salem, afterwards, in Danvers. He died March 1816, aged 77 years, Mrs. Martha Endicott in Sept. 1821.

781. i. SAMUEL, b. in 1763; m. Elizabeth Putnam and had 5 children; been selectman of Salem several years, and representative in the General Court. His son, William Putnam Endicott, b. in 1803, graduated at Harvard College in 1822, and living in Salem in 1885, and father of Hon. Wm. C. Endicott, who was appointed secretary of war in March 1885, by Pres. Cleveland.
782. ii. JOHN, JR., b. Jan. 13, 1765; m. twice, and had 10 children. He represented Danvers in the Legislature several times.
783. iii. MOSES, b. March 19, 1767; m. Anna Towne and had 7 children; was a sea captain. His son, Charles M Endicott, Esq., b. Dec. 6, 1791, was the author of Endicott's Genealogy.
784. iv. ANN, b. Jan. 1769; m. Solomon Giddings.
785. v. ELIZABETH, b. Aug. 1771; m. James Gray of Salem.
786. vi. JACOB, b. July 9, 1773; m. Ruth Hawkes of Boston; 5 children.
787. vii. MARTHA, b. Sept. 1775; m. Jeremiah Page of Danvers.

788. viii. NATHAN, twin, b. Sept. 1775; died young.
789. ix. SARAH, b. Sept. 1778; died unm.
790. x. REBECCA, b. May 20, 1780; m. Daniel Hardy.
791. xi. WILLIAM, b. in 1782; died in 1806.
792. xii. TIMOTHY, b. July 27, 1785; m. Harriet Martin.

(323½.) i. ISRAEL PUTNAM, b. in 1755; (son of Dea. Edmund Putnam of Danvers, who died in 1810, aged 86 years;) m. Anna Endicott, daughter of Elias Endicott, who was son of Capt. Samuel, and grandson of Samuel and Hannah (Felton) Endicott of Salem–Danvers.

Israel and Anna (Endicott) Putnam were the parents of Hon. Elias Putnam of Danvers, who was b. June 7, 1789; and died July 8, 1847, aged 58 years.

Hon. Elias Putnam was father of Rev. Alfred P. Putnam, D. D., a prominent Unitariam minister of Brooklyn, N. Y. Rev. Dr. A. P. Putnam is a descendant of the eighth generation, from the venerable John Putnam, Sen., the emigrant, who lived 79 years; also of the eighth generation from Gov. John Endicott of Massachusetts; also of the eighth generation from Rev. Samuel Skelton, the first settled minister of Salem, Mass., and also a descendant of the seventh generation from the venerable Lieut. Nathaniel Felton, Sen., the emigrant.

(329.) vi. STEPHEN PROCTOR, JR., b. Sept. 23, 1775; m. Mary Felton, b. Dec. 17, 1781, daughter of Timothy Felton, Sen., of Danvers, They lived in South Danvers. Mr. Proctor died Nov. 3, 1853, aged 78 years. Mrs. Mary Proctor died about two months before, Sept. 7, 1853, aged 71 years, 9 months. Had two sons.

793. i. NATHAN STEPHEN PROCTOR, b. Dec. 3, 1818; m. Martha A. Proctor. Mr. Proctor died Jan. 26, 1860, aged 41 years. Mrs Proctor m. second, Stephen Needham of South Danvers, and died in April 1882.
794. ii. EBENEZER WARREN PROCTOR, b. March 8, 1822; died Feb. 4, 1827, aged 5 years.

(336.) i. JONATHAN PROCTOR, JR., b. March 19, 1770, (son of Capt. Jonathan Proctor of South Danvers;) m. Phebe Gould in Nov. 1799; they lived in South Danvers near Felton Hill, or Mount Pleasant. They had 1 son and 7 dau's. Mr. Proctor died March 18, 1853, aged 83 years. His widow, Mrs. Phebe Proctor, about two months afterwards, May 28, 1853, aged 75 years. Mr. Proctor's relatives and neighbors, Stephen Proctor and wife, both died the same year, 1853.

Jonathan and Phebe Proctor's children were:

795. i. CLARISSA, b. Sept. 13, 1800; m. Benj. Earle; she died April 28, 1880, aged 79 years.
796. ii. ASENATH, b. May 10, 1803.
797. iii. BETSEY REED, b. April 26, 1806; m. Joel Brown; she died in 1883, aged 77 years.
797½. iv. PHEBE, b. July 5, 1807.
798. v. JONATHAN, JR., b. March 24, 1811; m. April 17, 1833, Sarah Colby. He was a soldier in the Union army; died or lost, aged about 51 years.
799. vi. MEHITABLE FELTON, b. Sept. 27, 1814; m. Caleb Strong Russell, b. in 1809; have several children; residence near Mount Peasant, Peabody, Mass.

(342.) vii. THORNDIKE PROCTOR, b. July 21, 1786; son of Capt. Jonathan Proctor of South Danvers; m. Eliza Wilson, b. Aug. 17, 1783, daughter of Robert and Sarah (Felton) Wilson of South Danvers. Was elected deacon of South Danvers church in 1837, and died in Peabody, near Mount Pleasant, Feb. 25, 1871, aged 84 years. Mrs. Eliza Proctor died Oct. 12, 1860, aged 77 years.

During the great New England gale of Sept. 8, 1869, (between 17 and 18 months before the demise of Dea. Proctor,) his "Big Tree," between his house and the road, was shattered by the storm, and soon afterwards cut down. The storm was very severe near the coast.

SIXTH GENERATION.

(350.) i. ABIJAH RICHARDSON, b. in Woburn, Mass., March 20, 1761; m. in 1788, Elizabeth Richardson, b. Feb. 23, 1763, daughter of Joseph and Abigail (Felton) Richardson, and grand-daughter of Dea. Malachi Felton of Danvers. They had 3 children at Woburn, and then moved in March 1794 or 1795, into the woods, the snow being about 3 feet deep, to a small hut in Dublin, N. H. The next June after they moved, Mr. Richardson had the misfortune to break his shoulder, which confined him to his home. Kind neighbors came in and relieved their necessities. Mr. Richardson died July 12, 1840, aged 79 years. Mrs. Richardson died Jan. 3, 1853, aged almost 90 years. They had 7 children.

800. i. ABIJAH, b. April 1, 1789; m. Mary Hay.

FELTON FAMILY.

801. ii. ELIZABETH, b. Aug. 24, 1791; died June 10, 1824, aged 33 years.
802. iii. RUEL, b. Sept. 2, 1791; m. Betsey Davis.
803. iv. LUKE, b. Aug. 4, 1795; m. twice.
804†. v. MALACHI, b. Sept. 25, 1798; m. Tamison Greenwood.
805. vi. MARY, b. Dec. 22, 1800; m. Rev. Daniel McClenring.
806. vii. JOSHUA, b. July 13, 1807; m. Rebecca Nurse.

About all these families settled in Cheshire County, N. H.

(357.) i. BENJAMIN KENT, JR., b April 8, 1768, son of Benjamin and Mary (Felton) Kent, (No. 147;) m. 1793, Elizabeth Fuller of Middleton, Mass., b. in Newburyport in 1770. Had 5 children. Mrs Kent died June 26, 1804. He m. second in 1805, Abigail Berry, b. June 16, 1763, at Newburyport; she died July 15, 1820. Mr. Kent m. third, Oct. 1821, Hannah Herrick of Topsfield, Mass. Benjamin Kent died Feb. 18, 1849, aged 80 years.

807. i. NANCY, b. Oct. 10, 1793; died young.
808. ii. BENJAMIN, b. Nov. 21, 1794.
809. iii. JOHN, b. Oct. 17, 1796; m. 1822, Hannah Tappan; had several children.
810. iv. NANCY, again, b. Oct., 1798.
811. v. CHARLOTTE, b. June, 1800.

(361.) i. ROBERT WILSON, JR., b. Sept. 5, 1776, son of Robert and Sarah (Felton) Wilson of Danvers; m. in 1800, Mary Southwick. They lived in Danvers where he died, Nov. 6, 1803, aged 27 years. Mrs. Mary Wilson died Aug. 15, 1854, aged 77 years. Had two children.

812. i. SAMUEL, b. Nov. 2, 1800.
813. ii. MERCY, b. June 17, 1803.

(362.) ii. JOHN WILSON, b. Jan. 18, 1778, son of Robert and Sarah (Felton) Wilson of Danvers; m. Clarissa Waldo, or Goldsmith, of Andover, Mass. Mr. Wilson settled in South Danvers, where he died June 26, 1863, aged 85 years. Had 2 sons.

814. i. JOHN, JR.; m.
815. ii. EDWARD, who died unm. about 1877, and left property for a chapel erected soon afterwards near Feltonville, in Peabody, Mass.

(363.) iii. JONATHAN BATCHELDER, m. April 12, 1804, Sarah Wilson, b. Jan. 6, 1780, daughter of Robert and

FELTON FAMILY.

Sarah (Felton) Wilson of Danvers. In 1805, Mr. Batchelder bought part of the late Benjamin Daland's estate. They settled in Danvers, and had 5 children.

- 816. i. MARTHA, b. Feb. 11, 1805.
- 817. ii. SARAH, b. Nov. 27, 1806.
- 818. iii. JONATHAN PRESCOTT, b. July 16, 1808; m.
- 819. iv. ELIZABETH, b. July 5, 1810.
- 820. v. MALACHI FELTON, b. April 22, 1812.

(366.) vi. MALACHI WILSON, b. July 25, 1785, son of Robert and Sarah (Felton) Wilson of South Danvers; m. Jan. 30, 1823, Sarah G. Tate, b. Jan. 1797; they had 7 children in Danvers. Mr. Wilson died Sept. 21, 1853, aged 68 years.

- 821. i. ABIGAIL, b. Dec. 15, 1823.
- 822. ii. ELIZABETH, b. Sept. 30, 1825.
- 823. iii. SAMUEL WALKER, b. April 22, 1827; m.
- 824. iv. MARY TATE, b. April 7, 1829.
- 825. v. MALACHI FELTON, b. Sept. 30, 1832.
- 826. vi. THOMAS TATE, b. Jan. 1834; died same year.
- 827. vii. THOMAS TATE, b. Aug. 22, 1836.

(369.) ix. NEWHALL WILSON, b. July 12, 1795, (son of Newhall Wilson, b. in Sept. 1755, who was son of Isaac Wilson of Salem;) m. Jan. 1825, Phebe Wilson, b. Jan. 25, 1793, daughter of Robert and Sarah (Felton) Wilson, (No. 73.)

- 828. i. ROBERT HENRY, b. May 25, 1829.
- 829. ii. THORNDIKE PROCTOR, b. Nov. 3, 1834; died July 3, 1849, aged 14 years.

(373.) iii. DEA. DAVID LINCOLN, of Hingham, b. Feb. 9, 1767, (son of David, b. 1734; son of David, b. 1695; son of David, b. 1668;) m. Nov. 10, 1793, Lucy Felton, b. July 31, 1770, daughter of Dea. Joshua Felton of Roxbury, Mass. Mrs. Lucy Lincoln died in Hingham, May 8, 1817, aged 47 years. (App. X.) Dea. David Lincoln died in the same town, Aug. 18, 1825, aged 58 years. Their children were:

- 830. i. JOSHUA FELTON, b. Aug. 22, 1794; died Oct. 20, 1812, aged 18 years.
- 831†. ii. DAVID, JR., b. Aug. 10, 1796; m. Hannah Souther.
- 832. iii. MARY WARDELL, b. Oct. 20, 1799; died Aug. 24, 1816, aged 17 years.

(381.) iv. WILLIAM FELTON⁶, (*William⁵, Nathaniel⁴, Nathaniel³, John², Nathaniel¹,*) b. June 12, 1779; m. in 1806,

Caroline Connable of Barnardston, Mass., b. June 24, 1784. Mr. Felton lived with Hon. Jonathan Hunt of Vernon, Vt., until 1803, when he moved to Franklin in the northern part of Vt. He was a selectman many years, and one of the leading men in the place. He was a delegate to two constitutional conventions, and a representative 6 or 7 years. Mr. Felton died Sept. 24, 1852, aged 73 years. Mrs. Caroline Felton, May 28, 1867, aged 83 years. They had 7 children.

 833†. i. EUNICE C., b. June 20, 1809 ; m. Otis Warner.
 834†. ii. CHARLES C., b. May 24, 1811 ; m. Orra Tracy.
 835†. iii. EDWIN, b. Aug. 24, 1813 ; m. Susan M. Knowlton.
 836†. iv. ADALINE, twin, b. Aug. 24, 1813 ; m. Lorenzo Olds ; she lived 69 years.
 837†. v. ALONZO, b. Aug. 8, 1815 ; m. Mary Tenny.
 838†. vi. AMELIA, twin, b. Aug. 8, 1815 ; m. Carmie Osgood ; she lived 50 years.
 839†. vii. WILLIAM C., b. Oct. 31, 1822 ; m. Fanny S. Todd.

(382.)   v. ELIJAH WILLIAMS FELTON^6, (*William^5, Nathaniel^4, Nathaniel^3, John^2, Nathaniel^1,*) b. about 1781, (was 17 years of age in 1798 ;) m. Oct. 1810, Almy Eliot, daughter of Col. Robert Eliot of Newport, R. I. Col. Eliot's will, dated Sept. 8, 1781, set up the same year. He left his estate to his widow, Abigail Eliott, for the purpose of educating, supporting and bringing up his family. After his widow's death, the estate to be divided equally among the surviving children. His wife and Christopher Ellery, executors. Mr. Felton settled in Dighton, Mass., where he bought some land in 1804. He was a saddler by trade ; also a merchant. In 1815, and 1816, Elijah W. Felton was a deputy sheriff in Bristol county, Mass. He died Feb. 10, 1833, aged 52 years. Mrs. Almy Felton died Nov. 13, 1843, aged 65 years. Had two daughters.

 840† i. CAROLINE LITCHFIELD, b. Feb. 16, 1812 ; m. George W. B. Atwood.
 841. ii. ELIZABETH ELLIOTT, b. Aug. 27, 1813 ; m. David W. Westcoat.

(383.) vi. CHARLES FELTON^6, (*William^5, Nathaniel^4, Nathaniel^3, John^2, Nathaniel^1,*) b. Dec. 10, 1783 ; he had a lawsuit with Obediah Dickinson, and gained the case. His father bound him out, when he was 14 years of age, for 200 dollars. When 21 years, he wanted the money ; Mr. Dickinson wanted him to take land in Vt. Charles Felton m. May 14, 1814, Catherine Felton, b. Aug. 26, 1784, (No. 274,) daughter of Amos Felton of New Salem. They moved in Feb. 1815, to Shutesbury, Mass., where he died April 28, 1820, aged 36 years. They had two children.

842†. i. CHARLES, JR., b. March 20, 1815; m. Esther T. Wheeler.
843†. ii. JOHN WILLIAMS, b. Dec. 23, 1817; m. Eunice Horr.

Widow Catherine Felton m. second, Levi Haskell; had two children.

344. iii. CATHERINE FELTON, b. about 1824; lived about 20 years.
845. iv. FRANKLIN, b. about 1826; m. —— Howard.

Mrs. Catherine (Felton) Haskell died Feb. 24, 1862, aged 77 years.

(389.) ii. JOSHUA FELTON[6], (*Edward J.*[5], *Nathaniel*[4], *Nathaniel*[3], *John*[2], *Nathaniel*[1],) b. April 15, 1787; m. Hepsy Skinner, (a sister of John Skinner of Charlestown, Mass.) Mr. Felton settled in Roxbury, where he died May 26, 1835, aged 48 years. Widow Felton died Sept. 8, 1854, aged 68 years. They had 5 children.

846†. i. SAMUEL, b. about 1809; m. Sarah A. Skinner.
847. ii. JOSHUA, JR., b. about 1820; died Aug. 1843, aged 23 years.
848†. iii. MARY ELIZABETH, b. Jan. 1824; m. Benjamin G. Pidgin.
849†. iv. JOHN RICHARDSON, b. Nov. 3, 1826; m. Mary E. Robinson.
850†. v. WILLIAM NATHANIEL, b. about 1828; m. Ann R. Lyons.

(391.) i. STEPHEN FELTON[6], (*Stephen*[5], *Stephen*[4], *Samuel*[3], *John*[2], *Nathaniel*[1],) b. May 28, 1769; m. April 2, 1806, Mehitable (Weston) Card, a widow with one daughter. They lived in Lyman, Me.; had 5 children. He died Feb. 17, 1851, aged 81 years, 9 months.

850†. *a.* i. STEPHEN, JR., b. 1807; m. Miriam Sawyer.
850†. *b.* ii. SALLY, b. April 7, 1809; m. Daniel Weymouth.
850. *c.* iii. HIRAM, b. Aug. 23, 1811; died Jan. 5, 1853, aged 41 years.
850. *d.* iv. NATHAN D., b. Nov. 15, 1815; living in Lyman, Me.
850. *e.* v. MEHITABLE ANN, b. Sept. 25, 1822; living in Lyman, Me.

(392.) ii. RICHARD SKIDMORE, JR., b. May 12, 1769; m. April 1793, Phebe Felton, b. May 28, 1769, (twin to Stephen

Jr.,) daughter of Stephen and Elizabeth Felton of Beverly and Wenham, Mass. (No. 160.) Mr. Skidmore was son of Lieut. Richard Skidmore, who was familiarly known as "Old Skid," a wheelwright and builder of gun carriages, and a man of much humor in Salem and vicinity. He was born in 1738, and was a drummer and a soldier in three wars. He m. in 1764, Rachel Wilkins, and had 10 children. Lieut. Skidmore died in Danvers, Oct. 26, 1820, aged 82 years. His son, Richard Skidmore died Sept. 11, 1832, aged 63 years, Mrs. Phebe Skidmore died Oct. 20, 1840, aged 71 years. They had 6 children born in Danvers, Mass.

- 851. i. SALLY, b. Aug. 2, 1794.
- 852. ii. BETSEY, b. Jan. 29, 1796.
- 853. iii. NANCY, b. Jan. 30, 1798.
- 854. iv. PHEBE, b. Jan. 22, 1802; sup. m. 1827, Daniel Gray.
- 855†. v. STEPHEN FELTON, b. Aug. 26, 1803; m. Mary Fiske.
- 856. vi. HENRY, b. Dec. 10, 1809.

(393.) JOHN DERBY, b. June 30, 1772, son of John Derby, m. in Wenham, May 23, or 26, 1796, Sarah Felton, b. March 2, 1772. Capt. John Derby, (not Capt. James Derby, as stated in my first edition in 1877,) who m. Miss Felton, was a mariner and died April 27, 1818; on a passage from Savannah to Batavia on board ship "Rubicon," aged 46 years; no issue. Their adopted daughter, Martha P. Derby, m. Joseph Ross, Jr., (860.) Capt. John Derby's brother, Capt. James Derby, b. Aug. 18, 1774; m. in 1798, Martha Parnell, died Feb. 2, 1814, aged 39 years. Mrs. Sarah Derby died in South Danvers, Oct. 14, 1857, aged 85 years, 7 months. She was cheerful and industrious in every good work.

(395.) i. JOSEPH ROSS, JR., son of Dea. Joseph and Sarah (Felton) Ross of Salem, m. Elsie Poor, and had 9 children; they lived in Salem and vicinity.

- 857. i. HENRY, m. Caroline Morgram; he died in Texas.
- 858. ii. SALLY FELTON; was living in 1865.
- 859. iii. ABIGAIL, m. Wm. Henry Brown; she died in 1865.
- 860. iv. JOSEPH, JR., m. Martha Parnell Derby, an adopted daughter of his Aunt Sarah Derby; had 4 children.
- 861. v. WILLIAM SPOFFORD, m. ——— Abbott.
- 862. vi. NATHANIEL FELTON, b. July 9, 1809; was a barber on Boston St., Salem, many years; he died about 1880, aged 71 years.
- 863. vii. PHILANDA COLTON, m. James S. Bell.

864. viii. HANNAH FELTON, m. William More.
865. ix. DAVID, m. Harriet Sias.

(397.) i. JOHN FELTON[6], (*John[5], Jacob[4], Samuel[3], John[2], Nathaniel[1],*) b. in Marlborough, N. H., Sept. 17, 1766; m. and had 4 or more children. Mr. Felton was constable and collector in Milford, N. Y., in 1796. He was civil engineer and was employed in the business in the western part of N. Y. State. He settled at Clarence, N. Y. before his parents moved to the place.

866. i. DAVID.
867. ii. THOMAS.
868. iii. LEVI.
869. iv. MARY.

(400.) iv. JEDEDIAH FELTON[6], (*John[5], Jacob[4], Samuel[3], John[2], Nathaniel[1],*) b. Feb. 1773, in Marlboro, N. H. He m. and had two daughters, and both deceased before 1881. He m. second a widow, who had two sons Mr. Felton had 7 daughters by his last wife. He resided at Otsego, Otsego County, N. Y. He died Dec. 27, 1824, aged 52 years. Mrs. Felton died soon afterwards. Four daughters living at Buffalo, N. Y., in 1881.

870. i. A daughter.
871. ii. The second daughter.
872. iii. SUSAN, b. Nov. 20, 1810; died March 11, 1811.
873. iv. ANN, b. Feb. 1, 1812; died before 1881.
874. v. MARIA, b. Oct. 30, 1813.
875. vi. LOVINA, b. April 29, 1816.
876. vii. ESTHER, b. July 2, 1818.
877. viii. HARRIET, b. June 11, 1820; died before 1881.
878. ix. BETSEY, b. Nov. 14, 1823.

(402.) vi. LEVI FELTON[6], (*John[5], Jacob[4], Samuel[3], John[2], Nathaniel[1],*) b. July 22, 1776 in Marlboro, N. H. About the year 1794, Levi Felton lived with his Uncle Stephen Felton, on the Felton homestead in Marlboro, Mass. He m. about 1802, and had 3 children. He died at Herkimer, or Clarence, N. Y. June 17, 1810, aged 34 years.

879†. i. STATICA, b. April 1, 1803; m. Bybie Luke Derrick.
880†. ii. BENJAMIN KEYES, b. at Clarence, N. Y., June 1, 1805; m. Julia Ann St. John.
881. iii. ELIZABETH, b. about 1808; died Oct. 1, 1867, aged 59 years.

(404.) viii. BARTHOLOMEW JOHNSON, b. Aug. 26, 1780; m. Sept. 22, 1803, Anna Sophia Felton, b. April 5,

1782, in Marlboro, N. H., daughter of John and Persis Felton (No. 162.) This family lived in Ohio. Mr. Johnson died in 1851, aged 71 years. Mrs. Anna Sophia Johnson died Sept. 26, 1866, aged 84 years. They had 9 children.

- 882. i. JOHN, b. July 14, 1804.
- 883. ii. FIDELIA, b. March 23, 1806.
- 884. iii. WAITY B., b. July 18, 1808.
- 885. iv. JEDEDIAH FELTON, b. July 14, 1811.
- 836. v. HARRISON, b. Oct. 1, 1813; he m. and settled in Mich. in 1836; in 1881, had 6 children, 3 sons and 3 daughters, the youngest aged 18 years in 1881.
- 887. vi. HIRAM B., b. Jan. 6, 1816.
- 888. vii. MARYETT, b. Oct. 4, 1818.
- 889. viii. DEWITT C., b. Dec. 28, 1820.
- 890. ix. SOPHIA FELTON, b. Feb. 4, 1824.

(405.) ix. SYLVANUS FELTON^6, ($John^5$, $Jacob^4$, $Samuel^3$, $John^2$, $Nathaniel^1$,) b. Aug. 22, 1785, in Marlboro, N. H.; his parents soon afterwards moved into N. Y. State. He m. Lydia Powers and had two children. He was an officer, Lieut., in the war of 1812, and was killed at Fort Erie in 1813; was taken to his home in Clarence, Erie County, N. Y., and buried with military honors. Lieut. Felton's age was 28 years.

- 891†. i. LEVI, b. about 1808; m. Laura Joslyn.
- 892. ii. ELIZA, b. about 1810.

(406.) i. SILAS FELTON^6, ($Stephen^5$, $Jacob^4$, $Samuel^3$, $John^2$, $Nathaniel^1$,) b. Feb. 24, 1776, the first year of American independence; m. Jan. 17, 1799, Lucretia Fay, b. March 3, 1778, daughter of Levi Fay, then of Marlboro, Mass. (App. Y for Fay.) The 31st day of March 1795, when 19 years of age, he commenced teaching school in his native town, Marlboro, and taught 250 weeks, within the next 8 years. One year he kept 46 weeks, 5½ days in a week; had in all 778 scholars. The last of June in 1799, Mr. Felton with Joel Cranston, Esq., who was 12 years his senior in age, opened a store in the north part of Marlboro, near Barnard's Mills, so called, afterwards Feltonville, under the firm name, Cranston & Felton. In March 1799, when Mr. Felton was 23 years of age, was chosen an assessor, and was re-elected 26 years. He was a land surveyor, and in 1801, surveyed all the roads in Marlboro; 69 roads, 89 miles in length; he followed surveying more or less every year afterwards. He had for many years the greatest share of the municipal business of the town. At the annual town meeting, March 1808, he was elected moderator; and was elected at the following March meetings in 1811, to 1815;

the last year named he resigned on being elected town clerk, which office he held for 13 years. In 1815, he was elected a selectman and held the office 11 years, and chairman the last 9 years. In 1820, Marlboro elected inspecting school committee for the first time, William Draper, Esq., Benj. Rice, Esq., Dr. John Baker, and Silas Felton were elected, and re-elected in 1821. Silas Felton was Justice of the Peace, and represented the town in the General Court three years, in 1821, 1823 and 1824. In May 1828, was appointed post-master in Feltonville, which took its name from Mr. Felton.

Silas Felton, Esq., died on Saturday, Aug. 16, 1828, aged 52 years, 6 months. His sickness was short, his disease was pleurisy. It is supposed he made more figures to count than any other person living in town before his departure.

The following extract from a newspaper printed in 1828:
"He sustained for several years, with honor to himself and the town, some of the highest offices in the gift of his fellow townsmen, and was a man universally respected for his probity and industry."

Widow Lucretia Felton m. April 13, 1831, Col. Lovell Barnes of Marlboro. He died Aug. 4, 1831, aged 67 years. Few years afterwards, Mrs. Barnes had her name changed to Felton by the Legislature. Mrs. Lucretia Felton died in Feltonville, July 17, 1862, aged 84 years.

Silas and Lucretia Felton had three children.

893. i. ALONZO, b. Feb. 14, 1801; died April 1, 1801.
894†. ii. HARRIET, b. Feb. 20, 1802; m. George E. Manson.
895† iii. CHARLOTTE, b. May 10, 1804; m. George W. Cook.

(409.) iv. WILLIAM FELTON[6], (Stephen[5], Jacob[4], Samuel[3], John[2], Nathaniel[1],) b. April 15, 1781; m. Feb. 1809, Lois Bartlett, b. April 8, 1785, daughter of Antipas and Lois (White) Bartlett of Northborough, Mass. (See Appendix Z for Bartlett.) He was a farmer and settled on the homestead in Marlboro, Mass.; also a cooper of barrels, tubs and butter-boxes. Was a self-educated performer on a violin. He was one of the sergeants of the West military company 6 or 8 years before 1812, when he was chosen orderly sergeant and clerk, and held the office 12 years. Had been juryman several times, prudential school committee man, and highway surveyor several years.

About 1810, Sergeant Felton transplanted an elm, at the homestead. It is now (1886,) standing, and its wide-spreading branches cover 20 square rods. William Felton died July 13, 1856, aged 75 years. Mrs. Lois Felton died Oct. 25, 1857, aged 72 years, 6 months.

896†. i. Sally Howe, b. June 26, 1809; m. Abel Brigham.
897†. ii. Lucy, b. Sept. 17, 1811; m. Leander Bigelow.
898. iii. Wm. Orison, b. Aug. 27, 1813.; he was a shoemaker. He died April 22, 1833, aged 19 years, 8 months. His illness was only two days. at the time the canker-rash and sore throat prevailed in town. The compiler of this Felton Family had not that day entirely recovered.
899†. iv. Cyrus, b. Nov. 20, 1815; m. Eliza R. Fay.
900. v. Elijah, b. Nov. 9, 1819; he was a shoe-maker; a violin player.
901†. vi. Jane B., b. Feb. 25, 1822; m. Charles H. Brigham.
902. vii. Lois White, b. May 18, died May 19, 1824.

(410.) v. LUTHER WOOD, b. Feb. 1778, son of Wm. Wood of Westborough, Mass.; m., Feb. 1804, Lydia Felton, b. Oct. 4, 1783, daughter of Stephen Felton of Marlborough, Mass, (No. 164.) Luther Wood was a tanner by trade, and in the month they were married, moved to Brookfield, Mass. He taught school few winters. After residing in few towns in Connecticut, they settled in Huntington in that State, where Mr. Wood died April 7, 1856, aged 78 years. Mrs. Lydia Wood died in the same town, Dec. 20, 1870, aged 87 years.

903†. i. Frederick Wm., b. May 25, 1805; m. Ann Maria Daily.
904†. ii. Lovinia Stowe, b. April 19, 1807; m. Ager Wheeler.
905†. iii. Alonzo Felton, b. June 27, 1824; m. Rachel Hodges.

(411.) vi. AARON FELTON[6], (Stephen[5], Jacob[4], Samuel[3], John[2], Nathaniel[1],) b. May 16, 1786; m. Sept. 1807, Lydia Bigelow, b. Aug. 19, 1788, daughter of Gershom and Mary (Howe) Bigelow, all of Marlboro. (Appendix A. A.) They settled in Marlboro about one mile north of his father's place. He died Dec. 13, 1827, (only a few weeks after his father's death,) aged 41 years; his death was hastened by a swelling on his hip. They had 7 children.

906†. i. Aaron Howe, b. Feb. 2, 1808; m. Martha A. Baker.
907. ii. Addison, b. March 27, 1810; died March 11, 1818, aged 8 years.
908. iii. Lydia, b. May 9, 1812; died Feb. 5, 1818, aged 6 years. Those two children died of throat distemper: several children died in town that year of the same disease.

909†. iv. LOVINAH STOWE, b. Feb. 13, 1817; m. Lewis T. Frye.
910†. v. LYMAN BIGELOW, b. Oct. 20, 1819; m. Eleanor Baker.
911† vi. LAMBERT ADDISON, b. March 8, 1822; m. Harriet Bliss.
912†. vii. LEWIS, b. Feb. 26, 1824; m. Mary L. Stowe.

Mrs. Lydia Felton m. second, Aug. 1829, William F. Holyoke, son of Capt. Wm. Holyoke, all of Marlboro. They had two children. Mrs. Holyoke died June 11, 1840, aged 52 years. Mr. Holyoke m. second, Miss Elizabeth Howe.

(412.) vii. JACOB FELTON[6], (Stephen[5], Jacob[4], Samuel[3], John[2], Nathaniel[1],) b. Nov. 15, 1790; (wanting only four days of being a year after his grandfather's death;) m. in June 1814, Lucinda Wilkins, b. Aug. 4, 1791, daughter of Edward and Sarah Wilkins of Marlboro, Mass. (For Wilkins, App. B. B.) In Sept. 1714, Jacob Felton went with a Marlborough company to Fort Warren, (during the war of 1812 to 1815,) and stopped one night, and returned home with the company the next day. Mr. Felton moved to Princeton, Mass., and carried on the carding machine business about 12 years. In 1828, they were living in Feltonville, Marlboro, and the next year removed and settled in the southwest part of Berlin, Mass., as a farmer. Mrs. Lucinda Felton died May 30, 1865, aged 74 years. Husband and wife 51 years. Mr. Felton m. second, March 1868, Mrs. Mary Wilkins of Hudson, b. April 4, 1802, daughter of Rufus Holman of Sterling, Mass. Her first husband was Edward Wilkins, a brother of Mr. Felton's first wife. Mrs. Mary Felton died in Wilkinsville, Hudson, May 18, 1875, aged 73 years. Mr. Felton afterwards moved back to Berlin, where he died Aug. 23, 1883, aged 92 years, 9 months.

913†. i. HENRY OTIS, b. Dec. 12, 1814; m. Charlotte Phelps.
914. ii. SYLVESTER, b. in Princeton, Mass., Sept. 5, 1818; died in Berlin, unm., Sept. 27, 1851, aged 33 years.
915†. iii. MERRICK, b. Aug. 31, 1823; m. Elizabeth Page.

(413.) viii. STEPHEN FELTON[6], (Stephen[5], Jacob[4], Samuel[3], John[2], Nathaniel[1],) b. July 10, 1795; m. in 1820; Sally Weeks, b. July 22, 1792, daughter of John and Betsey (Felton) Weeks of Marlboro, (No. 291.) She had been a school teacher several seasons in Marlboro. Mr. Felton taught school in Marlboro in 1819 and 1820. They moved to Constable, that part now Westville, near Malone, Franklin County, N. Y., where he was town clerk and postmaster. He taught school several winters, and as late as 1838. He also commanded a military company. Was a carpenter by trade. In 1842, Capt. Felton moved to Massena, St. Lawrence County, N. Y., and built him a house, between Racket and Grass rivers, in view of the River St. Lawrence. He declined to have his name used for a Justice of the Peace.

Mrs. Sally Felton died Jan. 3, 1873, aged 80 years. Husband and wife 52 years. Capt. Stephen Felton died in 1879, aged 84 years.

916†. i. HARIETTA N., b. Nov. 21, 1820; m. Herman Smith.
917†. ii. SILAS ADDISON, b. Feb. 7, 1825; m. Laura Day.
918. iii. MARY ELIZABETH, b. July 14, 1826; died unm. Sept. 9, 1876, aged 50 years.

(417.) iv. JACOB FELTON^6, ($Matthias^5, Jacob^4, Samuel^3, John^2, Nathaniel^1,$) b. July 16, 1787; m. March 20, 1814, Elizabeth Morse of Boston; she was a native of Exeter, N. H. Mr. Felton resided at Fitzwilliam, N. H., and Boston, Mass. Mrs. Elizabeth Felton died Aug. 28, 1848, aged sup. about 60 years. Jacob Felton died at or near Quincy, Ill., May 28, 1864, aged 76 years, 10 months.

919†. i. MARY E., b. Jan. 1, 1815; m. John Potter.
920. ii. JACOB HEWES, b. May 3, 1818; died Oct. 15, 1826, aged 8 years.
921. iii. ELIZABETH, b. in 1825; died May 28, 1841, aged 16 years.

(418.) v. ARTEMAS FELTON^6, ($Matthias^5, Jacob^4, Samuel^3, John^2, Nathaniel^1,$) b. April 2, 1789; m. Feb. 1812, Elizabeth Van Doom of Fitzwilliam, N. H. Mr. Felton m. second Jan. 1821, Sally Clark, b. July 27, 1794. He had 2 children by each wife. They resided in Fitzwilliam, N. H., and Boston, where they kept a boarding house several years. Artemas Felton died in Boston, Nov. 17, 1860, aged 71 years. Mrs. Sally Felton died Aug. 21, 1866, aged 72 years.

922†. i. ELIZABETH M., b. April 30, 1813; m. George C. Lord.
923†. ii. LYDIA RELIEF, b. May 21, 1816; m. Levi Haskell.
924†. iii. SARAH HEWES, b. July 23, 1822; m. Joseph B. Whall.
925†. iv. LOUISA CLARK, b. April 30, 1833; m. Daniel F. Long.

(419.) vi. MATTHIAS FELTON^6, ($Matthias^5, Jacob^4, Samuel^3, John^2, Nathaniel^1,$) b. March 12, 1792. He went South into Alabama, when a young man. One of his nephews, about 1850, heard of a Matthias Felton, a wealthy person in one of the southern states.

(420.) vii. LYMAN FELTON[6], (*Matthias[5], Jacob[4], Samuel[3], John[2], Nathaniel[1],*) b. in Jan. or Feb. 8, 1794; m. in 1814, Sarah Scott of Winchester, N. H., b. about 1791; she died July 22, 1820, aged 29 years, 6 months. Had two sons. He m. second, A. M. Bethune, and had 3 daughters. He m. third, Rachel ———, and had a daughter, Rachel Felton. Mr. Felton was a millwright; about the year 1854, he went to the western country, which was the last the family have known anything about him. His children were:

926†. i. LYMAN SCOTT, b. Jan. 1815; m. Clarissa Phillips.
927†. ii. MATTHIAS BRETT, b. Oct. 18, 1819; m. Lovina Bent.
928. iii. MARY E., b. Oct. 1823 or 1824; died aged 16 years.
929†. iv. SARAH R., b. Feb. 1826; m. Henry Case.
930. v. One daughter; died young.
931. vi. RACHEL, by the last wife.

(421.) i. EDWARD RICE, b. March 16, 1784, son of Gershom and Susanna (Howe) Rice of Marlboro, Mass.; m. Nov. 26, 1809, Susanna Felton, b. Oct. 29, 1788, daughter of Joel Felton of Marlboro, (No. 168.) (For Rice see App. C. C.) Mr. Rice was a farmer and resided in the west part, on the stage road between Marlboro and Worcester. He died May 18, 1871, aged 87 years. Mrs. Susanna (Felton) Rice died June 19, 1883, aged 94 years, 7 months; the oldest native born person in Marlboro. Had 6 children.

932†. i. SALLY, b. Oct. 5, 1810; m. Samuel B. Maynard.
933. ii. EMERSON, b. March 9, 1812; died Nov. 29, 1813.
934†. iii. EDWARD GERSHOM, b. Jan. 23, 1814; m. Sophia Huntington.
935†. iv. SUSAN BARNARD, twin, b. Jan. 23, 1814; m. Wm. Stratton.
936†. v. MARY, b. March 26, 1816; m. Ozias Huntington.
937†. vi. GEORGE EMERSON, b. May 29, 1818; m. Sarah A. Brigham.

(422.) ii. LUTHER FELTON[6], (*Joel[5], Jacob[4], Samuel[3], John[2], Nathaniel[1],*) b. in Marlboro, April 28, 1790; in 1811, he settled in Boston, where he was a distiller. He m. Nov. 10, 1816, Lydia Russell, b. Feb. 24, 1793, in Scituate, Mass. She died in Boston, March 27, 1838, aged 45 years. Mr. Felton m. second in Dec. 1838, Mrs. Mary Smith, widow of Cyrus Smith of Lexington, Mass., and daughter of Noah and Mary

Porter of Boston. She had 2 sons, Cyrus A. and Thomas J. Smith.

Luther Felton was an assistant assessor in Boston, 1834. He died in South Boston, Nov. 21, 1868, aged 78 years. Luther and Lydia Felton had 3 children.

- 938. i. LYDIA GRAY, b. in Charlestown, March 7, 1818; died in Boston, March 25, 1835, aged 17 years.
- 939†. ii. LUTHER HARVEY, b. Feb. 7, 1821; m. Sarah P. Withington.
- 940. iii. JOHN RUSSELL, b. Feb. 19, 1830; died in New York, unm., Oct. 8, 1869, aged 39 years.

(423.) iii. JOEL FELTON[6], (*Joel[5], Jacob[4], Samuel[3], John[2], Nathaniel[1],*) b. April 17, 1792; m. Nov. 1818, Widow Nancy Ann McDonnell, a sister of his brother Luther Felton's first wife; sup. she died May 1826, aged 36 years. Mr. Felton m. second, July 1828, Electa Spring, b. April 6, 1798, daughter of Wm. and Hannah Spring. They lived in Boston many years, and one season in Marlboro, Mass. In 1836, he purchased a farm in Bolton, on the side of Wattoquattoc Hill, where he has lived 50 years. Mrs. Electa Felton died Dec. 6, 1867, aged 69 years. They had 5 children. Joel Felton is living in his 95th year.

- 941. i. JOEL HENRY, b. June 10, 1829; died in Boston, Sept. 2, 1852, aged 23 years.
- 942. ii. WILLIAM SPRING, b. Aug. 2, 1831; died same month.
- 943†. iii. ANN SOPHIA, b. June 22, 1833: m. Rev. Joseph Barber.
- 944†. iv. WILLIAM NEWELL, b. Dec. 25, 1835; m. Sarah M. Blood.
- 945. v. ELIZA MARIA, b. Aug. 10, 1838; died April 20, 1860, aged 21 years.

(424.) iv. GEORGE FELTON[6], (*Joel[5], Jacob[4], Samuel[3], John[2], Nathaniel[1],*) b. May 3, 1796; m. in 1828, Betsey Hunting, who died Dec. 11, 1828, aged 34 years; left one daughter. Mr. Felton m. second, Rachel Perkins, b. in New Durham, N. H., Oct. 1811, or in 1803. He was a farmer and lived on his father's homestead in Marlboro, Mass. In Nov. 1874, his house was burned to the ground by an incendiary and Mr. Felton died about 4 months afterwards, March 15, 1875, aged 78 years. Mrs. Rachel Felton died at West Newton, Mass., Nov. 10, 1884, aged 73 or 81 years.

- 946. i. ELIZABETH, b. Nov. 1828; in 1882 her weight was 325 pounds; she died in Boston, Oct. 1885, aged 57 years; buried in Marlboro.

947†. ii. GEORGE NEWELL, b. Sept. 27, 1832; m. Sally Wing.
948†. iii. MARY BERRY, b. 1833; m. Minot Rice.
949. iv. LYDIA GRAY, b. 1836.
950. v. CHARLES PERKINS, b. Feb. 1838; m.
951. vi. CAROLINE F., b. 1843; m. Charles Augustus Littlefield.

(425.) v. LEVI FELTON$_5$ (*Joel$_5$ Jacob$_5$ Samuel$_5$ John^2, Nathaniel^1,*) b. Jan. 17, 1799; m. Judith Abbott of Billerica. Mr. Felton was a clothier, and was living in Lowell in 1826, the year the town was incorporated. He died in Westford, Mass., Oct. 21, 1829, aged 30 years and 9 months; buried in Marlboro, his native town. Mrs. Judith Felton of Chelmsford, died about 1870. They had two children.

952. i. MARIA, b. about 1827; m. S. Moulton.
953†. ii. GEORGE LEVI, b. about 1829; m. Martha ———.

(428.) viii. MATTHIAS FELTON^6, (*Joel$_5$ Jacob$_5$ Samuel^3. John^2, Nathaniel^1,*) b. Oct. 25, 1805; m. Lucy Hall, b. May 3, 1808; they lived in Grafton, Mass., several years, afterwards in Millbury, Mass., where he was one of the selectmen one year. In 1859, Matthias Felton and Company, said a newspaper, employ from 10 to 12 men in their iron foundry, constantly engaged in making castings for machinery; and do a heavy business in more than one sense. In 1861, Mr. Felton and son-in-law moved to Philadelphia, Pa. Mrs. Lucy Felton died in that city, April 29, 1869, aged 61 years. He m. second, Oct. 1872, Almira Pratt of Boston. Matthias Felton died in Philadelphia, Pa., in March 1881, aged 75 years, funeral March 8, at Millbury, Mass. Had 3 children by his first wife.

954†. i. FANNY, b. Aug. 14, 1833; m. Austin W. Goodale.
955. ii. LEVI AUGUSTUS, b. Oct. 7, 1837; died Oct. 31, same month.
956. iii. CHARLES, b. June 1841; died Oct. 14, 1847, aged 6 years.

(429.) ix. JOHN FELTON^6, (*Joel$_5$ Jacob$_5$ Samuel^3, John^2, Nathaniel^1,*) b. July 22, 1808; m. in 1835, Lydia Jenkins, dau. of Isaac Jenkins of Boston. Mrs. Lydia Felton's mother was sister to Luther, (No. 422,) and Joel Felton's, (No. 423,) first wives. John Felton was a distiller in Boston, where he died Jan. 1869, aged 60 years. Mrs. Felton died in Boston, March 12, 1864, aged 52 years. They had 4 children.

957. i. JOHN, JR., b. Oct. 22, 1837; died Dec. 1, 1857, aged 20 years.

94   FELTON FAMILY.

958†.   ii. GEORGE HENRY, b. about Aug. 1839; m. Euphemia A. Choate.
959.   iii. MARTHA BURROUGH.
960.   iv. ANNA H., died in No. Bridgewater, Dec. 10, 1870.

(430.) i. MOSES HOWE, b. in Holden, Mass., Oct. 13, 1774, son of Jonathan Howe, and grandson of Moses and Hannah (Felton) Howe of Marlboro, (No. 54); m. June 1801, Elizabeth Temple of Marlboro, where they lived a few years; then moved to Waterford, Me. They had 4 or 5 daughters and one son. Mr. Howe m. second, Esther ———, and had 2 or 3 daughters. Two of their children were.

961.   i. HANNAH BURNAP, bapt. in Marlboro, July 25, 1802.
962.   ii. ELMER HOWE was their son.

(431.) ii. AMOS NEWELL of Holden, Mass., m. in 1803, Hannah Howe, b. Jan. 23, 1777, daughter of Jonathan Howe of Holden, (No. 171.) Mr. Newell was son of Aaron and Sarah Newell of the same town. Mrs. Hannah Newell died aged 36 years. He m. second, Dec. 1813, Hannah Boynton of Paxton; she died in 1842, aged 60 years. Mr. Newell had 4 children by his first wife, and 3 by his last wife.
963.   i. MOSES, b. Sept. 29, 1803; m. Chloe Paddock in 1829, and had 5 children.
964.   ii. ELIZA, b. Oct. 29, 1807.
965.   iii. LUCY, b. Oct. 21, 1810.
966.   iv. NAHUM, b. Nov. 20, or 26, 1812; m. April 1836, Olive Davis, and had 5 children.

(433.) iv. ELIAS BLAKE, m. May 25, 1803, Lucy Howe, b. Sept. 25, 1780, daughter of Jonathan Howe of Holden, Mass., (No. 171.)
In 1791, an Elias Blake was one of the builders of the Unitarian meeting house in Worcester.

(434.) v. SAMUEL HOWE of Holden, b. Aug. 13, 1785, son of Jonathan Howe of Holden, (No. 171); m. Nov. 29, 1810, Persis Knight of Templeton, Mass. They lived in Holden and had 7 children, Mr. Howe died there, Feb. 16, 1862, aged 76 years. Mrs. Persis Howe died in McDonough, N. Y., at the residence of her son, A. J. Howe, March 30, 1877, aged 86 years, 10 months.
967.   i. SAMUEL NELSON, b. Oct. 12, 1811; m. in 1843, Persis E. Parker. He m. again in 1849; he died in 1861, aged 50 years.

968. ii. HANNAH MANDON, b. Dec. 14, 1813.
969. iii. MARTHA ARZINA, b. July 8, 1816; m. Aug. 1834, Wm. J. Watson.
970. iv. HOLLIS STILLMAN, b. July 3, 1818.
971. v. ADONIRAM JUDSON, b. Aug. 11, 182–; living in 1877, in N. Y. State.
972. vi. LaFAYETTE, b. Sept. 13, 1824.
973. vii. JANE VALINA, b. Dec. 9, 1826.

(436.) vii. JOEL BLAKE, m. June 30, 1811, Polly Howe, b. Feb. 18, 1793, daughter of Jonathan Howe of Holden. They had two or more children in Holden.

973. a. i. MARY EMELINE, b. April 21, 1818.
973. b. ii. ELIZA DODD, b. June 1, 1822.

(437.) viii. JOHN READ BOWLS, of Leicester, Mass.; m. April 22, 1813, Sarah Howe, b. June 17, 1796, daughter of Jonathan Howe of Holden, (No. 171.) They had one or more children. Their son Andrew E. Bowls, m. April 10, 1839, Ann Flagg of Holden; and had Sarah Elizabeth, b. March 8, 1843.

(438.) i. JOHN SWINTON FELTON[6], (*David[5] Samuel[4], Samuel[5] John[2], Nathaniel[1],*) b. Oct. 2, 1787; m. in 1814, Sally Wood, b. May 9, 1792, daughter of Israel Wood of Danvers. They had 5 children; the two oldest were born at Amesbury, Mass., where he was a merchant; the others b. at Danvers. Mr. Felton was a tanner in Danvers several years. The last years of his life were spent in Salem, where he died Feb. 1, 1875, aged 87 years.

974†. i. PHEBE M., b. Oct. 4, 1816; m. Daniel Haskell.
975†. ii. SALLY AUGUSTA, b. Sept. 29, 1818; m. Franklin Upton
976. iii. CHARLES F., b. Nov. 9, 1822; died Oct. 15, 1826.
977. iv. CAROLINE THATCHER, b. April 7, 1827; died Feb. 7, 1829.
978. v. CAROLINE ELIZABETH, b. Nov. 29, 1830.

(441.) iv. JAMES SLEEPER, b. in Brentwood, N. H., April 1783; m. Dec. 1822, Hannah Felton, b. Oct. 30, 1800, daughter of David Felton of Danvers, (No. 174.) They had 3 children in Danvers.

979. i. EMILY BATCHELDER, b. Dec. 12, 1823.
980. ii. JAMES HENRY, b. March 21, 1826.
981. iii. CHARLES FELTON, b. March 16, 1835.

(442.) i. RUFUS PUTNAM, b. July 17, 1774, was son

of Dr. James P. Putnam, and grandson of Dr. Amos Putnam, who lived at Felton's Corner in Danvers, now in Peabody. Rufus Putnam m. Feb. 1800, Polly Felton, b. June 1, 1782, daughter of Asa Felton of Danvers, (No. 175.) They lived at Hopkinton, N. H., and had 6 children. Rufus Putnam was a substantial farmer and a good man in every sense of the word, says Hon. Levi Bartlett of Warner, N. H. One of Mr. Putnam's grandsons was town clerk of Warner, N. H. in 1875. Rufus Putnam died May 12, 1855, aged 80 years, 10 months; Mrs. Putnam died Aug. 4, 1852, aged 70 years.

982†. i. MARTIN, b. Dec. 5, 1801; m. Margaret Butler.
983†. ii. HERRICK, b. Sept. 11, 1803; m. Rachel Kezer of Sutton, N. H.
984. iii. MARY, b. Nov. 1805; m. April 17, 1832, Hosea Clough of Webster, N. H.
985. iv. TRYPHENA, b. Oct. 5, 1808; d. Nov. 28, 1850, aged 42 years.
986†. v. RUFUS JR., b. Sept. 27, 1813; m. Apphia Clark.
987. vi. JOSEPH, b. April 20, 1817; died Sept. 24, 1843, aged 26 years.

(443.) ii. JAMES FELTON[6], (Asa[5] Samuel[4], Samuel[3], John[5] Nathaniel[1],) b. Sept. 10, 1786; m. Sophronia Webb, b. April 1808. Mr. Felton was a blacksmith and in 1810, was living in Hopkinton N. H. He returned to Danvers and followed his trade many years. He died in Danvers several years ago. Mrs. Sophronia Felton was living in 1885.

988†. i. JAMES PORTER, b. Feb. 15, 1828; died July 10, 1855, aged 27 years.
989. ii. MARGARET JANE, b. Jan. 25, 1830; m. ——— Wright.
990†. iii. LYDIA ANN, b. Sept. 1, 1832; m. Joseph W. Mead.
991. iv. SARAH ANN, b. Feb. 4, 1835.
992†. v. LEWIS EDWARDS, b. July 23, 1840; m. Martha J. Day.
993. vi. JOSEPH EPPES, b. Oct. 31, 1844; died Feb. 8, 1871, aged 26 years.

(455.) iv. DANIEL NICKERSON, m. Jan. 29, 1815, Phebe Felton, b. March 9, 1793, daughter of Asa Felton of Danvers, (No. 175.) In 1815, Mr. and Mrs. Nickerson were living at Orrington, Hancock County, Me. Sup. their daughter was m. in Lynn, Mass., in 1835.

994. i. SARAH FELTON NICKERSON, m. Jan. 1835, to Franklin Collins.

FELTON FAMILY.

(447.) vi. MOSES W. WILSON, b. May. 9, 1797; m. April 1818, Martha P. Felton, b. Oct. 23, 1797, daughter of Asa Felton, (No. 175.) They had 5 children in So. Danvers, Mr. Wilson died in Broadwick, Ga., Nov. 1, 1840, aged 43 years.

995. i. MARY HOWE, b. July 11, 1819; m.
996. ii. MOSES WILLIAM, b. Aug. 12, 1821.
997. iii. GEORGE HERRICK, b. Aug. 3, 1825; m.
998. iv. JOHN HENRY, b. Jan. 23, 1828.
999. v. CHARLES EDWARD, b. Nov. 27, 1834.

(448.) vii. ZACHARIAH FELTON[6], (Asa_5 $Samuel^4$, $Samuel^3$, $John^2$, $Nathaniel^1$,) b. Feb. 4, 1800; m. Dec. 1839, Abigail H. Towne of Lynn, Mass., b. Jan. 4, 1822. He resided on his father's homestead on Mount Pleasant, South Danvers, where he died March 22, 1842, aged 42 years. They had one son, posthumous. Mrs. Abigail H. Felton, m. second in 1843, George Warren Reed. Mr. Reed m. first in 1838, Eliza Ann Very; he m. third, Miss Proctor.

1000. i. ZACHARIAH FELTON, JR., b. June 22, 1842, (three months after his father's decease;) died March 4, 1843, aged 8 months.

(449.) i. SAMUL MacINTIRE, m. March 14, 1811, Sally Lander, b. June 8, 1788, daughter of Capt. Jonathan and Sarah (Felton) Lander of Salem. Their children recorded on South Danvers' records. Mr. MacIntire was b. Jan. 26, 1784, son of Samuel and Phebe MacIntire of Danvers.

1001. i. SAMUEL, JR., b. Dec. 1811.
1002. ii. SARAH, b. April 1814.
1003. iii. HENRY, b. July 1816.
1004. iv. JAMES FELTON, b. May 1819.
1005. v. INGALLS K., b. Dec. 1821.
1006. vi. WILLIAM, b. Feb. 1826.
1007. vii. NANCY, twin, b. Feb. 1826.
1008. viii. CHARLES, b. Sept. 1834.

(462.) i. WM. WEBBER FELTON[6], ($Daniel_5$ $David^4$, $Samuel_5$ $John^2$, $Nathaniel^1$,) b. July 4, 1775; m. in 1800, Sally Gary; she died in Batavia, N. Y., in 1817, aged 36 years. Mr. Felton lived in Hubbardston, Vt., before he moved to N. Y. State. Mrs. Felton was the mother of his children. Mr. Felton m. second, Mrs. Mehitable Whitlock, b. July 1777; she had 5 children by her first husband. They lived several years in Oneida County, N. Y. About 1837, Mr. Felton moved to Rome, Mich., where his wife and three of his daughters were buried before 1856. Wm. Webber Felton died about 1859, aged 83 years, 6 months. His children were:

1009†. i. LAURA M., b. Dec. 1801; m. William Filkin.
1010†. ii. ELIZA M., b. June 1805; m. Caleb Smith.
1011†. iii. WM. FLAGG, b. Sept. 1807; m. Annis Strong.
1012. iv. DANIEL W., b. in 1809; died in Batavia, N. Y., in 1814.
1013. v. LOYD DEXTER, b. May 1811; living in Wis in 1856.
1014†. vi. SARAH ANN, b. June 1813; m. Russell Clark.
1015†. vii. LUCINDA, b. Dec. 1816; m. Wm. Penfield.

(469.) viii. RUSSELL SHULES of Benson, Vt., m Polly Felton, b. March 9, 1785, daughter of Daniel and Lois (Wilder) Felton, (No. 183.) Mrs. Shules died about 1852, aged 67 years.

(470.) ix. JONATHAN BENNETT, m. Sally Felton, b. Jan. 21, 1787; she died before 1856. Mr. Bennett was living in Somerset, N. Y., in 1856, then aged 81 years.

(471.) x. LYMAN FELTON^6, (*Daniel$_5$ David^4, Samuel$_3$ John^2, Nathaniel^1,*) b. Nov. 5, 1788; m. Dolly Young. They lived at Orwell, Vt., and had 12 children. Mr. Felton died June 1869, aged 80 years, 7 months. He was one of the wealthy persons of the place.

1016. i. PERLINA, b. April 14, 1814; m.
1017. ii. MARIETTA, b. Dec. 25, 1815; m.
1018. iii. RHODILLA, b. March 1, 1818.
1019. iv. DARIUS, b. Aug. 29, 1820; died Sept. 1846, aged 26 years.
1020. v. FRANKLIN, b. Nov 18, 1822; in 1852 was living in Govanstown, Md., when he lost a valuable horse.
1021. vi. LYMAN W., b. Sept. 24, 1824; living in Ohio in 1849.
1022. vii. CHARLES Y., b. Feb. 11, 1826; m. He was a soldier, and was shot in the battle of the Wilderness, May 1864, aged 38 years
1023. viii. LOIS W., b. May 29, 1827; m.
1024. ix. LOUISA Y., twin, b. May 29, 1827; m.
1025†. x. SIMEON Y., b. Jan. 15, 1829; m.; living in Orwell, Vt.
1026. xi. WILLIAM, b. May 11, 1833; died in 1835.
1027†. xii. ASA YOUNG, b. Nov. 23, 1835; m. H. S. Douglas.

(472.) xi. LLOYD FELTON^6, (*Daniel$_5$ David^4, Samuel$_3$*

John², Nathaniel¹,) b. Feb. 2, 1790; m. Polly Woodard of Sudbury, Vt. Mr. Felton was a shoe-maker, and lived several years at Benson, Vt. They had 9 children; one son and two daughters died young. He moved to West Stockholm, N. Y., in St. Lawrence County, where Mrs. Felton died Sept. 6, 1855, aged 62 years.

1028. i.   MARY ANN, b. in 1814; living in Ill. in 1856.
1029. ii. GEORGE, b. in 1818; living in Wis. in 1856.
1030. iii. ROYAL, b. in 1820.
1031. iv. DANIEL, died before 1856.
1032. v.   HARRIET, b. in 1828.
1033. vi. LUCILIA, b in 1835.

(473.) xii. DANIEL FELTON⁶, (Daniel⁵, David⁴, Samuel³, John², Nathaniel¹,) b. in Athol, Mass., Aug. 5, 1791; m. Feb. 5, 1816, in Weathersfield, Vt. He m. second, Feb. 23, 1821, in Hinesburg, same state. He was a tanner and currier, and moved from Sudbury, Vt., about 1841, to Colton, St. Lawrence County, N. Y. They had several children.

1034. i. BERNETIA, a daughter, was living in Orwell, Vt., in 1856.
1035. ii. CASCIUS, in 1878, was a merchant at Norwood, N. Y.

(475.) ii. AARON JOHNSON, b. Oct. 21, 1775, son of Jonathan and Rachel (Felton) Johnson, (No. 184;) m. in 1804, Betsey Crossit, and had 4 children at Petersham, Mass.

1036. i.   ASA, b. Nov. 21, 1805.
1037. ii. ELIZA, b. March 21, 1808.
1038. iii. SUSANNA, b. Aug. 21, 1809.
1039. iv. DANIEL, b. Feb. 20, 1816.

(478.) v. AMOS JOHNSON, b. March 13, 1782, son of Jonathan and Rachel (Felton) Johnson, (No. 184;) m. in 1807, Mary Knapp, and lived in Phillipston and Petersham, Mass. Mrs. Mary Johnson died Nov. 8, 1826. They had 5 children.

1039½. i.   RACHEL FELTON, b. Oct. 8, 1808.
1040. ii. JAAZANIAH MASON KNAPP, b. Feb. 10, 1812.
1041. iii. LYDIA, b. Aug. 7, 1817.
1042. iv. AMOS D., b. Jan. 20, 1820.
1043. v.   LEVI, b. Sept. 27, 1821.

(479.) vi. HENRY JOHNSON, b. March 23, 1785, son of Jonathan and Rachel Johnson, (No. 184;) m. April 20, 1820, Lucy Clement, b. Jan. 1, 1791. Mr. Johnson died in

Athol, Mass., Dec. 14, 1846, aged 61 years. Mrs. Lucy Johnson died the same year, March 7, 1846, aged 55 years. They had five children.

 1044. i. EMILY, b. April 13, 1821; m. William A. Eaton.
 1045. ii. LUCY, b. March 1823; m. David S. Brock.
 1046†. iii. JONATHAN. b. Oct. 1, 1825; m. Climena Marsh.
 1047. iv. WARREN, b. Sept. 14, 1830; m. May 1855, Ellen E. Moulton.
 1048. v. DANIEL, b. Aug. 23, 1832; m. Sarah Bigelow.

(484.) i. AARON KEMP, m. Eunice Benjamin, b. Dec. 5, 1780; residence Fitchburg, Mass. Had several children who died young. Mrs. Kemp died June 20, 1820, aged 39 years. Mrs. Kemp was the oldest daughter of Daniel and Tamison (Felton) Benjamin, (No. 186.)

(485.) ii. DANIEL BENJAMIN, JR., b. March 6, 1782, son of Daniel and Tamison (Felton) Benjamin, (No. 168;) m. Rachel Wetherell of Mansfield. Had 2 sons and 2 dau's. He m. second time and had 4 more children.

(488.) v. SAMUEL KEYES of Roxbury, Mass., m. Abigail Benjamin b. June 17, 1789, daughter of Daniel and Tamison (Felton) Benjamin, (No. 186.) Had 8 children. One daughter m. a Mr. Cooper of Weston, Mass.

(489.) vi. JOHN HUNT of Boston, m. Sally Benjamin, b. March 14, 1792, daughter of Daniel and Tamison (Felton) Benjamin, (No. 186.) They had 8 children. Mrs. Hunt died March 31, 1836, or 37, aged 44 or 45 years. John Hunt was b. Nov. 20, 1792, son of John Hunt of Watertown. It is said Mr. Hunt m. in 1838, another Sarah Benjamin, a relative of his first wife. John Hunt was a soldier in the war of 1812 to 1815. He was a deacon of a church in Roxbury, Mass., where he died, July 10, 1883, aged 90 years. Dea. Hunt had a son, a soldier, in the late civil war.

 1049. i. JOHN M., b. Oct. 6, 1816; died Jan. 6, 1839, aged 22 years.
 1050. ii. SARAH ELIZABETH, b. Aug. 6, 1818; died July 9, 1821.
 1051. iii. HARRIET A., b. Jan. 18, 1821.
 1052. iv. MARIA CHARLOTTE, b. Feb. 5, 1825; m. Henry T. Hogan, a house-wright.
 1053. v. WM. A., b. March 13, 1827; m. Nov. 25, 1858, Inez M. White.
 1054. vi. EMILY, b. Sept. 26, 1829.

1055. vii. CLARISSA, died Nov. 3, 1835.
1056. viii. GEORGE E., b. Nov. 12, 1836.

(490.) vii. CHARLES DAMON of East Sudbury, b. Feb. 11, 1792, son of Dea. Aaron and Rachel Damon of East Sudbury; m. in 1814, Lydia Benjamin, b. May 11, 1794, dau. of Daniel and Tamison Benjamin, (No. 186.) Charles Damon was brother of Rev. David Damon of Lunenburg, Amesbury, and West Cambridge, Mass. Mr. Damon was a blacksmith, and died in Wayland, Mass., July 1871, aged 79 years. Mrs. Lydia Damon died in Cochituate, a village in the south part of Wayland, Oct. 25, 1876, aged 82 years. They had 10 children.

1057†. i. JANE ELIZABETH, b. Feb. 22, 1815; m. Tobin French.
1058†. ii. MARTHA TROWBRIDGE, b. July 22, 1817; m. James M. Bent.
1059†. iii. LYDIA ANN LUCY, b. July 17, 1819; m. Stephen Stanton.
1060†. iv. CHARLES ROSWELL, b. Oct. 3, 1821; m. Emily Estabrook.
1061. v. DANIEL BENJAMIN, b. Jan. 25, 1825; m. Elizabeth Jennison; he died at West Newton about 1853, aged 28 years.
1062. vi. GEORGE ALVIN, b. May 30, 1826; m. Orelia Farnum.
1063. vii. MIRICK FELTON, b. April 29, 1828; died in Wayland, aged 28 or 30 years.
1064. viii. AARON SANDFORD, b. June 21, 1830; m. Emily Esther Holbrook; he died in Peterborough, N. H., about 1858, aged 28 years.
1065. ix. SARAH AUGUSTA, b. June 12, 1832; m. in 1851, Nathaniel Whittemore.
1066. x. ADALINE ALTHEA, b. Sept. 22, 1835; m. Dearster Coolidge.

(492.) ix. JOHN CRAMM of Me., m. Lovice Benjamin, b. April 8, 1801, daughter of Daniel and Tamison Benjamin, (No. 186.) Had 2 children. Mrs. Cramm m. second, Joseph Moore; residence, Roxbury, Mass. They had 3 children.

(493.) x. EMERY WILLARD, b. in Ashburnham, Mass., Nov. 24, 1800; m. Irene Benjamin, b. Feb. 20, 1805, youngest child of Daniel and Tamison (Felton) Benjamin, (No. 186.) Mr. Willard resided in the north part of Brighton, Mass., and kept a lumber yard. He died of pneumonia, Feb. 25, 1872, aged 71 years. Mrs. Irene Willard died Jan. 16, 1874, aged 69 years. They had 12 children.

- 1067.   i. CAROLINE IRENE, b. Dec. 27, 1826; m. Edward Abbott.
- 1068. ii. CHARLES EMERY, b. May 10, 1829; died Aug. 9, 1830.
- 1069. iii. MARTHA MELLEN, b. June 13, 1831; living in 1874.
- 1070. iv. CHARLES EMERY, b. April 1, 1833; m. Mary E. Lovell, Oct. 1861.
- 1071.   v. GEORGE HENRY, b. Feb. 13, 1835; died Feb. 4, 1836.
- 1072. vi. GEORGE HENRY, b. Dec. 1, 1836; in California in 1872.
- 1073. vii. LOUISA MARIA, b. Jan. 3, 1839; died Jan. 19, 1841.
- 1074. viii. LOUISA MARIA, b. Jan. 4, 1841; m. Edward M. Simmons, April 1864.
- 1075. ix. ELLEN FRANCES, b. March 10, 1843; m. Charles C. Cobleigh, Oct. 1869.
- 1076.   x. CALVIN FELTON, b. Feb. 27, 1845; died April 28, 1849.
- 1077. xi. HARRIET AUGUSTA, b. March 24, 1847; died Sept. 21, 1847.
- 1078. xii. ALICE AMELIA, b. June 21, 1848; died Jan. 31, 1872, aged 23 years, 7 months.

(494.) i. JOSEPH POCORNEY, m. Feb. 28, 1808, Hannah Felton, b. April 2, 1736, daughter of George Webber Felton of Petersham, (No. 187.) They had one son. Mr. Pocorney died Oct. 5, 1812. Mrs. Hannah Pocorney m. second, March 22, 1815, Thomas Marshall Jacobs, b. Sept. 22, 1777, son of James Jacobs. (App. Jacobs, D. D.)

- 1079†.   i. JOSEPH POCORNEY, JR., b. Dec. 16, 1809; m. Lydia Clapp.

Thomas M., and Hannah (Felton) Jacobs had 5 children.
Thomas M. Jacobs, lived in West Scituate, Mass., where he died Nov. 4, 1845, aged 68 years. He was a carpenter by trade. He was a brother of the late Hon. Ichabod R. Jacobs of South Scituate. Mrs. Hannah (Felton) Jacobs died in West Scituate, May 28, 1878, aged 92 years.

- 1080.   ii. EUNICE H., b. Jan. 5, 1816; died Dec. 17, 1838, aged 23 years.
- 1081†. iii. JAMES M., b. March 12, 1818; m. Caroline E. Hendley.
- 1082†. iv. DAVID H., b. April 5, 1820; m. Elizabeth Ayres.

1083. v. AURELIA FELTON, b. June 22, 1823; took care of her aged mother.
1084. vi. THOMAS R, b. Nov. 24, 1825; m. Mary E. Hunt.

(495.) ii. AURELIA S. FELTON, b. Dec. 30, 1787, dau. of George Webber Felton Sr., of Petersham, (No. 187.) Miss Felton was betrothed to Augustine W. Newhall, but died unm. Sept. 2, 1819, aged 32 years. Mr. Newhall's sister m. Mr. Danforth, whose daughter, b. about 1819, named Aurelia Felton, m. a Mr. Raymond. Mrs. A. F. D. Raymond, has been a school teacher, a lecturer, and a physician in Syracuse, N. Y. Mr. A. W. Newhall afterwards married.

(496.) iii. GEORGE WEBBER FELTON^6, (George W.^{5}, David^4, Samuel^3, John^2, Nathaniel^1,) b. May 17, 1789; m. May 1814, Lydia Baker, b. Nov. 6, 1787, of Phillipston, Mass. They had 7 children. Mr. Felton died in Petersham, April 13, 1861, aged 72 years. Mrs. Lydia Felton was living in 1884, aged 97 years; she died in the northern part of N. H. in 1885, aged 98 years.

1085†. i. BETSEY FISH, b. March 22, 1815; m. Emery Shumway.
1086†. ii. EZRA BAKER, b. Nov. 16, 1816; m. Pamelia Cooley.
1087. iii. LYDIA, b. Dec. 2, 1818; living in 1863.
1088†. iv. GEORGE MERRICK, b. Nov. 10, 1820; m. Harriet Bigelow.
1089†. v. LEONARD ALEXANDER, b. Jan. 30, 1823; m. Sarah Dunton.
1090. vi. SILAS EDWARD, b. Sept. 7, 1825; died in 1848, aged 23 years.
1091†. vii. SARAH HOVEY, b. March 17, 1828; m. Ambrose A. Mason.

(497.) iv. NATHANIEL FARROW of Scituate, b. Nov. 4, 1788, son of Capt. Abiel Farrow of Hanover, Mass., m. Nov. 12, 1812, Elizabeth Alden Felton, b. March 19, 1791, dau. of George W. Felton of Petersham, (No. 187.) They settled at Shutesbury, and wrote their name Farrar. He died Nov. 27, 1841, aged 53 years; buried in his native town, Hanover. Mrs. Elizabeth A. Farrar died in Dorchester, Mass., May 14, 1873, aged 82 years; buried in Hanover, Mass. Their children were:

1092. i. GEORGE HOWE, b. Oct. 27, 1813; m. March 1835, Eveline Ewell; he died in Chicago, Ill., in March 1879, aged 65 years.

104   FELTON FAMILY.

1093.   ii. MARY OLIVER, b. Oct. 30, 1815; m. April 1836, Luther Edward Davis.
1094†. iii. ELIZABETH ALDEN, b. Feb. 10, 1818; m. Jonas H. Winter.
1095†. iv. AURELIA NEWELL, b. April 10, 1820; m. Edward Moody.
1096.   v. NATHANIEL FRANCIS, b. May 24, 1822.
1097.   vi. HANNAH ANN, b Dec. 21, 1824; m. Aug. 1842, Alden Moody.
1098.   vii. BETHIAH CUSHING, b. March 26, 1827; m. Feb. 1849, Dillon Francis Beebe.
1099.   viii. NATHANIEL NELSON, b. Nov. 4, 1829; died in Boston about 1880.
1100.   ix. ABBY JANE, b. Dec. 23, 1831; m. May 1854, Harrison Gray Otis Powers.
1101.   x. DIANTHA MERRILL, b. March 2, 1834; lived 15 years.
1102.   xi. EMILY ESTHER, b. Aug. 6, 1838; m. James M. Haskins.

(498.) v. DAVID HOWE FELTON[6], (*George W.*,[5] *David*[4], *Samuel*[3], *John*[2], *Nathaniel*[1],) b. Dec. 12, 1792; m. Feb. 1819, Nancy Fish of Athol, Mass. He was a blacksmith, and died in Athol, March 17, 1819, aged 26 years. He lived but six weeks after he was married. Widow Nancy Felton m. second, Henry Lee of Athol; she was living a widow in 1855.

(499.) vi. MOSES OLIVER FELTON[6], (*George W.*,[5] *David*[4], *Samuel*[3], *John*[2], *Nathaniel*[1],) b. March 14, 1794; m. July 1820, Susan Cummings of Shutesbury, Mass. Mr. Felton was a blacksmith and lived in that town. They had 10 children. Mr. Felton died in Whately, Mass., Jan. 6, 1882, aged 87 years, 10 months.

1103†. i. FREDERICK A., b. March 29, 1821; m. Mahalah A. Winter.
1104†. ii. SUSAN A., b. Dec. 21, 1822; m. Lucius L. Hyde.
1105†. iii. STEPHEN O., b. Dec. 18, 1824; m. Sarah D. Taylor.
1106.   iv. CAROLINE A., b. Feb. 26, 1827; m. Aug. 1850, Alonzo Crafts, (son of Erastus Crafts,) b. May 17, 1821; residence, Whately, Mass.
1107.   v. ELLEN S., b. May 25, 1829; m. James Logan; residence, Clinton, Mass. Mrs. Logan has been a milliner in Clinton many years.
1108.   vi. LUCY A., b. March 10, 1831; m. Sept. 1850, Henry Chilson.

1109. vii. LUCIA M., b. Feb. 23, 1833; m. Feb. 1860, in Clinton, Mass., Alexander Lord; she m. second, Mr. Fuller.
1110†.viii. FRANCIS A., b. March 19, 1835; m. Lydia Ann Chamberlin.
1111. ix. EDWARD W., b. April 29, 1838; left home early and never returned.
1112. x. EUNICE S., b. July 21, 1840; m. ——— Sparrow.

(500.) vii. ALEXANDER FELTON[6], (*George W.*[5], *David*[4], *Samuel*[3], *John*[2], *Nathaniel*[1],) b. April 8, 1795; m. Nov. 1819, Fanny Wells. In 1828, were living in Huntington, Ohio; afterwards settled in Ind. In 1853, they visited their friends in Mass. Mr. Felton died in Ind.. Sept. 2, 1854, aged 59 years. They had 9 children. Mrs. Fanny Felton died in Indianapolis, Feb. 17, 1883, aged 81 years, 4 months.

1113. i. NANCY, b. March 12, 1821; m. twice.
1114. ii. HANNAH, b. Aug. 29, 1824; m. D. C. Powell; she died July 13, 1882, aged 58 years.
1115. iii. GEORGE O., b. Jan. 21, 1826; died April 25, 1826.
1116. iv. MOSES O., b. March 14, 1828; living in Iowa in 1883.
1117. v. FLAVIUS J., b. Jan. 26, 1820; m. and has a son Alexander.
1118. vi. ELVIRA, b. July 27, 1834; died Oct. 27, 1873, aged 39 years.
1119. vii. ABRAHAM, b. Aug. 8, 1837; died Aug. 17, 1837.
1120. viii. SYLVANDER, b. March 13, 1839; living in Boone County, Ind.
1121. ix. LEANDER, b. July 29, 1843; living in Indianapolis, Ind.

(501.) i. ARTEMUS JACKSON of Newton, m. Jan. 1803, Polly Stimson, b. Nov. 6, 1780; the oldest child of Lemuel and Phebe (Felton) Stimson of Ashburnham, Mass. Mrs. Polly Jackson m. second, before 1806, Mr. Seaver. Mrs. Seaver died March 18, 1806, aged 25 years.

(503.) iii. JAMES WHITMORE, b. April 23, 1782; son of Isaac and Rebecca (Foster) Whitmore of Ashburnham; m. Oct. 1811, Phebe Stimson, b. Sept. 18, 1783, dau. of Lemuel and Phebe Stimson of Ashburnham, (No. 188.) They resided in several towns. He was deacon of the Baptist church in Framingham, where he died Jan. 7, 1869, aged 87 years. Mrs. Phebe Whitmore died in the same town July 16, 1838, aged 55 years. Had 2 sons.

1122†.   i. JAMES H., b. Aug. 17, 1812; m. Martha A. Stowe.
1123†. ii. CHARLES S., b. Dec. 6, 1815; m. Agnes S. Hyde.

(505.)   v. ROYAL STIMSON, b. March 6, 1788; son of Lemuel and Phebe Stimson, (No. 188;) m. Sept. 1813, Leaffa (or Relief) Walker of New Ipswich, N. H., b. at Merrimac, July 22, 1787, daughter of Capt. Zaccheus and Patty Walker. Mr. Stimson moved to Cambridge in 1834, where he died Nov. 4, 1860, aged 72 years. Mrs. Stimson died about 4 years afterwards, Aug. 22, 1864, aged 77 years. They had 6 children.

1124.   i. AMELIA H., m. Andrew Newell Wyeth who was b. April 1817.
1125. ii. FORDYCE M., Justice of the Peace in 1877, in Cambridge.
1126. iii. ROYAL W., living in Cambridge, Mass., in 1885.
1127. iv. ANN M., m. Daniel Chamberlain.

(507.) vii. EDWARD STIMSON, b. Oct. 3, 1792, son of Lemuel and Phebe Stimson. (No. 188;) m. in 1820, Sarah Foster; they were living in Winchester, N. H. in 1823. Mr. Stimson died Aug. 8, 1843, aged 51 years. They had 6 children.

(508.) viii. CHARLES STIMSON, b. May 9, 1795; son of Lemuel and Phebe Stimson of Ashburnham; m. May 1824, Beulah Whitmore, b. Aug. 8, 1799, daughter of Isaac Whitmore of Ashburnham. Charles Stimson died Feb. 26, 1830, in his 35th year. They had 2 children.

(509.) ix. ISAAC KEYES of Roxbury, m. Oct. 1817, Abigail Stimson, b. May 24, 1797, daughter of Lemuel and Phebe Stimson, (No. 188.) Had children in Cambridge, Mass. Mrs. Abigail Keyes died at Jamaica Plain, Roxbury, Jan. 22, 1861, aged 64 years. Sup. Mr. Keyes m. second, May 5, 1864, Miss Lucy W. Fuller of Watertown, Mass.

(510.)   x. JOHN CUSHING DAVIS, b. about 1800; m. Oct. 18, 1825, Lucy Stimson, b. Aug. 20, 1799, daughter of Lemuel and Phebe Stimson, (No. 188.) Mr. Davis was a prominent citizen of Ashburnham, and served as selectman of the town. Capt. Davis was a deacon of one of the churches in Ashburnham. He was the pioneer in the manufacture of chairs in that and neighboring towns. Capt. Davis died at Ocean Spray, Winthrop, Mass., at the residence of his son-in-law, Edward F. Rollins, June 19, 1883, aged 83 years. He left a widow and three daughters.

1128.   i. Lucy O., b. Nov. 22, 1826; m. in 1850, Charles Allen.
1129†. ii. Phebe E., b. Nov. 15, 1830; m. June 1851, Edward Fay Rollins.
1130·   iii. Elmira C., b. Dec. 9, 1834; m. in 1862, Frank N. Harris.

(511.) xi. BENJAMIN WHITNEY, b. about 1803; m. Oct. 1826, Elmira Stimson, b. Dec. 4, 1802, the youngest dau. of Lemuel and Phebe (Felton) Stimson of Ashburnham. Mr. Whitney settled in Marlborough, N. H., where he was a Justice of the Peace. He represented the town in the N. H. Legislature. Mrs. Whitney died May 12, 1865, aged 62 years. They had 3 children. Mr. Whitney m. second, Lydia H.——

1131.   i. Jared J., b. Aug. 1, 1833; m. Sarah J. Kidder.
1132†. ii. Elmira F., b. Jan. 18, 1836; m. Charles D. Tarbell.
1133·   iii. George E, b. Aug. 2, 1843; died March 12, 1861, aged 17 years.

(512.) xii. ELBRIDGE STIMSON, b. April 7, 1806, son of Lemuel and Phebe Stimson, (No. 188;) m. May 1833, Elizabeth Caldwell of Ashburnham, Mass. Mr. Stimson was one of the selectmen of Ashburnham in 1863; was town treasurer, 1862 to 1866. He has been a merchant. Has one son.

1134.   i. Charles Stimson.

(513.) xiii. MIRICK STIMSON, b. Aug. 15, 1808, youngest son of Lemuel and Phebe Stimson of Ashburnham, Mass.; he m. Sept. 1834, Sarah Barrett of Ashburnham. Sup. m. second, Charlotte Saulsbury of Brattleborough, Vt. Mr. Stimson was a merchant a few years in Gardner, South Village; he afterwards moved back to Ashburnham, and I believe followed the same business. They had a son born in Gardner. They had 3 children.

1135.   i. Charles B., b. in Gardner, Sept. 4, 1837.

(515.) ii. GEORGE CAMP, m. April 7, 1814, Nancy Felton of Tunbridge, Vt.; she was b. in Middleton, Mass., April 7, 1792; she died April 1848, aged 56 years.

(517.) iv. AMOS FELTON^6, (Amos^5, David^4, Samuel^3, John^2, Nathaniel^1,) b. Sept. 24, 1795; m. Aug. 29, 1832, Elsea Roberts. Their children b. in Tunbridge, Vt. Mr. Felton died April 12, 1833, aged 37 years.

(520.) vii. OSMAN P. FARNHAM, m. June 20, 1831, Lucy Felton, b. Feb. 20, 1802, in Middleton, Mass., daughter of Amos and Sarah (Putnam) Felton of Tunbridge, Vt. Mr. and Mrs. Farnham were living in Tunbridge in 1882. Mr. Farnham was b. in April 1801. Had 6 children.

1137. i. Amos P., b. Sept. 16, 1831.
1138. ii. Nancy A., b. Jan. 31, 1834.
1139. iii. Delia L., b. Aug. 4, 1836.
1140. iv. Laura B., b. May 8, 1839.
1141. v. Maria O., b. Sept. 27, 1841.
1142. vi. George D., b. Feb. 24, 1845.

(521.) viii. WILLIAM PUTNAM FELTON[6], (Amos[5], David[4], Samuel[3], John[2], Nathaniel[1],) b. April 26, 1804; m. in Reading, Vt., Oct. 26, 1836, Betsey Swain of that town; immediately after they were married started for Illinois, by the way of Whitehall, N. Y., Erie canal to Buffalo, thence by boat to Cleveland, O., by canal to Ohio river, to St. Louis, thence to Naples, Ill., near where he settled and lived 32 years. In 1836, they were 5 weeks and 4 days on their way from Vermont to Illinios; in 1851 he visited Tunbridge, Vt., and made the journey in 5 days. He visited Vermont in 1882, when 78 years of age. Mr. Felton was a farmer up to Nov. 1871, when he moved to Jacksonville, Ill., and was living there in 1884. Mrs. Elizabeth Felton died July 31, 1881, aged 78 years. Their children were:

1143. i. Sarah E., b. Feb. 23, 1840; died June 29, 1882, aged 42 years.
1144. ii. Byron A., b. Jan. 19, 1842; living in Jacksonville, Ill., in 1884.

(522.) ix. ABIJAH FELTON[6], (Amos[5], David[4], Samuel[3], John[2], Nathaniel[1],) b. May 27, 1806; m. May 28, 1837, by John Baldwin, Esq, in Sharon, Vt., to Phebe Baldwin. They lived in Sharon and Williamstown, Vt. They had 3 children. Mr. Felton died May 26, 1845, aged 39 years. Mrs. Phebe Felton m. second, Capt. Ariel Hall of Croydon, N. H.

1145†. i. Cornelia D., b. July 21, 1838; m. Daniel Ide.
1146. ii. Helen M., b. May 10, 1840; died in Williamstown, March 29, 1858, aged 18 years.
1147. iii. Sarah P., b. Aug. 24, 1842; died in Sharon, May 14, 1843.

(525.) xii. DAVID FELTON[6], (Amos[5], David[4], Samuel[3], John[2], Nathaniel[1],) b. Aug. 30, 1812; m. in Sharon, Vt., Aug. 30, 1840, by John Baldwin, Esq., Lucinda Baldwin of that town. They moved to Millersburg, Ill., in 1840, where he died suddenly, March 1849, aged 36 years. Mrs. Felton was living in the place in 1884. Had 4 children.

1148.   i. HERSCHEL, b. Aug. 14, 1841; was wounded in the Union army in 1862; m. in 1864, Miss E. Shafer; had 6 children, 5 living in 1884.

1149.   ii. JOHN B., b. Dec. 5, 1842; was a soldier and wounded in the army. He m. in 1866, Charlotte Howe; had 2 children in 1884.

1150.   iii. HIRAM H., b. April 1845; died Feb. 5, 1875, aged 30 years.

1151.   iv. DAVID JR., b. Aug. 16, 1847; contracted a disease in the war and died at home, April 6, 1864, aged 17 years.

(535.) ii. ELI BRIGHAM, b. July 18, 1794, (son of Ithamar Brigham, Jr., of Marlboro;) m. in 1819, Lydia Howe, b. in Sept. 1800, daughter of Jedediah and Lydia (Felton) Howe. Mr. Brigham was a farmer and settled in Marlboro, where he died Oct. 21, 1850, aged 56 years. Mrs. Lydia Brigham died in Northboro, Mass., in March 1885, aged 84 years. Had 5 children. (See App. E. E.)

1152†.   i. SARAH ANN, b Oct. 3, 1820; m. Jan. 1844, Alonzo Wood.

1153†.   ii. JONAS E., b. Jan. 17, 1823; m. Sarah Davenport.

1154†.   iii. SILAS E., b. Feb. 20, 1825; m. ——— Ellis.

1155.   iv. CAROLINE S., b. Oct. 19, 1831; m. Francis Brown of Ipswich, a carpenter. Mrs. Brown residing in Northboro, Mass., in 1885.

1156.   v. GEORGE W., b. June 20, 1833; a butcher and farmer in Northboro, Mass.

(536.) iii. LEE AMSDEN of Bolton, Mass., m. May 1830, Lucretia Howe, b. June 1806, daughter of Jedediah and Lydia (Felton) Howe, (No. 191.) Mr. Amsden was a wheelwright and settled in Boston, where he was living in 1885; he was b. in Southborough, Aug. 15, 1807, son of Wm. and Eunice (Fisher) Amsden of that town. They have had 6 children.

1157.   i. SUSAN E., b. in Bolton, June 1, 1831.

1158.   ii. MARTHA L., b. in Dedham, Dec. 22, 1833.

1159.   iii. MARIA V., b. in Dedham, Feb. 28, 1836; died Jan. 25, 1881, aged 45 years.

1160.   iv. SOPHIA V., twin, b. in Dedham, Feb. 28, 1836; m. A. L. Lovejoy.

1161. v. NELSON, b. in Dedham, Aug. 11, 1838.
1161½. vi. WALTER F., b. in Boston, July 18, 1849.

(537.) iv. REWELL HOWE, b. Sept. 1808, son of Jedediah and Lydia (Felton) Howe of Lunenburg, Vt.; m. March 1835, Mary Stone Rice, b. Aug. 29, 1811, daughter of Ephraim B. and Elizabeth (Howe) Rice of Lunenburg, Vt. Their two oldest children were born in that town. They lived in Marlboro, Mass., one year. For 15 years was warden of almshouses in the following towns in Mass.: Southborough, Westborough, Holden, West Boylston and Northborough; they have resided in Northborough, Mass. since 1870. Mrs. Mary S. Howe died in N., Feb. 26, 1885, aged 73 years.

1162. i.   CAROLINE H., b. May 29, 1836; m. 1857, John L. Darling, who was b. in Princeton, Mass; have one daughter, Jennie E. Darling, b. June 1859.
1163. ii. EPHRAIM B., b. April 10, 1840; living in Boston in 1885.
1164. iii. ANN ELIZA, b. in Southborough, July 10, 1849; m. Henry A. Cooper of Bellows Falls, Vt.; had a child born in 1870.

(538.) i. JOSEPH DALAND, b. Feb. 7, 1774, (son of Benjamin Daland, Jr., of Danvers, who was one of the 7 men from Danvers killed at Lexington, April 19, 1775;) m. in 1802, Phebe Guilford, b. in Danvers. They had 9 children.

1165. i.   BENJAMIN, b. July 1802; died July 1803.
1166. ii.   MARY, b. April 1804.
1167. iii. JOSEPH, JR., b. Nov. 1805.
1168. iv.   BENJAMIN, b. Feb. 15, 1808.
1169. v.   MOSES, b. March 1811.
1170. vi.   LEVI, b. May 1813.
1171. vii. LYDIA, b. Aug. 1819.
1172. viii. SALLY, b. July 1823.
1173. ix.   FRANKLIN, b. July 1826.

(539.) i. JOEL BROOKS, m. Tamison Howe, b. Aug. 31, 1770, daughter of Ebenezer and Elizabeth (Daland) Howe of Gardner, Mass., (No. 193.) They had 7 children. Mrs. Brooks died Jan. 13, 1806, aged 35 years. Mr. Brooks m. second, Azubah ———, and both died in Feb. and March 1841.

1174. i.   BETSEY, b. June 22, 1790.
1175. ii. LYDIA, b. March 7, 1792.
1176. iii. LUCY, b. Feb. 18, 1794.
1177. iv. JOEL, JR., b. April 5, 1796; m. Cynthia ———.
1178. v.   SILAS, b. July 8, 1800.

1179. vi. LUKE, b. July 20, 1803.
1180. vii. ANNA, b. Dec. 21, 1805.

(540.) ii, PERLEY HOWE, b. Nov. 7, 1772, (son of Ebenezer Howe of Gardner;) m. in Marlboro, Mass., at Stephen Felton's, Dec. 4, 1798, Jane Thompson Belcher of that town. They settled in Gardner, Mass. Mr. Howe died March 4, 1839, aged 66 years. Mrs. Howe died May 26, 1844, aged 69 years. Mr. Howe's mother was cousin to Stephen Felton. Their children were:

1181. i. BETSEY DEALAND, b. June 2, 1799; died June 5, 1822, aged 23 years.
1182. ii. SALLY, b. Sept. 18, 1801; m. Jonathan Harris.
1183. iii. ELI, b. April 2, 1804; m. Mary Severy.
1184. iv. FRANCES M., b. Nov. 24, 1806; m. Joel Derby.
1185. v. EBENEZER, b. April 7, 1809; m. Amy Ann Bly.
1186. vi. PERLEY JR., b. Sept. 17, 1811; m. Mary Whitney; had 2 or more children. Mr. Howe was a selectman in Ashburnham in 1863.
1187. vii. LYDIA, b. Sept. 22, 1813; died July 1, 1835, aged 22 years.
1188. viii. EMILY AUGUSTA, b. Oct. 2, 1819; m. Jonathan Burgess.

(541.) iii. EZEKIEL HOWE, b. March 20, 1775, son of Ebenezer Howe of Gardner. He m. Susanna Payson and had 9 children at Gardner, Mass. In the spring of 1810, Capt. Ezekiel Howe's house was struck by lightning. The house was not burned but so shattered that he built a new one. Capt. Howe died Jan. 13, 1842, aged 67 years.

1189. i. EZEKIEL, JR., b. Dec. 7, 1802; died July 15, 1829, aged 26 years.
1190. ii. FRANKLIN, b. Oct. 19, 1804; m. Mary Gill.
1191. iii. JOSEPH P., b. March 23, 1807; m. Maria Conant; had 4 children.
1192. iv. SAMUEL S., b. Oct. 8, 1808; m. Emeline Wood; 3 children. He was postmaster at South Gardner in 1851.
1193. v. STOWEL, b. Dec. 27, 1810.
1194. vi. MARY P., b. April 12, 1813; died Nov. 10, 1832, aged 19 years.
1195. vii. SUSANNA, b. Sept. 5, 1815; died Jan. 15, 1836 aged 20 years.
1196. viii. GEORGE, b. Nov. 6, 1817; m. Jerusha Howe.
1197. ix. DAVID M., b. March 30, 1820; m. Sarah B. Stratton.
1198. x. BETSEY, b. March 22, 1822.

(544.) i. BENJAMIN HOWE, b. Feb. 16, 1783, son of Ebenezer and Tamison Howe of Gardner, Mass.; he m. Keziah Hill and settled in Gardner, where his death was caused by a fall from a ladder in April 1835; he died three days afterwards, aged 52 years. Their children were:

 1199.   i. BENJAMIN, JR., b. July 9, 1804.
 1200.   ii. AMOS, b. Sept. 5, 1805; died in 1836, aged 31 years.
 1201.   iii. SARAH, b. May 5, 1808; m. Luke Bowker.
 1202.   iv. EBENEZER D., b. March 14, 1811; died Feb. 19, 1837, aged 26 years.
 1203.   v. SIMEON, b. May 14, 1813; m. Abigail Fairbanks, resides in Gardner, Mass., near the railroad station; had 6 children.
 1204.   vi. MARY ANN, b. Nov. 2, 1814; died Jan. 29, 1848, aged 33 years.
 1205.   vii. LUCY, b. June 23, 1816; died March 6, 1837, aged 21 years.
 1206.   viii. HARRISON, b. Oct. 5, 1818; m. Fanny Kendall.

(554.) ii. EBENEZER H. TUTTLE of Peru, Vt., b. June 21, 1800; m. Hannah Felton, b. Oct. 7, 1809; daughter of John and Lydia Felton of Landgrove, Vt. They settled in Peru, Vt., where Mr. T. was Justice of Peace. He died June 9, 1875, aged 75 years. Their children were:

 1207.   i. MARY M., b. Sept. 2, 1842; died Feb. 19, 1862, aged 19 years.
 1208.   ii. ABBY F., b. Dec. 3, 1843; m.
 1209.   iii. LUCY H., b. April 28, 1846; m.
 1210.   iv. LUTHER M., b. Aug. 4, 1848; m.
 1211.   v. EMMA M., b. Nov. 28, 1850; m.
 1212.   vi. IRENE M., b. Feb. 22, 1852; m.

(555.) iii. JOEL BARLOW FISKE, m. Sept. 30, 1830, Lydia M. Felton, b. Sept. 26, 1812; daughter of John and Lydia Felton of Landgrove, Vt. They formerly resided in or near Weston, Mass., afterwards in Weston, Vt. Their children were:

 1213.   i. JOSHUA B., b. Nov. 1831; he was a salesman of ready-made clothing in Boston many years in company with Isaac Fenno; and afterwards in Chicago, Ill., where he died of consumption, Jan. 21, 1877, aged 45 years.
 1214.   ii. ORLANDO W., b. May 13, 1834; m. and was living in Somerville, Mass., in 1879.
 1215.   iii. LYDIA, b. Oct. 16, 1838; died in Weston, Vt., May 31, 1839.

FELTON FAMILY. 113

1216.   iv. HANNAH, b. June 14, 1840; died March 4, 1847.
1217.   v. AMELIA C., b. Jan. 11, 1843; m.
1218.   vi. AZELIA L., twin, b. Jan. 11, 1843; m.

(556.) iv. JOHN FELTON[6], (*John[5], Elisha[4], John[3], John[2], Nathaniel[1],*) b. July 15, 1815; m. Sally Hall; they lived in Rutland, Vt., many years, afterwards in Weston, same state. They had 3 children.

1219.   i. HORACE E., b. ———; m.
1220.   . MARY C., m. ——— Shattuck.
1221.   iii. HATTIE, died in the spring of 1879, of diphtheria.

(558.) vi. WILLIAM H. ADAMS, m. Miranda Felton, b. Sept. 24, 1819, daughter of John and Lydia Felton of Landgrove, Vt. Mr. Adams also resides in that town and had 3 sons.

1221. *a.*   i. JOHN QUINCY.
1221. *b.*   ii. GEORGE.
1221. *c.*   iii. CHARLES.

(559.) i. GILMAN ROBERTSON, b. May 1800, son of Joseph and Rachel (Felton) Robertson; m. Dec. 29, 1829, Relief Wyman b. in 1809, and settled at Goffstown, N. H., where he died in the winter of 1882, or '83, aged nearly 83 years. Had 3 children.

1222.   i. LEONARD, m. and had two daughters living on their grandfather's farm in Goffstown in 1880.
1223.   ii. GILMAN F., m. and lives in Manchester, N. H.
1224.   iii. NOEL B., died young.

(560.) i. EZRA DEXTER CLARKE, m. April 1831, Harriet Felton, b. July 5, 1808, daughter of Elisha and Lydia Felton of Amherst, N. H.; they resided at Amherst, and had 3 sons and 3 daughters. It is said Mr. Clarke died about 1858.

1224. *a.*   i. CHARLES.
1224. *b.*   ii. RODNEY.
1224. *c.*   iii. WALTER.
1224. *d.*   iv. EMILY.
1224. *e.*   v. CAROLINE.
1224. *f.*   vi. LAURA.

(560½.) ii. HIRAM GRANVILLE FELTON[6], (*Elisha[5], Elisha[4], John[3], John[2], Nathaniel[1],*) b. Feb. 4, 1814; m. Jane Austin of Hollis, N. H. Mr. Felton was living in Amherst, N. H., in 1882.

(561.) ii. DANIEL CURRIER, m. Clarissa Felton, b. Feb. 16, 1791, daughter of Timothy Felton, Esq., of Warner, N. H. They resided in that town and had 4 daughters.

    1225.   i. HARRIET, m. Samuel Dow.
    1226.   ii. MATILDA, m. Samuel Dow. Mr. Dow is a leading farmer in Warner. He owns nearly 1000 acres of land, cuts annually 150 tons of hay and raised in 1881, about 800 bushels of corn; he winters upwards of 100 head of cattle and several horses.
    1227.   iii. MEHITABLE, m. Moses Story.
    1228.   iv. One daughter died unmarried.

Timothy Felton, Esq., had three great-grandchildren living at his decease in 1856.

(566 and 567.) iv.-v. WILLIAM PRICE, m. Lydia Felton, b. Sept. 25, 1804, daughter of Nathan Felton, Esq., of Danvers; she died Aug. 7, 1845, aged 41 years; she was the mother of his children. Mr. Price m. second, Eliza Matilda Felton, the youngest daughter of Nathan Felton, Esq., of Danvers. They reside on Andover St., in Peabody, Mass. Have 5 children.

    1229.   i. ELLEN F., b. March 12, 1835; m. Woodbury Hardy.
    1230.   ii. LYDIA A. P., b. June 13, 1836.
    1231.   iii. SARAH J., b. Dec. 5, 1838; m. Samuel F. Prey.
    1232.   iv. WM. H., b. Aug. 22, 1841.
    1233.   v. ELIZA F., b. Nov. 20, 1844.

(575.) i. WARREN SHELDON, b. March 4, 1810; m. in 1826, Serena Felton, b. on Mount Pleasant, Danvers, near Peabody, Oct. 16, 1803, daughter of Capt. John Felton of South Danvers. They lived on Danvers Plain, where Mrs. Sheldon died March 24, 1843, aged 39 years. They had 5 children. Mr. Sheldon m. second in 1843, and had 2 more children.

    1234.   i. CATHERINE E., b. March 24, 1827; died in 1843, aged 16 years.
    1235.   iii. SYRENA F., b. June 7, 1829; died Sept. 19, 1844, aged 15 years.
    1236.   iii. MARY ANN, b. Sept. 11, 1831; died April 4, 1844, aged 12 years.
    1237.   iv. CHARLES W., b. April 20, 1835; was a soldier in the civil war and died in the army hospital, Aug. 4, 1864, aged 29 years.
    1238.   v. EMILY C., b. July 29, 1838; living in 1882.

(576.) ii. JOSEPH MERRILL, m. Phebe Felton, b. April 17, 1805; daughter of Capt. John Felton, (No. 207.) Had 3 children. Settled at Danversport.

   1239.   i. JOHN A., b. about 1835; was a soldier and died in the army in 1863, aged 28 years.
   1240.   ii. GEORGE, m. and lives at Danversport.
   1241.   iii. MARY, m. Wm. Young; residence, Somerville, Mass; had 4 children.

(577.) iii. TIMOTHY PROCTOR FELTON^6, ($John^5$, $Timothy^4$, $John^3$, $John^2$, $Nathaniel^1$,) b. Jan. 14, 1807, on Felton Hill, Peabody; m. in 1834, Lydia Ann Haskell, b. June 20, 1817; had in Danvers two children. Mr. Felton died in San Francisco, Cal., Oct. 3, 1850, aged 43 years. Mrs. Felton and her daughter have lived in Providence, R. I.

   1242.   i. HENRY H., b. March 9, 1842.
   1243.   ii. LOIS A. A., b. April 4, 1845; taught school many years in Providence, R. I.

(578.) iv. GEORGE W. POUSLAND, b. in Beverly, May 13, 1814, (son of Capt. John Pousland;) m. May 1836, Elizabeth C. Felton, b. Oct. 25, 1811, daughter of Capt. John Felton, (No. 207.) They settled at Salem, where Mrs. Pousland died Dec. 31, 1880, aged 67 years. Capt. Pousland doing business in Boston of late years. Four of their children are settled near their father's residence in South Salem.

   1244.   i. ELIZABETH F., b. about 1837; m. March 8, 1870, Samuel F. Weeks of Cal.
   1245.   ii. GEORGE H., b. Oct. 4, 1839; m. Matilda Cornelius; he m. second, April 22, 1869, Ellen Potter, both of Salem, Mass.
   1246.   iii. DAVID N., b. about 1842; m.
   1247.   iv. SERENA A., b. about 1847; m.
   1248.   v. CHARLES F., b. about 1851; m.

(579.) v. WM. TAPLEY FELTON^6, ($John^5$, $Timothy^4$, $John^3$, $John^2$, $Nathaniel^1$,) b. Feb. 21, 1818; m. Harriet Stevens, b. Dec. 24, 1824; settled in Salem, Mass. Mr. Felton died in San Francisco, Cal., Feb. 29, 1852, aged 34 years.

   1249.   i. WILLIAM S., Aug. 16, 1845; m. June 17, 1868, Martha Ann Stone, daughter of Rev. Wm. R. Stone. He died in Salem, Aug. 19, 1878, aged 33 years, left a widow and two sons, William and Henry Felton.
   1250.   ii. HARRIET, b. May 1848; died Nov. 12, 1851, aged 3 years, 6 months.

(595.) ii. JOSEPH HOULTON, bapt. June 1760; was son of James and Lois Houlton, and grandson of Joseph and Rebecca (Felton) Houlton all of New Salem, Mass. Capt. Joseph Houlton m. Dec. 25, 1780, Sarah Putnam, daughter of Lieut. Amos Putnam of New Salem. Capt. Houlton was the founder of Houlton, Maine. He visited the place before the year 1804, says the History of Houlton, published in 1884. In the summer of 1804, Capt. Houlton with two persons left New Salem for the Houlton plantation. They started only a few weeks before Lewis and Clark's famous expedition to the Pacific Ocean. In the summer of 1807, Capt. Houlton, wife and eight children left New Salem to settle in the District of Maine. Capt. Houlton, Samuel Cook, Esq., his son-in-law, and James Houlton his son, who was married the day previous to their leaving New Salem, were the first three families of that forest home.

Capt. Houlton was a Justice of the Peace, and was living in Houlton in 1822. It is somewhat remarkable that the first school in Salem-Danvers was kept in James Houlton's house, before there was a school-house built in the place, and the first school in Houlton, Maine, was kept in his great-grandson's house, Joseph Houlton, Esq.

Capt. Joseph and Sarah Houlton's children were:

1250. *a*.   i. SALLY, m. Samuel Cook, Esq.; had 2 or more children.
1250. *b*.   ii. JAMES, m. in 1807, Sally Haskell of New Salem; had 2 or more children.
1250. *c*.   iii. POLLY, m. Ebenezer Warner; had 3 or more children.
1250. *d*.   iv. SAMUEL, m. Sarah Kendall, daughter of Dea. Samuel Kendall of New Salem and Houlton, and sister of school-master, Samuel Kendall, Jr.
1250. *e*.   v. LYDIA, m. Isaac Smith of New Brunswick.
1250. *f*.   vi. JOSEPH, JR., m. Elmira Ray; in 1824 was in the lumber business.
1250. *g*.   vii. LOUISA, m. Jesse Thompson of New Salem, Mass.
1250. *h*.   viii. HENRY, in company with his brother, Joseph Houlton. Houlton is the shire town of Aroostook County, Me.

(498.) i. WILLIAM PERRY, of Barre, Mass., m. in 1791, Mary Felton, b. April 12, 1768, daughter of Capt. Benj. Felton of Brookfield, Mass. Sup. they lived at Granville, Ohio; afterwards in Canton, St. Lawrence County, N. Y. It is said that Mr. Perry, or a son, lived on Gov. Silas Wright's farm. They had 8 children.

FELTON FAMILY. 117

1251. i. HEMAN.
1252. ii. WILLIAM, JR.
1253. iii. SOPHRONIA.
1254. iv. MARY.
1255. v. JANE.

(599.) ii. SAMUEL PARISH MOWER, b. in Barre, Mass., Dec. 22, 1766, (only son of Ebenezer and Susanna (Bent) Mower;) m. June 1791, Jane Felton, b. April 25, 1769, daughter of Capt. Benjamin Felton of Brookfield, (No. 222.) They moved to Granville, Ohio, about 1812, where he died March 9, 1838, aged 72 years. Mrs. Mower died March 7, 1836, aged 67 years.

 1259†. i. ISABELLA, b. Oct. 4, 1791; m. Dr. Wm. S. Richards.
 1260†. ii. LUCIUS D., b. May 1, 1793; m. Lucy Manson.
 1261. iii. SAMUEL, b. Oct. 6, 1795; left his home at 22 years of age, and never returned
 1262. iv. SHERLOCK, b. Oct. 23, 1797; died unm. July 30, 1837, aged 40 years.
 1263. v. HORATIO G., b. May 10, 1799; m. Jan. 1828, Mary G. Knight; he died March 29, 1833, aged 34 years.
 1264†. vi. SUSAN B., b. Oct. 18, 1800; m. Hiram Boardman.
 1265†. vii. JANE, b. Sept. 28, 1802; m. Alfred Avery.
 1266. viii. MARY ANN, b. March 5, 1805; died aged 7 years.
 1267. ix. MARIA, b. Jan. 1, 1808.
 1268. x. BENJAMIN F., b. Sept. 19, 1812; m. Esther Lockwood.

(600.) iii. BENJAMIN FELTON[6], (*Benjamin*[5], *Joseph*[4], *Skelton*[3], *Nathaniel*[2], *Nathaniel*[1],) b. July 20, 1771; m. Sept. 1794, Nancy Ellis. They lived at East Pelham, Mass., (incorporated a town, Prescott, in 1822,) in 1800 till 1810; he was a clothier by trade. In 1803, his brothers, Joseph, Nathan, John and Moses all lived there. Probably soon after 1810, Benjamin Felton moved to Wardsborough, Vt., where he was Justice of the Peace in 1822. In 1828, he moved to Jamaica, a town near Wardsborough, where Mrs. Nancy Felton died May 1, 1836. Mr. Felton lived a few years in Brookfield, Mass., before moving to Vt. Benjamin Felton, Esq., died in Jamaica, Oct. 18, 1858, aged 87 years. Had 8 children.

 1269†. i. ELIZA F., b. Nov. 2, 1795; m. Dr. Moses Chamberlain.
 1270†. ii. NATHAN B., b. Nov. 12, 1798; m. Ann Redding.

1271. iii. DWIGHT F., b. June 16, 1801; died unm. in New Orleans, La., May 20, 1847, aged 46 years; he was a merchant, first in Boston, afterwards in New Orleans.
1272†. iv. ASA E., b. April 6, 1804; m. Mary R. Ellis.
1273†. v. LUCY D., b Oct. 14, 1807; m. Col. Jonas Twitchell.
1274†. vi. HORATIO L., b. May 17, 1810; m. Nancy E. Pierce.
1275†. vii. HENRY H., b. Dec. 28, 1812; m. Eunice W. Sabine.
1276. viii. THEODOTIA R., b. May 6, 1815; living in Jamaica, Vt.

(601.) iv. JOSEPH FELTON[6], (*Benjamin*[5], *Joseph*[4], *Skelton*[3], *Nathaniel*[2], *Nathaniel*[1],) a twin, b. July 20, 1771; m. in 1794, Sally Bartlett of Salem, (sup. New Salem,) and after living several years at East Pelham, Mass., moved to Westford, Vt. It is said that Mr. and Mrs. Felton were cousins.

In 1803, Joseph and Benjamin Felton of Pelham were two of the 70 petitioners that were incorporated for building a bridge over Conn. river. Joseph Felton resided many years in Fairfax, Vt. Mrs. Sally Felton died in Dec. 1848, aged 78 years. Joseph Felton, a few months afterwards, April 9, 1849, aged almost 78 years. Lived husband and wife 54 years. Had 6 children.

1277†. i. JOSEPH C., b. about 1796; m. Lorena Crissey.
1278†. ii. LOUISA, b. about 1798; m. Nye Robinson.
1279†. iii. LODISA, b. about 1800; m. Loten Wilson.
1280†. iv. BENJAMIN S., b. in 1802; m. Amelia Russell.
1281†. v. MONTGOMERY B., m. Eliza Osborn.
1282†. vi. WILLIAM L., m. Sarah Buck.

(602.) v. NATHAN FELTON[6], (*Benjamin*[5], *Joseph*[4], *Skelton*[3], *Nathaniel*[2], *Nathaniel*[1],) b. June 25, 1775; m. Mary Hinds, b. in 1777, and had 9 children. Mr. Felton lived in the east parish of Pelham, Mass., which was made a town in 1822, and called Prescott, after the commander at Bunker Hill in 1775. He served as assessor in Pelham, and afterwards in Prescott, where he was a selectman 6 years, 1826 to 1828, 1832 to 1835. Nathan Felton moved to Northampton, where he died April 27, 1862, aged almost 87 years. Husband and wife 62 years. Mrs. Mary Felton died Oct. 23, 1868, aged 91 years, 9 months. Mr. Felton kept a hotel several years in East Pelham or Prescott.

1283. i. MARY P., b. 1801; m. Willard Barnes.

1284.   ii. ANNA C., b. in 1803; living in Northampton in 1876.
1285.   iii. NATHAN, JR., b. 1805; died unm. in New Braintree, aged 40 years.
1286.   iv. AUGUSTUS W., b. 1807; died in 1811.
1287.   v.   CHARLES S., b. in 1810; died in 1811.
1288†. vi. WILLIAM H., b. in 1813; m. Alice L. Barnes.
1289.   vii. LUETTA, b. in 1816; m. Willard A. Arnold.
1290.   viii. RUTH H., b. about 1818; living in Northampton in 1876.
1291†. ix. NEHEMIAH H., the youngest, m. Eliza Hooker.

(603.) vi. CALVIN PERRY of Shrewsbury, Vt., m. Dec. 1804, Ruth Felton b. April 15, 1778, daughter of Capt. Benj. Felton of Brookfield, (No. 222.) It is said they settled at Canton, St. Lawrence County, N. Y. Mrs. Ruth Perry died Dec. 1812, aged 34 years.

(604.) vii. JOHN FELTON[6], (*Benjamin*[5], *Joseph*[4], *Skelton*[3], *Nathaniel*[2], *Nathaniel*[1],) b. Dec. 3, 1780; m. in 1805, Mary Calhoun, b. May 24, 1788; they lived in Westford and West Fairfax, Vt. About 1835, moved to Plattsburg, N. Y., where he and several of his sons were manufacturers of iron. Mrs. Mary Felton died Jan. 7, 1843, aged 54 years. Mr. Felton died Jan. 14, 1852, aged 71 years. Had 8 children.

1292†. i.   ELBRIDGE G., b. in Pelham, Mass., June 15, 1806; m. Sarah Winslow.
1293†. ii. CAROLINE, b. Nov. 9, 1808; m. Jared L. Phillips.
1294†. iii. LUCY, b. Sept. 28, 1810; m. Jared L. Phillips.
1295†. iv. THOMAS S., b. Sept. 26, 1816; m. Anna Bromley.
1296.   v.   MOSES H., b. Jan. 26, 1818; m. Almeda Bromley.
1297†. vi. ALMON D., b. Dec. 22, 1821; m. Celinda Marsh.
1298.   vii. JAMES M., b. Jan. 25, 1823; m. Maria Tucker.
1299.   viii. LURA A., b. July 29, 1826; m. Warren Stackpole, in Aug. 1847; she died Jan. 16, 1848, aged 21 years.

(605.) viii. MOSES HAMILTON FELTON[6], (*Benjamin*[5], *Joseph*[4], *Skelton*[3], *Nathaniel*[2], *Nathaniel*[1],) b. Nov. 19, 1782. It is said when 7 years of age he went to New Braintree to live with his uncle, Moses Hamilton. Mr. Felton m. in 1805, Persis Thompson; had 3 daughters. Mrs. Felton died about 1817. He m. second, Sept. 25, 1821, Relief Pratt of Barre. b. in Shrewsbury, Mass., June 20, 1784; she died April 9, 1849, aged 65 years. He m. third, March 10, 1850, Widow Betsey Johnson aged 57 years. Mr. Felton was deputy sheriff a few years, and one of the selectmen of New Braintree in 1823.

He afterwards moved to Barre Plains, and kept a hotel and was a selectman in Barre in 1828, and chairman of the board in 1829 and 1836. He received premiums on cattle at cattle fairs. In 1838, had a fat cow weighing 1560 pounds. Had two sons by his second wife,

1300†. i. SERAPH, b. Sept. 23, 1809; m. John Bush Pratt.
1301†. ii. HARRIET, b. Nov. 5, 1812; m. Jotham Bush Pratt.
1302†. iii. ABIGAIL H., b. about 1815; m. Paul Wadsworth.
1303†. iv. NATHAN H., b. Jan. 10, 1822; m. Caroline A. Williams.
1304†. v. NYMPHUS P., b. April 27, 1825; m. Ann Chamberlain.

(606.) ix. SKELTON FELTON⁶, (*Benjamin⁵, Joseph⁴, Skelton³, Nathaniel², Nathaniel¹,*) b. Nov. 13, 1784; m. Oct. 1808, Lucinda Adams of New Braintree, b. May 1, 1783; they had 8 children. Mr. Felton was a school teacher many years. He was an officer in the war of 1812 to 1815. Lieut. Felton took charge of his father's farm in Brookfield in 1818; he was one of the examining school committee in 1821, and was re-elected 5 or more years. He was moderator at the annual March meetings in Brookfield in 1836 and 1838. He was a Justice of the Peace in 1837. He soon afterwards sold his farm in Brookfield to his youngest brother, and moved to Troy, N. Y., and was teaching in that city in 1848. His wife died May 1, 1848, on her birthday, aged 65 years. Lt. Felton died in or near Troy, N. Y., Dec. 26, 1851, aged 67 years.

1305. i. AMANDA, b. Nov. 4, 1809; died Sept. 3, 1811.
1306†. ii. LUCINDA, b. July 21, 1812; m. ——— Miller.
1307†. iii. AMORY, b. July 10, 1813; m. Nancy Perkins Boynton.
1308†. iv. SARAH C., b. Dec. 8, 1815; m. Asa B. Clark.
1309. v. ALMA, b. May 31, 1817; died June 27, 1844, aged 27 years.
1310. vi. BENJAMIN O., b. July 9, 1821; died Oct. 22, 1841, aged 20 years.
1311. vii. ALMIRA, b. Oct. 10, 1823; died April 10, 1841, aged 17 years.
1312. viii. HENRY N., b. Oct. 21, 1827; m. had one or more children; one son one of Vanderbilt's bookkeepers in 1875.

(607.) x. ANDREW BATCHELDER, b. April 16, 1772, (son of Ezra Batchelder of Danvers;) m. Feb. 13, 1802, Ruth Putnam, who died Nov. 5, 1805, aged 26 years. Had 2 children, Almira P., b. Oct. 6, 1802; m. Frederick Perley; John P., b. Nov. 26, 1803; m. Sarah A. Hollowell, and Mehitable Hollowell. He m. second, Jan. 7, 1807, Sally Felton, b. Feb. 27, 1787, daughter of Capt. Benjamin Felton of Brookfield, (No. 222.) Mr. Batchelder was a clockmaker and lived in Danvers. Had 11 children by his last wife.

1313. i. ANDREW P., b. Sept. 9, 1807; m. Bethiah Lee.
1314. ii. GEORGE F., b. Nov. 13, 1808; m. Ann Reed.
1315. iii. RUTH F., b. June 20, 1810; died July 25, 1811.
1316†. iv. SARAH F., b. Feb. 12, 1812; m. L. Martin.
1317. v. ABIGAIL P., b. Oct. 3, 1813; m. W. B. Henderson; m. second, Joseph Porter.
1318†. vi. OLIVER F., b. June 7, 1815; m. Sally Osborn.
1319. vii. LYDIA P., b. Dec. 23, 1816; m. Samuel Carter.
1320. viii. RUTH F., b. Dec. 3, 1818; m. Moses J. Currier, treasurer and collector of Maple street church, Danvers.
1321. ix. JAMES H., b. Oct. 3, 1820; m. Maria Ridout.
1322. x. HANNAH E., b. July 23, 1822; name changed in 1837, to Mary Jane; m. Mark Glidden.
1323. xi. ELIZA C., b. July 13, 1828; m. Ira P. Pope, b. Sept. 1823, son of Nathaniel Pope of Danvers.

(608.) xi. AMORY FELTON^6, (*Benjamin^5, Joseph^4, Skelton^3, Nathaniel^2, Nathaniel^1,*) b. April 10, 1789, m. Dec. 16, 1819, Mary S. Osborn, b. Nov. 16, 1791, in Danvers, where four of their children were born. He was a school teacher in Salem and Danvers, 1817 to 1822, or more years. In 1829, a merchant in Danvers. He moved to New Braintree about the time his brother Moses moved to Barre Plains. Mr. Felton was one of the inspecting school committee in 1843 and 1844, and postmaster several years in New Braintree. He was a Justice of the Peace and represented the town in the General Court in 1855. Mrs. Felton died Nov. 21, 1857, aged 66 years. She was the youngest of four Mrs. Feltons that deceased in Mass. that year. Amory Felton, Esq., died April 17, 1867, aged 78 years.

1324†. i. JOSEPH O., b. Jan. 1, 1822, m. Ellen B. ———.
1325†. ii. WM. A., b. Feb. 13, 1824; m. Susan Tyler.
1326. iii. MARY F., b. April 3, 1825; died Sept. 26, 1825.
1327. iv. ELIZA ANN, b. Dec. 31, 1826.
1328. v. ELIZABETH O., m. June 27, 1854, Lauriston White of Hardwick.

(609.) xii. JACIL KENDRICK of North Brookfield, m. Aug. 9, 1812, Hannah Felton, b. Oct. 1, 1791, daughter of Capt. Benjamin Felton of Brookfield, Mass., (No. 222.) Mr. Kendrick died in Enfield, Mass., May 5, 1874. Sup. he was a relation of Jacil Kendrick who died in Brookfield, Dec. 15, 1798, aged 82 years. Mrs. Hannah Kendrick died in Enfield, March 28, 1877; aged 86 years. They had 9 children.

1329. i. ORVILLA, b. in Brookfield, Feb. 17, 1813; m. in Enfield, April 1842, Samuel Brierly.
1330. ii. MARIA, b. in Brimfield, March 30, 1814; residence, Worcester.
1331. iii. BENJAMIN F., b. in Western, (now Warren,) May 11, 1817; m. Harriet Amelia Robinson, May 1844.
1332. iv. SARAH, b. in Western, July 22, 1819; m. Abraham Howe Newton of Princeton.
1333. v. ADALINE E., b. Sept. 11, 1822; m. David L. Emerson of Hollis, N. H.
1334†. vi. GEORGE P., b. Aug. 22, 1824; m. C. S. Stone.
1335†. vii. JANE, b. Nov. 12, 1827; m. Wm. Carlos Culver.
1336. viii. LEWIS B.; b. in Brookfield, Sept. 14, 1829; m. in Ware, Mass., Oct. 1855, Janette Tupper of Vt.
1337. ix. MARY E., b. in Ware, Aug. 28, 1834; died in Enfield, Jan. 22, 1859, aged 24 years.

(610.) xiii. OLIVER CROSBY FELTON[6], (*Benjamin*[5], *Joseph*[4], *Skelton*[3], *Nathaniel*[2], *Nathaniel*[1],) b. Sept. 15, or 19, 1795; he was named for Col. and Hon. Oliver Crosby of Brookfield, a relative of the Feltons of that town. He gave him a silver dollar to bear his name. Hon. Mr. Crosby died July 24, 1818, aged 53 years. Mr. Felton was many years, like several of his brothers, a school teacher. He taught in Danvers, where he m. Eliza Upton of that town. In 1829, he was teaching in Salem, where he continued several years, and was principal of the Phillips school in that city. Mr. Felton compiled and published, in 1842, a manual of English Grammar, a book of 140 pages. About 1837, he removed to Brookfield, his native town, where he was chairman of the school committee in 1838 and 1839, and an assessor many years. He was a contributor to the Boston Cultivator several years. He was a representative to the General Court from Brookfield in 1850, and a senator from Worcester county in 1858. He presided at several of the weekly meetings of the Legislative Agricultural Society, held in the House of Representatives in 1858. In 1856 was president of the Worcester South Agricultural Society. In 1859, he made a report on the renovation of exhausted pastures. His wife died Sept. 1864, aged 62 years. She was born Sept. 6, 1802, daughter of Jesse Upton of Danvers. Soon afterwards Mr. Felton sold his farm and moved into the village of Brookfield. He m. second about 1867, Widow Nancy Rice, daughter of Dr. Seth Knowlton, late of Shrewsbury, Mass. Mrs. Nancy Felton was born Nov. 23, 1814. Mr. Felton was a soldier in the war of 1812 to 1815, and the Widow Felton receives a pension.

Hon. Oliver C. Felton died at Brookfield, Jan. 21, 1875; aged 79 years, 4 months. The average living age of the eight brothers was 78 years, and 5⅓ months. A few years ago, W. B. Banister of N. Y. City, gave ten thousand dollars for a free public library building to be erected in Brookfiel·., Mass. Mrs. Nancy Felton of Brookfield gave a lot, 160 by 60 feet, on the southeast corner of the Common, valued at one thousand dollars, for the building. "This gift is made by Mrs. Felton as a memorial of her husband's interest and labor for the education of the young."

(611.) i. JOHN FRINK HOYT, b. in 1771; (son of Capt. Wyman and Hephzibah (Felton) Hoyt, No. 224); m., Nov. 17, 1799, Anna Bowman, b. in 1778. They had one or more children. Mr. Hoyt died April 3, 1823, aged 52 years. Mrs. Hoyt died June 7, 1851, aged 73 years.

1337½. i. HENRY A., was taxed in New Braintree, Mass., in 1876, for 6 acres of Bowman land. His taxes in 1876, $54.96. He was a fence viewer that year. He m. and had one or more children; his daughter Lizzie C. Hoyt.

(614.) ii. BARTHOLOMEW GREEN, m. Hannah Felton, b. Sept. 2, 1778, daughter of Skelton and Silence Felton (No. 227). They had one or more children. Their daughter, Silence Green, is named in widow Silence Felton's will of 1830. Mrs. Hannah Green died at Holden, Mass., in 1846, aged 68 years. In 1829, Mary Walker Green of Oakham, Mass., took the name of Mary Walker Felton, by Act of the Legislature.

1338. i. SILENCE GREEN.

(615.) iii. JOHN SMEAD, m. Lydia Felton, b. in Barre July 20, 1781, daughter of Skelton and Silence Felton (No. 227). Mrs. Smead m. second time and died at Obed, N. Y.

(616.) iv. JEREMIAH ROBINSON, m. Hephzibah Felton, b. June 2, 1783. Mrs. Robinson m. second ——— Carr. Mrs. Carr died at Corning, N. Y., in 1867, aged 84 years. (Sept. 7, 1849, Dea. Jeremiah Robinson of Worcester died in Boston, aged 85 years.)

(617.) v. SKELTON FELTON[6], (*Skelton*[5], *Joseph*[4], *Skelton*[3], *Nathaniel*[2], *Nathaniel*[1],) b. June 15, 1785, (seven months younger than his cousin of the same name), m., in 1808, Tryphosa Bullard. She died Aug. 26, 1827, aged 35 years. Major Feltou.m. second, May, 1828, Mrs. Eliza Walker Green. She died suddenly, May 2, 1829, aged 36 years. "Her death was caused by a slight scratch from a latch of the door, on the second joint of the first finger of the right hand," said a Worcester newspaper. Perhaps it was her daughter that took the name of Felton in 1829. Major Felton m. third. Sept., 1829, Mary P. Crawford, b. Nov. 7, 1807. Mr. Felton was called Major in 1822, and Justice of the Peace in 1827. Was one of the selectmen of Oakham, in 1824, and from 1826 to 1834. He died July 31, 1835, aged 50 years. His will dated May 22, 1835, names his wife and three daughters. He provided for Moses Bullard and wife a house and some land. He gave his sword and epaulets, valued at ten dollars, to his grandson, John F. Gray. Skelton Felton's property was valued at $4,390.30.

Skelton Felton Shepard, son of Samuel Shepard of Oakham, received of Major Felton five sheep for his name. S. F. Shepard m., in Barre in March, 1840, Miss MacIntire. They had 5 children. Felton Shepard died in Worcester several years ago. Mrs. Shepard and 3 children were living in that city in 1878.

Mrs. Mary P. Felton m., Oct., 1836, Simon S. Stevens of Paris, Me.; had one son and one daughter. She m. third time and was living in 1877. She d, Dec 16, 1892, a 92

The following from a newspaper printed in 1821:

ATTENTION!

The subscriber informs the selectmen of the several towns comprising the First Brigade in the Sixth Division, that he shall commence the inspection of their Magazines and Military Stores on the 17th of September next; and it is expected that the selectmen will have every article ready and in complete order, as is required by law they should have.

SKELTON FELTON, Jr.,
Brigade Quartermaster 1st Brigade, 6th Division.
Oakham, Aug. 28, 1821.

Major Felton's children were:

1339†. i. LUCINDA, b. Feb. 24, 1809; m. Dr. John H. Gray.
1340†. ii. ELIZA W., b. about 1830; m. Edward La Croix.
1341†. iii. LOUISA M., b. about 1833; m. Wells Bill.

(618.) vi. JOSIAH DANA FELTON[6], (*Skelton*[5], *Joseph*[4], *Skelton*[3], *Nathaniel*[2], *Nathaniel*[1],) b. March 13, 1788; m., Nov., 1816, Relief Smith. He died Sept. 15, in 1817 or 1819; was buried in Dana, Mass. Aug. 11, 1823, widow Relief Felton appointed guardian to her daughter. Mrs. Felton was a milliner in Worcester many years. She died April 12, 1867. They had one daughter.

1342†. i. CORDELIA M., b. Aug. 17, 1817; m. Charles C. Chamberlin.

(619.) vii. JONATHAN WALES FELTON[6], (Skelton[5], Joseph[4], Skelton[3], Nathaniel[2], Nathaniel[1],) b. June 17, 1790; m. Lydia Bullard June 1811. They had several children. Mr. Felton moved to Paris, Me., in 1827, and purchased a large farm. He died Dec. 25, 1866, aged 76 years. Mrs. Felton died Aug. 18, 1867.

1343†. i. ISABEL N., the oldest b. July 27, 1812, in Barre, Mass.; m. Jonathan Irish, residence, Buckfield, Me.
1344†. ii. STELLA J., b. Jan. 31, 1815; m. John Willis of Paris, Me.
1345†. iii. CHARLOTTE S., b. July 7, 1820; m. Marcellus Smith.
1346. iv. SKELTON, b. in Oakham, Mass., April 8, 1823; had his name changed to Charles Felton; m. Louisa G. Dunham; residence, Paris, Me. Had one son, died young.
1347†. v. ALBERT Q., b. in Paris, Me., March 7, 1828; m. twice.
1348. vi. JOHN D., b. April 13, 1832.

In 1865, Capt. John D. Felton of Paris, Me., of Company K., 13th Reg't, Me., was mustered out of service; was son of Jonathan Wales Felton. Capt. Felton went West; m. Sup. living in Col.

(620.) viii. BENJAMIN FELTON[6], (Skelton[5], Joseph[4], Skelton[3], Nathaniel[2], Nathaniel[1],) b. Sept. 6, 1792; m. Jan. 21, 1821, Lucretia Sturgis Nye, b. in Oakham, May 11, 1801, dau. of Timothy and Parnel Nye; she died in Barre, Mass., March 26, 1830, aged 29 years. Capt. Felton m. second, Nov. 4, 1830, Ruth Maranda Johnson, b. about 1808, daughter of Perrin Johnson. Had 6 children, 3 by each wife.

Capt. Felton was employed several years in teaming from Barre to Boston, through Marlborough. He died at Worcester, April 6, 1875, aged 82 years; buried in Oakham near Barre, Mass. Widow Ruth M. Felton died at Roxbury Highlands, March 5, 1884, aged 76 years.

1349†. i. CAROLINE N., b. Dec. 9, 1821; m. Elijah Hammond.
1350†. ii. JOHN, b. Oct. 6, 1824; m. Mary R. Swan.

1351†. iii. BENJAMIN F., b. Dec. 31, 1827; m. Ellen Chapman.
1352†. iv. CHARLES A., b. Sept. 18, 1831; m. Ellen J. Gale.
1353†. v. MARY L., b. Sept. 24, 1833; m. Josiah C. Bowker.
1354†. vi. ANN J., b. July 25, 1840; m. Frank J. Ward.

(621.) ix. JOSEPH FELTON[6], (*Skelton[5], Joseph[4], Skelton[3], Nathaniel[2], Nathaniel[1],*) b. Aug. 5, 1796; m. Deborah Foster, Oct. 28, 1819. They went to Chardon, Ohio; his wife died in that state, Sept. 20, 1834, aged 31 years. Mr. Felton returned to Barre, Mass., and died May 11, 1835, aged 38 years, 9 months. An inventory taken June 1835; was a carpenter by trade. They had two or more children.

1355. i. DWIGHT FELTON.
1356. ii. LUTHERA, a daughter.

(622.) x. SAMUEL CONE, m. Octavia Felton, b. March 18, 1799, youngest daughter of Skelton and Silence Felton, (No. 227.) They had one daughter. Mrs. Octavia Cone m. second, John Austick, and died at Schuyler Lake, N. Y., Aug. 1876, aged (75 years says the informant) 77 years, 6 months.

1357. i. HELEN CONE, died aged 14 years.

(625.) ii. PEMBERTON WARD, b. Jan. 15, 1778, (son of Rev. Ephraim Ward of Brookfield;) m. June 19, 1810, Isabel Wetherell, b. Dec. 1, 1791, daughter of Lieut. Sampson Wetherell, (No. 229.) They had 7 children at West Brookfield. Mrs. Isabella Ward died before 1878.

1357. a. i. MARY C., b. May 14, 1812; m. Jeremiah Myers, Nov. 1845.
1357. b. ii. GEORGE L., b. April 12, 1815; m. Dec. 1847, Caroline P. Jenkins.
1357. c. iii. SUSAN D., b. May 6, 1817; m. Francis W. R. Emery of Boston, May 1848.
1357. d. iv. MARIA H., b. Sept. 10, 1819; m. May 1843, George H. Dean of Boston.
1357. e. v. LUCY ANN, b. Dec. 27, 1822; m. Thomas Morey. Mrs. Morey was living in West Brookfield in 1878.
1357. f. vi. ELIZA J., b. March 3, 1827; m. Dec. 1848, Francis Houghton.
1357. g. vii. FRANCES J., b. March 2, 1832; living in West Brookfield in 1850.

(626.) iii. SAMPSON WETHERELL, JR., b. Aug. 5,

1795 ; sup. m. Lucy Kendall of Dana, Mass., in January 1822; had one or more children ; one dau. m. Capt. John G. Mudge of Petersham, Mass. Mr. Wetherell was postmaster in Petersham, in 1856. He died before April 1878.

(630.) i. FRANCIS FELTON⁶, (*John* or *Samuel*⁵, *Francis*⁴, *John*³, *Nathaniel*², *Nathaniel*¹,) m. about 1808, Sally Graves and settled in Marblehead. Mr. Felton was lost out of the schooner, William, Sept. 15, 1821, at Martinico, three days out of port, West Indies. Mrs. Sally Felton died about Nov. 1858, aged 80 years. They had 5 children.

1358.   i. SALLY, b. about 1809 ; m. Jan. 1828, Joseph C. Bowdin, and settled in Marblehead, where all her sisters resided.

1359.   ii. FRANCIS, JR., b. about 1811 ; died Nov. 22, 1813, aged 2 years.

1360.   iii. MARY R., b. May 11, 1815 ; m. Dec. 1834, Wm. T. High.

1361†. iv. ELIZABETH A., b. Dec. 1818 ; m. March 1850, Joseph H. Atkins.

1362.   v. HANNAH M., b. Sept. 7, 1820 ; m. July 1844, Levi Langley.

(631.) ii. THOMAS K. FELTON⁶, (*John* or *Samuel*⁵, *Francis*⁴, *John*³, *Nathaniel*², *Nathaniel*¹.) He was brother of Francis Felton, (No. 630 ;) he m. Mrs. Mary Tucker, widow of Amos Tucker, and sister of his brother Francis Felton's wife. Mr. Felton was lost at sea, Oct. 6, 1847, aged 56 years. Mrs. Mary Felton died March 6, 1865, aged 73 years. They lived in Marblehead, Mass.

(633.) i. JAMES FELTON⁶, (*James*⁵, *Francis*⁴, *John*³, *Nathaniel*², *Nathaniel*¹,) b. June 8, 1790 ; m. in Boston, Dec. 31, 1815, Sarah Hunt, b. June 7, 1795, daughter of Thomas and Sarah (Chapman) Hunt of Salem, and sister of Capt. Thomas Hunt of that city. Mr. Felton was a sail-maker and lived in Salem. Mrs. Sarah Felton died Feb. 26, 1826, aged 30 years. He m. second time in Boston, March 6, 1828, Sally Dodd, b Oct. 21, 1806. James Felton died April 18, 1854, aged 64 years. They had 5 children.

1363.   i. SARAH A., b. Dec. 3, 1816 ; was many years a school teacher; she died Feb. 13, 1852, aged 35 years.

1364.   ii. FRANCIS A., b. Feb. 19, 1819 ; died young.

1365.   iii. JAMES, JR., b. Sept. 10, 1821 ; died young.

1366†. iv. FRANCIS A., b. March 5, 1823 ; m. Sarah Elizabeth Churchell.

1367.   v. MARY E., b. Jan. 22, 1826.

(634.) ii. JOHN SMITH FELTON[6], (*James*[5], *Francis*[4], *John*[3], *Nathaniel*[2], *Nathaniel*[1],) b. about 1792; m. Dec. 1815, Nancy Crandall of Salem. Mr. Felton died about 1841. Mrs. Nancy Felton died in Salem, March 7, 1875, aged 83 years, 3 months, 20 days They had 4 daughters, all born within 3 years and 10 months.

 1368†. i. CAROLINE, b. April 2, 1816; m. Levi Wiggin.
 1369†. ii. MATILDA, b. July 1817; m. Levi Wyman.
 1370. iii. RUTH A., b. Sept. 1818; was a school teacher many years; died unm. about 1861, aged 43 years
 1371. iv. MARY J., b. Feb. 1820; m. April 26, 1870, Wm. Randall, b. in Vt. about 1825; his second m.

(637.) v. HOWARD BROWN, m. about 1846, Sarah Frances Felton, b. in Boston, March 12, 1826, daughter of James and Sally G. W. Felton of Boston, afterwards Salem. Mr. Brown lived in Salem, Mass., a few years, then moved to Stockton, Cal.

 1372. i. MATILDA, b. in Salem, June 3, 1847; m. George R. Martin.
 1373. ii. THOMAS B., b. in Salem, Mass., Nov. 21, 1853.
 1374. iii. FANNIE E., b. in Stockton, Cal., Feb. 27, 1856.
 1375. iv. ALICE, b. in Stockton, Cal. in 1858; m. John Peter Kafity.

(638.) vi. SAMUEL ADAMS, m. March 1847, Elizabeth G. Felton, b. in Boston, July 12, 1828, daughter of James and Sally G. W. Felton of Boston and Salem. Samuel Adams was of the firm of Adams & Dodge of Manchester, Mass. Mr. Adams had a fine brig called Elizabeth Felton, built by Charles Allen in the town of Essex, Mass., in 1847; it was launched in the autumn of that year. It was intended for the southern trade. In 1852, the brig was among the Cape Verde Islands. Samuel Adams died in the fall of 1867. They had 4 children.

 1376. i. FREDERICK, b. about 1864; living in Cal. in 1884.
 1377. ii. One daughter living in May 1884.

(639.) i. JACOB AMSDEN, b. Nov. 29, 1761, (son of Jacob Amsden, who was b. in Marlboro in 1728;) m. April 24, 1783, Sally Felton, sup. daughter of James Felton, (No. 262,) They resided in Petersham, Mass., and had 2 or more children.

 1378. i. EBENEZER, b. Feb. 1, 1784.
 1379. ii. SALLY, b. Dec. 23, 1785; m. March 1816, Shuball Shaw of New Salem.

(640.) ii. ASA POWERS of Shutesbury, m. Jan. 1788, Lois Felton, daughter of James Felton, Esq., of New Salem. Sup. Mr. Powers was son of Asa Powers, who m. Dec. 1764, Resinah Wheeler. In May 1825, Lois Powers, (sup. dau. of Asa and Lois above,) m. Archibald Wheeler.

In 1812 to 1814, Asa Powers, (No. 640,) was captain of a New Salem company. The following soldiers were from New Salem in 1814: Wm. Smith, John Shaw, Samuel Shaw, Joshua Shaw, Asa Powers, John Powers, John Frye, and Andrew Newell. Capt. Asa Powers was captain of a company in Col. Thomas Longley's reg't.

(641.) iii. SIMEON SOUTHWICK, bapt. in May 1766, was son of Benjamin and Sarah Southwick, and grandson of Dea. Benjamin and Abigail Southwick, all of New Salem, Mass. Simeon Southwick m. Dec. 1785, Ruth Felton, dau. of James and Sarah (Houlton) Felton of New Salem. They had one or more children.

1379½. i. SIMEON, JR., bapt. in 1791.

(646.) i. JAMES FELTON[6], ($James^5$, $David^4$, $Ebenezer^3$, $Nathaniel^2$, $Nathaniel^1$,) was not of age in 1792; he was appointed administrator of his father's estate in 1804. He m. Eunice Wheeler, a sister of Col. Wheeler of New Salem, or vicinity. Soon after the decease of his father, he moved into N. Y. State. It is supposed they had 10 children.

(648.) ii. DAVID HOULTON FELTON[6], ($Ebenezer^5$, $David^4$, $Ebenezer^3$, $Nathaniel^2$, $Nathaniel^1$,) b. Oct. 25, 1767; m. in New Salem, Sept. 26, 1796, Rebecca Hodskin, or Hotchkiss, b. Nov. 7, 1776. They lived a few years in Canada. In Feb. 1804, they moved to Sangerfield, Oneida County, N. Y., where he died about 1846, aged 79 years. Mrs. Felton was living in Eaton, N. Y. in 1856, aged 79 years. Had 3 sons and 3 daughters.

1380. i. ADIN; he died before May 1856.
1381. ii. SOPHIA, b. about 1799; m. —— Ward.
1382†. iii. DAVID, b. about 1804; m.; he lived 61 years.
1383. iv. SALLY. b. about 1806; m. —— Gaffin; Mrs. Gaffin living at Sangerfield, N. Y., in 1882; their son has been Mayor of Utica, N. Y.
1384. v. PARDON K., was postmaster at East Hamilton, Madison County, N. Y. in 1862.
1385. vi. Another daughter was living in 1856.

(649.) iii. ROBERT FELTON[6], ($Ebenezer^5$, $David^4$, $Ebenezer^3$, $Nathaniel^2$, $Nathaniel^1$,) bapt. Jan. 1771; he m. and moved into N. Y. State. They both deceased before May 1856; in 1856, one son and three daughters were living.

1386.   i. GILBERT.

(650.) iv. JOHN POWERS, Esq., of Shutesbury, Mass., m. Feb. 28, 1796, Hannah Felton of New Salem, bapt. April 11, 1773, daughter of Ebenezer Felton, (No. 263,) (or perhaps m. her mother, Mrs. Hannah (Page) Felton)

(651.) i. SAMUEL FOSTER, m. Abigail Felton b. July 12, 1778, oldest daughter of Stephen and Sarah Felton of New Salem, Mass., (No. 269.) They had 2 daughters. Mrs. Abigail Felton died Jan. 21, 1802, aged 23 years, 6 months. She died 14 months before her youngest sister, Abigail Felton, was born.

1390.   i. A daughter.
1391.   ii. Another daughter.

(652.) ii. EZEKIEL LEONARD, m. Rachel Felton, b. May 24, 1780, daughter of Stephen and Sarah Felton of New Salem. This family settled in Oakham, Mass. Mr. Leonard died about 1822. They had 5 daughters and 3 sons. Mrs. Rachel Leonard m. second; Dea. Andrew Sears of Greenwich, Mass. Mrs. Mehitable Sears, the mother of Dea. Sears, died in Greenwich, April 5, 1845, aged 100 years and 9 months. Dea. Sears died a year afterwards, April 14, 1846, aged 82 years. Mrs. Rachel Sears died Oct. 21, 1864, aged 84 years.

1392†. i. PRISCILLA E., b. May 14, 1802; m. Pliny Clifford.
1393. ii. LYDIA F., b. in Shutesbury, April 9, 1804; m. Washington Lamb; had 4 children. Mrs. Lamb living in 1884.
1394. iii. MINERVA, b. in Wendell, Mass., June 10, 1806; m. Lorenzo Billings in 1828; had 5 children. Mrs. Billings died in 1871, aged 65 years.
1395. iv. LUCY P., b. in Oakham, Dec. 25, 1810; m. Wm. Knox.
1396†. v. THORNDIKE, b. April 28, 1812; m. twice.
1397. vi. SALLY D., b. Oct. 1814; m. twice; had 8 children.
1398. vii. SULLIVAN, b. in 1816; died Dec. 7, 1816.
1399. viii. STEPHEN, b. about 1818; went West and m.

(653.) iii. STEPHEN FELTON[6], (*Stephen*[5], *Ebenezer*[4], *Ebenezer*[3], *Nathaniel*[2], *Nathaniel*[1],) b. May 18, 1782; m. Rhoda Ayers of Greenwich, Mass. Mr. Felton was a school teacher.

They had no children. Stephen Felton, Jr., died March 10, 1817, aged 35 years.

(655.) v. DANIEL FELTON⁶, (*Stephen⁵, Ebenezer⁴, Ebenezer³, Nathaniel², Nathaniel¹,*) b. March 9, 1787; m. Fanny Holden, daughter of Nathan Holden of Petersham, Mass. He resided at New Salem up to 1839, then moved to South Deerfield, near Mount Sugar-Loaf, where he purchased a farm. He was a merchant in New Salem, town clerk and parish clerk, constable and collector; deputy sheriff three years; was assessor and selectman in both towns. Daniel Felton, Esq., died Aug. 12, 1868, aged 81 years. Mrs. Fanny Felton died Aug. 24, 1874, aged 86 years, 8 months. They had 7 children.

1400†. i. MYRA H., b. Oct. 15, 1811; m. Charles Hager.
1401†. ii. ALVAN, b. Aug. 3, 1813; m. Mehitable Whitney.
1402. iii. LYDIA, b. Dec. 6, 1815; died aged about 13 years.
1403. iv. FRANKLIN, b. Nov. 3, 1817; m. Samantha Briant; he was living in Wendell in 1856; deceased before 1880; no issue.
1404. v. FANNY, b. Oct. 10, 1819; died aged about 20 years.
1405†. vi. LUCETTA, b. Jan. 14, 1822; m. David Austin Foot.
1406†. vii. JOSEPH P., b. Aug. 19, 1824; m. Harriet A. Bridges.

(656.) vi. THORNDIKE FELTON⁶, (*Stephen⁵, Ebenezer⁴, Ebenezer³, Nathaniel², Nathaniel¹,*) b. April 26, 1789; m. Nov. 1814, Joanna Chamberlain, b. Oct. 10, 1789. They settled in New Salem, where he died Oct. 19, 1825, aged 36 years. Mrs. Felton died in Hanover, Mass., Jan. 1875, aged 85 years. Had 5 children.

1407†. i. LANSFORD B., b. Aug. 29, 1815; m. Harriet A. Parker.
1408†. ii. STEPHEN, b. Feb. 6, 1817; m. Emily L. Bingham.
1409†. iii. LYDIA, b. Feb. 3, 1819; m. Daniel B. Felton, No. 671.
1410†. iv. REBECCA C., b. about 1821; m. Sylvanus Bates.
1411. v. WILLIAM, b. in 1824; died May 8, 1825.

(657.) vii. EBENEZER HOOPER, of Oakham, m. Sept. 1837, Sally Felton, b. June 26, 1791, daughter of Stephen and Sarah Felton of New Salem. Mrs. Hooper m. second, Samuel Macomber; no issue. Mrs. Sally Macomber died June 1, 1856, aged 65 years.

(658.) viii. PROCTOR FELTON[6], (*Stephen*[5], *Ebenezer*[4], *Ebenezer*[3], *Nathaniel*[2], *Nathaniel*[1],) b. May 17, 1794; m. Jan. 3, 1822, Mrs. Elizabeth (Libby) Prescott, b. Jan. 21, 1788. She had 4 children by her first husband, and 4 by her last. Mr. Felton had the misfortune to lose a leg in 1847. Mrs. Elizabeth Felton died in Cambridge, Mass., May 12, 1857, aged 67 years. Mr. Felton died in the same city, July 20, 1874, aged 80 years.

1412. i. FANNY D., b. Sept. 29, 1822, in Fredericton, N. B.; m. Nov. 1846, in Cambridge, to Daniel Farrell, b. about 1819, son of Daniel Farrell of Cornwallis, N. S. Mr. Farrell, Jr., a carpenter by trade. Mrs. Farrell m. second, James K. Southack.
1413. ii. RHODA A., b. in Calais, Me., Aug. 5, 1825; m. in Cambridge, June 1846, John G. Godfrey, b. at Edystone, Me., about 1824.
1414. iii. SARAH E., b. Oct. 10, 1827; m. Cyrus Phillips; they lived in Cambridge, Mass., where Mrs. Phillips died Jan. 16, 1874, aged 46 years.
1415. iv. GEORGE b. Nov. 30, 1829; m.; sup. lost in the late civil war.

Proctor Felton, when a small boy, grazed his knee-pan with a corner of a cooper's adze, and just escaped a stiff knee; many years afterwards wounded himself on the inside of that knee with a corner of a broad axe. Had his leg amputated when about 50 years of age.

(660.) x. EBENEZER FELTON[6], (*Stephen*[5], *Ebenezer*[4], *Ebenezer*[3], *Nathaniel*[2], *Nathaniel*[1],) b. May 21, 1800; m. Feb. 1, 1827, then of Boylston, to Phebe Rand Drury, b. in Shrewsbury, Mass., Nov. 6, 1804, daughter of Abijah Drury of that town They had 10 children. They resided in several towns before they settled in Enfield, Mass. Mrs. Phebe R. Felton died April 4, 1846, aged 41 years. He m. second, June 7, 1846, Sarah Topliff, and had 6 more children. Mr. Felton died in Enfield, April 21, 1882, aged almost 82 years.

1416. i. THORNDIKE P., b. Jan. 6, 1828; died Aug. 21, 1829.
1417. ii. LORENZO L., b. Feb. 8, 1830; m.
1418. iii. CHARLES A., b. Nov. 9, 1831; died June 14, 1837.
1419. iv. LAURA A., b. June 23, 1834.
1420. v. THORNDIKE P., b. April 23, 1836; died Jan. 28, 1847.
1421. vi. EDTHENA M., b. Aug. 6, 1837.
1422. vii. JOSEPH F., b. March 16, 1840; died April 4, 1840.

1423. viii. SARAH A., b. July 8, 1841.
1424†. ix. CHARLES A., b. Feb. 3, 1843; m.
1425. x. LOVIN L., b. Dec. 17, 1845; died May 23, 1846.

Children by his second wife:

1426. xi. GEORGE E., b. April 22, 1847; m. Nov. 1872.
1427. xii. EMILY M., b. Aug. 20, 1848; m. ——— Blair; she died Sept. 27, 1871. aged 23 years.
1428. xiii. MARY E., b. Sept. 21, 1849; died Sept. 23, 1372, aged 23 years.
1429. xiv. HIRAM A., b. Feb. 12, 1853; m. Nov. 1876.
1430. xv. FLORA A., b. Nov. 5, 1854; died Sept. 17, 1856.
1431. xvi. FLORA A., b. June 6, 1857; m. Dec. 21, 1882.

(661.) xi. DR. LEVI CHAMBERLAIN, (son of Zachariah Chamberlain of New Salem, Mass.;) m. May 18, 1823, Abigail Felton, b. March 22, 1803, (fourteen months after the decease of her oldest sister, Abigail,) youngest daughter of Stephen and Sarah Felton of New Salem. Dr. Chamberlain practised in several towns in Mass. He was one of the school committee of Greenwich in 1845-46. They had 4 sons and 2 daughters; three of their sons are physicians. Dr. Chamberlain died in his native town, New Salem, Dec. 21, 1864, aged 65 years. Mrs. Abigail Chamberlain died the next year, Dec. 16, 1865, aged 63 years.

1432†. i. DR. GEORGE F., b. in Brimfield in 1826; m.
1433†. ii. DR. CYRUS N., b. in Barnstable in 1829; enlisted in the Union army.
1434. iii. SARAH C., b. about 1832; m. Joseph Bowles; Mrs. Bowles died June 25, 1857, aged 25 years.
1435. iv. DR. MYRON C.; resides on Boylston St., Boston.
1436†. v. HELEN M., m. in 1862, Rev. Wm. A. Lloyd.
1437. vi. One son, died young.

(662.) xii. GEORGE D. FELTON[6], (*Stephen*[5], *Ebenezer*[4], *Ebenezer*[3], *Nathaniel*[2], *Nathaniel*[1],) b. Dec. 12, 1805; he taught school a few winters; two winters in Shrewsbury, one in Boylston. He attended the Franklin Academy at Shelburne Falls before he entered Brown University in Sept. 1835; he graduated with his class in 1839. Mr. Felton m. about 1839, Miss Emily Hurlburt, daughter of Aaron and Lucy Hurlburt of Sandisfield, Mass. Mr. Felton was a Baptist minister and was settled in Westminster, Mass., in 1840, where he preached between 2 and 3 years. On account of his wife's feeble health he removed to Chatham, Mass., where Mrs. Felton died Aug. 10, 1843. In May 1844, he m. second, Louisa M. Hurlburt, a sister of his first wife, and the same year was installed pastor of the Baptist church in Granville, Mass., where he was pastor 21 years. He was pastor of the Baptist church in Robertsville, Ct., 6 years, 1866 to 1872. The next two years he preached in Bloomfield, Ct. In April 1874, he returned to Granville, Mass., and purchased the parsonage as a home for his declining years. Many years was an active member of the school committee of the town of Granville, Mass. Rev. Mr. Felton died in that town, Jan. 31, 1885, aged 79 years. He had 3 children.

1438.   i. ELLA L., b. in 1840; m. Dea. Wm. H. Spelman of Granville.
1438½. ii. The second child died in 1843; soon after Mrs. Felton.
1439.   iii. DR. GEORGE H., b. Sept. 7, 1846; in St. Paul, Minn., 1886.

(666.) ii. DAVID BURNETT of Warwick, Mass., b. Oct. 18, 1802; m. Oct. 26, 1828, Lydia Felton, b. April 9, 1803, daughter of Amos and Lydia (King) Felton of New Salem, Mass. They lived in Warwick, where he was a captain and selectman in 1841 and '42. They had 5 children. In 1867, he moved back to New Salem, his native town. Capt. Burnett died in Sept. 1885, aged 83 years; Mrs. Burnett, two months afterwards, Nov. 27, 1885, aged 82 years. It is said she lost the thought of self in doing good.

1440.   i. JEHOADAN W., b. July 23, 1829; died Sept. 6, 1832.
1441.   ii. MERCIA G., b. July 11, 1831; m. Charles Frederick Carpenter, Feb. 15, 1860.
1442.   iii. JEHOADAN F., b. June 3, 1835; m. Amasa Gould, June 3, 1864; Mr. or Mrs. Gould died Aug. 30, 1867.
1443†. iv. LYDIA E., b. Nov. 16, 1837; m. Willard Putnam, (No. 1459.)
1444.   v. HANNAH K., b. June 28, 1840; died May 22, 1863, aged 23 years.

(667.) iii. ELI GROUT of Barre, Mass., m. Feb. 6, 1831, Betsey Felton, b. March 28, 1805, daughter of Amos and Lydia Felton of New Salem. Mr. Grout died March 20, 1860, aged 55 years. Mrs. Betsey Grout was living in Ill., in 1884.

(670.) vi. AMOS FELTON[6], (*Amos*[5], *Amos*[4], *Ebenezer*[3], *Nathaniel*[2], *Nathaniel*[1],) b. Feb. 17, 1812; m. April 14, 1835, Harriet Howard, b. Dec. 20, 1813. They were living at Leverett, Mass., in 1884; had two children.

1445. i. HOWARD K., b. Aug. 16, 1836; m. April 14, 1867, Eliza Ann Woods of Shutesbury, Mass., dau. of Daniel Woods. Mrs. Eliza Ann Felton died Oct. 29, 1869, aged 30 years.
1446. ii. MELISSA A., b. April 19, 1843; m. May 1868, Nathan Aaron Dudley, b. Aug. 27, 1837.

(671.) vii. DANIEL BOYCE FELTON[6], ($Amos^5$, $Amos^4$, $Ebenezer^3$, $Nathaniel^2$, $Nathaniel^1$,) b. Aug. 31, 1814; m. Lydia Felton, b. Feb. 3, 1819, daughter of Thorndike and Joanna Felton, (No. 1409.) Mrs. Lydia Felton died in Shutesbury, Feb. 18, 1847, aged 28 years; had 5 children. Mr. Felton m. second, Arvilla ———. They lived in several towns in western Mass. He died in Ware, Mass., Aug. 24, 1861, aged 47 years, buried in New Salem. His will dated Ware, July 2, 1861, set up Oct. 1861. He named in his will for executor, Ebenezer Felton of New Salem. Mrs. Arvilla Felton was appointed guardian for the 6 youngest children.

1447. i. MARY L., m. ——— Wheeler.
1448. ii. HATTIE A., was living in 1861.
1449. iii. HENRY C., b. in 1845; died July 18, 1863, aged 18 years.
1450. iv. DANIEL T.; living in 1884.
1451. v. LYDIA A. R.; living in 1861.
1452. vi. JOHN W.; he m. Feb. 2. 1876, Alice M. Tisdale; a dentist in Enfield, Mass., in 1884.
1453. vii. JOANNA B., b. in 1852; died Nov. 4, 1862, aged 10 years, 2 months.
1454. viii. IDA ESTHER.
1455. ix. CHARLES W, m. Jan. 13, 1880, Angenette J. Cogswell.
1456. x. WEBSTER F., m. ——— Pratt.
1457. xi. FRANK B., b. March 1861;. died May 7, 1862.

(672.) viii. JOHN FELTON[6], ($Amos^5$, $Amos^4$, $Ebenezer^3$, $Nathaniel^2$, $Nathaniel^1$,) b. May 4, 1817; m. Margaret Kellogg. They resided in New Salem, afterwards in Shutesbury, where they were living in 1884. They have had 5 children.

1458. i. CLARISSA J., b. in New Salem in 1839; died Aug. 3, 1841.
1458. *a.* ii. CLARA, sup. b. about 1842; m. ——— Coats.
1458. *b.* iii. ADOLPHUS; living in South Carolina in 1884.
1458. *c.* iv. HERBERT, m. before 1884.
1458. *d.* v. VICTORIA, living in 1884.

(675.) ii. WILLARD RICHARDSON, b. June 23, 1802; was son of Dr. Zaccheus and Elizabeth (Felton) Richardson.

Mr. R. m. Louisa Merell of Sumpter, S. C. He was an editor several years at Galveston, Texas. Mr. Richardson died July 26, 1875, aged 73 years.

(676.) iii. SAMUEL PUTNAM, b. in Danvers, Nov. 9, 1806, son of Amos and Lydia (Pierce) Putnam of Danvers, and afterwards of New Salem; m. Elizabeth Felton Richardson, b. Oct. 23, 1804, daughter of Dr. Zaccheus and Elizabeth (Felton) Richardson. Samuel Putnam resides in New Salem, Mass., and but few in that town pay a higher tax. He represented New Salem in the Legislature in 1847. They have one son.

1459†. i. WILLARD, b. Sept. 1838; m. Lydia Ellen Burnett, (No. 1443.)

(678.) ii. ALEXANDER CONKEY FELTON^6, (*Abraham^5, Benjamin^4, Ebenezer^3, Nathaniel^2, Nathaniel^1,*) b. in New Salem, April 1828. He studied law with Hon. Rufus Choate, and was familiar with his hand writing. When Mr. Choate delivered his eulogy on Daniel Webster at Dartmouth College, the N. Y. printers could not print it until it was rewritten by Mr. Felton. In 1856, Mr. Felton came to Marlboro. He m. the same year, Dec. 2, Maria B. Warren, b. in Boston, dau. of S. B. Warren of Leominster, Mass. In 1858, Gov. N. P. Banks appointed 100 Police Justices in the State, and 13 of them were in Middlesex county, and Alexander C. Felton of Marlboro was one of them. Mr. Felton practised law in Boston before and after he resided in Marlboro. Mr. Felton published a phonographic report of the second festival of the Sons of New Hampshire, held in Boston, Nov. 2, 1853; pp. 229.

1460. i. BENJAMIN T., b. in Marlboro, Dec. 30, 1857.
1461. ii. WILLIE A., b. March 7, 1860; died in Boston of diphtheria, March 31, 1864, aged 4 years.

(679.) iii. BENJAMIN R. FELTON^6, (*Abraham^5, Benjamin^4, Ebenezer^3, Nathaniel^2, Nathaniel^1,*) b. Nov. 20, 1830; he resides in Warwick, where he has been superintending school committee three or more years. Was a Justice of the Peace in 1874.

(685.) i. NATHANIEL FELTON^6, (*Nathaniel^5, Nathaniel^4, Ebenezer^3, Nathaniel^2, Nathaniel^1,*) b. Aug. 20, 1802; m. Abigail H. Bowker. They lived in Barre, and in towns in that vicinity. He was a shoe-maker and lived in Milford, Mass., a few years. They lived in Ohio a few years, and there buried a promising son. Mr. Felton died in Barre, June 5, 1875, aged 72 years, 9 months. (Before this date June 1875, six Feltons died in 1875 in Mass., all upwards of 73 years of age.) They had 4 or more children.

1462†.   i.   MABY A., b. about 1827; m. Joseph H. Stiles.
1463†.   ii.   WELCOME, b. April 6, 1832; m. Fidelia A. Thayer.
1464.   iii.   A son died in Ohio.
1465.   iv.   A daughter b. in Orange, Mass., Aug. 11, 1838.

(686.)   ii.   WILLIAM FRYE of New Salem, m. Eveline Felton, daughter of Nathaniel Felton of New Salem. They had 3 sons and 2 daughters; one son and two daughters living in 1867. About 1859, this family moved to Baraboo, Wis.

1466.   i.   WARREN, m.
1467.   ii.   One daughter, m. Andrew Tillotson.

(687.)   iii.   JAMES SHEPARD FELTON[6] (*Nathaniel[5], Nathaniel[4], Ebenezer[3], Nathaniel[2], Nathaniel[1],*) b. about 1805; m. about 1827, Mary E. Rawson, daughter of Dea. Elias Rawson of Nunda, N. Y.; had 2 children; she died Nov. 30, 1833, Mr. Felton m. second, Olive Bowers; residence, Norwalk, Ohio. Had 6 or 8 children by second wife.

1471.   i.   ELIAS R., b. about 1828, at Nunda, N. Y.; settled at Cleveland, Ohio ; of the firm of Felton, Bigelow, in penmanship.
1472.   ii.   MARY; died young.
1473.   iii.   One daughter, m. F. D. Bartley.
1474.   iv.   One daughter, m. Amon Canfield.
1475.   v.   GEORGE.
1476.   vi.   MOSES.

(688.)   iv.   JACOB VAUGHAN, b. about 1803; m. Clarissa Felton, daughter of Nathaniel Felton of New Salem. Mr. Vaughan m. second, her sister, Lucinda Felton. He m. third, Tirzah Shaw; he was living in 1884, in New Salem near Prescott. Had several children.

(690.)   vi.   CYRUS W. FELTON[6], (*Nathaniel[5], Nathaniel[4], Ebenezer[3], Nathaniel[2], Nathaniel[1],*) b. Feb. 15, 1819; m. July 1837, Harriet Hawes of Boston. He m. second, June 1842, Mary Jane Covell. Mr Felton was a painter and trunk-maker. They resided in Worcester and in Boston. He was a soldier from Boston in the Union army in 1861–62. He died in Boston, April 18, 1867, aged 48 years. Mrs. Mary Jane Felton died in Boston, Oct. 21, 1880, aged 57 years. They had 6 children.

1479. i. GEORGIANNA, b. in Boston, March 29, 1843; m. April 1860, Wm. H. Neal. Mr. Neal. died in the winter of 1880–81.
1480. ii. ABBIE J., b. in Boston, June 29, 1844; died young.
1481. iii. CLARA A., b. in Bridgewater, Dec. 8, 1846; died July 31, 1847.
1482. iv. MARY E., b. in Worcester, July 5, 1848; died young.
1483. v. ERASTUS W., b. in Worcester, July 10, 1850; m. in 1872, Sarah L. Littlefield of Boston; he m. second, July 1878, Mary A. Gould of Boston. He died April 4, 1882, aged 31 years.
1484. vi. ABBIE J., b. in Worcester, July 10, 1852; m.

(692.) i. LEVI PRESTON, JR., b. Dec. 5, 1783; m. Jan. 8, 1811, Rebecca Felton, b. March 20, 1789, daughter of Nathaniel and Hannah Felton of Danvers. Mr. Preston was a carpenter and in 1839, built the meeting house now standing, (in 1885,) in Danvers Centre. His father, Capt. Levi Preston, died Jan. 1850, aged 92 years, the oldest man in Danvers. Mrs. Rebecca Preston died Nov. 18, 1824, aged 35 years. Mr. Preston m. second, Abigail Abbot of Rowley. Had 3 children by his first wife.

1485. i. LEVI W., b. Dec. 11, 1812; died Aug. 1815.
1486. ii. REBECCA, b. Jan. 17, 1816; died Aug. 20, 1816.
1487. iii. LEVI A., b. July 3, 1818; died Feb. 21, 1819.

Mr. Preston had two sons and three daughters by his second wife. One son and one daughter living in 1886. Mr. Preston's brother, Dea. Samuel Preston, it is said was the inventor of the first shoe pegging machine in Mass.; it was patented March 1833. Mr. Levi Preston died March 25, 1867, aged 83 years. Mrs. Abigail Preston, living in 1885, aged about 87 years. Their youngest son, Levi Preston, Jr., b. Oct. 12, 1840; m. Mary Brown.

(693.) ii. NATHANIEL FELTON[6], (Nathaniel[5], Nathaniel[4], Jonathan[3], Nathaniel[2], Nathaniel[1],) b. Oct. 6, 1791; m. Polly Preston, b. April 7, 1795, daughter of Capt. Levi Preston of Danvers. He was a farmer and lived upon his father's place on Mt. Pleasant, now in Peabody. He received premiums on butter at Essex county agricultural fairs, almost every year from 1842 to 1853. Was captain of a Danvers company, 1814 to 1817, and rose to the rank of colonel. Col. Felton died Nov. 15, 1865, aged 74 years. Mrs. Polly Felton died Dec. 24, 1868, aged 73 years, 8 months. They had 7 children.

1488†. i. WILLIAM H., b. Dec. 25, 1821; m. Sarah Jane Sperry.
1489†. ii. REBECCA P., b. Feb. 19, 1824; m. Oren Frost.
1490. iii. MARY E., b. Aug. 16, 1826; died July 26, 1859, aged 33 years.
1491†. iv. HARRIET, b. Nov. 3, 1828; m. Capt. Charles B. Rhodes.
1492†. v. LEVI P., b. Jan. 10, 1831; m. Abby Rogers.
1493†. vi. NATHANIEL W., b. July 5, 1833; m. Maria L. Ferrin.
1494†. vii. MEHITABLE B., b. May 25, 1837; m. James Leverett Sperry.

(694.) iii. DANIEL FELTON[6], (*Nathaniel*[5], *Nathaniel*[4], *Jonathan*[3], *Nathaniel*[2], *Nathaniel*[1],) b. May 13, 1794; m. Feb. 20, 1825, Hannah P. Felton, b. Feb. 25, 1802, daughter of Nathan Felton, Esq., of Danvers. He was a merchant several years at his father-in-law's place, Felton's Corner, and a captain in the militia. Mrs. Hannah P. Felton died April 5, 1849, aged 47 years. Capt. Felton died March 28, 1861, aged 67 years. Had 7 children.

1495. i. MARTHA A., b. Dec. 10, 1825; died July 20, 1845, aged 19 years.
1496. ii. NATHAN A., b. April 6, 1828; kept a produce market in Boston many years.
1497. iii. SARAH D., b. Oct. 7, 1830; died Sept. 25, 1832.
1498†. iv. DANIEL H., b. March 6, 1836; a gardner, living at Felton's Corner, sometimes called Feltonville in Peabody.
1499. v. CAROLINE, b. March 23, 1839; died March 3, 1840.
1500. vi. HARRIET P., b. Dec. 1, 1842; in Feltonville, Peabody in 1885.
1501. vii. MARTHA A., b. Aug. 26, 1846; m. Warren S. Pike, b. Feb. 26, 1838; son of John Pike; resides near Feltonville in Peabody; have 4 children.

(696.) v. JAMES MARSH, b. March 7, 1803, (son of John Marsh,) m. April 5, 1825, Mary Prince Felton, b. June 30, 1799, daughter of Nathaniel and Hannah Felton of Mount Pleasant. Mr. Marsh settled in South Danvers, now Peabody, where Mrs. Marsh died Nov. 6, 1868, aged 69 years. Had 7 children. Mr. Marsh m. second, Caroline Mudge. Mr. Marsh is a farmer.

1502. i. HANNAH F., b. Sept. 17, 1825; living in 1886.

1503. ii. JAMES, JR., b. Oct. 26, 1827; m. May 1843, Mary A. Ranney of Lawrence.
1504. iii. JOHN B., b. Oct. 16, 1829; m. in Cal., Kate J. Baldwin, Aug. 1856.
1505. iv. NATHANIEL F., b. Dec. 11, 1831; m. in Cal., Mary A. Walsh, Aug. 1864.
1506. v. CALEB W., b. May 3, 1834; m. Dec. 31, 1854, Clara E. Brown.
1507. vi. GEORGE E., b. May 22, 1836; m. Elizabeth N. Floyd of Lynn, Dec. 31, 1864.
1508. vii. FRANCIS, b. Aug. 18, 1838; m. Feb. 13, 1867; Caroline E. Pope, daughter of Zephaniah and grand-daughter of Amos Pope, the Danvers Almanac maker.

(697.) vi. JASPER POPE, b. July 1802; m. Dec. 15. 1830, Harriet Felton, b. Sept. 19, 1803, daughter of Nathaniel and Hannah Felton of Felton Hill, in Peabody. Mrs. Pope died Nov. 24, 1844, aged 41 years. He m. second, Feb. 9, 1846, her sister, Sarah Felton; b. Jan. 4, 1807; she died June 17, 1882, aged 75 years. Mr. Pope a farmer in Danvers, near the line of West Peabody. He was son of Elijah Pope, who sold the celebrated Oakes cow to Caleb Oakes, that received a premium at the Brighton fair in 1816, of 20 dollars for the best milch cow. Jasper Pope is a nephew of Amos Pope the Danver's Almanac maker. Mr. Pope is now living with his third wife. He had one son.

1509. i. JASPER E., b. Feb. 12, 1847; died March 5, 1873, aged 26 years.

(699.) i. DANIEL FELTON^6, (*Jedediah^5, Anthony^4, Jonathan^3, Nathaniel^2, Nathaniel^1*,) m. Mary (Stickney) Gilman, sister of Dr. Orville Gilman and daughter of Daniel Gilman, who m. Mary B. Stickney, b. Jan. 29, 1781, daughter of Moses Stickney, who died at Jaffrey, N. H., in 1852, aged 100 years 6 months. In 1845, and 46 Daniel Felton was in Chilicothe, Ohio. Sup. they had one or more children.

1509½. i. MARY E., of Mason, N. H., m. Jan. 1, 1863, Henry Kendall of Shirley, Mass.

(700.) ii. AMOS ELIOT, b. March 8, 1799, (son of Andrew Eliot of Mason, N. H.,) m. Feb. 22, 1821, Betsey Felton, daughter of Jedediah and Mary (Proctor) Felton of Mason, N. H. Amos Eliot of Amherst, N. H., died in 1826, leaving children, Amos, Jr., Catherine, Nancy, Abigail, and Martha.

(701.) iii. IRA HADLEY, m. Mary Felton, daughter of

Jedediah and Mary Felton, (No. 289.) They were living in 1845, and had several children.

(Family, No. 98; the grandparents of the three following families were overlooked and not printed on page 98; we will insert it here:)

(98.) v. JONATHAN FELTON⁴, (*Jonathan³, Nathaniel², Nathaniel¹,*) bapt. Feb. 1736-7; m., May 24, 1772. Mrs. Anna Whittemore, (or Whitredge,) both of Danvers. Mr. Felton was a soldier in the revolutionary army. He died in Danvers, Feb. 23, 1811, aged 75 or more years. Mrs. Anna Felton died in Salem, Jan. 9, 1821, aged 78 or 80 years. They had one son born in Danvers.

(290.) i. JONATHAN, JR., b. Nov. 17, 1779; m. Sept. 12, 1801, Betsey Wood of Rowley, Mass. See page 71.)

(702.) i. GEORGE W. FELTON⁶, (*Jonathan⁵, Jonathan⁴, Jonathan³, Nathaniel², Nathaniel¹,*) b. Jan. 3, 1803; m. Jan. 31, 1830, Mrs. Mary (Crandall) Beals, a sister to the wife of John Smith Felton, (No. 634.) Mr. Felton was a shoe manufacturer in Salem, and for a number of years one of the members of the Salem brass band. He moved to Malden, and was for some 25 years in the employ of the Boston Rubber Company, and was an expert in the branch of the business that he followed. He died suddenly at Malden, June 14, 1882, aged 79 years, after a short but severe sickness of 8 days. A Boston newspaper said he was a man of sterling integrity and will be missed by all who knew and associated with him. They had 3 children.

1510. i. SUSIE B., b. about 1831; died April 12, 1882, (about two months before her father's decease,) aged 50 years.
1511†. ii. GEORGE W., JR., b. Aug. 6, 1833; a graduate of Salem high school.
1512. iii. MARY A.; an invalid living in Malden, Mass., in 1883.

(703.) ii. JOHN BURNHAM, JR., m. Jan. 17, 1826, Sophia Jane Felton, b. July 10, 1805, daughter of Jonathan Felton the third of Salem. They had 4 children. Mr. Burnham was lost at sea, off Trieste, Nov. 14, 1835, aged 35 years. Mrs. Sophia J. Burnham died Aug. 1, 1858, aged 53 years.

1513. i. SOPHIA J., b. Dec. 25, 1827; m. Oct. 11, 1855, David Allyn of Chelsea, Mass. Mr. Allyn is a carpenter and resides at North Andover, Mass.

1514. ii. JOHN M., b. April 12, 1831; m. Oct. 21, 1855, Ann Maria Patterson. Mr. Burnham died March 28, 1863, aged 32 years.
1515. iii. WILLIAM F., b. June 16, 1833; m. June 5, 1855, Harriet Sherman of Boston. In Cal. in 1883; went there about 1859.
1516. iv. LIZZIE W., b. Aug. 12, 1835; died Oct. 12, 1835.

(705.) iv. JONATHAN NEEDHAM FELTON[6], (Jonathan[5], Jonathan[4], Jonathan[3], Nathaniel[2], Nathaniel[1],) b. Nov. 3, 1817; he was a shoe manufacturer in Salem and captain of the Salem military company. He m. Dec. 31, 1847, Harriet Grant of Salem, Mass. Capt. Felton moved to Colchester, Conn. in 1855. He lost some property by a fire in Colchester Village a few years ago. Have had 3 or more children.

1517. i. CHARLES, m. and has 5 children.
1518. ii. ZAIDEE, a daughter, died several years ago.
1519. iii. ANNA, living in 1883.

(707.) i. JOHN PRIEST MAYNARD, b. June 2, 1791, (son of Simon Maynard of Marlboro, and uncle to Amory Maynard, the founder of the town of Maynard, Mass.;) m. in 1812, Betsey Weeks, b. Aug. 21, 1789, daughter of John and Betsey (Felton) Weeks of Marlboro. They had 3 children. Mr. Maynard died Sept. 29, 1818, aged 27 years. Mrs. Maynard m. second, April 1821, Ira Temple of Marlboro, b. Jan. 4, 1794, son of John and Dorothy Temple; she had 4 more children. Mrs Betsey Temple died July 19, 1828, aged 39 years. Mr. Temple m. twice afterwards and died in Fayville, Southboro, April 23, 1878, aged 84 years.

1520. i. WILLIAM, b. March 11, 1813.
1521. ii. A son, b. July 28, 1815; died Sept. 21, 1815.
1522†. iii. LUCY, b. ———; m. in 1837, Wm. Bigelow.
1523†. iv. ELEANOR, b. Feb. 26, 1822; m. Elbridge G. Parmenter.
1524. v. JOHN A., b. Aug. 25, 1824.
1525. vi. LYDIA, b. April 26, 1826; m. ——— Drake; m. second, ——— Hunt.
1526. vii. ELIZABETH, b. May 3, 1828; died Aug. 23, 1828.

(709.) iii. JABEZ S. WALCOTT, m. in 1820, Thankful Weeks, b. Jan. 22, 1795, daughter of John and Betsey (Felton) Weeks of Marlboro. They settled at Waltham, Mass. Mr. Walcott died Sept. 18, 1858, aged 66 years. Had 4 or more children.

1527. i. MARY; m. ——— Cobley.

FELTON FAMILY. 143

1528.   ii. GEORGE; died in California.
1529.   iii. THEODORE; m. June 26, 1851, Olive A. Emerson of Waltham.
1530.   iv. SUSAN.

(714.) viii. WILLIAM RICE WHEELER, of Sudbury, b. June 4, 1804, son of Israel Wheeler and grand son of Wm. Rice, Esq., of Sudbury; m. in 1826, Lucy Weeks, b. Sept. 8, 1807, daughter of John and Betsey (Felton) Weeks of Marlboro. Mr. Wheeler died July 23, 1831, aged 27 years. Mrs. Wheeler m. second. Nov. 1842, Lyman Morse Bigelow, b. July 26, 1811, son of Ephraim Bigelow of Marlboro. They resided at Feltonville, now town of Hudson. Mr. Bigelow died June 2, 1882, aged 71 years. Mrs. Lucy W. Bigelow died in Dorchester, at the residence of her daughter, Feb. 26, 1884, aged 76 years, 5 months. She had 4 children by her two husbands.

1531.   i. JOHN W, b. July 5, 1826; m. Anna ———; had one son.
1532.   ii. WM. H., b. Feb. 24, 1828; m. Margaret Cassidy; had one daughter.
1533.   iii. LYMAN A., b. March 15, 1830; died at Feltonville, Oct. 31, 1851, aged 21 years.
1534.   iv. ABBY J., b. Jan. 2, 1845; m. June 27, 1867, Lorenzo O. Walcott, son of Truman Walcott of Marlboro; have 2 sons.

(715.) ix. JOHN WEEKS, JR., b. April 12, 1810; m. June 1831, Nancy Hager, b. April 17, 1809, daughter of Wm. Hager of Marlboro. They lived at Sudbury, Mass.; where Mrs. Weeks died July 26, 1884, aged 75 years. They had 3 children.

1535.   i. MARY E.; m. William Moore.
1536.   ii. NANCY M.; m. Abner Vose.
1537.   iii. SARAH A., b. about 1842; m. May 1862, Elbridge A. Ladd, b. about 1839; had Osgood J. Ladd, b. in Marlboro, Oct. 29, 1863.

(716.) i. DANIEL FELTON[6], (*William*[5], *Archelaus*[4], *Jonathan*[3], *Nathaniel*[2], *Nathaniel*[1],) b. April 23, 1792; he was at work in Leominster, where he was accidentally drowned, April 18, 1815, aged 23 years; funeral in Marlboro.

(717.) ii. ISAAC TEMPLE STEVENS, b. Jan. 1798, (son of Daniel Stevens, Esq., of Marlboro; m. Oct. 17, 1817, Catherine Felton, b. Dec. 16, 1794, daughter of Wm. and Catherine Felton of Marlboro, (No. 292.) Mr. Stevens was a farmer and resided with his father, on the Bent place, near the outlet of Marlboro Lake. He drove a butcher's cart for his father several years. Mr. Stevens held the office of coroner several years. Mrs. Catherine F. Stevens died Sept 20, 1873, aged 78 years, 9 months. Mr. Stevens died April 16, 1876, aged 78 years. They had 13 children.

Within two furlongs of Mr. Steven's place is probably the oldest and largest chestnut tree in Mass. Its circumference, a few feet from the ground, 33 feet; its trunk is hollow, being a mere shell; part of its branches and limbs broken off; the tree is near the outlet of Marlboro Lake.

 1538. i. MARY E., b. Feb. 28, 1818; died Sept. 3, 1819.
 1539†. ii. DANIEL W., b. Jan. 18, 1820; m. Caroline Partridge.
 1540†. iii. ISAAC E., b. Jan. 30, 1822; m. Susan C. Burdett.
 1541†. iv. JOHN S., b. Feb. 26, 1823; m. Mary Elizabeth Perry.
 1542†. v. LEVI L., b. Oct. 22, 1824; m. Mary Elizabeth Bispham.
 1543†. vi. MARY T., b. Sept. 14, 1827; m. Samuel S. Townsend.
 1544†. vii. ABRAHAM G., b. June 19, 1829; m. Charlotte Weeks.
 1545†. viii. ANN B., b. March 28, 1831; m. Thomas W. Bispham.
 1546. ix. SUSANNA C., b. May 16, 1833; unm. 1885.
 1547. x. CATHERINE A., b. Oct. 2, 1835; died Nov. 2, 1835.
 1548. xi. WILLIAM A., twin, b. Oct. 2, 1835; died Nov. 4, 1835.
 1549†. xii. WILLIAM R., b. April 10, 1838; m. Sarah S. Lamson.
 1550†. xiii. JANE C., b. July 10, 1840; m. Henry A. Holyoke.

(718.) iii. WILLIAM FELTON[6], (*William*[5], *Archelaus*[4], *Jonathan*[3], *Nathaniel*[2], *Nathaniel*[1],) b. Feb. 17, 1796; m. Mary Ann Stow, b. in Stow, Mass., Sept. 1802. They were m. in Southboro, Feb. 1825, and called both of that town; they lived in several towns. Mr. Felton died in Providence, R. I., May 1847, aged 51 years. They had 9 children. Mrs. Felton m. second in 1849, John Hawes of Stow, Mass.; he died about 1862, aged 88 years.

 1551†. i. SUSAN A., b. Jan. 13, 1826; m. Ebenezer V. Stowe.
 1552†. ii. SOPHRONIA A., b. June 17, 1827; m. Ebenezer Oakes.
 1553. iii. DANIEL W., b. in Northboro, Feb. 6, 1829; living in 1885.
 1554†. iv. CHARLOTTE M., b. Sept. 17, 1830; m. Wm. H. Chamberlain.

1555†. v. MARY M., b. June 20, 1832; m. Luke Bowers.
1556. vi. SARAH J., b. in Marlboro, Dec. 26, 1834; died in the same town, Jan. 5, 1844, aged 9 years.
1557†. vii. CHARLES A., b. Aug. 10, 1836; m. Hannah D. Whitney.
1558. viii. GEORGE W., b. in Northboro, Jan. 16, 1839; died Nov. 25, 1855, aged 17 years.
1559†. ix. LEVI L., b. about 1841; m. Susan W. Hapgood.

(719.) iv. JAMES POTTER, b. in 1799, (son of Stephen Potter of Marlboro;) m. April 1825, Elizabeth Felton, b. Feb. 19, 1805, daughter of Wm. and Catherine Felton of Marlboro, (No. 292.) Mr. Potter was a shoe-maker, and settled at Northboro, where he was one of the selectmen 1846–47–48. He died May 15, 1864, aged 65 years. Mrs. Elizabeth Potter died March 15, 1871, aged 66 years. They had 5 children.

1560†. i. MERRICK, b. April 7, 1826; m. Elizabeth S. Twitchell.
1561†. ii. LYDIA F., b. Aug. 26, 1828; m. Henry Bartlett.
1562†. iii. CHARLES, b. June 24, 1830; m. Mary Maria Holyoke.
1563†. iv. CYRUS, b. Feb. 19, 1832; m. Sarah A. Burdett.
1564†. v. ELIZABETH E., b. Aug. 12, 1840; m. Horace L. Peverly.

(720.) v. EDWARD FELTON[6], (*William*[5], *Archelaus*[4], *Jonathan*[3], *Nathaniel*[2], *Nathaniel*[1],) b. July 6, 1807; m. July 1849, Lydia Ann Stone, b. about 1825, daughter of James Stone of Northboro. He is a farmer and settled on his father's place in Marlboro. They have 4 children.

1565. i. LAURA A., b. June 23, 1851; m. Aug. 10, 1884, Charles A. Andrews.
1566. ii. EDWIN A., b. June 19, 1853.
1567. iii. ADALAIDE M., b. Sept. 13, 1857.
1568. iv. ARTEMAS, b. Oct. 9, 1859.

(721.) vi. WILLIAM GILES, b. Sept. 1815, (son of Luther Giles of Concord, Mass;) m. Dec. 1846, Susan Ann Felton, b. Feb. 1817, daughter of Wm. and Catherine Felton of Marlboro, (No. 292.) They settled in Marlboro, where Mrs. Giles died Jan. 5, 1876, aged 59 years. Had 2 children.

1569. i. MARY A., b. Feb. 18, 1848; m. Feb. 8, 1876, Alfred E. Wallace, (son of Wm. Wallace of Marlboro, who died in 1876.)
1570. ii. JOEL W., b. Feb. 27, 1850; m. Jan. 10, 1879, Minnie E. Riley; he is a good taxidermist and resides in Marlboro, Mass.

(722.) i. JAMES OTIS. MORSE, b. in Marlboro, Mass., Feb. 13, 1788, son of Aaron and Sarah (Felton) Morse, (No. 293.) Mr. Morse graduated at Union College, N. Y., in 1809, and the same year commenced the study of law, under the direction of the late Isaac Sedge, Esq., of Cherry Valley. He m. in 1812, Mrs. Mary G. Phillips, daughter of Rev. Andrew Oliver of Springfield, and settled in Cherry Valley, Otsego County, N. Y., where he was the first Judge of Otsego Co. courts, appointed about 1828. He died at the residence of his daughter, Mrs. A. G. Story, at Little Falls, Herkimer Co., Monday, Dec. 4, 1847, aged almost 50 years. His remains were interred at Cherry Valley. His death was not less sudden and unexpected than it was afflicted, says one writer, for he left home the 22d of Nov., and was arrested on the way by typhus fever and died Dec. 4, following. "He was a learned and upright judge, an affectionate husband, a tender and indulgent father, a humble and fervent Christian, a generous and devoted friend, a public-spirited citizen, and an active, enterprising and extensively useful man. He left a widow, three sons and two daughters," says Morse Memorial.

- 1571†. i. OLIVER A., b. about 1813; m. Ann Clark.
- 1572†. ii. JAMES O., JR.; m. Georgie A. Whitwell.
- 1573. iii. SARAH, m. in 1835, Albert G. Story.
- 1574. iv. ELIZABETH; died at Cherry Valley since 1837.
- 1575†. v. STEWART, b. Feb. 10, 1824; a lawyer and physician.

(726.) ii. JOHN FELTON[6], (*John*[5], *Archelaus*[4], *Jonathan*[3], *Nathaniel*[2], *Nathaniel*[1],) b. July 23, 1797; m. Feb. 1823, Lucinda Ward. In 1836, this family moved from Massena, St. Lawrence County, N. Y., to Elyria, Lorain County, Ohio; afterwards moved to Northampton, Summit County, in the same state. John Felton died Aug. 27, 1851, aged 54 years. They had 9 children.

- 1576. i. MARIAH, b. Oct. 13, 1825.
- 1577. ii. SARAH, b. Oct. 8, 1827; died Oct. 17, 1864, aged 37 years.
- 1578. iii. LEWIS, b. June 18, 1829.
- 1579. iv. LOVINIA, b. July 3, 1831.
- 1580. v. ANN, b. Feb. 13, 1833.
- 1581. vi. LAURA, b. Jan. 14, 1836.
- 1582. vii. JOHN, JR., b. July 18, 1839; died May 6, 1864, aged 25 years.
- 1583. viii. ELLEN, b. June 17, 1841; died Sept. 1, 1868, aged 27 years.
- 1584. ix. HATTIE, b. May 9, 1847; died May 17, 1872, aged 25 years.

(728.) iv. JOSHUA PAINE of Massena, N. Y., m. Oct. 6, 1825, Nancy Felton, b. May 22, 1801, daughter of John and Olive Felton. They settled in that township and had 4 children. Mrs. Nancy Paine died Sept. 9, 1843, aged 42 years.

1585.   i. LEVI; was living in 1853.
1586.   ii. MALINDA; died before 1848.
1587.   iii. CHANDLER; died before 1843.
1587½. iv. ALVIRA; died young.

(729.) v. LYMAN FELTON[6], (*John*[5], *Archelaus*[4], *Jonathan*[3], *Nathaniel*[2], *Nathaniel*[1],) b. March 6, 1804; m. Dec. 11, 1835, Eliza Sampson. He moved from Massena, in N. Y., to Ohio with his brother, John Felton, in 1836. He died in Northampton, Ohio, Oct. 15, 1843, aged 39 years. They had one or more children.

1588.   i. CHARLES, was living in Ohio in 1880.

(730.) vi. ABEL SPAULDING, m. March 27, 1827, Eliza Felton, b. Sept. 28, 1806, daughter of John and Olive Felton, (No. 294.) They had 5 children. In 1855, Mr. and Mrs. Spaulding were living at Painesville, Ohio.

(734.) iv. MARK FISHER, m. Josepha (or Josephine) Guild, b. Dec. 28, 1801, daughter of Joseph and Rebecca (Felton) Guild of Dedham, Mass. Had several children. In 1878, one son and two daughters were living. Mr. Fisher died about 1861. Mrs. Josephine Fisher died in Roxbury, (Boston) Feb. 27, 1885, aged 83 years. The following item taken from a newspaper in 1882: "Mark Fisher, a Boston boy, (a painter of scenes, signs and pictures in Boston,) a successful painter in English Art Circles." Perhaps a relative of the above-named Mark Fisher.

(735.) i. FRANCIS McINTOSH, b. Jan. 27, 1791, (son of Ebenezer and Jemima McIntosh of Needham;) m. May 17, 1821, Julia Felton, b. Oct. 22, 1802, daughter of Isaac and Anna Felton of Needham, Mass. Mr. McIntosh died Aug. 24, 1829, aged 38 years. His widow m. second, —— Slade, and died in France many years ago.

1589.   i. ANN F.; died Nov. 19, 1824.
1590.   ii. ANN L., b. Oct. 5, 1824.

(737.) iii. CHARLES COOK FELTON[6],(*Isaac*[5], *Daniel*[4], *Jonathan*[3], *Nathaniel*[2], *Nathaniel*[1],) b. Dec. 16, 1808; m., May 1834, Mary C. Smith of Lexington, Mass., b. March 25, 1817; she died in

Dedham, June 10, 1853, aged 36 years. Had 11 children. Mr. Felton was a carpenter; he procured a patent for a window fastener in 1852. He m. second, Mary Wilder of Hingham, and had two children. Mr. Felton lived in Dedham, where he died Oct. 9, 1864, aged almost 56 years.

    1591.   i. CHARLES E., b. Nov. 28, 1835; died June 10, 1839.
    1592 .   ii. WILLIAM H., b. Aug. 16, 1838; died April 11, 1840.
    1593†.   iii. DANIEL C., b. July 19, 1840; m., Dec. 25, 1865, Caroline H. Horton.
    1594.   iv. MARY A., b. May 17, 1842; died.
    1595.   v. CLARA C., b. March 29, 1844; died Aug. 28, 1844.
    1596.   vi. JANE, b. July 13, 1845; died Sept. 23, 1845.
    1597.   vii. SARAH J., b. Oct. 8, 1846; died May 20, 1849.
    1598.   viii. GEORGE H., b. Nov. 14, 1847; died July 17, 1850.
    1599.   ix. HORACE, b. April 25, 1849; died March 17, 1865, aged 16 years.
    1600.–1601.   x.–xi. Twins, b. May 17, 1851; died July 2, 1851.
    1602.–1603.   xii.–xiii. Two children by his last wife.

(738.) iv. JAMES P. TOLMAN, m. Mary Ann Felton, b. March 2, 1813, daughter of Isaac and Anna Felton of Needham. Their children were born in Needham, Mass. About 1854, they moved to Oshkosh, Wis., where they were living in 1884. Mr. Tolman was formerly of Lynn.

    1604.   i. CYNTHIA B., b. Dec. 9, 1843.
    1605.   ii. B. FRANKLIN.
    1606.   iii. LUCY A.; m. ——— Forbes.
    1607.   iv. WILLIAM H.

(739.) v. HORACE FELTON^6, (*Isaac^5, Daniel^4, Jonathan^3, Nathaniel^2, Nathaniel^1,*) b. Sept. 1811, is a blacksmith, formerly of the firm of Smith & Felton of Boston. In Aug. 1853, the firm of Smith & Felton had the contract for the cast and wrought iron work for the enlargement of the State House in Boston awarded to them. Mr. Felton m. Charlotte Lewis of Dedham, Mass. He lived in Portland, Me., several years; moved to Boston in Nov. 1851. In Jan. 1849, H. Felton, Cummings & Hinckley of Portland, Me., obtained a patent for improvement in railroad car wheels. Had 2 children.

    1607. *a.*   i. CHARLOTTE A.; living in Boston.

(740.) i. SAMPSON FELTON⁶, (*James⁵, Daniel⁴, Daniel³, Nathaniel², Nathaniel¹,*) b. in New Salem, Mass., Feb. 26, 1784. He was a blacksmith as were his ancestors for three generations. He m. and had 8 children. He settled in Warsaw, Clark Township, Coshocton County, Ohio. In 1856, had 5 children, 24 grandchildren and 3 great-grandchildren living. He died about the year 1865, in Coshocton, aged about 80 years. His death took place soon after he was butted by a buck as he was passing through a field.

Sampson Felton thought he had discovered a remedy for the potato rot about the time of its first appearance, by mixing dry fresh-burnt charcoal with potatoes in the fall, and covering them with dry straw and earth, and the coal would draw the disorder from the potatoes.

1607. *b.* ii. SAMUEL L., b. about 1844; was a soldier from Boston in the 47th Reg't, Co. H., in 1862; he died of typhoid malaria, Aug. 27, 1863, aged about 19 years.

In 1851, the Commonwealth of Massachusetts offered a reward of ten thousand dollars to any person, within the limits of the State, for a remedy for the potato rot. Sampson Felton thought "within the State" ought to have been left out of the reward, and the reward go to the person who found the remedy. Mr. Felton did not give me the names of his children. A nephew of Mr. Felton gave me the name of one son.

1608. i. ALEXANDER; was living a few years ago.

(741.) ii. ANDREW WEATHERWAX, m. Lydia Felton, b. about 1786, daughter of James and Olive (Sampson) Felton, (No. 298.) They had 3 or more sons and several daughters. Mrs. W.'s sister, Betsey Felton, m. Adam Weatherwax and had several children. These families, it is said, resided in Ohio. In 1856, Capt. John Weatherwax and his cousin, Andrew Weatherwax, were living near Plattsburg, N. Y.

(742.) iii. JAMES FELTON⁶, (*James⁵, Daniel⁴, Daniel³, Nathaniel², Nathaniel¹,*) b. about 1788; m. and had a large family. He was a blacksmith in early life, afterwards followed farming. He died Jan. 15, 1876, near Brooklyn, Iowa, aged 88 years. Some of his children were:

1609. i. DERRICK, the oldest, died about 1840.
1610†. ii. JAMES, JR., b. Feb. 23, 1821; m. Mary Smith; died during the late civil war.
1611†. iii. AUSTIN; m.; living in Iowa, town of Victor.

1612. iv. WILLIAM; m.; had several children; one son Joseph.
1613. v. EZRA; living a few years ago in Palo, York County, Neb.
1614. vi. PAMELIA; m. Benhadal Winchester, son of Elhanan Winchester.
1615. vii. MARTHA; m. Solomon Casebeer.

(744.) v. EZRA FELTON⁶, (*James⁵, Daniel⁴, Daniel³, Nathaniel², Nathaniel¹,*) b. March 7, 1791; m. Hannah Sherman in Pottstown, N. Y., about 1815. He m. second, March 24, 1830, Abigail ———, b. Jan. 20, 1812. Had 2 children by each wife. In 1856, they were living at West Ellery, N. Y. Ezra Felton died March 18, 1877, aged 86 years.

1616. i. ELIZABETH, b. May 8, 1818; m. ——— Scofield.
1617†. ii. ALONZO L., b. Sept. 25, 1819; m. Caroline M. Olmstead.
1618†. iii. HANNAH A., b. June 5, 1832; m. ——— Nobles.
1619†. iv. LAURETTA A., b. Sept. 17, 1839; m. ——— Farlow.

(746.) vii. DAVID FELTON⁶, (*James⁵, Daniel⁴, Daniel³, Nathaniel², Nathaniel¹,*) was a blacksmith; lived many years near Blissfield, Mich.; he died about Nov. 1, 1882. He had one son, and four daughters.

1619. a. i. SAMPSON.
1619. b. ii. MARY A.
1619. c. iii. LOUISA.
1619. d iv. BETSEY.
1619. e. v. NANCY.

(747.) viii. DANIEL FELTON⁶, (*James⁵, Daniel⁴, Daniel³, Nathaniel², Nathaniel¹,*) b. in Rensselaer County, N. Y.. May 7, 1802; he m. Mary Ann Hall; she died about one year after marriage. Mr. Felton m. second, Esley Emma Brownell, b. March 9, 1811, daughter of Joseph Browrell of Rensselaer County, N. Y. They lived many years in Chautauqua County, N. Y. They had 10 children. Mrs. Felton died Dec. 8, 1862, aged 50 years. Daniel Felton died at the residence of his oldest son at Granite Falls, Minn., July 13, 1880, aged 78 years. Three of their sons, Daniel Jr., Israel and Ezra, were soldiers during the late civil war.

1620†. i. JAMES S., b. Oct. 17, 1827; m. Amelia F. Cowles.
1621. ii. A daughter, b. in 1829; died young.
1622†. iii. JOSEPH, b. May 12, 1831; m. Sarah Francis———.
1623. iv. DANIEL, JR., b. March 12, 1833; m. and had a son, Daniel, Jr.

1624. v. ISAAC, b. April 28, 1835; m.; has two daughters.
1625. vi. ISRAEL B., b. July 25, 1838; was a Union soldier.
1626. vii. EZRA, b. March 19, 1840; m.; has two sons and two daughters.
1627. viii. MARY A., b. Feb. 10, 1842; died July 11, 1842.
1628. ix. ALONZO, b. Aug. 29, 1843; died July 30, 1844.
1629. x. GEORGE W. A., b. Sept. 12, 1853; died Nov. 6, 1865, aged 12 years.

(748.) ix. ALEXANDER W. FELTON[6], (*James[5], Daniel[4], Daniel[3], Nathaniel[2], Nathaniel[1]*,) b. June 19, 1804; m. Rachel ——— who was b. Feb. 6, 1806. They had 8 children. Mr. Felton died in Clark Township, Coshocton County, Ohio, Feb. 23, 1853, aged 49 years. Mrs. Rachel Felton died in the same Township, Sept. 21, 1862, aged 56 years.

1630. i. SALLY A., b. Dec. 13, 1827.
1631. ii. MINERVA, b. Oct. 5, 1829.
1632. iii. JAMES A., b. Oct. 10, 1832.
1633. iv. DANIEL, b. March 11, 1836.
1634. v EMMA, b. Nov. 21, 1838.
1635. vi. LYDIA, b. Oct. 23, 1842.
1636. vii. JONATHAN, b. June 2, 1844.
1637. viii. EZRA, b. May 25, 1850.

(751.) xii. JONATHAN MAXON, m. Nancy Felton, daughter of James and Olive Felton, (No. 298.) Were living in Wis. in 1856, and 1882. They had 7 children.

1637. 1. i. ALEXANDER.
1637. 2. ii. DANIEL.
1637. 3. iii. DAVID.
1637. 4. iv. GEORGE.
1637. 5. v. EMILY.
1637. 6. vi. LYDIA.
1637. 7. vii. MERCY.

(754.) i. SYLVANUS GOODNOUGH, m. Susan Felton, daughter of Daniel and Polly (Darling) Felton, (No. 299.) They had 13 children, 7 living in 1878. Part of the children were b. at Ellery, N. Y. Mr. or Mrs. or both were preachers of the Free-will Baptist denomination. Mrs. Susan Goodnough died at Defiance, Ohio, May 1855, sup. aged about 65 years. Their children are said to have been, though probably not all in this order.

1637. *a.* i. JOHN, W., m. living at Defiance, Ohio., in 1878; died in 1883.
1637†. *b.* ii. MARY A., b. in Sodus, N. Y., 1810; m. James McClelland.

1637. c.   iii. CHLOE; m. Cornelius Winchester; living at Brooklyn, Iowa, in 1883; had several children, one named James Winchester.
1637. d.   iv. MARIA; m. —— May at Lottsville, Pa.; living in New Jersey in 1883.
1637. e.   v. CHARLES W.; enlisted in the U. S. service 3 years; afterwards settled in Iowa.
1637. f.   vi. ANGELINE; m. —— Green; she was a widow in 1883, and living in Ill.
1637. g.   vii. ELMAN; left home in early life.
1637. h.   viii. SYLVANUS JR., sup. b. about 1828; living in Brooklyn, Iowa, in 1883
1637. i.   ix. EDWIN; m.; living in Defiance, Ohio, in 1883; had 3 children.
1637. j.   x. DANIEL; living in Texas in 1878 and 1883.

(757.) iii. DARLING FELTON[6], (Robert[5], Daniel[4], Daniel[3], Nathaniel[2], Nathaniel[1],) b. Sept. 6, 1795; m. Sarah —— and had 3 children.

1637. k.   i. ELAM.
1637. l.   ii. ELIZABETH.
1637. m.   iii. EMMA.

(762.) viii. ROBERT FELTON[6], (Robert[5], Daniel[4], Daniel[3], Nathaniel[2], Nathaniel[1],) b. Jan. 31, 1810; m. Caroline Raymond, and had 5 children, viz:

1637. n.   i. EDWARD.
1637. o.   ii. WALTER.
1637. p.   iii. AMBROSE.
1637. q.   iv. WILLARD.
1637. r.   v. JENNIE.

Robert Felton m. second, Jerusha Stevens, b. May 16, 1826, daughter of Joseph and Amy Stevens; were married April 1850. Mr. Felton lived at Fond du Lac, Wis., and had 3 more children.

1637. s.   vi. CHARLES.
1637. t.   vii. ADELBERT.
1637. u.   viii. HATTIE.

(763.) ix. NELSON FELTON[6], (Robert[5], Daniel[4], Daniel[3], Nathaniel[2], Nathaniel[1],) b. July 17, 1812; m. Emily Raymond, b. Oct. 28, 1815; a sister of his brother Robert's first wife. Nelson Felton moved from Oneida County, N. Y., to Rosendale, Wis., about 1852. He died in 1878, aged 66 years. Had 6 children.

1637. v.   i. MERRITT B., b. Aug. 6, 1837; living at Rome, N. Y. in 1883.
1637. w. ii. ALANSON D., b. Sept. 23, 1841; living in Cooleysville, Minn., in 1884.
1637. x. iii. GEORGE G., b. Sept. 28, 1843; living in Granby, Iowa, in 1884.
1637. y. iv. ALBERT N., b. Aug. 13, 1845; living in Fond du Lac County, Wis.
1637. z.   v. THEODORE F., b. Dec. 9, 1848.
1637. aa. vi. HORACE W., b. Nov. 14, 1852; is a physician in Wis.

(769.) iii. CORNELIUS CONWAY FELTON[6], (*Thomas*[5], *Thomas*[4], *Daniel*[3], *Nathaniel*[2], *Nathaniel*[1],) b. June 28, 1784; m. Anna Morse b. Sept. 1781, daughter of David and Abigail (Bayley) Morse of Newbury, Mass. They had 7 children, 3 in Newbury, and 4 in Chelsea, Mass. Mrs. Felton died Dec. 27, 1824, aged 43 years Mr. Felton m. second, Dec. 25, 1825, Mrs. Lucy (Torrey) Boynton of Saugus and had 3 children. Mrs. Boynton had two daughters by her first husband. Mr. Felton was a chaise-maker by trade. After the war of 1812 to 1815, was a toll-keeper at Chelsea. He helped build Warren Bridge, and was one of the toll-keepers. After the Fitchburg railroad was constructed, Mr. Felton contracted for all the wood used on said road. He purchased a place in Littleton, Mass., in Nov. 1846, where he died July 23, 1849, aged 65 years. He was named for his grandfather, Capt. Cornelius Conway.

1638†.   i. CORNELIUS C., JR., b. Nov. 6, 1807; m. Mary Whitney.
1639†. ii. SAMUEL M., b. July 17, 1809; m. Eleanor Stetson.
1640. iii. LYDIA B., b. Nov. 29, 1811; a school teacher; principal of Female Seminary at South Boston about 12 years. Now living at Lancaster, Mass.
1641†. iv. MARTHA C., b. Oct. 12, 1815; m. George E. Bent.
1642.   v. ANNA M., b. Sept. 10, 1817; died Feb. 27, 1832, aged 14 years.
1642½. vi. JOHN B., b. May 9, 1820; died May 2, 1826, aged 6 years.
1643†. vii. HARRIET N., b. Aug. 15, 1822; m. George A. Parker.
1644†. viii. JOHN B., b. June 9, 1827; m. Kate Baldwin.
1645†. ix. FRANKLIN E., b. April 7, 1829; graduated at Harvard College in 1851.
1646.   x. GEORGE E., b. March 13, 1831; died May 8, 1834, aged 3 years.

(772.) vi. THOMAS FELTON[6], (*Thomas*[5], *Thomas*[4], *Daniel*[3], *Nathaniel*[2], *Nathaniel*[1],) b. Sept. 2, 1791 ; m. Oct. 29, 1823, Hannah Morse, b. at Londonderry, N. H., Feb. 13, 1798, dau. of Humphrey Morse; they had 3 sons. Mrs. Felton died Aug. 19, 1837, aged 39 years. Mr. Felton was a carpenter and lived in Chelsea, Cambridge and Charlestown. He m. second, Mrs. Thankful Jewell, daughter of Ephraim and Lydia Bumpus of Readfield, Me. Mr. Felton was cured of salt rheum of twenty years standing by using two bottles of Kennedy's Medical Discovery. He afterwards told Mr. K. he was as rugged as a bear. In 1854, he moved to Belgrade, Me., on to a farm, where he died July 3, 1858, aged 67 years. Mrs. Thankful Felton died in Charlestown, Mass., Aug. 17, 1877, aged almost 80 years.

1647†. i. JOSHUA M., b. Nov. 3, 1825 ; m. Emily L. Jewell.
1648†. ii. ALBERT H., b. March 9, 1827; railroad engineer.
1649†. iii. CORNELIUS C., b. Feb. 22, 1829; railroad engineer.

SEVENTH GENERATION.

(804.) v. MALACHI RICHARDSON, b. in Dublin, N. H., Sept. 25, 1798, (a great-grandson of Dea. Malachi Felton;) m. March 1837, Tamison Greenwood, b. March 10, 1810, dau. of Aaron and Mary Greenwood. Mr. Richardson was living in 1882, on the Richardson homestead in Dublin, N. H. They had 7 children, two of them sons, Luke Felton and Malachi M. Richardson. Mr. Richardson has a pewter tankard which holds about one quart, with the name of Felton inscribed or engraved on it. It was his great-grandfather, Dea. Malachi Felton's, and was used by him in communion services. Mr. Richardson's son, Luke Felton Richardson, has a large pewter platter which was owned by his great-grandmother, Elizabeth (Felton) Richardson.

(831.) ii. DAVID LINCOLN, JR., b. Aug. 10, 1796, (son of Dea. David and Lucy (Felton) Lincoln of Hingham;) m. Hannah Souther, b. in Feb. 1798, daughter of John Souther, a noted ship builder. They had 3 daughters. Mr. Lincoln was a Justice of the Peace and president of the Hingham bank a few years. David Lincoln, Esq., died Oct. 22, 1873, aged 77 years. Mrs. Hannah Lincoln is living in Hingham.

1650†. i. LUCY F., b. Nov. 24, 1826; m. Nathan Lincoln, a music teacher, and resides in Cambridge, Mass. They have one son, Nathan F. Lincoln, and two daughters.

1651. ii. HANNAH S., b. Jan. 24, 1830; m. Thomas F. Whiton. Have one son, Morris F. Whiton. Mrs. Whiton, and her mother, Mrs. Lincoln, are living in Hingham. Thomas F. Whiton died several years ago.

1652. iii. MARY W., b. Jan. 30, 1839; m. Dr. Frank Nickerson of Lowell, Mass. Have several children.

(833.) i OTIS WARNER of Bernardston, Mass., m. Nov. 1831, Eunice C. Felton, b. June 20, 1809, daughter of Wm. and Caroline Felton of Franklin, Vt. They had one daughter, Carrie M., who m. Squire Shedd. Mrs. Eunice C. Warner died Sept. 30, 1838, aged 29 years. Mr. Warner was living in Bernardston in 1881. Mr. Shedd died during the civil war in the army.

1653. i. CARRIE M., and one son, Merton Shedd, were living in 1881.

(834.) ii. CHARLES FELTON[7], ($Wm.^6$, $Wm.^5$, $Nathaniel^4$, $Nathaniel^3$, $John^2$, $Nathaniel^1$,) b. May 24, 1811; m., March 1836, Orra Tracy and had 6 sons and 1 daughter. He settled at Franklin, Vt. He was a delegate in the Constitutional Convention in 1850; was a representative in Oct. 1855, in all four years. At the age of 74 years, Charles Felton is found among the Vermont Legislative Reunionists of Oct. 1885.

1654. i. WALTER W., b. about 1839; resided in California and Mexico.
1655. ii. HOWARD, b. about 1841; died in 1880.
1656. iii. EMERSON; living in Chicago, Ill., in 1881.
1657. iv. EMELINE; twin to Emerson; died aged 16 years.
1658. v. LYMAN H., b. in 1843; lives on his father's place. In March 1884, he was fattening 51 steers for market.
1659. vi. HERBERT; in Mexico with his brother Walter Felton.
1660. vii. CHARLES S., b. in 1850; m. Clara Palmer of Janesville, Wis.

(835.) iii. EDWIN FELTON[7], ($Wm.^6$, $Wm.^5$, $Nathaniel^4$, $Nathaniel^3$, $John^2$, $Nathaniel^1$,) b. Aug. 24, 1813; m. March 1835, Susan M. Knowlton. They have had 3 children. Mr. Felton died April 20, 1875, aged 61 years; sup. lived at Franklin, Vt., as no town was named in the record of this family.

1661. i. MAYNARD; living in Minn. in 1881.
1662. ii. MARSHALL; died before 1881.
1663. iii. MARIA; died before 1881.

(837.) v. ALONZO FELTON[7], (*Wm.*,[6] *Wm.*[5], *Nathaniel*[4], *Nathaniel*[3], *John*[2], *Nathaniel*[1],) b. Aug. 8, 1815; m., March 1839, Mary Tenny. They had 4 daughters. and 2 sons. He died Oct. 18, 1866, aged 51 years. A few of the children living in Franklin.

   1664.   i. HARRIET; died in 1881.
   1665.   ii. SARAH.
   1666.   iii. AMELIA.
   1667.   iv. MARY.
   1668.   v. GEORGE.
   1669.   vi. WILLIAM.

(839.) viii. WILLIAM C. FELTON[7], (*Wm.*[6], *Wm.*[5], *Nathaniel*[4], *Nathaniel*[3], *John*[2], *Nathaniel*[1],) b. Oct. 31, 1822; m. in 1845, Fanny S. Todd. He was a Justice of the Peace in Franklin, Vt., where he died Aug. 18, 1866, aged 44 years. They had 2 sons.

   1670.   i. A. D., b. about 1847; living in Cedarville, N. J.
   1671.   ii. BRYAN; sup. in Franklin, Vt.

(840.) i. GEORGE W. B. ATWOOD, of Dighton, Mass., m. Dec. 27, 1832, Caroline Litchfield Felton, b. Feb. 16, 1812, daughter of Elijah W. and Almy Felton of Dighton, (No. 382.) Had 4 children.

   1672.   i. GEORGE W., b. Dec. 2, 1834; m. Nellie M. Root in Cal.
   1673.   ii. JOHN C., b. Oct. 14, 1844.
   1674.   iii. ROBERT E, b. Nov. 10, 1846; m. Abbie J. Briggs of Dighton.
   1675.   iv. ALMY, b. Dec. 1, 1848; living in 1886.

George W. B. Atwood died June 21, 1884.

(841.) ii. DAVID WOOD WASTCOAT of Dighton, m. Sept. 1838, Elizabeth Elliott Felton, b. Aug. 27, 1813, dau. of E. W. and Almy Felton of Dighton, Mass. In 1886, were living in Taunton, Mass. Had four children, all born in Taunton.

   1675. *a.*   i. MORTIMER, b. Aug. 20, 1843; m. Feb. 17, 1875, Emeline F. Billings; have 3 sons, Richard, Edward, Roy Washburn.
   1675. *b.*   ii. HERBERT, b. Oct. 10, 1845.
   1675. *c.*   iii. ARTHUR F., b. June 9, 1851; m. June 19, 1878, Hattie Maria Leonard of Dighton; had one son, Carlton, b. June 6, 1880.
   1675. *d.*   iv. EDGAR E., b. June 13, 1853.

(842.) i. CHARLES FELTON[7], (*Charles*[6], *Wm.*[5], *Nathaniel*[4], *Nathaniel*[3], *John*[2], *Nathaniel*[1],) b. March 20, 1815; m. April 24, 1838, Esther T. Wheeler. He settled near Lock's Village, Shutesbury, Mass. He has owned a saw-mill many years; is also a farmer. Had 5 children.

   1676.   i. DWIGHT S., b. Dec. 21, 1839; m. May 1862, Jennie M. Harris. He was a soldier in the Union army from Orange, Mass.

   1677.   ii. ALBERT F., b Dec. 17, 1842; m. March 1866, Betsey J. Moor. Was a box-maker in North Leverett, Mass., in 1876.

   1678.   iii. EDWIN O., b. Dec. 20, 1846; m. Nov. 1868, Etta N. Gates; she died in Northfield, Mass., June 23, 1870, aged 23 years; he m. second, May 1872, Mary A. Burrows. In 1876, he had a saw and grist mill in West Northfield.

   1679.   iv. ORA H., b. Aug. 12, 1849; m. Sept. 1870, Clara E. Whittaker of New Salem. Was a miller in Shutesbury several years. In 1884, a merchant in Orange, Mass.

   1680.   v. CARRIE A., b. Sept. 27, 1857; m. Dec. 28, 1881, Walter A. Bryant.

(843.) ii. JOHN WILLIAMS FELTON[7], (*Charles*[6], *Wm.*[5], *Nathaniel*[4], *Nathaniel*[3], *John*[2], *Nathaniel*[1],) b. Dec. 23, 1817; m. Eunice Hoar, and had 4 children. He died May 7, 1854, aged 36 years. His brother, Charles Felton, settled the estate. They lived in Shutesbury, Mass.

   1681.   i. MARY C.
   1682.   ii. CLARA A.
   1683.   iii. CHARLES E.
   1684.   iv. VIOLA W., b. in 1854.

(846.) i. SAMUEL FELTON[7], (*Joshua*[6], *Edward J.*[5], *Nathaniel*[4], *Nathaniel*[3], *John*[2], *Nathaniel*[1],) b. about 1809; m. Oct. 1832, his cousin, Sarah A. Skinner. He settled in Roxbury, and had 4 sons and 4 daughters; 7 of them living in 1875. Mrs. Felton died at Boston Highlands, June 8, 1874, aged 62 years, 10 months. Samuel Felton died March 31, 1877, aged 68 years.

   1685.   i. SARAH A., b. Sept. 1833; m. June 1859, George S. Darling; they had 3 children in 1875.

   1686†.   ii. SAMUEL JR., b. Dec. 22, 1835; m. Abby W. Richardson.

   1687.   iii. CAROLINE L.; m. Nov. 1861, Thomas J. Higgins of Chicago, Ill.; have a daughter, Carrie, b. about 1869.

1688. iv. REUBEN H.; m. Sarah Pratt; he died March 1876, in Warren, Me. Had one son, Wm. Churchill Felton, b. March 1867.
1689. v. ISABELLA, b. June 1842.
1690. vi. JOSHUA, b. Sept. 1844; m. Maria Stevens.
1691. vii. EDWARD; a janitor in Boston; has a son, Edward, Jr.
1692. viii. EMMA, b. about 1850.

(848.) iii. BENJAMIN GORDON PIDGIN, m. Mary Elizabeth Felton, b. Jan. 1824, daughter of Joshua and Hepsy Felton of Roxbury. They lived near the Felton place at Boston Highlands, where Mr. Pidgin died June 24, 1882. They had 3 children.

1693. i. CHARLES F., b. Nov. 11, 1844; m. first, Lizzie Anne Dane; m. second, Lucy T. Gardner.
1694. ii. MARY F., b. in 1848; lived 3½ years.
1695. iii. NANCY C.; lived 1 year.

(849.) iv. JOHN RICHARDSON FELTON[7], ($Joshua^6$, $Edward$ $J.^5$, $Nathaniel^4$, $Nathaniel^3$, $John^2$, $Nathaniel^1$,) b. Nov. 3, 1826; he is a mason by trade; has lived in Boston, Roxbury, Neponset. He m. Mary E. Robinson, b. in Bath, Me; had 4 children. He m. second, Ruth C. Cox, b. in Dorchester, dau. of Isaac and Mary Cox. Mrs. Ruth C. Felton died Jan. 13, 1878, aged 49 years. Mr. Felton m. third, Ellen Snyder.

1696. i. MARY E., b. Aug. 1856; died in Boston, Dec. 8, 1878, aged 22 years.
1697. ii. FANNY, b. about 1859.
1698. iii. ANNA, b. about 1862.
1699. iv. JOHN C., b. in 1863; died Feb. 1864, aged 7 months.
1700. v. HATTIE, by his last wife.

(850.) v. WILLIAM NATHANIEL FELTON[7], ($Joshua^6$, $Edward$ $J.^5$, $Nathaniel^4$, $Nathaniel^3$, $John^2$, $Nathaniel^1$,) b. about the year 1828; he was a mason by trade. In Aug. 1848, he had one of his hands accidentally shot. He was m. in 1850, to Ann R. Lyons. In 1852, he was chosen city messenger in Roxbury, and was re-elected every year to 1865. Mrs. Annie R. Felton died March 9, 1886, aged 55 years, 8 months.

(850a.) i. STEPHEN FELTON[7], ($Stephen^6$, $Stephen^5$, $Stephen^4$, $Samuel^3$, $John^2$, $Nathaniel^1$,) b. in 1807; m. Dec. 1846, Merriam Sawyer, b. Sept. 16, 1810; she was living in Woodford, Cumberland County, Me., in 1886. Mr. Felton died Sept. 21, 1878, aged 71 years. Residence, Woodford, Me. Had one or more children.

1700. *a.*   i. STEPHEN A., b. ———; died, aged 3 months.

(806.) ii. DANIEL WEYMOUTH, b. April 1806; m. Sept. 18, 1834, Sally Felton, b. April 7, 1809, daughter of Stephen and Mehitable Felton of Lyman, Me. They had 4 daughters. Mrs. Weymouth died Feb. 4, 1844, aged 35 years. Mr. Weymouth died Sept. 12, 1885, aged 79 years, 5 months.

1700. *b.*   i. HANNAH[8]; m. Nathaniel Woodman.
1700†. *c.*   ii. SARAH J.[8]; m. first, Francis Clough; had 2 children; m. second, his brother, George Clough; had 4 children.
1700†. *d.*   iii. LORETTA[8], b. April 15, 1839; m. Christopher W. Davis.
1700. *e.*   iv. ESTHER[8]; m. Charles E. Scammon.

(855.) v. STEPHEN FELTON SKIDMORE, b. in Danvers, Aug. 26, 1803, (son of Richard and Phebe (Felton) Skidmore of Danvers;) m. Mary Fish, b. in Marblehead in 1809; they had 10 children. Their son, Stephen Felton, Jr., was found drowned in Duck's Pond in Danversport in 1846, aged 4 years. Mr. Skidmore died in the winter of 1876–77, in Danversport, aged 73 years.

(879.) i. BYBIE LUKE DERRICK, b. Aug. 12, 1796; m. April 4, 1820, Statica Felton, b. April 1, 1803, daughter of Levi Felton, b. in 1776, in Marlboro, N. H. They had 10 children. Mr. Derrick died in Buffalo, N. Y., April 10, 1865, aged 68 years. Mrs. Statica Derrick died in the same city, April 21, 1884, aged 81 years.

1701.   i. DELIA E., b. Aug. 9, 1821.
1702.   ii. MARY E., b. Feb. 27, 1823.
1703.   iii. LUCINDA S., b. Dec. 26, 1825.
1704.   iv. WINFIELD S., b. Aug. 8, 1827.
1705.   v. LEVI F., b. June 21, 1829.
1706.   vi. MORRIS B., b. May 14, 1831.
1707.   vii. BRYANT B., b. July 21, 1833.
1708.   viii. HELEN M., b. June 16, 1835.
1709.   ix. FREDERICK R., b. Nov. 26, 1837.
1710.   x. HARRIET S., b. Sept. 9, 1841.

(880.) ii. BENJAMIN KEYES FELTON[7], (*Levi[6], John[5], Jacob[4], Samuel[3], John[2], Nathaniel[1],*) b. June 1, 1805; m. Dec. 3, 1826, Julia Ann St. John, b. March 7, 1808; they had 4 children. They lived in N. Y. State, and in Mich. Mrs. Julia

Ann Felton died June 30, 1867, aged 59 years. Mr. Felton died in Clinton, Mich., March 19, 1874, aged almost 69 years.

   1711†. i. CHARLES N., b. Jan. 1, 1828; m. Charlotte A. Ashley.
   1712†. ii. MARY C., b. Jan. 3, 1830; m. Henry M. Vaughan.
   1713. iii. EZRA St. J., b. July 7, 1832; died in California, Oct. 25, 1854, aged 22 years.
   1714†. iv. ELIZA H., b. Dec. 15, 1838; m. George A. Rowland.

(891.) i. LEVI FELTON[7], (Sylvanus[6], John[5], Jacob[4], Samuel[3], John[2], Nathaniel[1],) b. about 1808; m. Laura Joslyn. Resided at Machias, N. Y. Mr. Felton died June 1843, aged 35 years. Mrs. Felton and her two sons moved to Dorr, Mich., before 1872.

   1715. i. SYLVANUS, b. April 7, 1839; m.; is a farmer in Mich.
   1716. ii. ENOS B., b. March 18, 1842; died in Cattaraugus County, N. Y., in 1862, aged 20 years.
   1717. iii. JAMES L., b. Dec. 20, 1843; m. and their dau., Laura Gay, b. in 1878. Mr. Felton is a farmer in Dorr, Mich.

(894.) ii. GEORGE EDDY MANSON, b. Nov. 6, 1797, in Marlboro, Mass., (son of Loring Manson then of Marlboro;) m. Nov. 1821, Harriet Felton, b. Feb. 20, 1802, daughter of Silas and Lucretia (Fay) Felton. Mr. Manson was a merchant with his father-in-law, and afterwards many years under the firm name of Manson & Brigham. Mr. Manson was the second postmaster in Feltonville, and held the office 27 years. He was chosen a selectman of Marlboro in 1835, and served 9 years; chosen again in 1857, and served 4 years. He was Justice of the Peace several years. Mrs. Harriet Manson died June 25, 1868, aged 66 years. He m. second, Oct. 1873, Sarah Jane Phelps, b. April 1827. Mr. Manson died March 17, 1874, aged 76 years. Mrs. Sarah J. Manson, m. second, Nov. 1875, Harrison Leland of North Attleborough, Mass. Mr. Manson's children were:

   1718. i. SILAS F., b. Aug. 7, 1824; died Sept. 4, 1826, aged 2 years.
   1719†. ii. GEORGE L., b. Nov. 6, 1827; m. Lucy Haskell.
   1720. iii. FRANCIS D., b. June 27, 1830; died Sept. 30, 1835, aged 5 years.
   1721†. iv. SILAS F., b. March 25, 1824; m. Josephine L. Priest.

(895.) iii. GEORGE WASHINGTON COOK, b. in Harvard, Mass.; m. Jan. 1, 1827, Charlotte Felton, b. May 10, 1804, daughter of Silas and Lucretia Felton of Feltonville in Marlboro. Mr. Cook was a comb maker, and died in Feltonville, Sept. 3, 1830, aged 31 years. Mrs. Cook m. second, May 20, 1833, Col. Silas Stuart of Boston. He was Lt.-Col. Stuart in 1825, at the time Gen. LaFayette visited Boston and Charlestown. Col. Stuart was a tailor in Boston, and afterwards in Feltonville. Several of his last years he had a sawmill and made shoe boxes. Col. Stuart had several children by a former wife, and his son, Silas H. Stuart, was chosen in 1866, the first town clerk in the new town of Hudson, Mass. Col. Stuart died March 10, 1859, aged 65 years. Mrs. Charlotte Stuart died Aug. 30, 1872; her monument has it: " Entered the Unseen World, August 30, 1872, aged 68 years, 3 months, 20 days." She gave, by will, $500 to the Universalist Publishing House, Boston, Mass. The compiler has a sampler, 16x21 inches, that she worked when 12 years of age.

(896.) i. DEA. ABEL BRIGHAM, b. in Marlboro, Feb. 13, 1797, (youngest son of Ithamar Brigham, Jr.;) m. Jan. 3, 1844, Sally Howe Felton, b. June 26, 1809, daughter of William and Lois (Bartlett) Felton of Marlboro. Mr. Brigham was a farmer in his native town. He had one son and one daughter by a former wife. Dea. Brigham died March 16, 1871, aged 74 years. Mrs. Brigham died Feb. 13, 1878, aged 68 years. She was among the last to use a hand-power loom, and very industrious.

(897.) ii. LEANDER BIGELOW, b. April 13, 1812, (eldest son of Levi Bigelow, Sen., of Marlboro;) m. Nov. 4, 1835, Lucy Felton, b. Sept. 17, 1811, daughter of William and Lois Felton of Marlboro, (No. 409.) When 19 months old she had the misfortune to lose her right hand. She could write, knit and sew. She taught school five summers in Marlboro. The compiler has a Family Record, 28x30 inches, which she worked when 13 years of age.

Mr. Bigelow was formerly a market man in Marlboro, and drove a team weekly to Boston. In 1871, he moved to Worcester, where Mrs. Bigelow died April 5, 1873, aged 61 years. Their children were b. in Marlboro. Mr. Bigelow m. second, Oct. 1876, Mrs. Ann Maria Howe of Marlboro. For several years Mr. Bigelow has been supt. of the Worcester & Shrewsbury railroad at Washington Square, Worcester.

1722. i. MARION O., b. Aug. 17, 1836; m. Jan. 1859, Elbert Leighton, b. in Westford, Mass , in 1837, (son of Albert Leighton,) a shoe manufacturer of the firm of Frank Leighton & Co., of Pepperell, Mass.
1723. ii. ELECTA J., b. Nov. 29, 1839; died Feb. 10, 1842.
1724. iii. VALENA J., b. June 21, 1842; m. May 1867, James L. Mock, a shoe-maker in Pepperell, Mass.
1725. iv. ALTHEA M., b. July 15, 1844; died July 29, 1861, aged 17 years.
1726†. v. JULIAN F., b. April 18, 1846; m. Adelaide Speller.
1727. vi. ORIANA L., b. March 20, 1850; m. Nov. 4, 1880, Albert E. Russell.
1728. vii. LOUIS E., b. June 5, 1852; died Oct. 12, 1853.

(899.) iv. CYRUS FELTON[7], ($William^6$, $Stephen^5$, $Jacob^4$, $Samuel^3$, $John^2$, $Nathaniel^1$,) b. Nov. 20, 1815, (just 26 years after the decease of Jacob Felton, No. 31,) and resides on the homestead, within two furlongs of Marlboro Lake. He m. Feb. 1858, Eliza R. Fay, b. Oct. 5, 1837, in Enfield, Conn., daughter of Elisha R. and Lois (Holkins) Fay, and granddaughter of Daniel Fay of Westboro, Mass. Lived together about 10 years. They had one daughter. Cyrus Felton followed farming till within a few years. In Aug. 1877, had published the Felton Family pamphlet of 19 pages. In 1879 and 1880, he compiled and had printed, in two pamphlets of between 60 and 70 pages, a record of one thousand remarkable events, with the dates of their occurrence, in Marlboro and neighboring towns. Since 1859, has written many articles on antiquarian topics, for the Marlboro newspapers. He is the compiler of this Felton Family Genealogy.

1729. i. LOIS CYRELLA, b. Sept. 21, 1859; died July 13, 1865, aged 5 years, 10 months.

The following lines are on her gravestone:

> Farewell, darling, cherished one, adieu;
> Great our loss, but angels loved you too;
> Sweetly called, to yonder blissful shore;
> To bloom in fresh youth, forevermore.

(901.) vi. CHARLES HASTINGS BRIGHAM, b. June 1, 1822, (son of Hastings and Nancy Brigham;) m. Nov. 1849, Jane B. Felton, b. Feb. 25, 1822, daughter of William and Lois Felton of Marlboro, (No. 409.) Mr. Brigham was a shoe-maker; since 1872, took out a number of patents in the leather business. He resided in Marlboro, where Mrs. Brigham died Oct. 10, 1869, aged 47 years. Had 3 sons. He m. second, June 1, 1870, Mrs. Kezzie (Wood) Johnson of Northboro, b. Oct. 17, 1838, daughter of Miles Wood. She had one son and one daughter by her first husband, Joseph P. Johnson, who was a soldier and wounded Sept. 17, 1862, at Antietam, and died Oct. 4, 1862. Mr. Brigham died Jan. 16, 1877, aged 54 years.

- 1730. i. CHARLES H., b. Aug. 3, 1852; m. June 1879, Hattie A. Blodgett of Leominster, Mass. They reside in that town.
- 1731†. ii. EUGENE O., b. July 25, 1855; m. April 1878, Annie F. Cotting, daughter of John F. Cotting of Marlboro.
- 1732. iii. MORRELL F., b. April 5, 1857; m. Mary E. Grant, Jan. 1883.

By his second wife: Elbert I., b. July 12, 1871, and Ruth M., b. March 28, 1874.

(903.) i. FREDERICK WILLIAM WOOD, b. May 25, 1805, (son of Luther and Lydia (Felton) Wood;) m. about 1829, Ann Maria Dailey of New Berne, N. C., and had 3 dau's. He worked at the leather belting business in N. Y. City, where he died June 1848, aged 43 years.

- 1733. i. LYDIA E., b. Dec. 1829; m. James Perkins, and had two or more children.
- 1734. ii. ANN M., b. Feb. 1832; died Dec. 14, 1855, aged 24 years.
- 1735. iii. HENRIETTA, b. about July 1833; lived about 5 months

(904.) ii. AGER WHEELER of Huntington, Conn., m. Lovinia Stowe Wood, b. April 19, 1807, daughter of Luther and Lydia Wood. Mr. Wheeler was a farmer in that town, and died Feb. 18, 1858, aged 53 years. His mother died in the same place six days afterwards, aged 78 years. Mrs. Wheeler living in 1886, aged 79 years. Had 5 children.

- 1736. i. JULIA A., b. July 23, 1833; m. Nov. 1857, Theodore Beard. They have had 6 or more children.
- 1737. ii. FREDERICK A., b. Jan. 1835; died Feb. 8, 1860, aged 25 years.
- 1738. iii. LOVINIA M., b. in 1837; died Jan. 9, 1856, aged 19 years.
- 1739. iv. LEANDER J., b. Sept. 1843; m. Nov. 1865, Anna A. Chatfield.
- 1740. v. WILLIAM L., b. in 1845; m.

(905.) iii. ALONZO FELTON WOOD, b. June 27, 1824, (son of Luther and Lydia (Felton) Wood;) m. Rachel Hodges and had 8 children. Mr. Wood has been a druggist and apothecary at New Haven, Conn., one-third of a century, and at his decease was the oldest druggist in New Haven. His dwelling house is in West Haven, a village in the town of Orange, and he has represented the town two years in the Legislature. He died of lung trouble, Aug. 28, 1885, aged 61 years.

1741†. i. LUTHER H., b. in 1847; m. Mary V. Townsend.
1742. ii. MARGARET L., b. Jan. 1849; died Sept. 1849.
1743. iii. WALLACE A., b. Aug. 1850; died Jan 9, 1851.
1744. iv. IDA M., b. Nov. 1854; m. June 18, 1884, Edwin A. Hill of New Haven, Conn.
1745. v. FREDERICK W., b. July 23, 1857; died 1863, aged 6 years.
1746. vi. HARRY C., b. Dec. 4, 1859; died Feb. 1861.
1747. vii. ALONZO F., JR., b. March 1862.
1748. viii. JAMES P., b. 1864.

The two youngest sons continue the business at their father's place in New Haven.

(906.) i. AARON HOWE FELTON[7], (Aaron[6], Stephen[5], Jacob[4], Samuel[3], John[2], Nathaniel[1],) b. Feb. 2, 1808; m. April 1829, Martha Adaline Baker, b. Nov. 24, 1811, daughter of Dr. John Baker of Marlboro. He lived several years on his father's place, and took the fourth premium of Middlesex County on his farm one year. He followed teaming several years before he moved to the West Village in Marlboro. He carted many thousand of bricks from Northboro to help make the Cochituate Aqueduct at Natick. They had 12 children; the twins were born at his grandmother's place, Mrs. Lovinah Felton's. Mr. Felton died suddenly, March 31, 1870, aged 62 years.

1749†. i. CAROLINE B., b. April 29, 1830; m. Andrew Phelps.
1750†. ii. CATHERINE B., b. April 29, 1830; m. Frederick Jewett.
1751†. iii. SILAS A., b. Sept. 4, 1832; m. Mary E. Dudley.
1752†. iv. HARRIET A., b. Sept. 16, 1834; m. Roger Boyd.
1753†. v. SARAH D., b. March 26, 1836; m. Elbridge Lewis.
1754. vi. LOVINAH D., b. June 2, 1838; m. April 1857, Levi Cutting; he died in Marlboro, Mass., Jan. 10, 1882, aged 46 years; was a shoe maker.
1755†. vii. JOHN S., b. March 11, 1841; m. Lucia A. Gibbs.

1756†. viii. HENRY F., b. June 25, 1843; m. Jennie Webb.
1757. ix. ANN M., b. July 21, 1845; m. Nov. 1866, Wm. H. Bullard.
1758. x. CHARLES M., b. May 7, 1848; m. Mrs. ——— Twitchell. When in his teens and afterwards a good base ball player.
1759. xi. MARTHA J., b. March 5, 1850; m. Dec. 1876, Fred H. Kirk.
1760. xii. WILLIAM L., b. Aug. 24, 1852; m. Feb. 1877, Etta Atwood.

(909.) iv. LEWIS T. FRYE, b. in Bolton, Dec. 15, 1817, (son of Jonathan and nephew of Thomas Frye of the Bolton Frye School;) m. Dec. 1838, Lovinah Stowe Felton, b. Feb. 13, 1817, daughter of Aaron and Lydia (Bigelow) Felton of Marlboro, (No. 411.) Mr. Frye was a shoe manufacturer in Marlboro, and represented the town in the General Court in 1855. He died Aug. 8, 1856, aged 38 years. Mr. Frye failed once and went through chancery, and afterwards paid the principal of his old debts, and I believe the interest also. They had 4 children.

1761†. i. JOHN A., b. Nov. 27, 1839; m. Elvira F. Russell.
1762‡. ii. CHARLES L., b. April 4, 1842; m. Lucinda E. Howe.
1763†. iii. LUCY, b. Dec. 1, 1844; m. Sept. 1867, Charles Cutting.
1764. iv. MARY L., b. Feb. 17, 1848; died Aug. 18, 1848.

(910.) v. LYMAN BIGELOW FELTON[7], ($Aaron^6$, $Stephen^5$, $Jacob^4$, $Samuel^3$, $John^2$, $Nathaniel^1$,) b. Oct. 20, 1819; m. Eleanor Baker, daughter of Joseph Baker of East Pharsalia, N. Y. Mr. Baker m. Aug. 1812, Pamelia Bartlett, both of Princeton, Mass. Mr. Felton is a carpenter and settled in East Pharsalia.

1765. i. SARAH J., b. in Marlboro, Mass., Sept. 3, 1842; m. Feb. 1869, Floyd C. Childs, b. in Exeter, N. Y., March 1831.
1766. ii. JOSEPH H., b. April 1844; m. Ellen Sumner, b. April 2, 1848, daughter of Daniel Hill Sumner of Chenango County, N. Y.
1767. iii. LEWIS E., b. July 25, 1846; died Aug. 26, 1849.
1768. iv. MARY L., b. Oct. 23, 1848; died Oct. 2, 1849.
1769. v. MARY L., b. Sept. 1850; living in 1881.
1770. vi. ELLEN A., b. Sept. 1852, or 1854; m. J. Newton.
1771. vii. CARRIE E., b. Sept. 1857, or 1858; m. Willie Brooks.
1772. viii. LYDIA A., b. July 1862.

(911.) vi. LAMBERT ADDISON FELTON[7], ($Aaron^6$, $Stephen^5$, $Jacob^4$, $Samuel^3$, $John^2$, $Nathaniel^1$,) b. March 8, 1822; m. Harriet E. Bliss of Marlboro, b. in 1822. He was a shoemaker and lived in several places in Marlboro, his native town, where he died June 10, 1859, aged 37 years. Mr. Felton and his family lived a few years in Westboro and Upton. They had 4 children. Mrs. Harriet E. Felton m. second, Sylvanus Stone of Sturbridge, Mass.; his second m.; he had 10 childen by his former wife, the youngest born in 1846.

1773. i. ANGELINE E., b. June 12, 1843; m. July 1860, Daniel H. Sawyer of Berlin, Mass.
1774. ii. LAMBERT E., b. Sept. 24, 1846; under the name of Edgar L. Felton, he enlisted in the army from Leicester, Mass., June 1864, and was discharged July 1865, at the close of the war. He died at Worcester, April 1871, aged 24 years, and was buried at Marlboro.
1775. iii. ELLA B., b. March 27, 1849; m. Charles Fay of Southboro, Mass.
1776. iv. MARY S., b. June 1, 1851; m. Jan. 1870, Charles Henry Johnson. Mrs. Susie M. Johnson died in Marlboro, Aug. 18, 1879, aged 28 years; left one child. Mr. Johnson m. second, Jan. 1882, Mrs. Lelia, daughter of Dr. Charles Putnam of Marlboro, Mass.

(912.) vii. LEWIS FELTON[7], ($Aaron^6$, $Stephen^5$, $Jacob^4$, $Samuel^3$, $John^2$, $Nathaniel^1$,) b. Feb. 26, 1824; m. March 1847, Mary Lewis Stowe, b. Nov. 15, 1826, daughter of Rufus and Thankful (Brigham) Stowe of Marlboro. He was a shoe manufacturer, formerly of the firm of Whitney, Felton & Chipman of Marlboro, and all three died within one year. Mr. Felton deceased last, April 1, 1877, aged 53 years; the three between 50 and 60 years of age. Their children were:

1777. i. HARRIET A., b. Feb. 28, 1848; m. Dec. 1868, Dallas Polk Mahan of Marlboro.
1778. ii. ARTHUR I., b. July 6, 1851; m. Feb. 1876, Katie C. Davis, daughter of Benj. Davis of Warren, Me.
1779. iii. FREDERICK L., b. July 27, 1857.

(913.) i. HENRY OTIS FELTON[7], ($Jacob^6$, $Stephen^5$, $Jacob^4$, $Samuel^3$, $John^2$, $Nathaniel^1$,) b. in Marlboro, Dec. 12, 1814; m. May 1840, Charlotte Phelps of Lunenburg, Mass., b. July 21, 1818. He was a carpenter, and had charge of a saw-mill in Lunenburg several years, and lost a few of his fingers. Some 30 years ago he purchased what was known as Barber's grist and saw-mills, and later Pollard's mills at West Berlin, Mass., and moved to the place. Since Mr. Felton has so thoroughly repaired them, are sometimes called Felton's mills.

1780.	i.	MARIA C., b. March 23, 1841, in Townsend, Mass.; m. Jan. 1869, Levi Babcock of Berlin. Mrs. Babcock died Aug. 15, 1885, aged 44 years.
1781.	ii.	MARY E., b. April 21, 1843; a school teacher; taught in Lancaster, Clinton, Hudson and Maynard, Mass.
1782.	iii.	GEORGE H., b. Aug. 2, 1847; m. Aug. 1884, Mrs. Sarah Mackey of Northboro, Mass.
1783.	iv.	SARAH A., b. April 22, 1850; died March 2, 1852.
1784.	v.	ADDIE L., b. Nov. 6, 1854.

(915.) iii. MERRICK FELTON[7], (Jacob[6], Stephen[5], Jacob[4], Samuel[3], John[2], Nathaniel[1],) b. in Princeton, Mass., Aug. 31, 1823; m. Elizabeth Page b. March 18, 1824, daughter of Enoch and Hannah Page of Lunenburg, Mass. He was a carpenter and has worked in Southboro, Clinton and Lawrence, Mass. Some 30 years ago he settled on his father's farm in west part of Berlin, Mass., where he built him a good substantial barn. Mrs. Felton died Sept. 30, 1871, aged 47 years. Had 6 children. He m. second, Aug. 31, 1872, Mary B. Priest of Clinton.

1785.	i.	CHARLES M., b. Jan. 25, 1850; died Jan. 27, same month.
1786.	ii.	MARTHA E., b. Oct. 14, 1852; m. Sept. 1869, George H. Dyer. Was divorced and in April 1873, had her name changed to Martha E. Felton.
1787.	iii.	ABBOTT S., b. Aug. 14, 1855; m. March 1882.
1788.	iv.	MARION A., b. Aug. 30, 1858; m. April 1885, Charles G. Learned.
1789.	v.	TRUMAN P., b. Jan. 25, 1862.
1790.	vi.	LUCINDA E., b. Oct. 10, 1864.

(916.) i. HEMAN SMITH, of Massena, N. Y., m. in 1851, Henrietta N. Felton, b. Nov. 21, 1820, daughter of Stephen and Sally (Weeks) Felton of Massena, (No. 413.) They settled in the place. Mrs. Smith died Jan. 11, 1865, aged 44 years. They had 2 daughters. About 1869, Mr. Smith with his youngest daughter moved to Faribault County, Minn.

1791. i. MARY, b. in 1852; m. March 1875, Frederick Freeman of Westville, N. Y. They lived a few years on their great-grandfather's place in Massena, St. Lawrence County, N. Y.
1792. ii. IDA, b. in 1855; went to Minn. with her father.

(917.) ii. SILAS ADDISON FELTON[7], (*Stephen*[6], *Stephen*[5], *Jacob*[4], *Samuel*[3], *John*[2], *Nathaniel*[1],) b. Feb. 7, 1825; m. Laura Day, b. Aug. 27, 1825, daughter of Edward Day of Massena. They lived many years on Mr. Day's farm. In 1873, they moved to Potsdam, in the same county, and soon he was engaged in the grocery trade in that town, as one of the firm of Stinson & Felton. In May 1878, the firm name of Felton & Senter was formed. Had one son.

1793†. i. LUCIUS E., b. in 1849; graduated at Burlington College.

(919.) i. JOHN POTTER, m. Aug. 17, 1836, Mary E. Felton, b. Jan. 1, 1815, daughter of Jacob and Elizabeth (Morse) Felton of Fitzwilliam, N. H., (No. 417.) After living several years in that town, they moved to Quincy, Ill., where they now reside. They had one son b. in Fitzwilliam.

1794. i. JOHN F., b. Oct. 17, 1838.
1795. ii. A daughter.

(922.) i. GEORGE CHRISTOPHER LORD of Wiscasset, Me., b. May 26, 1807; m. Oct. 11, 1832, Elizabeth Monroe Felton, b. April 30, 1813, daughter of Artemus Felton of Fitzwilliam and of Boston. Mr. Lord was a merchant in Boston; he died at West Roxbury, May 13, 1864, aged 57 years. They had 9 children, all b. in Boston. Mrs. Lord died Oct. 11, 1882, aged 69 years, just 50 years after she was married.

1796. i. GEORGE A., b. Feb. 15, 1834; m. Mary Elizabeth Wason, Sept. 18, 1862.
1796½. ii. CHARLES M., b. July 28, 1836; died Dec. 3, 1846, aged 10 years.
1797. iii. FRANCIS C., b. July 11, 1838; m. Juliette Thompson Longee, June 21, 1883.
1798. iv. WILLIAM H., b. Aug. 20, 1840; he was a soldier in the Union army; he m. Dec. 29, 1870, Mary Augusta Endicott; reside at Dedham, Mass.; they have two sons.
1798½. v. HORACE F., b. Dec. 3, 1843; died March 19, 1845.
1799. vi. SARAH E., b. May 16, 1846.

1800. vii. ADELAIDE M., twin, b. May 16, 1846.
1801. viii. JANET C., b. April 16, 1850; m. Horace Moody, June 1882; reside in Lowell, Mass.
1801½. ix. CHARLES H., b. Feb. 21, 1853; died Aug. 9, 1853.

(923.) ii. LEVI HASKELL, b. in 1806, (son of Levi Haskell who died suddenly in Fitzwilliam, Nov. 1830, aged 61 years,) m. Lydia Relief Felton, b. May 21, 1816, daughter of Artemus Felton, (No. 418.) They lived in Fitzwilliam, where Mrs. Haskell died June 21, 1847, aged 31 years. Had one son. Mr. Haskell m. second, Sarah Amelia ———, and had several children. He died Aug. 4, 1865, aged 59 years.

1802. i. FREDERICK H., b. Feb. 27, 1842.

(924.) iii. JOSEPH B. WHALL of Boston, m. Sept. 30, 1841, Sarah Hewes Felton, b. July 23, 1822, daughter of Artemus and Sally (Clark) Felton of Boston. Mrs. Whall died Feb. 1845, aged 22 years. Had one son.

1802½. i. A son, b. Dec. 22, 1844; died Feb. 3, 1876, aged 31 years.

(925.) iv. DANIEL F. LONG of Boston, m. Nov. 17, 1857, Louisa Clark Felton, b. April 30, 1833, daughter of Artemus and Sally (Clark) Felton of Boston. They have one son. In 1885, Mr. Long was the proprietor of "The Phinney Book Store," Montpelier, Vt.

1802¾. i. FREDERICK D., b. Nov. 15, 1864.

(926.) i. LYMAN SCOTT FELTON[7], (*Lyman*[6], *Matthias*[5], *Jacob*[4], *Samuel*[3], *John*[2], *Nathaniel*[1],) b. Jan. 1815; m. Clarissa Phillips of Fitzwilliam, N. H. No issue. He m. second, Sarah Bruce, daughter of Dexter and Harriet (Gates) Bruce of Winchendon, Mass. Had 3 children. He was a harness maker and has resided in several places, but most of the time since 1866, in West Boylston, Mass. He died there in the fall of 1883, aged nearly 68 years.

1803. i. ALBERT W., the first child, lived 5 years, 10 months.
1804. ii. ELLA M., b. June 24, 1860; a school teacher, commenced teaching in 1879.
1805. iii. ARTHUR M., b. Sept. 1864; died Oct. 1865.

(927.) ii. MATTHIAS BRETT FELTON[7], (*Lyman*[6], *Matthias*[5], *Jacob*[4], *Samuel*[3], *John*[2], *Nathaniel*[1],) b. Oct. 18, 1819; m. Aug. 1841, Lurena Bent of Fitzwilliam. He was a trunk and harness maker in F. two years. In 1843, moved to Winchendon, Mass.; in 1851, was clerk of the fire engine company. In 1859, moved to Northfield, Mass. Was in Vineland, N. J., in 1866, and in Camden, N. J., in 1869, where he had a provision market. Have had 5 children.

- 1806. i. CLARENCE M., b. July 9, 1842; died Dec. 26, 1842.
- 1807. ii. GEORGE G., b. May 21, 1845; was in the Union army from Northfield, Mass., in 1862 and 1863. He m. Esther M. Long, and had one son, Willie Allan, b. at Camden, N. J., April 27, 1872.
- 1808. iii. ALDEN P., b. Sept. 5, 1849; died Oct. 26, 1849.
- 1809. iv. CHARLES H., b. Aug. 24, 1855; m. Sept. 4, 1879, Mary J. Sanderson of Camden, N. J. Have two children.
- 1810. v. ERNEST E., b. June 28, 1860; died at Gardner, Mass., Oct. 1881, aged 21 years.

(929.) iv. HENRY CASE of South Orange, Mass., m. Sarah R. Felton, b. Feb. 1826, daughter of Lyman Felton of Fitzwilliam and Winchester, N. H. They had one son. Mrs. Case m. second, Albert P. Thompson of Swansea, N. H., and had 4 children. Mrs. Thompson m. third, Stillman Holden of Gardner, Mass. They now reside in Erving, Mass.

- 1810½. i. A son by Mr. Case.
- 1811. ii. FRANK P, b. May 1851.
- 1812. iii. ELLA E., b. Dec. 1852.
- 1813. iv. GEORGE L., b. Aug. 1856.
- 1814. v. ANNA M., b. June 1858; m. Frank Dame.

(932.) i. SAMUEL BROWN MAYNARD, b. July 20, 1807, son of Hollon Maynard, Jr., of Northboro; m. Feb. 1840, Sally Rice, b. Oct. 5, 1810, daughter of Edward and Susanna (Felton) Rice of Marlboro, (No. 421.) Mr. Maynard m. first, Merena Stratton of Northboro, and had one son, Wm. Henry, b. Oct. 31, 1832; died Aug. 23, 1836. Mrs. Merena Maynard died in Marlboro, June 25, 1839, aged 33 years. He was a sleigh maker and moved to Marlboro, in 1832, and resided the north side of Marlboro Lake. He was an insurance agent 25 years before 1880, and rode most every day on the cars between Marlboro and Boston. He was a deacon in the West (Unitarian) church, and a Justice of the Peace. Deacon Maynard died Jan. 31, 1882, aged 74 years.

- 1815†. i. SARAH M., b. June 23, 1842; m. Joseph V. Jackman.
- 1816. ii. SAMUEL N., b. Dec. 12, 1843; died Nov. 22, 1844.

1817. iii. EDWARD R., b. March 16. 1846 ; m. Marion Park; he died Oct. 1882. Mrs. Maynard died Oct. 1881, aged 28 years; left 2 daughters.
1818. iv. CHARLES F., b. March 5. 1848 ; m. May 1874, Carrie B. Wilson.
1819. v. SAMUEL B., JR., b. Dec. 6, 1849 ; died Sept. 5, 1852.
1820. vi. STEPHEN H., b. Aug. 24, 1852.

(834.) iii. EDWARD GERSHOM RICE, b. Jan. 23, 1814, son of Edward and Susanna Rice of Marlboro, m. May 1844, Sophia Huntington of Spencer, Mass. Mr. Rice is a farmer on his father's place in the west part of Marlboro. Had 7 children ; the three oldest died in one month of scarlet fever and canker. Mrs. Sophia Rice was b. March 26, 1816.

1821. i. HARRIET A., b. April 16, 1845 ; died Aug. 7, 1851, aged 6 years.
1822. ii. SUSANNA S., b. Feb. 13, 1848 ; died Aug. 14, 1851, aged 3 years.
1823. iii. CORDELIA H., b. Oct. 25, 1849 ; died Aug. 17, 1851.
1824. iv. JULIA A. H., b. Dec. 16, 1851; taught school several terms ; m. Dec. 1874, John Calvin Hastings, b. Aug. 17, 1849, son of Calvin Hastings, Jr., of Northboro ; is a merchant at Oakdale, West Boylston, Mass. Mrs. Hastings died May 22, 1884, aged 32 years.
1825. v. CORDELIA H., b. Jan. 25, 1854 ; died Aug. 23, 1877, aged 23 years.
1826. vi. HENRIETTA A., b. March 17, 1857 ; died Aug. 22, 1884, aged 27 years.
1827. vii. EDWARD H., b. May 16, 1859 ; m. Feb. 1882, Anella L. Bruce ; she died in Hudson, March 4, 1885, aged 23 years. He m. second, June 1885, Josie L. Tubbs.

(935.) iv. WILLIAM STRATTON, b. Jan. 16, 1809, (son of Windsor Stratton of Northboro ;) m. Jan. 1844, Susan Barnard Rice, b. Jan. 23, 1814, daughter of Edward and Susanna (Felton) Rice of Marlboro. He was a farmer on his father's place in Northboro, near Bartlett's mills. He was a selectman in 1845, 1847 and 1848. He died in 1875, aged 66 years. Mrs. Susan B. Stratton died Sept. 18, 1878, aged 64 years ; was a twin. They had 4 children.

1828. i. GEORGE D., b. Aug. 14, 1845; m. June 1879, Ellen Maria Ballou; was a farmer on his father's place in Northboro, Mass.; he died Feb. 22, 1886, aged 41 years. He fell through an elevator well about a week before his death. Had two children.
1829. ii. ELLEN M., b. Dec. 10, 1850; died Feb. 16, 1852.
1830. iii. WILLIAM E., b. Sept. 28, 1853.
1831. iv. SUSAN M., twin, b. Sept. 28, 1853; m. Jan. 1880, George F. Rice, son of Curtis Rice of Northboro.

(936.) v. OZIAS HUNTINGTON, b. Nov. 10, 1812, (son of Azel and Hannah Huntington of Spencer, Mass.;) m. June 1844, Mary Rice, b. March 26, 1816, daughter of Edward and Susanna Rice, (No. 421.) They settled at Spencer. Moved to Marlboro before 1860. A shoe-maker and farmer. Had 4 children.

1832. i. MARY A., b. May 20, 1845; m. June 1870, Henry Coffeen; she died at Troy, N. Y., Aug. 4, 1871, aged 26 years.
1833. ii. WILLIAM B., b. Feb. 3, 1847.
1834†. iii. EMMA S., b. Oct. 4, 1851; m. Ira E. Parmenter.
1835. iv. HERBERT R., b. Sept. 4, 1861, in Marlboro.

(937.) vi. GEORGE EMERSON RICE, b. May 29, 1818, (son of Edward and Susanna Rice, (No. 421);) m. Jan. 1851, Sarah Ann Brigham b. Dec. 1, 1824, daughter of Henry Brigham, of Northboro. They had 4 children. Mrs. Rice died Aug. 30, 1862, aged 37 years. He m. second, Nov. 1863, Mary Augusta Allen, b. Aug. 21, 1840, daughter of Silas Allen of Marlboro. Mr. Rice was a shoe-maker and farmer. His place was adjoining his father's farm on the north side. Had 6 children by his last wife. He died May 6, 1880, aged 62 years. Mrs. Rice, with her children, soon afterwards moved to Northboro.

1836. i. MARY S., b. Feb. 5, 1852.
1837. ii. CHARLES E., b. Jan. 16, 1854; died July 19, 1877, aged 23 years.
1838. iii. SARAH E., b. Sept. 2, 1857; m. Oct. 1881, Chas. H. Sloan.
1839. iv. A son b. Aug. 1862; died Oct. 12, 1862, aged 9 weeks.
1840. v. HATTIE L., b. Nov. 25, 1864.
1841. vi. BERTHA M., b. Aug. 28, 1866.
1842. vii. WALTER E., b. July 4, 1868.
1843. viii. GEORGE H., b. Aug. 12, 1871.

1844. ix. EDITH E., b. June 16, 1873.
1845. x. HERMAN F., b. June 22, 1876.

(939.) ii. LUTHER HARVEY FELTON[7], (*Luther*[6], *Joel*[5], *Jacob*[4], *Samuel*[3], *John*[2], *Nathaniel*[1],) b. in Boston, Feb. 7, 1821; m. Oct. 13, 1845, Sarah P. Withington, b. Dec. 10, 1824, daughter of Josiah Withington of Boston. Mr. Felton is a distiller in Boston. He was at first of the firm of Luther Felton & Son; for the last 20 years, Luther H. Felton & Son. Mr. Felton's step-mother, Mrs. Mary Felton, (named on page 91,) died in May 1886, aged 87 years.

 1846. i. CLARA A., b. Jan. 1847; died July 31, 1847, aged 6 months.
 1847†. ii. FREDERICK L., b. Sept. 9, 1849; m. Laura B. Woodworth.
 1848. iii. ARTHUR W., b. Aug. 25, 1853.
 1849. iv. HARRIET G., b. Sept. 17, 1855; m. May 4, 1876, Charles William Leatherbee of West Newton, son of William H. Leatherbee of Boston. One son, Clifton Felton, b. Dec. 15, 1879.

(943.) iii. REV. JOSEPH BARBER of Bolton, Mass., b. in Medway about 1831, (son of Cyrus and Martha Barber;) m. Nov. 27, 1870, Ann Sophia Felton, b. June 22, 1833, dau. of Joel and Electa Felton of Bolton. Mr. Barber is a Baptist minister. He m. first, Julia A. Putnam, daughter of Silvanus Putnam of Sutton; she died in Bolton, Dec. 2, 1869, aged 36 years, 10 months. Mr. Barber preached in Bridgewater, Mass., a few years, and in 1876 removed to Westminster, Mass. In 1885, he removed to Fayville, (Southboro,) Mass.

 1850. i. ESTELLA S., b. Oct. 29, 1874.

(944.) iv. WILLIAM NEWELL FELTON[7], (*Joel*[6], *Joel*[5], *Jacob*[4], *Samuel*[3], *John*[2], *Nathaniel*[1],) b. Dec. 25, 1835; m. July 1859, Sarah Melinda Blood, b. Jan. 10, 1840, daughter of Amos Fiske Blood. He is a farmer in Bolton, and has been president of the Farmers and Mechanics' Club in that town. Had 4 children.

 1851. i. WILLIAM H., b. Feb. 28, 1860; m.
 1852. ii. EVERETT M., b. July 9, 1865; m. Oct. 1885, Gertrude Hodges of Clinton.
 1853. iii. A child born and died in Jan. 1867.
 1854. iv. ARTHUR S., b. Dec. 17, 1870.

(947.) ii. GEORGE NEWELL FELTON[7], (*George*[6], *Joel*[5], *Jacob*[4], *Samuel*[3], *John*[2], *Nathaniel*[1],) b. Sept. 27, 1832; m. Jan.

1854, Sally M. Wing, daughter of Nelson Wing of Savoy, Mass. She died in Northfield, Mass., in 1856, aged 26 years. He m. second, Jan. 1857, Mrs. Margaret Lyman of Northfield; she died in 1867. He m. third, Jan. 1868, Amelia Lyman, daughter of Joseph and Margaret Lyman. His children were :

 1855. i. NEWELL M., b. Dec. 1854; m. June 1879, Mabel Nellie Johnson, b. May 18, 1860, daughter of Joseph P. Johnson.
 1856. ii. LIZZIE A.
 1857. iii. MARY E.
 1858. iv. GEORGE W.
 1859. v. CHARLES H., b. Aug. 1861; died next month.
 1860. vi. EFFIE G.

(948.) iii. MINOT RICE, b. in Marlboro, June 11, 1823, a twin, son of Abel Rice of that town; m. Sept. 1851, Mary Berry Felton, b. in 1833, daughter of George and Rachel Felton of Marlboro. After living in his native town several years, they moved to Worcester. Several years ago kept a a provision market in that city. Had one son.

 1861†. FRANKLIN P., b. in Marlboro, July 29, 1852.

(953.) ii. GEORGE LEVI FELTON^7, ($Levi^6$, $Joel^5$, $Jacob^4$, $Samuel^3$, $John^2$, $Nathaniel^1$,) b. about 1829; m. Martha L. ———. He was living at Brooklyn, N. Y., several years before 1856. He purchased a place in Wilbraham, Mass., and resided there from 1858 to 1867; soon afterwards moved back to Brooklyn or N. Y. City, and established an "Agents' Supply Depot," where he died suddenly in 1875, aged 46 years. They had 5 children, three living in 1875.

 1862. i. LEWIS D.
 1863. ii. GEORGE L., JR.
 1864. iii. One daughter, living in 1875.

(954.) i. AUSTIN W. GOODALE of Millbury, Mass., m. Nov. 27, 1854, Fanny Felton, b. Aug. 14, 1833, daughter of Matthias Felton then of that town. Mrs. Fanny Goodale died Nov. 29, 1860, aged 27 years. Left one child. Mr. Goodale moved to Philadelphia, Pa., in 1861, with his father-in-law.

(958.) ii. GEORGE HENRY FELTON^7, ($John^6$, $Joel^5$, $Jacob^4$, $Samuel^3$, $John^2$, $Nathaniel^1$,) b. about Aug. 1839; m. June 2, 1862, Euphema A. Choate of Boston, daughter of Isaac C. Choate of Kendall's Mills, Me.; he died at Providence, R. I.,

March 19, 1871, aged 31 years. 7 months. It is said Mrs. E. A. Felton m. second ―――― Johnson. Mr. and Mrs. Felton left one son.

1864½.   i. Edward B., b. Aug. 4, 1865.

(974.)   i. DANIEL HASKELL, b. July 15, 1813; m. June 11, 1851, Phebe M. Felton, b. Oct. 4, 1816, daughter of John S. and Sally (Wood) Felton of Danvers, Mass., (No. 438.) They had one son. Mr. Haskell m. first, in 1831, Lucy B. Mansfield ; had 4 children.

1865.   i. George F., b. May 11, 1852.

(975.)   ii. FRANKLIN UPTON, b. in Salem, Jan. 28, 1819, (son of Robert Upton ;) m. Jan. 28, 1840, (just 21 years of age,) to Sarah Augusta Felton, b. Sept. 29, 1818, daughter of John S. and Sally (Wood) Felton. Their children were born in South Danvers, now Peabody.

1866.   i. Albert F., b. Aug. 18, 1842.
1867.   ii. Isabel A., b. Sept. 17, 1844 ; m. Nov., 1865, George H. Burt.
1868.   iii. Oscar W., b. Nov. 6, or 14, 1846.
1869.   iv. Willard D., b. Dec. 1, 1849 ; drowned July 28, 1851.
1870.   v Caroline E., b. Dec. 23, 1852 ; died Dec. 27, 1852.

(982.)   i. MARTIN PUTNAM, b. Dec. 5, 1801, son of Rufus and Polly (Felton) Putnam of the north part of Hopkinton, N. H. He m. Margaret Butler, daughter of Bela and Sarah Butler of Hopkinton, Nov. 24, 1831. They had 5 children. Mr. Putnam was a farmer and blacksmith. He was captain of the militia, and selectman of Hopkinton. He died May 6, 1845, aged 44 years. They had several children. One daughter married a son of Moses and Martha (Felton) Wilson of Danvers. Capt. Martin Putnam's children were :

1870. *a.*   i. Margaret E.; sup. m. ―――― Wilson.
1870. *b.*   ii. James M.; m. Sarah C. Davis of Hopkinton, N. H.
1870. *c.*   iii. Amos.
1870. *d.*   iv. Charles ; m. ―――― Eastman of Hopkinton, N. H.
1870. *e.*   v. Eliza J.

(983.)   ii. HERRICK PUTNAM, b. Sept. 11, 1803, son of Rufus and Polly (Felton) Putnam of Hopkinton, N. H,

He m. Sept. 27, 1827, Rachel Keyer of Sutton, N. H. Had several children. Their son, Augustus R. Putnam was town clerk of Warner from March 1872 to March 1877, and represented the town in the Legislature, 1881 and 1882.

Herrick Putnam died July 14, 1861, aged 58 years. His widow was living in Warner, N. H., in 1883.

(986.) v. RUFUS PUTNAM, JR., b. Sept. 27, 1813, son of Rufus and Polly (Felton) Putnam, and grandson of Dr. James P. and Molly (Herrick) Putnam of Danvers, Mass.; m. Nov. 17, 1835, Apphice Clark of Warner; she died Jan. 12, 1837. He m. second, June 1839, Harriet Bailey, or Daily, of Warner, N. H.; she died Oct. 11, 1848; left two sons, Joseph and William. Rufus Putnam m. third, Dec., about 1850, to Lydia C. Goss of Henniker, N. H., and had one son, Charles R. Putnam of Contoocook, N. H.

(988.) i. JAMES PORTER FELTON[7], (*James*[6], *Asa*[5], *Samuel*[4], *Samuel*[3], *John*[2], *Nathaniel*[1],) b. Feb. 15, 1828; supposed m. Caroline R. ———. Mrs. Felton was a widow in Danvers in 1865. He died July 10, 1855, aged 27 years.

(990.) iii. JOSEPH W. MEAD of Salem, m. Dec. 1853, Lydia Ann Felton of North Danvers, b. Sept. 1, 1832, dau. of James and Sophronia (Webb) Felton of Danvers.

(992.) v. LEWIS EDWARD FELTON[7], (*James*[6], *Asa*[5], *Samuel*[4], *Samuel*[3], *John*[2], *Nathaniel*[1],) b. July 23, 1840; m. Jan. 28, 1862, Martha J. Day, b. Dec. 17, 1843. He was, a few years ago, of the firm of Day & Felton, brick-makers, of Danversport, Mass.

1871. i. ANNIE P., b. Feb. 1, 1863; a school teacher in 1882.
1872. ii. CARRIE E., b. Nov. 25, 1868.

(1009.) i. WILLIAM FILKINS, m. Laura M. Felton, b. Dec. 1801, daughter of William W. and Sally (Garry) Felton, (No. 462.) They resided many years in N. Y. State; moved to Mich., about 1837. They have had five children; one son.

1873. i. JAMES; living at Pittsford, Hillsdale County, Mich., in 1878.

(1010.) ii. CALEB SMITH of Orwell, Vt., m. second, Eliza M. Felton, b. June 1805, daughter of William W. and Sally Felton, (No. 462.) They resided at Orwell, Vt.; they had 4 children, 3 living in 1878. After Mr. Smith's decease, Mrs. Smith m. second, Solomon Millington of Vt., his second wife. and moved to Joliet, Ill., where they were living in 1856. Caleb Smith's first wife was Abigail Pierce, daughter of Caleb and Abigail (Felton) Pierce.

(1011.) iii. WILLIAM FLAGG FELTON[7], (*William W.[6], Daniel[5], David[4], Samuel[3], John[2], Nathaniel[1],*) b. Sept. 1807; m. Annis Strong, Sept. 5, 1815, in McArthur, Ohio. Mr. Felton lived with Caleb Smith of Orwell, Vt., (No. 543,) 1821 to 1828. When he was 21 years of age Mr. Smith gave him $100 and two suits of clothes made of homespun cloth. He worked a few years for 10 to 11 dollars per month in summer and 6 dollars in winter till 1833, when 26 years of age, he went to Ohio with 300 dollars. In Ohio, was either a farmer or a merchant. Mrs. Annis Felton died Feb. 27, 1868, aged 52 years. He m. second, Martha J. McCabe of Vinton County, Ohio. They were living a few years ago. Their 6 children were:

1874. i. JEHIEL; a merchant in McArthur, Ohio.
1875. ii. ELIZABETH; died at the age 19 years.
1876. iii. WILLIAM F., JR.; died young, aged one year.
1877. iv. JOSEPH; a merchant in McArthur.
1878. v. NETTIE, b. July 4, 1873.
1879. vi. THOMAS, b. April 1876.

(1014.) vi. RUSSELL CLARK, m. Sarah Ann Felton, b. June 1813, daughter of William W. and Sally Felton, (No. 462.) Mrs. Clark died in Mich., Nov. 1853, aged 40 years. They had 2 children, one living in 1878.

(1015.) vii. WILLIAM PENFIELD, m. Lucinda Felton, b. Dec. 1816, youngest daughter of William W. and Sally Felton. They had 7 children, 5 of them sons and two of them in the late Union army.

(1025.) x. SIMEON Y. FELTON[7], (*Lyman[6], Daniel[5], David[4], Samuel[3], John[2], Nathaniel[1],*) b. Jan. 15, 1829; m. and settled on his father's place in Orwell, Vt.

(1027.) xii. ASA YOUNG FELTON[7], (*Lyman[6], Daniel[5], David[4], Samuel[3], John[2], Nathaniel[1],*) b. Nov. 23, 1835; m. Oct. 15, 1861, Hortensia Saloma Douglas, b. Oct. 15, 1840, daughter of Amos Douglas. She died at Plainview, Minn., Sept. 11, 1863, aged 23 years. He m. second, and had 4 children living in 1880.
Feb. 9, 1875, Asa Y. Felton of Plainview, Minn., obtained a patent for a "Fanning Mill," No. 159–569.

(1046.) iii. JONATHAN JOHNSON, b. Oct. 1, 1825, in

Petersham, son of Henry Johnson of Athol, and grandson of Jonathan and Rachel (Felton) Johnson of Petersham, Mass. He m. Dec. 26, 1854, in Montague, Climena Marsh. He is agent for several newspapers, and resides at Greenfield, Mass. He is in height, I believe, 6 feet, 5 inches. They have 4 children.

- 1880. i. CALVIN H., b. Oct. 18, 1855, in Montague.
- 1881. ii. JAMES C., b. Aug. 3, 1857, in Montague.
- 1882. iii. JULIA I., b. July 20, 1859, in Sunderland.
- 1883. iv. DARWIN M., b. Jan. 27, 1861, in South Deerfield.

(1057.) i. TOBIN FRENCH of Brighton, m. Aug. 1835, Jane Elizabeth Damon, b. Feb. 22, 1815, daughter of Charles and Lydia Damon of Wayland, Mass., (No. 490.) They reside at Cochituate, south part of Wayland. Had 4 children.

- 1884. i. CHARLES; m. Mary Parks.
- 1885. ii. ADALINE; m. George Barrett.
- 1886. iii. JOHN; m. Sarah Clark.
- 1887. iv. EMILY; m. Albert King.

(1058.) ii. JAMES M. BENT, b. May 19, 1812; m. in 1838, Martha T. Damon, b. July 22, 1817, daughter of Charles and Lydia Damon of Wayland. Mr. Bent is a shoe manufacturer at Cochituate and represented the town of Wayland in the General Court in 1857.

About 1830, William and James M. Bent commenced the manufacture of shoes and continued 50 years, being the leading business house in the village. The following from a newspaper of 1879: "James M. Bent, the Cochituate boot and shoe manufacturer, has put a pleasure steamer upon the Sudbury river to run between Wayland and Billerica as he pleases." Their children were:

- 1888. i. ANN M.; m. William Lovejoy.
- 1889. ii. WILLIAM H., b. March 1, 1840; m. Theresa Loker; is a shoe manufacturer, and represented Wayland in the Legislature in 1875.
- 1890. iii. JAMES A.; m. Anna Dudley.
- 1891. iv. THOMAS D., b. Nov. 14, 1844.
- 1892. v. ABBY; m. George M. Fairbanks.
- 1893. vi. MYRON W., b. Sept. 19, 1849; m. Cornelia Dudley; he was a representative from Wayland in 1878.
- 1894. vii. RALPH, b. about 1853; m. Isabella Bond.

(1059.) iii. STEPHEN STANTON, m. Dec. 2, 1839, Lydia Ann Lucy Damon, b. July 17, 1819, daughter of Chas.

and Lydia Damon. They had 11 children at Cochituate; buried 9 before 1872, part of them in 6 months of diphtheria. Two living.

 1895. i. FRANCES ; a daughter living in 1872.
 1896. ii. ELIZABETH ; living in 1872.

(1060.) iv CHARLES ROSWELL DAMON, b. in Wayland, (then called East Sudbury,) Oct. 3, 1821, son of Charles and Lydia Damon; m. in 1845, Emily Estabrook of New Ipswich, N. H. He was the first postmaster in Cochituate, appointed in 1846, and held the office in 1856. He was a representative from Wayland in 1866 and 1867 ; was Justice of the Peace in 1877. Mr. Damon m. second, Mary Walker ; she died in Cochituate, Oct. 1, 1876, aged 48 or 49 years. Sup. he m. third, June 1879, Jennie M. Alexander of South Framingham, Mass.

(1079.) i. JOSEPH PECORNEY, b. Dec. 16, 1809, son of Joseph and Hannah (Felton) Pecorney, (No. 494;) m. May 1832, Lydia Clapp. They had 6 children. He was landlord of the tavern at Hanover Four Corners, and the only one in operation in that town in 1853. He died June 6, 1854, aged 44 years. Mrs. Lydia Pecorney died March 12, 1857, aged 45 years.

 1897. i. JOSEPH E.; died in 1834.
 1898. ii. AUGUSTINE P., b. Dec. 22, 1835 ; drowned Aug. 29, 1850, aged 14 years.
 1899. iii. CERENA C., b. Jan. 3, 1838 ; m. before Sept. 1859.
 1900. iv. EUNICE A., b. Aug. 8, 1841 ; m. Sept. 1859, Samuel Loring of Hingham.
 1901. v. JOSEPH E., b. in 1843 ; died in 1846.
 1902. vi. LYDIA A., b. April 7, 1847.

(1081.) iii. JAMES M. JACOBS, b. March 12, 1818, son of Thomas M. and Hannah (Felton) Jacobs of West Scituate, Mass.; m. Sept. 9, 1849, Caroline E. Handley ; she died March 26, 1852, aged 26 years. He m. second, March 31, 1857, Harriet C. Johnson. He was a merchant tailor in Boston many years, of the well-known house of Jacobs & Deane. He was one of the deacons of Rev. A. A. Miner's church. Dea. Jacobs died suddenly Sept. 23, 1883, aged 65 years. Had one child by his first wife and 5 by his last.

 1903. i. FRANCES A., b. Nov. 25, 1851 ; m. April 29, 1875, Frederick O. Mendum.
 1904. ii. ADDIE R., b. Jan. 31, 1858 ; m. Oct. 30, 1884, Arthur Philip French.

1905. iii. HATTIE C., b. Dec. 12, 1860; m. Feb. 4, 1885, Edward F. Keeleo.
1906. iv. MINNIE J., b. May 13, 1862; died Feb. 4, 1869.
1907. v. JAMES M., JR., b. Aug. 16, 1863; died Feb. 1, 1869.
1908. vi. BELLE D., b. July 31, 1870; died Nov. 29, 1879.

(1082.) iv. DAVID HOWE JACOBS, b. April 5, 1820, son of Thomas M. and Hannah (Felton) Jacobs; m. April 25, 1847, Elizabeth Ayres; she died May 26, 1853. He m. second, June 20, 1855, Caroline Leonard. Mr. Jacobs is a master mason and contractor in Boston. Had two or more children.

1909. i. JAMES A., b. Oct. 15, 1848.
1910. ii. ANNA E., b. Jan. 14, 1852.

(1084.) vi. THOMAS R. JACOBS, b. Nov. 24, 1825, son of Thomas M. and Hannah (Felton) Jacobs of West Scituate, (No. 494;) m. Aug. 28, 1859, Mary E. Hunt. He was a clerk several years in Jacobs & Deane's clothing house, Boston. In 1870, was a member of the Boston Common Council. He died suddenly of apoplexy, April 14, 1876, aged 50 years. Mrs. Mary E. Jacobs, b. about 1831, daughter of Edward Hunt and grand-daughter of John Hunt of Gilmanton, N. H.

(1085.) i. EMERY SHUMWAY, m. in 1845, Betsey Fish Felton, b. March 22, 1815, daughter of George W. and Lydia Felton of Petersham. In March 1839, Emery Shumway of Rutland, sup. same person as above, m. Eliza F. Felton Phillipston, Mass.

(1086.) ii. EZRA BAKER FELTON[7], (*George W., Jr.*[6], *George W., Sr*[5], *David*[4], *Samuel*[3], *John*[2], *Nathaniel*[1],) b. Nov. 16, 1816; m. Mrs. Pamelia (Cooley) Cutter. In 1863, their residence was in Cooleyville, New Salem, Mass. Mr. Felton was a blacksmith and machinist. His death was accidental in Framingham, Mass., Jan. 24, 1869, aged 52 years. They had 4 or more children.

1911. i. ELLEN E., b. about 1846; m. July 21, 1864, John Abbott Allen, Jr., of Boston, b. in Jaffrey, N. H. in 1842.
1912. ii. EDWARD S.; living in 1869.
1913. iii. FRANK B., b. May 12, 1858; living in Saxonville in 1869.
1914. iv. CARRIE JANE W.

(1088.) iv. GEORGE MERRICK FELTON[7], (*George W.,*

Jr.⁶, *George W., Sr.⁵, David⁴, Samuel³, John², Nathaniel¹,*) b. Nov 10, 1820; m. before 1849, Harriet Bigelow. He is a mason by trade, and living in Holyoke, Mass., in 1848; the last 10 or more years in Phillipston, Mass. Had 5 children.

1915. i. GEORGE M., JR.; lived about 16 years.
1916. ii. HATTIE M.; m. Alvin Parker; residence, Orange, Mass., in 1884.
1917. iii. CARRIE B.; m. Aldes Parker; residence, Gardner, Mass., in 1884.
1918. iv. WILLIAM; living in Phillipston in 1884.

(1089.) v. LEONARD A. FELTON⁷, (*George W., Jr.⁶, George W., Sr.⁵, David⁴, Samuel³, John², Nathaniel¹,*) b. Jan. 30, 1823; m. Sarah Dunton, daughter of Warren Dunton of Newcastle, Me. He is a mason by trade, and lived in several places in Mass. and N. H. He was in the Union army from Boston in 1864, then aged 41 years. The last 10 years has resided at Clarksville, in Stewartstown, Coos County, N. H. His moth- is with him, aged 98 years. Has one son.

1919. i. CHARLES.

(1091.) vii. AMBROSE A. MASON of Clinton, Mass., m. May 1848, Sarah Hovey Felton, b. March 17, 1828, youngest child of George W. and Lydia Felton. Mrs. Mason died in Troy, N. Y., before 1863; left one son and one daughter.

(1094.) iii. JONAS HUMPHREY WINTER, b. Nov. 29, 1813; m. Sept. 25, 1836, Elizabeth Alden Farrar, b. Feb. 11, 1818, daughter of Nathaniel and Elizabeth A. (Felton) Farrar; she died June 6, 1855, aged 37 years. Mr. Winter m. second, Harriet N. Kellogg of Amherst, Mass. Mr. Winter was a boot and shoe manufacturer in Shutesbury, Mass., and has been one of the selectmen of that town. He represented the town in the Legislature in 1849. In 1883, Mr. Winter was living at Faribault, Minn. They had 4 children.

1920. i. MARY E., b. May 2, 1838; m. April 1866, E. N. Leavens.
1921. ii. JONAS A., b. Oct. 19, 1839; m. Feb. 1861, Nellie Stephens.
1922. iii. ELLA J., b. Jan. 26, 1849; m. Feb. 1871, W. W Howard.
iv. HATTIE K., b. Jan. 27, 1860.

(1095.) iv. EDWARD MOODY, m. Dec. 19, 1837, Aurelia Newell Farrar, b. April 10, 1820, daughter of Nathaniel and Elizabeth A. (Felton) Farrar of Shutesbury, Mass. Mrs.

Aurelia N. Moody m. second, Nov. 25, 1847, Seneca Haskins. Mrs. Haskins was living in 1883.

(1103.) i. FREDERICK AUGUSTUS FELTON[7], (Moses O.[6], George W.[5], David[4], Samuel[3], John[2], Nathaniel[1],) b. March 29, 1821; m. Mahalah Angeline Winter, Sept. 1844; residence in 1883, in Faribault, Minn. Has lived in the West many years. Had 4 children.

 1923. i. HENRY A., b. in 1846; residence in 1883, LaFayette, Ind.
 1924. ii. MYRA A., b. in 1848; m. —— Davis; residence LaFayette, Ind.
 1925. iii. HERBERT W., b. in 1855.
 1926. iv. SUSIE M., b. in 1881; (sup. 1861.)

(1104.) ii. LUCIUS LYMAN HYDE, m. Sept. 1844, Susan Amelia Felton, b. Dec. 21, 1822, daughter of Moses O. and Susan C. Felton, (No. 499.) Residence, Springfield, Mass. They have two children.

 1927. i. DELLA, b. in 1845; m. —— Redington,
 1928. ii. ANNA, b. in 1854; m. —— Percival.

(1105.) iii. STEPHEN OLIVER FELTON[7], (Moses O.[6], George W.[5], David[4], Samuel[3], John[2], Nathaniel[1],) b. Dec. 18, 1824; was a carpenter; lived in Boston several years; was one of the builders of Tufts College. He m. in Boston, Oct. 4, 1852, Sarah D. Taylor. Some 30 years ago he moved to one of the western states.

(1110.) viii. FRANCIS ALEXANDER FELTON[7], (Moses O.[6], George W.[5], David[4], Samuel[3], John[2], Nathaniel[1],) b. March 19, 1835; m. March 2, 1854, Lydia Chamberlain, both of Dana, Mass. Mr. Felton and family resided in St. Louis, Mo., many years. About 1883, moved to Texarkana, Ark., where he had a saw-mill.

(1122.) i. JAMES HERVEY WHITMORE, b. at Londonderry, Vt., Aug. 17, 1812, son of Dea. James and Phebe (Stimson) Whitmore of Framingham, Mass; he m. April 9, 1835, Martha A. Stowe, b. Sept. 14, 1813, daughter of Dana and Martha Stowe of Southboro, Mass. They resided in Framingham several years; were living in Milford in 1853. He died Jan. 28, 1866, aged 54 years. They had 5 children.

 1929. i. MARTHA E., b. Oct. 26, 1836.
 1930. ii. PHEBE S., b. Oct. 19, 1838.
 1931. iii. ANNE C., b. June 2, 1841.

1932. iv. MARY C., b. April 9, 1343.
1933. v. WALLIE G., b. in Milford, Jan. 22, 1853.

(1123.) ii. CHARLES STIMSON WHITMORE, b. Oct. 6, 1815, son of Dea. James and Phebe (Stimson) Whitmore of Framingham, Mass; m. Oct. 6, 1842, Agnes S. Hyde. He settled near the center of Framingham, where he was town clerk 20 years, 1855 to 1876. He is deacon in the Baptist church and represented the town in the General Court two years, 1877 and 1878. No children, but one adopted daughter, Agnes M. Whitmore, who m. March 1877, Frank C. Day of Worcester, Mass.

(1124.) i. ANDREW NEWELL WYETH, b. April 29, 1817, son of John Wyeth of Cambridge; m. Amelia H. B. Stimson, daughter of Royal and Leaffa Stimson of Cambridge, Mass. They resided at Cambridge and had several children.

1934. i. AMELIA A., b. Jan. 4, 1846.
1935. ii. SUSAN E., b. Dec. 28, 1847.
1936. iii. ANDREW N., JR.; m. Dec. 21, 1881, Hattie Zimgiebel.

(1125.) ii. FORDYCE MIRICK STIMSON, son of Royal Stimson of Cambridge. He was an alderman in Cambridge in 1864; Justice of the Peace in 1877.

(1129.) ii. EDWARD FAY ROLLINS, m. June 1851, Phebe E. Davis, b. Nov. 15, 1830, daughter of Capt. John C. and Lucy (Stimson) Davis of Ashburnham, Mass. Mr. Rollins was a soldier in the 12th Mass. Regiment, and promoted to lieutenant in 1864. They have had 3 children. Lt. Rollins is a printer and business manager, also one of the editors of The Bivouac, an independent military monthly published in Boston.

(1132.) ii. CHARLES D. TARBELL, b. July 20, 1832, son of Reuben Tarbell; m. Nov. 18, 1856, Elmira F. Whitney, b. Jan. 18, 1836, daughter of Benjamin and Elmira (Stimson) Whitney of Marlborough, N. H. In 1876, Mr. Tarbell was living in Littleton, N. H.; a lumber merchant. Had 4 children.

1936. a. i. FRANK L., b. March 20, 1859; died Feb. 7, 1867, aged 8 years.
1936. b. ii. MARY E., b. March 17, 1861.
1936. c. iii. ANNA M., b. Sept. 6, 1868.
1936. d. iv. FLORA E., b. March 6, 1871.

(1145.) i. DANIEL IDE, b. March 25, 1832, son of Joshua Ide; m. May 8, 1860, Cornelia D. Felton, b. in Sharon, Vt., July 21, 1838, daughter of Abijah and Phebe (Baldwin) Felton of Sharon, Vt. Mr. Ide is a wealthy farmer in Croydon, N. H. They have had 4 children.

1937.   i. JASIAL, b. Sept. 25, 1862; graduated at Steven's High School at Claremont, N. H., June 1882, and the same month was admitted to Dartmouth College.
1938.   ii. SIDNEY W., b. Nov. 19, 1867.
1939.   iii. OSCAR M., b. Feb. 14, 1871.
1940.   iv. One child died young.

(1152.) i. ALONZO WOOD, b. Aug. 17, 1817, son of Capt. Jedediah and Betsey (Wilkins) Wood of Feltonville, Marlboro; m. in 1844, Sarah Ann Brigham, b. Oct. 3, 1820, daughter of Eli and Lydia (Howe) Brigham of Marlboro. Mr. Wood settled in Feltonville. They had 4 children. He was an assessor in Feltonville in 1867, then the new town of Hudson. He died Oct. 16, 1873, aged 56 years. Mrs. Wood a few years afterwards moved to Northboro. where she died March 15, 1884, aged 63 years.

1941.   i. ANN E., b. July 27, 1845; died May 1857, of erysipelas, aged 12 years.
1942.   ii. ALONZO, JR., b. Jan. 18, 1847.
1943.   iii. FRANK J., b. Aug. 23, 1851; m. Oct. 1873, Kittie A. Howe, daughter of Albin P. Howe, Esq., of Marlboro.
1944.   iv. HIRAM H.; living in Hudson in 1876.

(1153.) ii. JONAS EDWARD BRIGHAM, b. Jan. 17, 1823, son of Eli and Lydia Brigham of Marlboro; m. Sarah Davenport and settled on his father's place in Marlboro. They have 3 children.

1945.   i. ELIZA, b. Nov. 10, 1853; a school teacher in Marlboro since 1871.
1946.   ii. EDWIN, b. Aug. 10, 1856.
1947.   iii. HATTIE E., b. March 7, 1862; graduated at Marlboro High School in 1879.

(1154.) iii. SILAS EDWIN BRIGHAM, b. Feb. 20, 1825, son of Eli and Lydia Brigham of Marlboro; m. Nov. 1858, Martha A. Ellis, daughter of Elisha and Betsey Ellis of Westboro. He settled on his great-uncle's, Silas Brigham's, place in Southboro, Mass. Had 3 sons.

1948.   i. SILAS O., b. March 1862; died Aug. 8, 1875, aged 13 years.
1949.   ii. CHARLES E., b. Sept. 19, 1864.
1950.   iii. HERBERT E., b. Feb. 25, 1867.

(1259) i. WILLIAM S. RICHARDS of Granville, Ohio, m. Sept. 1813, Isabella Mower, b. Oct. 4, 1791, daughter of Samuel P. and Jane (Felton) Mower of Granville, Ohio. Mr. Richards was a physician and settled in that town. They had 4 children.

1951†.   i. REV. HENRY L., b. in 1814; m. Cynthia Cowles.
1952†.   ii. MARY A., b. in 1816; m. Virgil Hillyer.
1953†.   iii. WILLIAM, b. in 1819; m. Hannah Ralston.
1954†.   iv. ISABELLA, b. in 1821; m. J. B. Howell.

(1260.) ii. LUCIUS DOOLITTLE MOWER, b. May 1, 1793; m. April 15, 1826, Lucy Manson. He died at St. Augustine, Florida, Feb. 19, 1834, aged 40 years and buried there. At Granville, Ohio is a monument to his memory. His widow, Mrs. Lucy Mower, deceased before 1879.

(1264.) vi HIRAM BOARDMAN, m. Jan. 15, 1828, Susan Bent Mower, b. Oct. 18, 1800, daughter of Samuel P. and Jane (Felton) Mower, (No. 599.) They had 4 children. Mrs. Boardman died at Springfield, Ill., June 6, 1878, aged 77 years.

1955.   i. LUCIUS M.; living at Springfield, Ill., in 1879.
1956.   ii. ANNA M., or B.; m. ——— Morse; residence, Warrensburg, Ill.
1957.   iii. SAMUEL P.; died before 1879.
1958.   iv. JANE; died before 1879.

(1265.) vii. ALFRED AVERY, m. April 8, 1824, Jane Mower, b. Sept. 28, 1802, daughter of Samuel P. and Jane (Felton) Mower, (No. 599.) They had 6 children. Mrs. Avery died Jan. 24, 1836, aged 33 years.

1959.   i. HORATIO M., b. April 2, 1825; died at Orange, N. J., Feb. 13, 1860, aged 35 years.
1960.   ii. HENRIETTA B., b. July 27, 1826; m. A. S. Hutchins of Wis.
1961.   iii. LLYOD, (or Lloyd;) died in infancy.
1962.   iv. FRANK G., b. Feb. 22, 1829; died at Marquette, Lake Superior, Dec. 17, 1858, aged 30 years.
1963.   v. SARAH J., b. Aug. 24, 1834; m. J. Drown of Wis.
1964†. vi. ALLYN A., b. Dec. 19, 1835; m. H. Louisa Billings in 1868.

(1268.) x. BENJAMIN FELTON MOWER, b. Sept. 19, 1812, the youngest child of Samuel Parish and Jane (Felton) Mower; m. July 1833, Esther Lockwood. They had 3 children, all married and living in the State of Mo., in 1879. Mr. B. F. Mower died May 21, 1842, aged 29 years, 8 months.

   1965.   i. MARIA J., b. Nov. 10, 1835; m.
   1966.   ii. SUSAN A., b. June 14, 1837; m.
   1967. iii. SAMUEL L., b. Sept. 7, 1840; m.

(1269.) i. DR. MOSES CHAMBERLAIN, m. May 18, 1825, Eliza F. Felton, b. Nov. 2, 1795, daughter of Benjamin Felton, Esq., of Wardsborough, Vt., (No. 600.) Dr. Chamberlain practised a few years in Halifax, Vt., but most of his life in Jamaica, Vt., where he died July 9, 1842. They had 8 children, Mrs. Chamberlain died Feb. 1882, aged 86 years.

   1968.   i. An infant, b. and died June 10, 1826.
   1969.   ii. FRANCES, b. July 10, 1827; m. Oct. 14, 1846, Lorenzo Waterman.
   1970. iii. FISK, b. Dec. 29, 1828; died Aug. 26, 1834, aged 5 years.
   1971†. iv. ANN, b. May 10, 1830; m. Nymphus P. Felton, (No. 1304.)
   1972†. v. LAURETT, b. March 25, 1832; m. George O. Fessenden.
   1973†. vi. JANE, b. Jan. 18, 1834; m. John Q. Fessenden.
   1974. vii. MARY, b. Dec. 6, 1836; died Jan. 20, 1837.
   1975. viii. HENRY M., b. Oct. 18, 1839.

(1270.) ii. NATHAN BUCKMAN FELTON[7], (Benjamin[6], Benjamin[5], Joseph[4], Skelton[3], Nathaniel[2], Nathaniel[1],) b. Nov. 11, or 12, 1798, in Pelham, Mass., the part now Prescott, Mass. In 1805, his parents, with their family, moved to Windham County, Vt. In 1818, he entered Middlebury College, one year in advance, whence, in 1821, he graduated with high honors. He read law with Martin Field, Esq., of Newfane, Vt., 1821 to 1823; with Jonathan Hunt, Esq., of Brattleboro, 1823 and 1824, and in the office of W. C. Bradley, Esq., of Westminster, Vt.; was admitted to the Bar in 1825, and moved to Lebanon, N. H. and commenced the practice of his profession. He was postmaster in Lebanon about 10 years, 1825 to 1835. In 1835, was appointed clerk of the Supreme Court of Grafton County, N. H., and moved to Haverhill in that county. He held the office 12 years. In Sept. 1852, was appointed Probate Registrar of the same county, and continued till 1856. He represented Haverhill in the General Court in 1853, and probably other years. The late

Hon. Edmund Burke, member of Congress from N. H., said, June 1853, that Mr. Felton " was one of the most intelligent and able members of the House of Representatives of that State."

At a celebration in Lebanon, July 4, 1826, Nathan B. Felton was the orator of the day. The oration was published the same month in the New Hampshire Patriot. It said, " Mr. Felton has done great credit to himself, both as a patriot and scholar. His topics were well chosen." In July 1876, Centennial year, fifty years after the oration was delivered, it was republished in the Granite State Free Press, a newspaper published in Lebanon, N. H. Mr. Felton m. May 22, 1836, Ann Redding. No issue.

In January 1875, then 76 years of age, he was a magistrate of Haverhill, and presided in the examination of the Piermont tragedy. A correspondent of the Boston Journal then said of Mr. Felton that he was " a gentleman of discriminating mind and excellent judgment." He died Dec. 22, 1876, aged 78 years.

Below are two extracts from the White Mountain Republic published at Littleton, Grafton County, N. H., of Dec. 28, 1876. " The town of Haverhill, N. H., has suffered a great loss in the death of one of the most esteemed citizens, Nathan B. Felton, who died at his residence on the 22d inst. of apoplexy." " As a member of the legal fraternity Mr. Felton was one whose counsel was sought by the wisest and best. He was not only learned in the law but a long and remarkably industrious life had made him familiar with the sciences and arts. He had for a long time been one of the leading lawyers of the State, and his name was ever a synonym for honesty and integrity. Probably no man lives who possesses to a fuller extent the entire confidence of every one who knew him than did Mr. Felton." He died at the ripe age of 78 years, leaving a bereaved widow and a large number of mourning friends. " Funeral services were held at the Congregational church on Christmas day, at which time Hon. Evarts W. Farr and Hon. Wm. H. Duncan, as representatives of Grafton County Bar, spoke in fitting praise of him who for more than half a century had been the ' Alpha and Omega ' of the profession."

(1272.) iv. ASA E. FELTON[7], (*Benjamin*[6], *Benjamin*[5], *Joseph*[4], *Skelton*[3], *Nathaniel*[2], *Nathaniel*[1],) b. April 6, 1804, in Mass., and is living in Jamaica, Vt., in 1886, aged 82 years. He m. Jan. 31, 1837, Mary R. Ellis of Jamaica. He is a farmer; their children were:

1976. i. Lucy M., b. Nov. 18, 1837.

1977. ii. FREDERICK B., b. Aug. 7, 1839.
1978. iii. ADELAIDE F., b. Sept. 8, 1841; m. March 12, 1868, Charles Grey.

(1273.) v. COL. JAMES TWITCHELL, m. Feb. 21, 1841, Lucy D. Felton, b. Oct. 14, 1807, daughter of Benjamin Felton, Esq., of Jamaica, Vt. They settled at Townshend, in Vt. Col. Twitchell died in Jan. 1879. They had 3 children.

1979. i. MARY T., b. Oct. 9, 1842; m. May 6, 1868, Pardon D. Holbrook; living in Athol, Mass., in 1883.
1980. ii. ELLEN M., b. Oct. 18, 1844.
1981. iii. FREDERICK F., b. Aug. 10, 1849.

(1274.) vi. HORATIO LYMAN FELTON[7], (Benjamin[6], Benjamin[5], Joseph[4], Skelton[3], Nathaniel[2], Nathaniel[1],) b. May 17, 1810; m. Feb. 14, 1849, Nancy E. Pierce; have one son. Mr. Felton was a tanner and currier, in company with his youngest brother, till about 1866, when he withdrew from the firm.

1982. i. EDWARD O., b. June 24, 1859.

(1275.) vii. HENRY H. FELTON[7], (Benjamin[6], Benjamin[5], Joseph[4], Skelton[3], Nathaniel[2], Nathaniel[1],) b. Dec. 28, 1812; m. June 22, 1843, Eunice W. Saben; he is a tanner and currier in Jamaica, and was a Justice of the Peace in 1863. They had two children.

1983. i. FRANCIS H., b. Sept. 28, 1844; died Nov. 13, 1864, aged 20 years.
1984. ii. NELLIE, b. Oct. 1, 1858; died Sept. 11, 1859, aged 11 months.

(1277.) i. JOSEPH CHENEY FELTON[7], (Joseph[6], Benjamin[5], Joseph[4], Skelton[3], Nathaniel[2], Nathaniel[1],) b. about 1796; m. Lorana Crissey of Fairfax, Vt. Had two children. He died about 1822, aged 25 years. Mrs. Lorana Felton was living in Fairfax in 1876,

1985†. i. JAY, b. about 1819; m. Chloe Sherman.
1986†. ii. JOSEPH C., JR., b. about 1821; m. and had several children.

(1278.) ii. NYE ROBINSON, m. Lovisa Felton, b. about 1798, daughter of Joseph and Sally (Bartlett) Felton, (No. 601.) Mr. Robinson died in the winter of 1875-76; Mrs. Robinson was then living aged nearly 80 years. They had 3 children; one daughter died young.

1987.   i. A daughter; m. George Hobart; had one son and one daughter. Mr. Hobart died before 1876.
1988.   ii. HENRY; m. and living at Nevada, Iowa, in 1876.

(1279.) iii. LOTEN WILLSON, b. about 1796; m. Lodisa Felton, b. about 1800, daughter of Joseph and Sally (Bartlett) Felton, (No. 601.) Mr. and Mrs. Willson were living in 1876 at Lost Nation, Iowa. They had 7 children.

1989.   i. MYLON; m. and had 4 sons, Mylon, Jr., Preston King, James and Benjamin G.; father and sons, living at Burlington, Vt., in 1876.
1990†. ii. MARION; m. Norvell D. Waite.
1991.   iii. LOUISA; m. John Scott; residence Lost Nation, Iowa.
1992.   iv. HELEN; m. H. L. Cotlee of Highgate, Vt.; had two children, Hattie and Homer.
1993.   v. HENRY L.; m. and had two daughters; residence in 1876, in Oliver, Iowa.
1994.   vi. SILAS W.; m.; had in 1876, one son, Willie; residence, Wyoming, Iowa.
1995.   vii. ANNIE; m. —— Robinson; had two children in 1876; residence Bodega, Cal.

(1280.) iv. BENJAMIN SEARS FELTON[7], (*Joseph*[6], *Benjamin*[5], *Joseph*[4], *Skelton*[3], *Nathaniel*[2], *Nathaniel*[1],) b. in Barre, Mass., in 1802; m. Amelia Russell, and had 8 children. He m. second, after 1834, Lucia Parker, and had two daughters. Mr. Felton died in 1863, aged 61 years. Mrs. Lucia Felton was living in Fairfax, Vt., in 1876.

1996.   i. JOSEPH; died aged 1 year.
1997.   ii. WELLINGTON; died aged 2 years.
1998.   iii. LODISA; m.
1999.   iv. HANNAH; m.
2000.   v. SARAH; m.
2001.   vi. MARION; m.

These four daughters reside in Marshalltown, Iowa.

2002.   vii. FLORETTA, b. in 1831; died in 1858, aged 27 years.
2003†. viii. BENJAMIN W., b. in 1833; m. Angeline E. Moore.
2004.   ix. LUCIA, b. in Fairfax, Vt.
2005.   x. ARMINA; m. —— Robinson; residence, Fairfax, Vt.

(1281.) v. MONTGOMERY BARTLETT FELTON[7], (*Joseph*[6], *Benjamin*[5], *Joseph*[4], *Skelton*[3], *Nathaniel*[2], *Nathaniel*[1],)

m. first, Eliza Osborne; she died 6 months afterwards; he m. second, Emma Hall; had 5 children. Mrs. Emma Felton died before 1876. Mr. Felton was living with some of his children in Wisconsin in 1876.

2006†. i. MARCIA, b. about 1835; m. Rev. Willard W. Ames.
2007. ii. ADALINE; m. I. Hodge; had one daughter, Adaline; residence, Oshkosh, Wis. Mrs. Hodge died several years before 1876.
2008. iii. CAROLINE; m. and had children living in 1876.
2009. iv. CARLOS; m. and had a family in 1876.
2010. v. SAMUEL; m. and had a family in 1876.

(1282.) vi. WILLIAM LOREN FELTON^7, (*Joseph^6, Benjamin^5, Joseph^4, Skelton^3, Nathaniel^2, Nathaniel^1,*) m. Sarah Buck. They lived in Chicago, Ill., where Mr. Felton was accidentally killed by the falling of a building several years before 1876. They had one son. Mrs. Sarah Felton m. second, Jones Bellows; he died and the Widow Bellows was living in Fairfax, Vt., in 1876.

2011. i. FOSTER, b. about 1854; was living in 1876.

In 1876, Montgomery B. Felton was living, and his two sisters and the widows of his three brothers; also the widow of Joseph Cheney Felton, Jr.

(1288.) vi. WILLIAM HENRY FELTON^7, (*Nathan^6, Benjamin^5, Joseph^4, Skelton^3, Nathaniel^2, Nathaniel^1,*) b. in Pelham, the part now Prescott, Mass., in 1813; m. Alice Lincoln Barnes and lived there till about 1845, when he moved to Northampton, Mass., where he has been a merchant many years. Mrs. Alice L. Felton is sister to Willard Barnes, the husband of Mr. Felton's oldest sister. They had 3 children.

2012†. i. WILLARD B., b. Nov. 26, 1837; m. Fannie A. Burbank.
2013. ii. MARY J.
2014. iii. NATHAN A.

(1291.) ix. NEHEMIAH HINDS FELTON^7, (*Nathan^6, Benjamin^5, Joseph^4, Skelton^3, Nathaniel^2, Nathaniel^1,*) b. in Prescott, Mass.; m. July 1844, Eliza Hooker of Watertown, Mass. In 1876, they were living in Detroit, Mich., and had two or more children.

2015. i. MARY E.
2016. ii. CLARENCE.

FELTON FAMILY. 191

(1292.) i. ELBRIDGE GERRY FELTON[7], (John[6], Benjamin[5], Joseph[4], Skelton[3], Nathaniel[2], Nathaniel[1],) b. in Pelham, now Prescott, Mass., June 15, 1806; m. Feb. 15, 1829, or 1830, in Barre, Mass., Sarah Winslow. They have lived many years at Schuyler Falls, N. Y.

- 2017. i. LUCIUS; died aged 2 years.
- 2018. ii. SOPHIA; m. Ebenezer Ryder; have 2 children.
- 2019. iii. MARIA; m. Abel Dorchin in 1868; had 1 child.
- 2020. iv. CARRIE; m. James Raymond in 1865; had 2 children.
- 2021. v. HENRY J.; m. Lovina Lorlett.
- 2022. vi. LUCIUS M., b. March 7, 1842; m. —— Good of Schuyler Falls.
- 2023. vii. CELINDA; m. Wm. H. Adams in 1868.

(1293.) ii. JARED L. PHILLIPS, m. in 1829, Caroline A. Felton, b. Nov. 9, 1808, daughter of John and Mary (Calhoun) Felton of northern Vt. They had 2 children. Mrs. Caroline Phillips died Jan. 9, 1833, aged 24 years.

- 2024. i. ARMINA, b. about 1829.
- 2025. ii. SABRA; died aged 18 months.

(1294.) iii. JARED L. PHILLIPS, m. second, Lucy A. Felton, b. Sept. 28, 1810, daughter of John and Mary Felton, (No. 604.) They had 8 children. This family was living in Kansas in 1884.

- 2026. i. RASSELAS W., lives at Sturgeon Bay, Wis.
- 2027. ii. PHILETUS O., in Buffalo, Kansas.
- 2028. iii. DORLISKA L.; died aged 3 years.
- 2029. iv. THEODOTIA R.; died young.
- 2030. v. ELISHA A.; living in Green Bay, Wis., in 1884.
- 2031. vi. JARED L., JR.; died young.
- 2032. vii. ORMON T.; died young.
- 2033. viii. SIGNOR, was killed by the bursting of a steam boiler when 18 years of age.

(1295.) iv. THOMAS SKELTON FELTON[7], (John[6], Benjamin[5], Joseph[4], Skelton[3], Nathaniel[2], Nathaniel[1],) b. Sept. 26, 1816; m. Anna Bromley and settled at Schuyler Falls, N. Y. Had 2 children. He was kicked by a colt, which caused his death Jan. 5, 1866, aged 49 years.

- 2034. i. CORNELIUS.
- 2035. ii. LEROY.

(1296.) v. MOSES H. FELTON[7], (John[6], Benjamin[5], Joseph[4], Skelton[3], Nathaniel[2], Nathaniel[1],) b. Jan. 16, 1818, in Petersham, Mass.; m. Almeda Bromley; had 2 or 3 children. Residence, N. Y. State.

 2036. i. A daughter.
 2037. ii. A son.

(1297.) vi. ALMON D. FELTON[7], (John[6], Benjamin[5], Joseph[4], Skelton[3], Nathaniel[2], Nathaniel[1],) b. in Wardsborough, Vt., Dec. 22, 1821; m. July 26, 1844, Celinda Marsh, b. Sept. 26, 1818. He was in the iron business several years; was a farmer in Beekmantown, Clinton County, N. Y., 1855 till 1876, when he moved to Plattsburg, N. Y. Was Justice of the Peace 12 years and a side judge several years. Have had 5 children.

 2098. i. Isaac M., b. Sept. 26, 1845; died July 29, 1857, aged 11 years.
 2099. ii. Elam, b. Dec. 10, 1846; died Sept. 20, 1847.
 2100. iii. Marshall A., b. Feb. 23, 1849; m.
 2101. iv. Susan S., b. Nov. 5, 1850.
 2102. v. Mary J., b. Feb. 4, 1859.

(1298.) vii. JAMES M. FELTON[7], (John[6], Benjamin[5], Joseph[4], Skelton[3], Nathaniel[2], Nathaniel[1],) b. Jan. 25, 1823; m. in 1844, Maria Tucker; settled in Kansas; had 6 children in 1884.

 2103. i. Charles.
 2104. ii. Albert.
 2105. iii. John.
 2106. iv. Julia.
 2107. v. Mary.
 2108. vi. Menoe.

(1300.) i. JOHN BUSH PRATT, b. July 26, 1809, (son of Dr. Elnathan and Cornelia (Bush) Pratt of Worcester;) m., May 9, 1832, Seraph Felton, b. Sept. 23, 1809, daughter of Moses H. Felton of Barre, Mass., (No. 605.) Mr. Pratt is a farmer and gardner at Worcester. Mrs. Pratt died and he m. second, March 1855, Emmeline D. W. Curtis. Had 4 children by his first wife.

 2109. i. Elnathan, b. March 24, 1833.
 2110. ii. Theodore, b. Dec. 19, 1834; died Dec. 27, 1844.
 2111. iii. Abigail, b. June 18, 1839; died Jan. 5, 1857, aged 17 years.

2112. iv. JOHN B., JR.. b. March 28, 1841; m. Nov. 1862, Sarah Jane Davis of Syracuse, N. Y.; she died April 12, 1864, aged 21 years. He m. second, Mary Elizabeth Orcutt of Waltham. He died Sept. 30, 1868, aged 27 years. Mrs. Pratt died Oct. 7, 1869, aged 27 years. Had one son, John Theodore H. Pratt, b. May 26, 1868.

(1301.) ii. JOTHAM BUSH PRATT, b. Jan. 1812, son of Dr. Elnathan and Cornelia (Bush) Pratt of Worcester; m. Harriet Felton, b. Nov. 5, 1812, daughter of Moses H. Felton of Barre, Mass. They lived in Worcester and had 3 children. Mr. Pratt died at Kingston, Jamaica, on his way home from California, May 18, or 19, 1850, aged 38 years. Mrs. Pratt is living at Worcester.

2113. i. HENRY, b. Feb. 23, 1840; m. Julia Healey; had 3 children in 1881.
2114. ii. ELIZABETH, b. June 16, 1842; m. Henry B. Keith.
2115. iii. LOUISA, b. May 16, 1846; a clerk in Worcester in 1881.

(1302.) iii. PAUL WADSWORTH, (son of John and Lois (Warren) Wadsworth of Barre;) m. Abigail H. Felton, b. about 1815, daughter of Moses H. Felton of Barre, Mass. They resided at Barre where their children were born and Mr. Wadsworth was one of the selectmen in 1837. He was a farmer and trader in Barre; about 1859, moved to Holden, Mass., and resided there several years. They afterwards went to Weston, Mass., where he died about 1870. Mrs. Wadsworth died in that town Jan. 4, 1876, aged 60 years. Had 3 children.

2116. i. MARCUS M., b. in 1836; m. Maria Henry of Westboro, Mass.
2117. ii. JOHN, b. in 1842; m. Lucy Turner of Holden.
2118. iii. SERAPH F.; m. Joseph Ballard of Weston.

(1303.) iv. NATHAN H. FELTON[7], (*Moses H.*[6], *Benjamin*[5], *Joseph*[4], *Skelton*[3], *Nathaniel*[2], *Nathaniel*[1],) b. Jan. 10, 1822; m. Caroline A. Williams, daughter of George Williams, Esq., of Hubbardston, Mass. They reside in Hubbardston, where he has been an assessor. In the winter of 1881–82, lost some of his buildings by fire. They have had 5 children.

2119. i. GEORGE W., b. in Barre, Jan. 31, 1845; was a soldier in the Union army, 1864–65; m. Lucinda Savage. Has been a stable keeper.
2120. ii. SUSIE A.; lived 20 years.
2121. iii. CARRIE A.; m. A. G. Williams.

2122.   iv. ARTHUR P., b July 18, 1860; traveling agent for a Boston firm.
2123.   v. MARY B., b. in 1862.

(1304.) v. NYMPHUS PRATT FELTON[7], (*Moses H.[6], Benjamin[5], Joseph[4], Skelton[3], Nathaniel[2], Nathaniel[1],*) b. April 27, 1825; m. Jan. 1849, Ann Chamberlain, b. May 10, 1830, daughter of Dr. Moses and Eliza (Felton) Chamberlain of Jamaica, Vt. He was a soldier in the Union army in 1864–65 from Westfield, Mass. They had 5 children. Mrs. Felton died Sept. 14, 1862, aged 32 years. He m. second, Nov. 8, 1863, Lidea A. Bates.

2124.   i. ELIZA R., b. in Barre, Jan. 19, 1850.
2125.   ii. FRANCES J., b. in Barre, Dec. 2, 1852.
2126.   iii. ADA C., b. May 29, 1854.
2127.   iv. BENJAMIN O., b. April 30, 1857.
2128.   v. ALBERT, b. March 25, 1862.

(1306.) ii. CHARLES MILLER, m. Lucinda Felton, b. July 21, 1812, daughter of Skelton and Lucinda (Adams) Felton of Brookfield, Mass., and Troy, N. Y. They had 3 children. Mrs. Miller died March 3, 1871, aged 58 years. Mr. Miller had charge of an orange grove in Florida in 1885. Their two sons are traveling through the country selling stores or store goods.

2128. *a.*   i. FELTON.
2128. *b.*   ii. CHARLES, JR.

(1307.) iii. AMORY FELTON[7], (*Skelton[6], Benjamin[5], Joseph[4], Skelton[3], Nathaniel[2], Nathaniel[1],*) b. July 10, 1813; m. Jan. 1849, Nancy P. Boynton, and had 4 children. He was a merchant in Troy, N. Y. He died March 3, 1864, aged 50 years. In 1855, Mr. Felton was patentee for grinding mills. Mrs. Felton lived, since Mr. Felton's death, in Chicago; now living in western N. Y.

2129†.   i. WILLIAM A., b. Dec. 27, 1836; m. Mary Ann Faxon.
2130†.   ii. CHARLES H., b. Feb. 18, 1840; m. Lydia R. Barthwick.
2131†.   iii. HERBERT C., b. Nov. 3, 1846; m. Harriet Louisa Job.
2132.   iv. EMMA, b. Dec. 27, 1852; m. Frederick Lyon. Residence, Dunkirk, N. Y. in 1885.

(1308.) iv. ASA B. CLARK of Vernon, Vt., m. April 1836, Sarah C. Felton, b. Dec. 8, 1815, daughter of Skelton and Lucinda Felton of Troy, N. Y. They had one daughter. Mrs. Clark died Feb. 25, 1850, aged 34 years.

 2132½. i. JANE; m. Thomas J. Bowers of Troy, N. Y.; he is a lawyer, now in California; they have a large family.

(1316.) vi. L. MARTIN, m. Sarah Batchelder, b. Feb. 12, 1812, daughter of Andrew and Sally (Felton) Batchelder of Danvers, (No. 607.) After Mr. Martin's death, Mrs. Sarah Felton Martin m. second, Oct. 12, 1847, Amos Proctor Perley of Windham, N. H.; he was b. at Boxford, Mass., Jan. 15, 1807, and died in Danvers, Aug. 17, 1881, aged 74 years. They had 2 or more children in Danvers, Mass.

 2133. i. EMMA, b. July 22, 1848; died Sept. 13, 1848.
 2134. ii. HENRY, b. July 13, 1849; died July 17, aged 4 days.

(1318.) viii. OLIVER FELTON BATCHELDER, b. June 7, 1815, son of Andrew and Sally (Felton) Batchelder of Danvers; m. Nov. 4, 1844, Sally Osborn; they reside at South Danvers, now Peabody; been a trader many years. Have 5 children.

 2135. i. WILLIAM O., b. Oct. 10, 1845; a merchant in Peabody.
 2136. ii. EMILY, b. Dec. 28, 1846.
 2137. iii. CHARLES, b. Feb. 22, 1849.
 2138. iv. EVELINE, b. July 8, 1852.
 2139. v. SARAH, b. March 30, 1859.

(1324.) i. JOSEPH OSBORN FELTON[7], (*Amory*[6], *Benjamin*[5], *Joseph*[4], *Skelton*[3], *Nathaniel*[2], *Nathaniel*[1],) b. in Danvers, Jan. 1, 1822; he was in Amherst College 1838–39; again 1841 to 1843; read law in Worcester with Mr. Torrey. He was a lawyer in Wilmington, Ohio, 1849 to 1852; editor of Dayton (Ohio) Gazette, 1852 to 1855. In 1855, Mr. Felton moved to Chicago, Ill., where he was a lawyer and legal reporter of the Chicago Tribune. He m. Nov. 1857, Ellen Brandt of North Brookfield, Mass. He died at Chicago of pneumonia, March 1, 1864, aged 42 years, 2 months.

(1325.) ii. WILLIAM AMORY FELTON[7], (*Amory*[6], *Benjamin*[5], *Joseph*[4], *Skelton*[3], *Nathaniel*[2], *Nathaniel*[1],) b. Feb. 13, 1824; m. Susan Tyler. He resides in New Braintree, Mass., and was one of their selectmen in 1862 and 1863; one of the 9 jurors in 1876. Is a butcher by trade. Their children were:

 2140. i. WILLIAM T.; a cabinet maker.

2141. ii. HENRY H., b. about 1854.
2142. iii. CHARLES A.
2143. iv. SUSIE A. In 1882, says a newspaper, Miss Susie A. Felton had not been absent or tardy from school for 9 years in succession.

(1334.) vi. GEORGE PERRY KENDRICK; b. in Western, (now Warren,) Mass., Aug. 22, 1824, son of Jacil and Hannah (Felton) Kendrick, (No. 609.) He resides at Worcester, and represented the city in the General Court 1871 and 1872; was an alderman in 1877 and 1878. He is a stable keeper, and had his stable with 15 horses burnt in the winter of 1881-82. Mr. Kendrick m. Sept. 23, 1850, Caroline S. Holman, b. about 1829. They have 2 sons.

2144. i. GEORGE A., b. May 16, 1853.
2145. ii. EDWARD H., b. Nov. 28, 1858.

(1335.) vii. WILLIAM CARLOS CULVER of N. H., m. in Enfield, Mass., July 3, 1845, Jane Kendrick, b. in Western, (now Warren,) Mass., Nov. 12, 1827, daughter of Jacil and Hannah (Felton) Kendrick. Mr. Culver resides in Boston, Mrs. Jane K. Culver is a physician in that city. They have children.

(1339.) i. DR. JOHN H. GRAY, m. Lucinda Felton, b. Feb. 24, 1809, daughter of Maj. Skelton and Tryphosa (Bullard) Felton of Oakham, Mass. He was a physician and sup. settled in N. Y. State. Had 2 or more children.

2146. ii. JOHN F., sup. b. about 1830; was living at Schuyler Lake a few years ago.
2147. ii. SARAH A., b. in 1833; m. ——— Durpee. Mrs. Sarah A. Durpee died at Schuyler Lake, Otsego County, N. Y., Jan. 31, 1878, aged 44 years.

(1340.) ii. EDWARD LaCROIX of Southbridge, Mass., (b. in Medway,) m. July 1849, Eliza Walker Felton, b. about 1830, daughter of Skelton Felton, Esq., of Oakham. They had 7 children. A few years ago were living in Needham. Mr. LaCroix was b. about 1825, son of William and Lois LaCroix.

2148. i. WILLIAM E., b. about 1851; m. Georgianna Hoyt; have 3 children.
2149. ii. HENRY L.; died aged 5 months.
2150. iii. FREDERICK W., b. about 1854; m. Jennie Dexter.
2151. iv. EDWARD W., b. about 1856.

2152. v. LAURA, b. about 1859 ; m. Frederick H. Tucker.
2153. vi. MARY F., b. about 1862.
2154. vii. JAMES.

(1341.) iii. WELLS BILL, m. Louisa Malvina Felton, b. about 1833, daughter of Maj. Skelton and Mary P. (Crawford) Felton of Oakham, Mass. Had several children.

2155. i. IDA M.
2156. ii. FRANK F.; died, aged 18 months.
2157. iii. HENRY W.; died in 1883, aged 24 years.
2158. iv. ALICE O.; died young.
2159. v. ANNIE C., b. about 1863 ; one daughter m. James DeCamp.
2160. vi. HELEN A., b. about 1865 ; m. Walker Houston.
2161. vii. ELIZABETH, b. about 1870.
2162. viii. BERTHA LaC., b. in 1873.

(1342.) i. CHARLES CHURCH CHAMBERLIN of Bangor, Me., b. June 30, 1815 ; m. Sept. 15, 1837, (or 1836) Cordelia Maria Felton, b. Aug. 17, 1817, daughter of Josiah D. and Reliet Felton. Mr. Chamberlin died Dec. 24, 1851, aged 36 years. Mrs. Chamberlin died March 23, 1872, aged 54 years. Their children were :

2163†. i. CORDELIA C., b. July 15, 1838 ; m. Frederick B. Deane.
2164†. ii. MARY C., b. Sept. 23, 1840 ; m. James C Chittendon.
2165†. iii. SOPHIA H., b. Sept. 23, 1843 ; m. David H. McIvor.
2166. iv. CHARLOTTE, b. July 23, 1847 ; m. Herbert H. Fairbanks in 1872.
2167. v. ELLEN D., b. Aug. 23, 1850 ; died July 29, 1852, aged 2 years.

(1343.) i. JONATHAN IRISH of Buckfield, Me., m. Isabella Nye Felton, b. in Barre, Mass., July 27, 1812, dau. of Jonathan W. Felton of Paris, Me. Have had 5 children, only 2 living in 1886. Mrs. Irish died in Phillips, Me., Sept. 27, 1878, aged 66 years. Their children were :

2167. *a.* i. GEORGE P.
2167. *b.* ii. ELIZABETH L.; m. Willard Russell ; residence, Weld, Me.
2167. *c.* iii. MARY J.
2167. *d.* iv. FRANCIS.
2167. *e.* v. NETTIE ; m. Frank Russell ; residence, Avon, Me.

(1344.) ii. JOHN W. WILLIS of Paris, Me., m. Stella Jane Felton, b. Jan. 31, 1815, in Barre, Mass., daughter of Jonathan W. Felton of Paris, Me. Had 5 children.

2167. *f.*   i. FRANCIS L., b. July 26, 1840; m. Marietta Bird of Paris, Me. One daughter.
2167. *g.*   ii. LORRAINE F., b. Jan. 13, 1843; m. Ellen A. Usher of Gorham, Me. Have 4 children.
2167. *h.*   iii. GEORGE DEK., b. March 2, 1847; m. Katie W. Hutchinson of Paris, Me. He died in Oct. 1875; have 2 children.
2167. *i.*   iv. ELIZA J., b. Aug. 28, 1849; m. Parker C. Green; residence, Athol, Mass.
2167. *j.*   v. STELLA L., b. Dec. 5, 1859; m. George P. Burnham; residence, Gilead, Me.

(1345.) iii. MARCELLUS SMITH of Wellington, Vt., m. Charlotte Selina Felton, b. July 7, 1820, daughter of Jonathan W. Felton of Paris, Me. Mrs. Smith died Feb. 1867, aged 46 years; left one child.

2167. *k.*   i. HATTIE L.; living in Norway, Me.

(1347.) v. ALBERT QUINCY FELTON[7], (*Jonathan W.*[6], *Skelton*[5], *Joseph*[4], *Skelton*[3], *Nathaniel*[2], *Nathaniel*[1],) was b. in Paris, Me., March 7, 1828; m. second, Mrs. Mary Jane Libbey, widow of Frederic Libbey, and daughter of Wm. Bent. They reside in Paris, Me. They have one son.

2167. *l.*   i. GEORGE F., b. March 6, 1865; m. Agnes Robbins.

Albert Quincy Felton m. first Columbia Decortes; no issue.

(1349.) i. ELIJAH HAMMOND, b. in Oakham, Oct. 9, 1819, son of John Hammond who was a representative of Worcester in 1841. Elijah Hammond m. Dec. 19, 1843, Caroline Nye Felton, b. Dec. 9, 1821, daughter of Capt. Benjamin and Lucretia Felton of Barre, Mass. He is a farmer on Moreland street, Worcester. Mrs. Hammond died June 6, 1882, aged 60 years. They had 5 children.

2168†.   i. ADALINE S., b. in Oakham, Jan. 17, 1845; m. Vernon Long.
2169.   ii. ALICE M., b. in Worcester, Dec. 19, 1849.
2170.   iii. ELLEN C., b. in W., Jan. 12, 1853.
2171.   iv. JOHN, b. Dec. 8, 1856; died March 6, 1864, aged 7 years.
2172.   v. ALBERT E., b. Dec. 16, 1859; died just 6 hours after his brother, March 6, 1864, aged 4 years.

(1350.) ii. JOHN FELTON[7], (*Benjamin*[6], *Skelton*[5], *Joseph*[4], *Skelton*[3], *Nathaniel*[2], *Nathaniel*[1],) b. Oct. 6, 1824; m. April 6, 1852, Mary R. Swan of Barre, Mass., where he was a trader and draper several years. He was a soldier in the Union army in 1864, enlisted for 3 years. He is now a merchant in Buffalo, N. Y. In 1879, one of the board of trustees of the Unitarian society of that city. Had one daughter.

2173.   i. ANNA C.

(1351.) iii. BENJAMIN F. FELTON[7], (*Benjamin*[6], *Skelton*[5], *Joseph*[4], *Skelton*[3], *Nathaniel*[2], *Nathaniel*[1],) b. Dec. 31, 1827; m. Ellen Chapman. He drove a milk wagon in Worcester a few years. Now resides at Buffalo, N. Y. Have had 7 children.

2174.   i. JOHN C., b. Aug. 1858; died aged 6 years.
2175.   ii. CAROLINE E.
2176.   iii. GRACE A.
2177.   iv. LILLIAN DEGAFF; lived 5 months.
2178.   v. CHARLES A.
2179.   vi. ROBERT W.
2180.   vii. WILLARD H.

(1352.) iv. CHARLES EMORY FELTON[7], (*Benjamin*[6], *Skelton*[5], *Joseph*[4], *Skelton*[3], *Nathaniel*[2], *Nathaniel*[1],) b. Sept. 18, 1831; m. Ellen J. Gale of Buffalo, N. Y.; she died in Chicago, Ill., June 13, 1872. They moved to Chicago about 1870. He m. second, Jan. 26, 1874, Mrs. Ellen Maria (Britnall) Compton of that place. In 1871, Mr. Felton was appointed superintendent of the house of correction of the City of Chicago; has held the office 15 years. Have had 5 or more children.

2181.   i. CHARLES E., JR., b. Jan. 1854; died Oct. 9, 1854.
2182.   ii. GEORGE G., b. about 1855; living in Chicago a few years ago.
2183.   iii. ELLEN J; m. Jan. 29, 1880, Charles E. Willard.
2184.   iv. MARY L.
2185.   v. FRANCIS W; lived 9 weeks.

(1353.) v. JOSIAH CHARLES BOWKER, b. in Conway, Mass., July 31, 1814, (son of Josiah Bowker;) m. Jan. 1 1854, Mary Louisa Felton, b. Sept. 24, 1833, daughter of Capt. Benjamin Felton of Barre, (No. 620.) They lived in Worcester several years; in Marlboro, 1860 to 1863, a shoemaker; the latter year moved to Dorchester. Mrs. Bowker died at Boston Highlands, April 12, 1878, aged 44 years; buried in

Phillipston, Mass., and the same day, April 12, 1878, died in Phillipston, Mr. Bowker's sister, Mrs. Harriet B., wife of Hon. Jason Goulding, aged 60 years. Funerals of both April 16. Less than two months afterwards, June 4, 1878, died in Phillipston, Josiah Charles Bowker, aged 64 years. Had 1 son.

2186. CHARLES F., b. Oct. 1858; m. about 1881, Florence J. ——, and had a son Charles Felton, Jr., b. March 1882.

(1354.) vi. FRANCIS JACKSON WARD, b. Sept. 17, 1830, son of Nahum Ward of Roxbury, who was of the 6th generation of Dea. Wm. Ward, one of the first settlers in Marlboro, Mass. Mr. Ward m. Aug. 2, 1860, Ann Jane Felton, b. July 25, 1840, the youngest daughter of Capt. Benjamin Felton of Barre, Mass. Mr. Ward had two or more children by a former wife; buried a daughter in 1877, aged 18 years and another daughter in 1879, aged 24 years. Mr. Ward is a provision dealer in Boston; his house at Boston Highlands.

2187. i RUTH F., b. Jan. 30, 1866.
2188. ii. ESTHER H., b. April 8, 1870.

(1361.) iv. JOSEPH H. ATKINS, b. about 1822, son of Isaac and Sarah Atkins of Marblehead; m. March 10, 1850, Elizabeth A. Felton, b. Dec. 1818, daughter of Francis and Sally Felton of Marblehead. They had one or more children.

2188½. i. FRANCIS F. b. about 1854; m. Sept. 25, 1877, Mary Ellen Giles, all of Marblehead.

(1366.) iv. FRANCIS A. FELTON[7], (James[6], James[5], Francis[4], John[3], Nathaniel[2], Nathaniel[1],) b. March 5, 1823; m. Sarah Elizabeth Churchill; he was a sail-maker in Salem, Mass. He died Jan. 15, 1867, aged 44 years. Mrs. Felton died suddenly in the same city of heart disease, Dec. 19, 1882. They had 8 children.

2189. i. FRANCIS A., b. April 17, 1846; died in Cal., April 1875, aged 29 years.
2190. ii. MARY E., b. May 9, 1848; m. Albert McCully.
2191. iii. JOHN S., b. June 23, 1849.
2192. iv. SARAH A., b. Sept. 2, 1850; m. Robert Price of Lynn.
2193. v. CHARLES H., b. March 28, 1853; died Sept. 4, 1855.
2194. vi. LOUISA W., b. Oct. 19, 1855.

2195. vii. LAURA E., b. Jan. 18, 1858; m. Charles B. Merrill, Jan. 1877.
2196. viii. WILLIAM E., b. May 18, 1862.

(1368.) i. .LEVI WIGGIN of Salem, m. in Boston, Jan. 1849, Caroline Felton, b. April 2, 1816, daughter of John Smith Felton of Salem. They resided in Salem and had 5 children.

2197. i. ANN E., b. Aug. 25, 1849; living in 1883.
2198. ii. JOHN S. F., b, Nov. 2, 1853; unm. in 1883.
2199. iii. LAWRENCE P., b. May 16, 1855; died Oct. 15, 1855.
2200. iv. FRANK H., b. Oct. 8, 1857; died Sept. 1861.
2201. v. CAROLINE F., b. Aug. 25, 1858; died Sept. 8, 1858.

(1369.) ii. LEVI WYMAN, m. Matilda Felton, b. July 1817, daughter of John Smith and Nancy (Crandall) Felton of Salem, Mass. Mr. Wyman died several years ago. Mrs. Wyman is living in Salem. Had 3 children.

2202. i. MATILDA F., b. about 1844; m. Josiah M. Crocker.
2203. ii. RUTH A., b. about 1846; died unm.
2204. iii. LEVI, JR., b. Nov. 1848; died Jan. 1879, aged 30 years.

(1371.) iv. WILLIAM RANDALL, b. in Vt., about 1822; m. second, April 26, 1870, Mary Jane Felton, b. in Jan. 1820, daughter of John S. and Nancy Felton of Salem. Mr. Randall died Jan. 1883, aged 61 years. No issue by last wife.

(1382.) ii. DAVID FELTON[7], (*David H.*[6], *Ebenezer*[5], *David*[4], *Ebenezer*[3], *Nathaniel*[2], *Nathaniel*[1],) b. in 1805; he m. and had one daughter. He lived in N. Y. State, and died July 22, 1865, aged 61 years.

2204. *a.* i. MARTHA G., m. Levi J. Richardson and moved to Wisconsin in 1867. Had no children in 1882; had an adopted son, John Edward Richardson, b. about 1865.

(1392.) i. PLINY CLIFFORD m. Priscilla Elvira Leonard, b. May 14, 1802, daughter of Ezekiel and Rachel (Felton) Leonard, (No. 652.) Had one son.

2204. *b.* i. PLINY JR.; he was living in Hampshire County, Mass., a few years ago.

Mrs. P. E. Clifford was married three times; she lived 68 years.

(1396.) v. THORNDIKE LEONARD, b. April 28, 1812, son of Ezekiel and Rachel (Felton) Leonard of Oakham, Mass.; m. Sarah Elizabeth Temple, b. in Marlboro in 1814. He lived in several towns, Greenwich, Hopkinton, Westboro, Northboro, and the last 25 years in Grafton, Mass. Mrs. Leonard died in Greenwich; they had 3 children. Mr. Leonard m. second, Mrs. Hannah (Claflin) Gibson and had 3 more children. Mrs. Hannah Leonard is cousin to ex-Gov. William Claflin of Mass.

 2205. i. LUCY A.; m. Lewis Freeman; have 5 children.
 2206. ii. RUTH A.; m. John H. Johnson.
 2207. iii. JOHN L.; lived 6 or 8 months.
 2208. iv. SARAH J., b. about 1849; m. Levi N. Leland, Jr.; had 2 children.
 2209. v. CHARLES L., b. about 1850; m. Ella C. Brewer; residence, Grafton; have 4 children.
 2210. vi. SUMNER F., b. in 1857; m. Mabel G. Thurston.

(1400.) i. CHARLES HAGER, b. in Wendell, Mass., Oct. 9, 1809, (son of Martin Hager, who was born in Marlboro in 1778;) m. Myra H. Felton, b. Oct. 15, 1811, daughter of Daniel and Fanny (Holden) Felton of Deerfield, Mass. Mr. Hager has a large farm near Mount Sugar Loaf in South Deerfield, Mass. He moved from Wendell to Deerfield in 1855, and in 1857, bought his father-in-law's farm. He was a selectman in Deerfield in 1872. They have had 5 children. All the sons are married and live near or upon their father's farm.

 2211. i. DEXTER F., b. May 4, 1840; was a soldier in the late civil war. In May 1883, was commander of South Deerfield Post, G. A. R.
 2212. ii. FANNY F., b. March 17, 1842; died Jan. 6, 1866, aged 23 years.
 2213. iii. LYDIA E., b. March 23, 1845; m. L. L. Eaton of Whately, Mass.
 2214. iv. OTIS, b. Oct. 20, 1849; m.
 2215. v. MARTIN, b. Sept. 16, 1851; m.

(1401.) ii. ALVIN FELTON[7], (*Daniel*[6], *Stephen*[5], *Ebenezer*[4], *Ebenezer*[3], *Nathaniel*[2], *Nathaniel*[1],) b. Aug. 3, 1813; m. Mehitable A. Whitney. He was a blacksmith and has lived in Barre, Dana and Orange. He is now a farmer at South Deerfield, Mass. Have had 5 or more children.

 2216. i. ELLEN; died aged 10 years.

2217. ii. LORENZO G., b. in Orange, Jan. 1838; m. Ellen or Helen A. Lincoln; they lived at Leverett several years. He died in Deerfield of heart disease, April 14, 1873, aged 35 years; was a farmer. No issue. Mrs. Felton m. second, Augustine Holden, a relative of Mr. Felton's grandmother, Mrs. Fanny Felton.

2218. iii. PERRY, b. about 1841; died young.

2219. iv. RUBY W., b. in 1844; m. May 1867, Clement E. Bates, b. 1845, son of Daniel H. Bates.

2220. v. MELISSA E., b. about 1847; m. March 1878, Newton R. Hawkes, son of Almon Hawkes; he is a farmer.

(1405.) vi. DAVID AUSTIN FOOT, b. in 1810, son of David Foot; m. July 1857, Lucetta Felton, b. Jan. 14, 1822, daughter of Daniel and Fanny Felton of Deerfield; his second marriage: they reside in Deerfield, Mass. Had one child.

2220½. i. ELLEN F., b. in 1861: died in 1879, aged 18 years.

(1406.) vii. JOSEPH P. FELTON^7, ($Daniel^6$, $Stephen^5$, $Ebenezer^4$, $Ebenezer^3$, $Nathaniel^2$, $Nathaniel^1$,) b. Aug. 19, 1824; m. Harriet A. Bridges; they resided a few years in Deerfield, and in Sunderland a few years. About 1861, moved to Greenfield, where he has a meat market. In 1865 and 1866, was on the school committee; has been deputy sheriff 3 years, and justice of the peace. Had 5 children.

2221. i. JENNIE L., b. in 1850; m. Albert Julius Smead; residence, Greenfield, Mass.

2222. ii. FANNIE E., b. in Deerfield; died aged about 15 years.

2223. iii. FREDERICK B., b. about 1856; m.

2224. iv. One daughter, b. in Sunderland, Oct. 29, 1859.

2225. v. GEORGE F., b. in Greenfield, April 24, 1862.

(1407.) i. LANSFORD BURR FELTON^7, ($Thorndike^6$, $Stephen^5$, $Ebenezer^4$, $Ebenezer^3$, $Nathaniel^2$, $Nathaniel^1$,) b. Aug. 29, 1815; m. May 1836, Harriet A. Parker, b. Sept. 13, 1819, daughter of Samuel and Hannah (Fay) Parker of Hardwick, Mass. He was a harness-maker in Barre several years. He moved to Milford, Mass., about 1847, and was landlord of Felton Hotel in that place several years, also kept a livery stable. He moved out on a farm a few years before he deceased. He died in Milford, March 29, 1880, aged 64 years. Mrs. Felton died about 4 years afterwards, in the winter of 1883-84, aged 64 years.

2226. i. FISK A., b. in Barre, May 18, 1844; m. June 1872, Lizzie M. Chase of Boston; have two or more children.
2227. ii. FRANK B., b. in Milford, June 3, 1853; m. Jan. 1876, Katie Elizabeth Smith.
2228. iii. LENA F., b. Jan. 22, 1855; died March 5, 1855.
2229. iv. ETTA L., b. March 25, 1856; died Jan. 19, 1858.

Maria A. Felton, b. in Rindge, N. H. about 1834, lived in Mr. Felton's family a dozen years and took the surname of Felton; she m. June 1860, Hiram W. Eames of Boston, son of Aaron Eames of Grafton, Mass.

(1408.) ii. STEPHEN FELTON[7], (*Thorndike*[6], *Stephen*[5], *Ebenezer*[4], *Ebenezer*[3], *Nathaniel*[2], *Nathaniel*[1],) b. Feb. 6, 1817; m. July 3, 1849, Emily L. Bingham and settled at Towanda, Pa., where he died Sept. 15, 1864, aged 47 years. They had 5 children. Mrs. Emily L. Felton was living in Towanda a few years ago.

2230. i. HARRIET E., b. Feb. 19, 1853; m. May 19, 1875, W. J. Young, Esq., an attorney-at-law and auditor at Towanda, Bradford County, Pa.
2231. ii. GEORGE B., b. May 1, 1855; died Feb. 28, 1856.
2232. iii. JOHN B., b. Jan. 2, 1857; m. Dec. 7, 1881, Miss Frank Morley. He is a printer in Towanda.
2233. iv. FREDERICK S., b. Nov. 1, 1858; a printer in Towanda.
2234. v. CHARLES L., b. Jan. 30, 1862; a book-keeper.

(1410.) iv. SYLVANUS WING BATES, b. Dec. 23, 1818, (son of Capt. Thomas M. Bates of Hanover, Mass., and grandson of Capt. Clement Bates of that town;) m. Rebecca Chamberlain Felton, daughter of Thorndike and Joanna (Chamberlain) Felton of New Salem, Mass. They resided in Hanover, Mass., and had two sons.

2235. i. LYSANDER F., b. March 8, 1843; m.
2236. ii. LUCIUS W., b. Aug. 24, 1849; m.

(1424.) ix. CHARLES A. FELTON[7], (*Ebenezer*[6], *Stephen*[5], *Ebenezer*[4], *Ebenezer*[3], *Nathaniel*[2], *Nathaniel*[1],) b. Feb. 3, 1843; m. Sept. 9, 1865, Mrs. Sarah A. Albee, both of Wendell, Mass. Mrs. Felton was killed at the disaster (boiler explosion) in Wendell, Dec. 8, 1880; there were several men killed at the same time. They had one son.

2236½. i. LEROY, b. about 1866.

(1434.) ii. DR. GEORGE F. CHAMBERLAIN, b. in

Brimfield, Mass., in 1826, and settled in that town, (a son of Dr. Levi Chamberlain and Abigail Felton, who were born and died in New Salem, Mass.) Dr. George F. Chamberlain buried his twin daughters in 1879, aged 25 years; Alice died in April and Annie in Dec.; Annie was married and left one child.

(1435.) iii. DR. CYRUS N. CHAMBERLAIN, b. in Barnstable, Mass., March 8, 1829, (son of Dr. Levi Chamberlain, who died in New Salem in 1864;) he graduated at the Medical College in 1850; settled at Granby, Mass.; afterwards in Northampton, Mass. In June 1861, enlisted in the Union army; was surgeon in the 10th Mass. Regiment. After the war, in 1865, settled in the city of Lawrence, Mass.

(1436.) iv. WILLIAM A. LLOYD was a teacher in 1856, in Sanderson Academy, in Ashfield, Mass. He m. in 1862, Helen M. Chamberlain of New Salem, Mass. Mr. Lloyd is a minister and resides in Ill. In 1862 in Ringwood, in Morris in 1865, in Ravenswood, Cook County, since 1870. Mrs. Helen M. Lloyd, a daughter of Dr. Levi and Abigail (Felton) Chamberlain, who died in New Salem, Mass., in 1864 and 1865.

(1443 and 1459.) i. WILLARD PUTNAM, b. in Sept. 1838, son of Samuel and Elizabeth Putnam of New Salem, Mass. He fitted for college at New Salem Academy, and graduated at Amherst College in 1860. He taught school two years, served on the school board of New Salem and represented the town in the Legislature in 1875. He m. June 14, 1862, Lydia Ellen Burnett, b. Nov. 16, 1837, daughter of Capt. David and Lydia (Felton) Burnett of New Salem, Mass. They have two sons.

2239. i. WILLARD A., b. July 22, 1865.
2240. ii. BERTRAND F., b. Feb. 9, 1871.

(1462.) i. JOSEPH H. STILES, m. Nov. 18, 1852, Mary A. Felton, b. about 1827, daughter of Nathaniel and Abigail H. (Bowker) Felton of Barre, Mass. They had two children. Mr. Stiles died before 1864.

2240. a, i. MARY A. F., b. in Barre, Aug. 22, 1853.
2240. b. ii. JOSEPH H., JR.

(1463.) ii. WELCOME FELTON[7], (Nathaniel[6], Nathaniel[5], Nathaniel[4], Ebenezer[3], Nathaniel[2], Nathaniel[1],) b. April 6, 1832; m. Aug. 24, 1854, Fidelia A. Thayer, daughter of Asa Thayer, Esq., of Winchester, N. H. He was a bookseller and stationer in Brattleborough, Vt., in 1854, and several years afterwards. They have been in Boston several years. Have had two or more children.

2241. i. Percy T.
2242. ii. Warren B.

(1488.) i. WILLIAM HENRY FELTON[7], (Nathaniel[6], Nathaniel[5], Nathaniel[4], Jonathan[3], Nathaniel[2], Nathaniel[1],) b. Dec. 25, 1821; m. June 1851, Sarah Jane Sperry, daughter of Charles Sperry of Lowell, Mass. Had 4 children. Mrs. Felton died July 20, 1864, aged 38 years. He m. second, June 1866, Hattie Palmer, b. June 9, 1835, daughter of Asa P. Palmer of Orford, N. H. He resided on Mt. Pleasant, in Peabody, until April 1877, when the family moved to Marlboro, Mass. Mr. Felton is a farmer.

2243. i. Sarah F., b. May 1, 1852; died July 3, 1860, aged 8 years.
2244. ii. Susie W., b. Feb. 15, 1855; a school teacher a few years; m. in Marlboro, Jan. 1881, Walter W. Howe of Marlboro.
2245. iii. Mabel S., b. Aug. 31, 1857; m. Oct. 1881, Winslow B. Howe of Marlboro.
2246. iv. Nathaniel H., b. Oct. 31, 1861.

(1489.) ii. OREN FROST of Tewksbury, Mass., m. Rebecca Preston Felton, b. Feb. 19, 1824, daughter of Col. Nathaniel Felton of Felton Hill, South Danvers. Mr. Frost was town treasurer of Tewksbury 4 years, 1862 to 1866. Had 5 children. He m. first, Jane Sperry, a cousin of Sarah Jane Felton named above, and had Oren, Jr., and one daughter. Mr. Frost died Jan. 27, 1874, aged 54 years. Mrs. Rebecca P. Frost died in the summer of 1884, aged 60 years.

2247. i. Nathaniel F., b. Jan. 31, 1853; m.
2248. ii. Horace W., b. Aug. 6, 1856.
2249. iii. Mary P., b. Nov. 7, 1857; died before 1877.
2250. iv. Susan A., b. Nov. 19, 1860; died in 1879.
2251. v. Aaron A., b. Aug. 2, or 3, 1863.

(1491.) iv. Capt. CHARLES B. RHODES, m. Harriet Felton, b. Nov. 3, 1828, daughter of Col. Nathaniel Felton of South Danvers. She taught school in Danvers a few years before she was married. Capt. Rhodes was lost at sea, Feb. (about 25) 1862, aged 50 years. Since 1862, Mrs. Rhodes resided several years in California; she is now living in Mass.

(1492.) v. LEVI PRESTON FELTON[7], (Nathaniel[6],

Nathaniel⁶, Nathaniel⁴, Jonathan³, Nathaniel², Nathaniel¹,) b. Jan. 10, 1831; he studied law at Albany, N. Y., a few years; m. May 1865, Abby Rogers of Tewksbury, Mass. About 1867, they moved to Cal, He was police judge at Stockton, Cal., several years. Mrs. Felton died in 1875. They had two sons. He died at Murphy's, Cal., July 5, 1881, aged 50 years.

 2252. i. BURTON R., b. in Tewksbury, Mass., March 24, 1866.
 2253. ii. CHARLES R., b. in Cal March 17, 1869.

(1493.) vi. NATHANIEL WARD FELTON⁷, (*Nathaniel⁶, Nathaniel⁵, Nathaniel⁴, Jonathan³, Nathaniel², Nathaniel¹,*) b. July 5, 1833; m. June 20, 1866, Maria L. Ferrin of Beverly, Mass., b. Feb. 7, 1845. All of his Felton ancestors had the name Nathaniel but one. Mr. Felton now resides on the Felton farm and homestead, on Mt. Pleasant, in Peabody, Mass.

(1494.) vii. JAMES LEVERETT SPERRY, b. in N. H., son of Charles Sperry of Lowell, Mass; m. Mehitable Berry Felton, b. May 24, 1837, the youngest daughter of Col. Nathaniel Felton of South Danvers, Mass. They settled in Calaveras County, Cal., and kept the Sperry Hotel, near the big tree grove in that county. Mrs. Sperry has written several pieces of poetry for the California newspapers; she composed one of 27 verses on their family horse, " Selem " that died in Nov. 1873; " Selem " was well known to tourists and visitors to the Calaveras Big Tree Grove.

 2254. i. WILLARD F., b. in Danvers, Mass., Sept. 24, 1865.
 2255. ii. HARRIET E., b. in Cal., July 7, 1868.
 2256. iii. MARION P., b. June 1871.
 2257. iv. JAMES C., b. in 1874.

In June 1883, The Stockton (Cal.) *Independent* said that J. L. Sperry, proprietor of the hotel near the wonderful big trees, the mammoth monarchs of the forest, had one of the finest hotels in the State. The Grove Hotel can accommodate one hundred guests.

The grove contains ten trees, each thirty feet in diameter, and over seventy that are between fifteen and thirty feet. In 1853, one of the largest trees, 92 feet in circumference and over 300 feet high, was cut down. Five men worked 25 days in felling it, using large augers. The stump of this tree easily accommodates 32 dancers. " Hercules " was the largest tree standing in the grove until 1862, when, during a heavy storm, it fell. It was 325 feet long, and 97 in circumference. Near the Grove Hotel stand the "two sentinels" each over 300 feet high, and the larger 23 feet in diameter. The carriage road approaching the hotel passes directly between the "two sentinels."

(1498.) vii. DANIEL HENRY FELTON⁷, (*Daniel⁶, Nathaniel⁵, Nathaniel⁴, Jonathan³, Nathaniel², Nathaniel¹,*) b. March 6, 1836, and resides at Felton Corner, where his father, also his maternal grandfather, Nathan Felton, Esq., lived and died. He is a gardener and owns some land on Felton Hill, Mt. Pleasant. Mr. Felton has taken considerable interest in collecting information about the early settlers in his vicinity.

(1516.) ii. GEORGE W. FELTON⁷, (*George⁶, Jonathan⁵, Jonathan⁴, Jonathan³, Nathaniel², Nathaniel¹,*) b. in Salem, Mass., Aug. 6, 1833; was a graduate of Salem High School. He was a photographer in Salem several years. He has been several years superintendent of the Western Union Telegraph Company and resides in Chicago, Ill. He m. Harriet Payson and has 3 children.

- 2258.   i. ANNA E.
- 2259.   ii. ALBERT E.
- 2260.   iii. BETSEY M.

(1522.) iii. WILLIAM BIGELOW, b. April 12, 1809, son of Ephraim Bigelow of Marlboro; m. Lucy Maynard in 1837, daughter of John P. and Betsey Maynard of Marlboro. They had one daughter. Mr. Bigelow died Sept. 11, 1843, aged 34 years. Mrs. Bigelow m. second, in 1846, his brother, Granville Bigelow, and had 2 more children. Mr. Bigelow is a farmer in Marlboro.

- 2260. *a.*   i. ELIZABETH, b. Jan. 22, 1838.
- 2260. *b.*   ii. WILLIAM G., b. in Nov. 2, 1847; died July 20, 1849.
- 2260. *c.*   iii. EMILY G., b. July 2, 1850.

(1523.) iv. ELBRIDGE G. PARMENTER, b. Dec. 2, 1814, (son of Ezekiel Parmenter of Marlboro;) m. May 1840, Eleanor Temple, b. Feb. 26, 1822, daughter of Ira and Betsey Temple of Marlboro. They settled on their father's place in Marlboro, and had 9 children. Mr. Parmenter died Dec. 3, 1882, aged 68 years. He was a farmer in the extreme northeast part of the town. Mrs. Parmenter now resides near the village of Marlboro.

- 2261.   i. ALBERT G., b. Nov. 21, 1841; died May 12, 1874, aged 32 years.

FELTON FAMILY. 209

2262.   ii. ALTHEA H., b. Feb. 22. 1843; m. Dec. 1868, Charles B. Greenwood.
2263.   iii. WILLIAM A., b. Nov. 8, 1844.
2264.   iv. GEORGE D., b. Nov. 14, 1846; died Feb. 23, 1852, aged 5 years.
2265†. v. IRA E., b. Dec. 19, 1848; m. Emma S. Huntington, (No. 1834.)
2266.   vi. LUCY E., b. April 20, 1851; m. Sept. 1877, Chas. T. Berry of Marlboro.
2267.   vii. GEORGE D., b. Feb. 23, 1853; died June 2, 1883, aged 30 years.
2268.   viii. FREEMAN M., b. Nov. 7, 1857.
2269.   ix. LYDIA I., b. Jan. 19, 1865; died July 26, 1866.

(1539.) ii. DANIEL WALDO STEVENS, b. Jan. 18, 1820, son of I. T. and Catherine (Felton) Stevens of Marlboro; m. Caroline Partridge of Medway; had one son; he m. second, Mrs. Esther Sumner; he m. third in 1863, Anna Frances Fairbanks; she died May 1871. He graduated at Harvard College in 1346; read theology and was a Unitarian preacher and settled at Mansfield, Mass. Mr. Stevens has for several years had the charge of the Seaman Society at Martha's Vineyard.

2270.   i. DANIEL; m. Oct. 23, 1872, Mary E. Young, dau. of Rev. Joshua Young of Cambridge, Mass.
2271.   ii. CAROLINE, by his third wife; died young in 1871.

(1540.) iii. ISAAC EMERSON STEVENS, b. Jan. 30, 1822, son of Isaac Temple Stevens of Marlboro; m. about Jan. 1846, Susan C. Burditt of Malden, Mass. Settled in Marlboro, near his father's place, and had 7 children. Mrs. Stevens died in Boston, Aug. 13, 1878, aged 58 years; buried in Marlboro. Mr. Stevens has resided for several years in Ky.

2272.   i. CHARLES E., b. Oct. 4, 1846; m. Albertine Honey.
2273.   ii. LOUIS F., b. June 17, 1848; m. Dora Frances Paine, Jan. 1872.
2274.   iii. CAROLINE E., b. July 26, 1850; m. Nicholas Doyle.
2275.   iv. MARY A., b. July 1852; m. Edward Lyon.
2276.   v. ALBERT, b. Sept. 12, 1854.
2277.   vi. ALFRED, twin, b. Sept. 12, 1854.
2278.   vii. FREDERICK E., b. Nov. 26, 1857; m.

(1541.) iv. JOHN SULLIVAN STEVENS, b. Feb. 26, 1823, son of Isaac T. and Catherine Stevens of Marlboro; m.

in 1846, Mary Elizabeth Perry, b. in Marlboro, Sept. 17, 1828, daughter of Capt. Jesse Perry, then of Marlboro. He settled in Marlboro, and in 1853, lost some of his fingers by blasting rocks; has since become a tin peddler. Their children were:

- 2279. i. JOHN J., b. April 11, 1847; drowned in Marlboro Lake, July 18, 1857, aged 10 years.
- 2280.-81. ii.-iii. In 1854, twins, born and died in Dec.
- 2282. iv. EDDIE P., b. Sept. 3, 1859.
- 2283. v. EUNICE E., b. May 5, 1861.
- 2284. vi. LAURA A., b. Oct. 21, 1867; died young.
- 2285. vii. LAURA A., b. July 28, 1869.

(1542.) v. LEVI LINCOLN STEVENS, b. Oct. 22, 1824, son of Isaac T. Stevens of Marlboro; m. Mary Elizabeth Bispham; she died in childbed, July 9. 1849, aged 22 years; had 2 children. He m. second, Ellen Abigail Salisbury; had 5 children. Mr. Stevens was a shoe-maker many years; he is now a dentist with his son Oscar H. Stevens. They have had 7 children.

- 2286. i. One child, b. in 1848; died Oct. 19, 1848, aged 5 months.
- 2287. ii. One child, b. July 1849; died Oct. 1849.
- 2288. iii. WALDO L., b. in Medfield, May 4, 1852; m. Jan. 1874, Emma Wood; settled in Stevensville, near his father's place.
- 2289. iv. OSCAR H., b. Nov. 16, 1854; a dentist in Marlboro; m. May 6, 1885, Charlotte A., daughter of S. Herbert Howe, Esq.
- 2290. v. JOHN S., b. May 20, 1858; m. Abbie M. Daily in 1883.
- 2291. vi. GEORGE H., b. June 5, 1863; m. Florence H. Wilkins in Sept. 1885.
- 2292. vii. HARRIET H., b. April 13. 1865.

(1543.) vi. SAMUEL STILLMAN TOWNSEND, b. March 5, 1823, in Dixfield, Me.; m. March 1855, Mary Temple Stevens, b. Sept. 14, 1827, daughter of Isaac Temple and Catherine (Felton) Stevens of Stevensville, Marlboro. He was a farmer and settled in Marlboro, where Mrs. Townsend died of a cancer, Oct. 11, 1871, aged 44 years. They had 4 children. He m. second, June 1872, Charlotte Wood, b. Dec. 11, 1840, daughter of Miles Wood of Northboro. They reside near the center of Marlboro.

- 2293. i. WILLIAM S., b. Jan. 2, 1856; m. July 1882, Grace O. Barker.

2294. ii. HENRY S., b. March 30, 1857; Nellie Francis Fay, June 1876.
2295. iii. AUGUSTUS E., b. March 24, 1859; m. Lucretia J. Kelly.
2296. iv. AUGUSTA C., twin, b. March 24, 1859; m. Frederick B. Gleason, Oct. 1881.

(1544.) vii. ABRAHAM GATES STEVENS, b. June 19, 1829, son of I. T. and Catherine Stevens of Marlboro; m. Jan. 1, 1850, Charlotte Weeks, b. in Worthington, Mass., daughter of Alfred and Betsey Weeks. He was a carpenter, and resided in Marlboro, where he died May 7, 1879, aged 50 years. Mrs. Charlotte Stevens moved to Worthington a few years ago.

2297. i. FRANK G., b. Jan. 31, 1851.
2298. ii. CHARLOTTE E., b. June 18; 1853; died Sept. 15, 1855.
2299. iii. ERNEST F., b. Oct. 1, 1864; died Sept. 10, 1865.
2300. iv. FRED M., b. Jan. 16, 1868.

(1545.) viii. THOMAS WOODWARD BISPHAM, b. Dec. 1829; m. Nov. 1857, Ann Bent Stevens, b. March 6, 1831, daughter of I. T. and Catherine (Felton) Stevens, (No. 717.) He is a tin peddler, and his home in Marlboro, Mass. Have 3 children.

2301. i. MARY W., b. May 1860.
2302. ii. WALTER M., b. Oct. 21, 1869.
2303. iii. CARRIE P., b. Aug. 1872.

(1549.) xii. WILLIAM ROBINSON STEVENS, b. April 10, 1838, son of Isaac T. and Catherine F. Stevens of Marlboro; m. in 1863, Sarah S. Lamson. He is a farmer and resides on his father's homestead, near the outlet of Marlboro Lake. Had 4 children.

2304. i. STILLMAN R., b. Aug. 28, 1865; graduate of Marlboro High School in 1883.
2304½. ii. CORA L., b. July 17, 1867; died Dec. 17, 1875, aged 8 years.
2305. iii. BERTHA, b. Nov. 11, 1870.
2305½. iv. CLARENCE A., b. March 25, 1873.

(1550.) xiii. HENRY ALFRED HOLYOKE, b. Oct. 14, 1835, son of Capt. Jacob and Lydia (Howe) Holyoke of Marlboro; m. Sept. 8, 1864, Jane Catherine Stevens, the youngest child of Isaac Temple and Catherine (Felton) Stevens of

Marlboro. He was a soldier in the late civil war. Is a farmer in Marlboro. Mrs. Holyoke died Jan. 19, 1884, aged 43 years. Had two sons.

 2306. i. ARTHUR P., b. Nov. 20, 1865.
 2307. ii. GEORGE A., b. March 9, 1871.

At a reunion of the Stevens family at the old homestead on the last Wednesday in May 1886, (the Bay State "old Election Day") the party went to the old chestnut tree, near the homestead, (a brief account of which is found on page 144,) and nineteen members of the family found shelter at the same time within its trunk.

(1551.) i. EBENEZER VINAL STOWE, b. Nov. 16, 1817, son of Jere and Lovinah (Howe) Stowe of Marlboro; m. in Nov. 1847, Susan Almira Felton, b. in Framingham, Jan. 13, 1826, daughter of William and Mary Ann Felton. He was a shoe-maker in Marlboro many years. He is now living in Hudson, Mass. Had two sons.

 2308. i. ALFRED E., b. July 29, 1849; m. Nov. 1871, Alice A. Clough, daughter of John P. and Lydia O. Clough of Boston.
 2309. ii. HERBERT P., b. Oct. 10, 1851; died May 18, 1867, aged 15 years.

(1552.) ii. EBENEZER OAKES, b. in Phillips, Me., in 1823; m. Jan. 1846, Sophronia Ann Felton, b. in Marlboro, June 17, 1827, daughter of William and Mary A. Felton. Mrs. Oakes died Dec. 20, 1847, aged 20 years, leaving one daughter; when the child was three weeks of age, was adopted by Capt. Reuben Hapgood of Feltonville, and took the name, Hapgood.

 2310. i. LUELLA; died in Hudson, Mass., in Sept. 1881, aged 34 years.

Mr. Oakes m. second, June 1848, Francilla Octavia Simpson.

(1554.) iv. WILLIAM H. CHAMBERLAIN, b. about 1822; m. May 1848, Charlotte M. Felton, b. in Northboro, Sept. 17, 1830, daughter of William and Mary Ann Felton, (No. 718.) He is a shoe manufacturer in Hudson, Mass. Has been Overseer of the Poor of that town.

 2311. i. FRANK H., b. Jan. 26, 1850; has been a clerk; m. and moved to Elgin, Ill. He is now, 1885, of the firm of Moulton & Chamberlain, Boot and Shoe Manufacturers, Hudson, Mass.

2312. ii. EMMA, b. July 5, 1852.
2313. iii. One child; died before 1866.

(1555.) v. LUKE BOWERS of Harvard, m. Mary Maria Felton, b in Berlin, Mass., June 20, 1842, daughter of Wm. and Mary Ann Felton, (No. 718.) He enlisted from Acton, and was wounded in the late civil war. Mrs. Bowers died in April 1863, aged 31 years. They buried two children.

(1557.) vii. CHARLES AUGUSTUS FELTON[7], (*William*[6], *William*[5], *Archelaus*[4], *Jonathan*[3], *Nathaniel*[2], *Nathaniel*[1],) b. in Bolton, Mass., Aug. 18, 1836; m. Hannah Cordelia Whitney, of Stow, Mass. He was a soldier in the army from Northboro; enlisted in 1863, for 3 years.

2314. i. FANNIE S., b. in Northboro, Aug. 8, 1861.
2315. ii. LAURA, b. in Northboro, March 2, 1863; died April 4, same year.
2316. iii. A daughter, b. in 1864.
2317. iv. A daughter, b. in 1866.
2318. v. ALVIN O., b. in Northboro, May 12, 1870.

June 3, 1882, Mr. Felton fell into an elevator well, (dropped four stories,) at Wilkinsville, Sutton, Mass., and died soon afterwards, aged 46 years.

(1559.) ix. LEVI LUTHER FELTON[7], (*William*[6], *William*[5], *Archelaus*[4], *Jonathan*[3], *Nathaniel*[2], *Nathaniel*[1],) b. in 1841; m. June 17, 1863, Susan W. Hapgood, daughter of Moses Hapgood then of Marlboro. He was a soldier in the Union army from Marlboro, and from Feltonville in Marlboro. He was a shoe-maker and died in Hudson, Mass., Jan. 28, 1875, aged 34 years. Mrs. Felton died the same year, Oct. 21, 1875, aged 31 years. They had 3 children.

2319. i. LESLIE, b. June 1866; died at Milton Mills, N. H., Nov. 1885, aged 19 years; buried in Hudson, Mass.
2320. ii. FREDERICK, b. about 1868; died July 1877, aged 9 years.
2321. iii. ALBERT L., b. Jan. 13, 1871; died Aug. 24, 1871.

(1560.) i. MERRICK POTTER, b. April 7, 1826, son of James and Elizabeth (Felton) Potter of Northboro, (No. 719;) m. Oct. 1847, Elizabeth S. Twitchell; he is a shoe-maker. They have lived in Northboro, Berlin, and in 1879, bought a place in the west part of Marlboro. They have had 13 children.

2322. i. ELLA J., b. Jan. 19, 1849; m. Daniel Richard Montague.

2323. ii. ELWYN L., b. June 25, 1850; died Dec. 21, 1850.
2324. iii. EDWIN A., b. Jan. 22, 1852; m. Fannie J. Allen.
2325. iv. FREDERICK H., b. Nov. 18, 1853; died Aug. 21, 1854.
2326. v. JENNIE F., b. March 2, 1855; m. David Lynch.
2327. vi. EMMA A., b. March 25, 1857; m. George Bucklin.
2328. vii. GEORGE L., b. April 12, 1859.
2329. viii. CHARLES H., b. May 22, 1861.
2330. ix. JAMES E., b. July 14, 1863.
2331, x. CHARLOTTE E., b. Aug. 4, 1865; m. Roscoe Lincoln in 1881.
2332. xi. OLIVE F., b. Sept. 3, 1867.
2333. xii. ROBERT L., b. Nov. 13, 1869,
2334. xiii. ELSIE M., b. Jan. 29, 1872.

(1561.) ii. HENRY BARTLETT, a Boston merchant, m. Lydia Felton Potter, b. Aug. 28, 1828, daughter of James and Elizabeth (Felton) Potter of Northboro, Mass. Mr. Bartlett was son of Henry Bartlett, who married Mrs. Gilbert, the mother of John Gilbert, the actor. The widely-known Bartlett pear was named for Henry Bartlett, Jr.'s, uncle, Enoch Bartlett, Esq., of Roxbury. Henry and Lydia Felton Bartlett of Boston had one son.

2335. i. HENRY, JR., b. about 1858; died before 1885.

(1562.) iii. CHARLES POTTER, b. June 24, 1830, son of James and Elizabeth (Felton) Potter; m. Nov. 29, 1866, Mary Maria Holyoke, b. March 24, 1833, daughter of Capt. Jacob and Lydia (Howe) Holyoke of Marlboro. He is a farmer in the west part of Northboro; was a selectman in 1871 and 1872, and again in 1884 and 1885.

2336. i. MARY E., b. Dec. 9, 1868; graduated at Northboro High School in 1885.
2337. ii. ANNA M., b. Nov. 1871.

(1563.) iv. CYRUS POTTER, b. Feb. 19, 1832, son of James and Elizabeth (Felton) Potter; m. May 1857, Sarah A. Burdett of Northboro. He resides in Northboro, and was a selectman in 1876 and 1877. Have one son.

2338. i. WILLIAM J., b. April 20, 1859; graduated at Northboro High School in 1876; m. in Feb. 1884, Florence Brigham of Northboro.

(1564.) v. HORACE L. PEVERLY, (son of Mr. and Mrs. Anna Peverly formerly of Charlestown, N. H.;) m. in

1860, Elizabeth E. Potter, b. Aug. 12, 1840, daughter of James and Elizabeth (Felton) Potter of Northboro, (No. 719.) He was a soldier from Northboro, and was wounded in both legs at the battle of Sharpsburg, Md., Sept. 17, 1862. He now, 1885, resides in or near Rutland, Vt. Had two sons.

2339. i. WALTER, b. Nov. 27, 1860.
2340. ii. HENRY, b, Jan. 18, 1864.

(1571.) i. HON. OLIVER A. MORSE, b. in Cherry Valley, N. Y., b. about 1815, son of James Otis Morse, Esq., (No. 722;) graduated at Hamilton College in Clinton, N. Y., in 1833; studied law and entered upon the practice of the profession. He lived a few years in Perrysburg, Ohio. He returned to Otsego County, where he was a prominent citizen, and was a member of Congress from Otsego District two years, 1857 to 1859. He was always opposed to slavery; first a Democrat, then a Republican. It is said he was a well-read man; always a thinker, a writer and useful member of Congress. He m. in 1839, Ann Clark of Cherry Valley, N. Y. He died April 20, 1870, aged about 56 years.

(1572.) ii. JAMES OTIS MORSE, JR., b. about 1817, son of James Otis Morse, Esq., (No. 722;) graduated at Hamilton College, N. Y., in 1836. He m. Georgia A., a dau. of Furman R. Whitwell, Esq., of Fairhaven, Mass. In 1850, he resided at Brooklyn, N. Y. In 1879, it was said that Mr. Morse was living in N. J., and doing business in New York City.

(1573.) iii. ALBERT G. STORY, m. in 1835, Sarah Morse, the oldest daughter of James Otis Morse, Esq., of Cherry Valley, N. Y. In 1850, he resided at Little Falls, N. Y., and was cashier of Herkimer County Bank. Had 5 children.

2341. i. MARY, b. April 17, 1836; died April 1, 1845, aged 9 years.
2342. ii. JAMES O. M., b. July 27, 1838; died July 28, 1838.
2343. iii. SARAH b. June 17, 1839.
2344. iv. ALBERT, b. Aug. 1, 1841.
2345. v. EMILY W., b. June 30, 1845.

(1575.) v. STEWART MORSE, b. Feb. 10, 1824, son of James Otis Morse, Esq., of Cherry Valley, N. Y.; educated at Lawrenceville Seminary, N. J. Was a member of the N. Y. bar in 1846; in 1850, resided in Cherry Valley and was cashier of a bank; in 1853, was a physician.

(1593.) iii. DANIEL C. FELTON[7], (*Charles C.[6], Isaac[5], Daniel[4], Jonathan[3], Nathaniel[2], Nathaniel[1],*) b. July 19, 1840; he was a soldier in the Union army from Dedham, 1861 to 1864; m. Dec. 25, 1865, Caroline H. Horton of Camden, Me. He is a shoe-maker and resides in Natick, Mass. Have 3 children.

    2346.   i. Lewis E., b. Aug. 18, 1867.
    2347.   ii. Maude F., b. Oct. 1, 1872.
    2348.   iii. Mabel R., b. Feb. 15, 1874.

Daniel C. Felton's cousin, Samuel L. Felton, a soldier in the Union army from Boston in 1862, is printed with Sampson Felton's family on page 149; it should have been placed after his sister, Charlotte A. Felton of Boston, on page 148.

(1610.) iii. JAMES FELTON[7], (*James[6], James[5], Daniel[4], Daniel[3], Nathaniel[2], Nathaniel[1],*) b. Feb. 23, 1821; m. June 27, 1844, Mary Smith, b. Feb. 19, 1824; he was a soldier in Co. B. of 16th Regiment of Ohio Volunteers; he died Sept. 5, 1863, at Columbus, Ohio, and was buried with military honors in Green Lawn Cemetery, near Columbus, Ohio, aged 42 years, 6 months. James and Mary Felton had 8 children; they were born in Coshocton and Holmes Counties, Ohio.

    2349.   i. Philip S., b. Oct. 24, 1845; died of diphtheria, July 13, 1858, aged 13 years.
    2350.   ii. Ezra W., b. May 30, 1847; living in 1886, in Ladora, Iowa.
    2351.   iii. James M., b. May 4, 1849; m. July 20, 1871, Annie Stedry.
    2352.   iv. Mary b. Jan. 14, 1852; died Dec. 13, 1853, aged almost 2 years.
    2353.   v. Jonathan F., b. Oct. 13, 1854; died July 31, 1858, aged 4 years, of diphtheria.
    2354.   vi. Lucy M., b. Aug. 13, 1859; died March 6, 1863, of diphtheria.
    2355.   vii. John C., b. May 31, 1861; died March 8, 1863, of diphtheria.
    2356.   viii. Joshua B., b. Feb. 14, 1863.

Mr. and Mrs. Felton were born in Ohio, Holmes and Wayne counties.

(1611.) iii. AUSTIN FELTON[7], (*James[6], James[5], Daniel[4], Daniel[3], Nathaniel[2], Nathaniel[1].*) He is a farmer in Victor, Poweshiek County, Iowa. He was living in 1885. He m. first, Margaret Given, and had a son, Robert. He m. second, Miss Given, a cousin of his first wife, and had several daughters and one son, Frederick.

2357. i. ROBERT.
2358. ii. FREDERICK.

(1617.) iii. ALONZO L. FELTON[7], (*Ezra*[6], *James*[5], *Daniel*[4], *Daniel*[3], *Nathaniel*[2], *Nathaniel*[1],) b. Sept. 25, 1819; m. Caroline M. Olmstead, b. Sept. 22, 1823. In 1856, was postmaster at West Ellery, N. Y. Had 5 children.

2359. i. GEORGE E., b. Feb. 17, 1844.
2360. ii. JULIA M., b. Oct. 12, 1847; m. ——— Clark.
2361. iii. MARY C., b. July 4, 1850; m. ——— Chase.
2362. iv. EMMA H., b. Sept. 6, 1856.
2363. v. ADA F., b. Dec. 24, 1862.

(1618.) iv. MR. NOBLES, m. Hannah A. Felton, b. June 5, 1832, daughter of Ezra Felton, (No. 744.) Residence, Bemus Point, western part of N. Y. State. Their children were:

2364. i. CHARLES E., b. June 4, 1850.
2365. ii. WILLIS A., b. June 18, 1856.
2366. iii. RALPH A., b. Dec. 29, 1859.

(1619.) v. MR. FARLOW, m. Lauretta A. Felton, b. Sept. 17, 1839, daughter of Ezra Felton, (No. 744.) Residence, western part of N. Y. State. Had 2 children.

2367. i. ADDIE R., b. April 2, 1858.
2368. ii. CHARLES B., b. Oct. 2, 1860.

(1620.) i. JAMES S. FELTON[7], (*Daniel*[6], *James*[5], *Daniel*[4], *Daniel*[3], *Nathaniel*[2], *Nathaniel*[1],) b. Oct. 17, 1827; m. in Jefferson County, Wis., Oct. 24, 1847, Amelia F. Cowles, b. at Henderson, Jefferson Co., N. Y., Aug. 8, 1829; she died April 19, 1861, aged 32 years. Had 6 children. He m. second, Aug. 18, 1875, Martha Jane Bonesteel, b. May 4, 1836, daughter of David Bonesteel, formerly of N. Y. State. Mr. Felton resides at East Granite Falls, Minn.; he is a farmer; he has kindly aided me by giving information of families in the Western States. Two of his sons are living in Dakota.

2369. i. CHARLES H., b. Jan. 5, 1849; m. Nov. 1870, Catherine A. Sargent; had 3 children.
2370. ii. ADELBERT S., b. Jan, 25, 1851; m. Dec. 1870, Margaret E. Ritchie; had 3 children.
2371. iii. HELENA A., b. Aug. 8, 1852; m. Feb. 1873, Lewis C. Ewing; had 2 children in 1880.
2372. iv. JAMES E., b. July 17, 1854; m. Dec. 1879, Addie L. McLyman.

2373. v. GEORGE B., b. June 26, 1856; died June 21, 1865, aged 9 years.
2374. vi. EVIE A., b. Jan. 8, 1859.

(1622.) iii. JOSEPH FELTON[7], (*Daniel[6], James[5], Daniel[4], Daniel[3], Nathaniel[2], Nathaniel[1],*) b. May 12, 1831; m. Sarah Frances ———, and had 2 daughters. Mrs. Felton died March 16, 1862. He m. again, and since his decease, his widow has married.. Mr. Felton died Jan. 7, 1876, aged 44 years.

2375. i. SARAH E., b. Oct. 19, 1855; m. W. T. Williams; had 2 children.
2376. ii. MINNESOTA F., b. Sept. 23, 1857; died Nov. 1, 1880, aged 23 years.

(1637. *b.*) ii. JAMES McCLELLAND, b. May 1807; m. May 24, 1838, Mary Ann Goodnough, b. in 1810, at Sodus, N. Y., daughter of Sylvanus and Susan (Felton) Goodnough. Mrs. McClelland died at Girard, Pa., March 17, 1873, aged 62 years. Mr. McClelland was living at Girard in 1883. They had 3 children.

2377. i. HELEN A., b. Sept. 1842; living at Girard in 1883.
2378. ii. A son; living in Buffalo, N. Y., in 1878, in Girard in 1883.
2379. iii. A daughter; living at Girard in 1883.

(1638.) i. CORNELIUS CONWAY FELTON[7], (*Cornelius C.[6], Thomas[5], Thomas[4], Daniel[3], Nathaniel[2], Nathaniel[1],*) b. in Newbury, Mass., Nov. 6, 1807; graduated at Harvard College in 1827; he taught school a few winters when in college; one winter in Bolton and one in Concord, Mass.; had charge of Livingston County, N. Y., high school two years 1827 to 1829. He was an instructor in Harvard College as tutor, professor, and president about one-third of a century; he was tutor from 1829 to 1832; from 1832 to 1834, professor of Greek language; 1834 to 1860, Eliot professor of Greek literature. In 1849, he was chosen faculty regent of the college by Pres. Jared Sparks, a new office, and next to the president. In 1860, by the unanimous approval of the friends of the college, Prof. Felton was chosen the 20th president.

In 1851 and 1852, Prof. Felton delivered a course of lectures before the Lowell Institute in Boston on the Greek language and Greece, "filled with interesting information in regard to that classic land." Twice he visited Greece, and a volume of nearly 400 pages of his letters was published in 1864. He was called one of the finest Greek scholars America has ·yet produced. He was the author of a number of works. Felton's Greek Reader; Felton's Agamemnon, with notes; Felton's Translation of Homer's Iliad, with notes, pages 598. Translated works from German and from French. He contributed to Appleton's New American Cyclopædia, eight articles, viz: Agassiz, Athens, F. Bowen, Demosthenes, Euripides, Greece, Greek Literature and Homer. He was the author of a life of Gen. William Eaton in Sparks' American Biography and in 1852, he edited a selection from the writings of Prof. Popkin, his predecessor in the Eliot professorship, with an introductory biographical notice. In 1848, he received from Amherst College the honorary degree of Doctor of Laws. He had served on the school committee in Cambridge, been a member of the Board of Education of the State of Massachusetts, appointed in 1854, and one of the Regents of the Smithsonian Institution at Washington, D. C., appointed Feb. 13, 1856, by the United States Senate.

Prof. Felton m. in 1838, Mary Whitney, b. May 5, 1815, daughter of Asa and Mary Whitney; she died April 12, 1845, aged 30 years. He m. second, Sept. 28, 1846, Mary Louisa Cary, daughter of Hon. Thomas G. Cary of Boston. Some of the newspapers said in speaking of the wealth of the literary men of Cambridge, that Prof. Felton had been equally fortunate in his matrimonial connections in regard to wealth with the other professors, viz: Everett, Palfrey, Longfellow, Lowell and Norton, by marrying fortunes in expectancy or possession. Pres. Felton died at the residence of his brother at Chester, Pa., Feb. 26, 1862, of enlargement of the heart, aged 54 years, three months and 20 days. The announcement of his death was received with general regret throughout the country.

The following lines are extracts from a sermon preached in the Appleton chapel, Cambridge, March 9, 1862, being the Sunday after the funeral of Pres. Cornelius Conway Felton, by Rev. Andrew P. Peabody, preacher to the Cambridge University:

In the estimate of our late President's claims on our grateful remembrance, we cannot forget how large and unique a place he filled in the world of letters. Few men have attained so high a position in one department, with so generous a culture in all. While he was unsurpassed in the language and literature to which his labors were given for so many years, it was impossible to point out his deficiencies in any branch of learning.

Among his moral traits we are first reminded of the genial elements of his social nature. He can never have made an enemy; he never forgot or lost a friend. And who ever had so many friends, or friends more devoted and loving? There was no possible claim on his regard or kindness which he was not prompt and persistent in recognizing. He loved those near his own plane, because he could enter into their thoughts, and they into his,—those far below it, because he could lift them up,—the prosperous, because they could aid his beneficent plans,—the poor and depressed, because he could give them help and comfort,—the aged, from natural reverence,—the young, from sympathy with their exposures, difficulties, and temptations.

We who have known him the longest can recall not an act or a word which we do not love to remember. Steadfast in the right no power on earth could make him swerve from his convictions of duty. His force of character, hidden on ordinary occasions by his gentle and sunny temperament, appeared impregnable whenever it was put to the test. From the most arduous, thankless, and painful duties he never shrank; and in prompt decision and fearless energy for difficult emergencies he was no less conspicuous and admirable, than in those amiable and graceful qualities which adorned his daily life.

An extract from Prof. Parker's address, of the Law School at Cambridge.

The acquisition and diffusion of knowledge was not only the business of his life,—it was a passion with him. Whether in the professorial chair, pouring forth his rich stores of Grecian literature,—or among the Regents of the Smithsonian Institution, diffusing the blessings of science through that great national instrumentality,—or as a member of the Board of Education of the State of Massachusetts, devising the best means for advancing the character of the instruction in the common schools,—or in the State Normal Schools, uttering words of encouragement to those who were there qualifying themselves to become instructors,—or in the hall of the Lowell Institute, delivering courses of lectures on literature and science to the inhabitants of a great city,—or in the occasional assemblages of persons met together for the purpose of listening to his addresses on science, literature, art, agriculture, or politics,—and even in the more humble duty of a member of the committee for examining schools in this city, he was sure to instruct and delight his auditory by the accuracy of his knowledge, the fulness of his illustrations, the humor of his anecdotes, his manifest and great interest in his subject, his evident pleasure in imparting information to others, and the geniality and friendship of his general deportment.

In the pure gold of his character, as thus portrayed, there was none of the alloy of an unworthy selfishness.

The loss of such a man is beyond estimation.

March 12, 1862, Hon. Edward Everett addressed the Board of Overseers of Harvard College, and then offered the following resolutions:

I hold, Sir, in my hand, a resolution, which I beg leave to offer to the acceptance—I venture to hope the unanimous acceptance—of the Board:—

Whereas, It has pleased Divine Providence to remove by death the late honored and beloved head of the University at Cambridge,—

Resolved unanimously by this Board, that the Overseers of the College, in common with its officers and members of every degree, and the friends of the institution throughout the country, have suffered in the decease of President Felton the loss of a devoted and faithful head of the University, whose whole life has been consecrated, with rare singleness of purpose, to its service; a zealous friend and supporter of education in every department; an efficient promoter of every liberal and public-spirited enterprise; an active and patriotic citizen and member of the community, who added to his great merit as a public servant the most amiable personal qualities, and all those virtues and graces which adorn and dignify every relation of social and private life, and constitute the model character of a man and a Christian.

Mrs. Mary Louisa Felton died May 31, 1864.

Prof. Felton had 2 daughters by his first wife, and one daughter and two sons by his last wife.

2380. i. MARY S., b. April 30, 1839; she served for a long time with her friend, Miss Anna Lowell of Cambridge, Mass., at the Amory Square Hospital, Washington, during the late civil war.

2381. ii. JULIA W., b. Aug. 24, 1842; she died in Florence, March 8, 1884, aged 42 years.

2382, iii. LOUISA C., b. March 16, 1849.

2383. iv. CORNELIUS C., JR., b. Dec. 1851; graduated at Harvard College, in 1872. He m. Sept. 20, 1877, Miss E. W. Farley, daughter of Gustavus Farley, Esq. Have one daughter.

2384. v. THOMAS C., b. Sept. 15, 1855; graduated at Harvard College in 1875.

There is a Felton School, a Felton Building and Hall, and a Felton Street in Cambridge, Mass.

(1639.) ii. SAMUEL MORSE FELTON[7], (*Cornelius C.*[6], *Thomas*[5], *Thomas*[4], *Daniel*[3], *Nathaniel*[2], *Nathaniel*[1],) b. July 17, 1809, in Newbury, Mass.; graduated at Harvard College in 1834. He studied civil engineering. In 1839, he was appointed a commissioner with Prof. Simon Greenleaf and Dea. Levi Farwell to make boundary lines in regard to taking ice on Fresh Pond, Cambridge. Mr. Felton was civil engineer and superintendent of the Fitchburg Railroad from its commencement in 1842 until 1851. In Feb. 1851, the employes on the Fitchburg Railroad presented Samuel M. Felton, the retiring superintendent, with a service of silver plate, valued at about 265 dollars, as a testimonial of their regard. In 1846, Mr. Felton, with Hon. J. M. Williams and Eliab Gilman, was a referee in the suit against the Maine Extension Railroad; $20,000 involved in the decision; counsel, Bell, Bartlett, and Farrar for the plaintiff; Choate, Derby, and H. W. Fuller for defendants. He has been one of the referees in several somewhat similar cases. In 1850, Mr. Felton and Mr. Edwards were appointed agents by the Troy and Greenfield Railroad Company to go to Europe on business.

In Feb. 1851, Mr. Felton was chosen president of the Philadelphia, Wilmington and Baltimore Railroad and moved to Philadelphia, and served as president until after the close of the late civil war. He was president at the time President Lincoln made his wonderful entrance into Washington, before his inauguration, at the peril of his life, in Feb. 1861.

When the first troops passed through Pennsylvania and Maryland in April 1861, Gen. B. F. Butler had interviews with Pres. Felton and said "I may have to sink or burn your boat," "Do so," replied Mr. Felton and immediately wrote an order authorizing its destruction if necessary.

Several years ago a writer speaking of railroad managers, said, "Great praise is also due Mr. Felton of the Philadelphia, Wilmington and Baltimore Railroad for the able management of that line of travel. The accommodations furnished by that road, the promptness with which the troops and supplies have been despatched, and the alacrity with which the repairs were made after the destruction of the bridges by the Baltimore secessionists, entitle Mr. Felton to the gratitude of the people. We are apt to forget valuable services done off the field of battle, but the railroad manager, who faithfully and energetically does his duty, is as much entitled to the praise of the people as the general who wins the victory. To Messrs. Smith and Felton the country owes a debt of gratitude which can never be paid, because their services are not likely to be rightly estimated."

In 1876, Mr. Felton was president of the Pennsylvania Steel Company, near Harrisburg, for manufacturing hammered steel rails. It is said it is the largest and one of the most successful establishments of the kind in the country.

In 1879, Mr. Felton was one of the Board of Arbitrators with Judge Brigham and Pres. Phillips of the Eastern Railroad, to whom was referred the question of deciding what rebate, if any, should be allowed the Fitchburg Railroad by the State, in order to operate the Troy and Greenfield Railroad through the Hoosac Tunnel.

In 1884, Mr. Felton attended the semi-centennial reunion of the Harvard College class of 1834, in Mass.

Mr. Felton m. May 1836, Eleanor Stetson, b. Aug. 12, 1813, daughter of David and Sarah Stetson; she died Aug. 24, 1847, aged 34 years. He m. second, Oct. 1850, Maria Low Liffitt, daughter of Warren Liffitt, Esq., of Providence, R. I. Had 3 daughters by his first wife; one daughter and 3 sons by his present wife. Mrs. M. L. Felton was b. Jan. 26, 1826.

2385. i. ELEANOR S., b. June 21, 1837; m. Jan. 12, 1871, Capt. Eben Francis Barker of Charlestown, Mass., son of Ebenezer and Sarah (Fuller) Barker.
2386. ii. ANNA M., b. Jan. 1, 1839.
2387. iii. MARY S., b. Jan. 11, 1842; m. in Thurlow, Pa., Jan. 12, 1871, Maj. Luther Stedman Bent of Boston, b. Dec. 6, 1829, son of Ebenezer and Nancy (Stedman) Bent.
2388. iv. HARRIET P., b. Aug. 16, 1851; m. June 30, 1874, Richard Peters, b. Nov. 2, 1848, son of Richard and Mary (Thompson) Peters.
2389†. v. SAMUEL M., JR., b. Feb. 3, 1853; m. Dora Hamilton.
2390†. vi. EDGAR C., b. April 13, 1858; m. Abbie Bent.
2391. vii. CORNELIUS C., b. Dec. 29, 1863; entered Harvard College in 188–.

The town of Felton in Delaware, sup. named for Samuel M. Felton. The following items are from the *American Cultivator* of Sept. 6, 1879. In Aug. 1879, a single peach grower in Felton, Del., picked 800 baskets of good fruit from 600 trees, and expects to secure 500 baskets more from the same source. The same month, Aug. 1879, a New York speculator bought at Felton, Del., 80,000 baskets choice peaches for $40,000 and shipped them to Cincinnati, Ohio.

(1641.) iv. GEORGE E. BENT, b. in South Boston, July 28, 1811, son of Adam and Sukey F. (Blake) Bent of Boston; m. Aug. 31, 1843, Martha Conway Felton, b. Oct. 12, 1815, daughter of Cornelius C. and Anna M. Felton of Charlestown, Mass. Mr. Bent's children were born in South Boston. In 1861, Mr. Bent with his family moved to Thurlow, near Philadelphia. Mrs. Bent deceased Feb. 15, 1877, aged 61 years.

2392. i. GEORGE C., b. July 11, 1844.
2393. ii. CLARA F., b. Nov. 12, 1846.
2394. iii. CORNELIUS C. F:, b. July 3, 1848.
2395. iv. ANNIE M., b. April 6, 1851,
2396. v. MARY B., b. Dec. 2, 1855.

(1643.) vi. GEORGE A. PARKER, b. in Concord, N.

H., May 9, 1821; m. Harriet N. Felton, b. Aug. 15, 1822, daughter of Cornelius C. Felton, Sen., (No. 769.) They resided at Charlestown, Mass., till about 1857, when they moved to Lancaster, Mass., and settled on George Hill. Mr. Parker fitted for college, but entered the office of Mr. ——— Baldwin, civil engineer, where he studied his profession, civil engineering. He was subsequently associated with his brother-in-law, Samuel M. Felton, Esq. Mr. Parker has been identified with the building of some of the leading railroads in the country. He built the bridge across the Susquehanna River at Havre de Grace, which is justly regarded as a work of great merit.

It is said that at one time during the war, he acted, at the request of Secretary Stanton, as superintendent of the military railroads. He and his family lived at Chester, Pa., about two years. He was representative to the General Court from Lancaster in 1870, 1871 and 1872. Had 7 children; the first four children were born in Charlestown, the next two at Lancaster.

In 1877, Mr. Parker's Lancaster tax was 291 dollars, and the next highest tax payer after Nathaniel Thayer the wealthiest citizen in the town.

2397. i.   EDITH, b. in Charlestown, Mass., Aug. 2, 1848.
2398. ii. GEORGE A., JR., b. May 22, 1852; died Feb. 18, 1853.
2399. iii. HAROLD, b. June 17, 1854; m. July 29, 1884, Elizabeth W. Bartol, only daughter of Rev. George M. Bartol of Lancaster, Mass. He is a civil engineer, and in 1885, moved to Zanesville, Ohio.
2400. iv. HERBERT, b. March 2, 1856; in 1885, one of the school committee of Lancaster, Mass.; in 1886, an associate justice of the eastern Worcester District court.
2401. v.   BERTHA, b. March 16, 1858.
2402. vi. FELTON, b. Oct. 8, 1860.
2403. vii. CHESTER, b. at Chester, Pa., Aug. 10, 1862.

(1644.) vii. JOHN BROOKS FELTON[7], (*Cornelius C.[6], Thomas[5], Thomas[4], Daniel[3], Nathaniel[2], Nathaniel[1],*) b. in Saugus, Mass., June 9, 1827. He graduated at Harvard College in 1847, and was a tutor in Greek there in 1849 and 1850. In 1849, he delivered a poem at Cambridge called "The Horse shoe," and had it published in a pamphlet. He graduated in the law school at Cambridge in 1853, with the degree of L. L. B. He settled in San Francisco, Cal., where he was a prominent lawyer. His legal attainments were of the highest character, and he was probably the leading member of the San

Francisco bar, says a California newspaper, and it also says, "As a Supreme Court petitioner he had no superior, and before this tribunal he had always a very large practice, and was generally successful in his cases."

It is said he probably received as large fees as were ever paid any lawyer in the United States; his fee in one case where employed by James Lick, the millionaire, was $100,000. Some newspapers have it, Mr. Felton once received one of the greatest fees on record, one quarter of a million of dollars for the management of a single suit.

In politics he was a Union man, acting with the Republican party after the advent of the rebellion.

Mr. Felton was an elector in two presidential elections, and twice ran in the nominating conventions for the candidacy for the United States Senate. It is said he was a fine scholar in both the French and Spanish languages. He was a member of the Board of Regents of the University of California.

Mr. Felton was a resident of Oakland and served one term as mayor of the city, and always evinced a great deal of pride and interest in its local government and prosperity.

He m. in 1862, Kate Baldwin, daughter of the late J. G. Baldwin, Justice of the Supreme Court of California. Hon. John B. Felton died in Oakland of paralysis, May 2, 1877, aged almost 50 years; left a widow and two daughters.

2404. i. One daughter, b. about 1865.
2405. ii. A daughter, b. about 1872.

Two more extracts from a California paper; In a very quiet and unostentatious manner Mr. Felton gave a great deal to charitable objects. His most intimate friends say he was a wit of the highest order—a flashing, brilliant wit, which they enthusiastically declare to have equalled Curran's and was of that high-minded generous quality which never wounded the feelings of its subject.

(1645.) viii. FRANKLIN ELIOT FELTON[7], (*Cornelius C.*[6], *Thomas*[5], *Thomas*[4], *Daniel*[3], *Nathaniel*[2], *Nathaniel*[1],) b. in Charlestown, Mass., April 7, 1829. He graduated at Harvard College in 1851. In 1853, the degree of Bachelor of Laws was conferred on 52 persons by Harvard College and one was Franklin Eliot Felton. He delivered an oration, July 4, 1867, at Valejo, Cal., on purification and reconstruction of the Southern States; it was published by request and made a pamphlet of 22 pages.

In 1869, Mr. Felton edited the *Secrets of Internal Revenues*, by a detective, exposing the whiskey ring, etc., published in 1870; 543 pages.

It was said a few years ago, Mr. Felton was living at Washington, D. C.

(1647.) i. JOSHUA MORSE FELTON[7], (*Thomas*[6], *Thomas*[5], *Thomas*[4], *Daniel*[3], *Nathaniel*[2], *Nathaniel*[1],) b. in Hampstead, N. H., Nov. 3, 1825; he m. Emily L. Jewell, b. in 1828, daughter of Nathaniel and Thankful (Bumpus) Jewell. They had 7 children. He was a soldier in the Union army from Charlestown; he died in Bunker Hill District, June 12, 1880, or 1881, aged 54 or 55 years.

  2406. i. IMOGENE; lived 11 years.
  2407. ii. WILLIAM T.; was a soldier in the late civil war; lived 21 years. He enlisted in Charlestown in Jan. 1865.
  2408. iii, EMILY L., b. about 1850; m. Nov. 6, 1878, Geo. O. Brentnall.
  2409. iv. ABBY M.; died about 1882, aged 27 years.
  2410. v. ALBERT H., b. Aug. 28, 1856; m. Jan. 8, 1880, Lizzie F. Norton.
  2411. vi. ESTELLE, (STELLA), b. Jan. 1859.
  2412. vii. SAMUEL M., b. Feb. 1, 1868.

(1648.) ii. ALBERT HUMPHREY FELTON[7], (*Thomas*[6], *Thomas*[5], *Thomas*[4], *Daniel*[3], *Nathaniel*[2], *Nathaniel*[1],) b. in Chelsea, Mass., March 9, 1827; was an engineer several years on the Fitchburg Railroad; when his cousin, Samuel M. Felton, Esq., moved to Philadelphia, Pa., in 1851, Albert H. Felton went to Baltimore, Md., and followed engineering; as an engineer, he went to Rio Janeiro, South America, about 1857, and there died of a fever, April 29, 1858, aged 31 years.

(1649.) iii. CORNELIUS CONWAY FELTON[7], (*Thomas*[6], *Thomas*[5], *Thomas*[4], *Daniel*[3], *Nathaniel*[2], *Nathaniel*[1],) b. in Chelsea, Mass., Feb. 22, 1829; was also an engineer on the Fitchburg Railroad; he went to Charleston, S. C., about the time his brother moved to Baltimore, as an engineer; about 1857, to Rio Janeiro, South America, and died of a fever, March 29, 1858, just a month before his brother's death, aged 29 years.

Their father, Thomas Felton died in Maine, the same year, July 3, 1858, aged 67 years.

EIGHTH GENERATION.

(1650.) i. NATHAN LINCOLN, b. Jan. 22, 1822, (son of Barnabas and grandson of Nathan Lincoln of Hingham, Mass.;) m. Lucy Felton Lincoln, b. Nov. 24, 1826, daughter of David Lincoln, Esq., (No. 831.) Mr. Lincoln is a music teacher and resides at Cambridge, Mass.

  2413. i. NATHAN F., b. March 21, 1853; a merchant on Commercial St., Boston.

2414. ii. MARY E., b. May 18, 1856.
2415. iii. MARTHA, b. July 21, 1864.

(1686.) ii. SAMUEL FELTON[8], (*Samuel[7], Joshua[6], Edward J.[5], Nathaniel[4], Nathaniel[3], John[2], Nathaniel[1],*) b. in Roxbury, Dec. 22, 1835; m. Abby W. Richardson. He was a soldier in the Union army 3 years, 1861 to July 1864, from Belchertown, Mass. They settled at Worcester and had 3 children. In 1878, moved to Leominster, Mass., where Mrs. Felton died before Oct. 1883.

 2416. i. GERTRUDE H.; graduated at Leominster High School in 1885.
 2417. ii. CARRIE.
 2418. iii. ARTHUR.

(1700. *d.*) iii. CHRISTOPHER W. DAVIS; m. Loretta Weymouth, b. April 15, 1839, daughter of Daniel and Sally (Felton) Weymouth of Maine. They had one daughter living in 1836. Mrs. Davis is a nurse; residence, Woodford, near Portland, Me.

 2419. NELLIE I.; m. Alton E. Stevens; have two children of the tenth generation from Nathaniel Felton, Sen.

(1711.) i. CHARLES NORTON FELTON[8], (*Benjamin K[7], Levi[6], John[5], Jacob[4], Samuel[3], John[2], Nathaniel[1],*) b. in Buffalo, N. Y., Jan. 1, 1828; m. Feb. 1852. Charlotte A. Ashley of Syracuse, N. Y.; she died in San Francisco, Cal., Jan. 1875. They have two children.

Mr. Felton was sub-treasurer at San Francisco, 1869 to 1872. In Nov. 1880, chosen a representative in San Mateo County. In Nov. 1884, chosen a member of Congress, 1885 to 1887.

 2420. i. KATE, b. Aug. 20, 1862.
 2421. ii. CHARLES N., JR., b. April 11, 1869.

It is reported that Mr. Felton is one of the richest men of the Golden State.

The following from the Congressional Directory of the 49th Congress: "Mr. Felton received an academic education; after having retired from active business, was assistant treasurer and treasurer of the Mint of San Francisco for six years; was elected to the Legislature of Cal., for two terms."

The town of Felton in Santa Cruz County, Cal., (and eight miles from Santa Cruz,) on the Southern Pacific Railroad, we suppose was named for Mr. Felton.

The Big Tree Grove in Felton and Camp Felton are 7½ miles from Santa Cruz. One writer says, "the Big Tree

Grove of Felton is one of the most beautiful and interesting places to visit in the State. Running through the grove is the San Lorenzo river, where good fishing can be had. The trees are magnificent in proportion and the forest grand and extensive. Camp Felton, among the red woods of Santa Cruz County, is about one mile from the big-tree grove, in the heart of one of the most picturesque regions of California. No one has really seen the beauties surrounding the beautiful watering place of Santa Cruz, unless a visit is paid to the grove in Felton."

(1712.) ii. HENRY M. VAUGHAN, m. Sept. 13, 1849, Mary Corintha Felton, b. Jan. 3, 1830, daughter of Benjamin K. and Julia Ann (St. John) Felton, (No. 880.) Had two daughters. Mr. Vaughan died in Detroit. Mich., May 30, 1854. Mrs. Mary C. Vaughan m. second, Sept. 13, 1866, to Welcome V. Fiske. They now reside in Clinton, Mich.

2422. i. Mary E., b. Sept. 8, 1850; m. Willis Mann.
2423. ii. Eva C , b. May 24, 1854; m. Feb. 2, 1874, Chas. M. Hinsdale.

(1714.) iv. GEORGE A. ROWLAND, m. Nov. 1, 1860, Eliza Hicks Felton, b. Dec. 15, 1838, daughter of Benjamin K. Felton, (No. 880.) They reside at Clinton, Mich. Have had 2 children.

2424. i. Frank E., b. Oct. 27, 1862; died next month, Nov. 7, in Clinton.
2425. ii. Lua H., b. April 8, 1864.

(1719.) ii. GEORGE LORING MANSON, b. Nov. 6, 1827, (the day his father was 30 years of age,) son of George E. and Harriet (Felton) Manson of Feltonville; m. Jan. 1852, Lucy Haskell, b. Dec. 22, 1831, daughter of Phineas and Betsey (Brigham) Haskell of the same village. Mr. Manson was a merchant and postmaster a few years at Feltonville in Marlboro, Mass. Have one daughter.

2426. Sarah R., b. Dec. 11, or 19, 1852.

(1721.) iv. SILAS FELTON MANSON, b. March 25, 1834, son of George E. and Harriet (Felton) Manson of Feltonville, Marlboro. He m. Nov. 1858, Josephine L. Priest, daughter of Silas Priest; she died March 3, 1882, aged 45 years. He m. second, Sept. 23, 1885, Annie E. Valentine. Mr. Manson was postmaster in the village, now town of Hudson, 19 years, 1865 to Oct. 1884.

FELTON FAMILY. 229

2427. i. GRACE B., b. Sept. 18, 1860; a graduate of Hudson High School, June, 1879; she died Dec. 1, 1884, aged 24 years.
2428. ii. A son, b. March 5, 1868; died same day.
2429. iii. FRANK S. E., b. Dec., 1872; died Sept. 6, 1873.

(1726.) v. JULIAN FELTON BIGELOW, b. in Marlboro, April 18, 1846, son of Leander and Lucy (Felton) Bigelow, (No. 897.) He m. Adelaide Speller of Malden, Mass. They reside at Worcester. He has been superintendent of the Worcester and Shrewsbury railroad. He is now, 1886, manager of Bigelow's Rink in that city.

2430. i. ALTHEA, b. Nov. 26, 1870.
2431. ii. GLENNIE D., b. March 31, 1876.
2432. iii. LUCY H., b. Sept. 5, 1880.

(1731.) ii. EUGENE ORISON BRIGHAM, b. July 25, 1855, son of Charles H. and Jane (Felton) Brigham of Marlboro, (No. 901.) He m. April 1878, Annie F. Cotting, dau. of Dea. John F. Cotting of Marlboro. He is assisting his father-in-law, who is depot master. Mr. Brigham has been collector of taxes in Marlboro a few years. Have one son.

2433. i. CHARLES H., b. Feb. 9, 1880.

(1741.) i. LUTHER HODGES WOOD, b. in New Haven, Ct., in 1847, son of Alonzo Felton Wood, (No. 905.) He graduated at New Haven Medical College in 1868. He m., April, 1869, Mary W. Townsend and went to Monroe, Ct.; he moved to Southington in the fall of 1871. Dr. Wood is practicing in Denver, Col., in 1886.

2434. i. HENRY T., b. March 5, 1870; died July, 1870.
2435. ii. HENRY C., b. April 26, 1871.
2436. iii. WILLIAM, b. Jan., 1875; died next month.

(1749.) i. ANDREW J. PHELPS, (son of Samuel Phelps of Fitchburg;) m. April 1850, Caroline B. Felton, b. April 29, 1830, daughter of Aaron H. Felton, (No. 906.) He died in Marlboro of heart disease, May 3, 1854, aged 25 years. Had two children. Mrs. Phelps m. second, July 6, 1862, Nahum A. Gay of Feltonville; he died May 24, 1881, aged 60 years.

2437. i. WILLIS H., b. Dec. 31, 1850; died July 3, 1876, aged 25 years, of heart disease.
2438. ii. LILLIE A., b. Aug. 12, 1853; died Feb. 23, 1854.

(1750.) ii. FREDERICK JEWETT, m. Oct. 1856, Catherine B. Felton, b. April 29, (a twin,) 1830, daughter of Aaron H. Felton of Marlboro. Have lived in Marlboro and Hudson. Have one son.

    2439.   i. JESSE G., b. in Marlboro, Sept. 4, 1864; graduated at Marlboro High School in June 1882.

(1751.) iii. SILAS ADDISON FELTON[8], (*Aaron H.*[7], *Aaron*[6], *Stephen*[5], *Jacob*[4], *Samuel*[3], *John*[2], *Nathaniel*[1],) b. in Marlboro, Sept. 4, 1832, (just 57 years after the first Silas Felton died in Marlboro;) m. Jan. 20, 1861, Mary E. Dudley. Mr. Felton was a shoe manufacturer in Marlboro several years. For the last 10 or more years, a manufacturer of brushes at Manchester, N. H.

    2440.   i. DAVID D., b. Dec. 27, 1861.
    2441.   ii. HENRY C., b. in Marlboro, Sept. 29, 1869; died Aug. 10, 1870.
    2442.   iii. FRANK P., b. June 10, 1878.

(1752.) iv. ROGER BOYD, b. Dec. 5, 1827, (the youngest son of John and Sophia (Phelps) Boyd of Marlboro;) m. May 1856, Harriet Augusta Felton, b. Sept. 16, 1834, dau. of Aaron H. and Martha Adaline Felton. Mr. Boyd was employed many years in Boyd & Corey's shoe factory in Marlboro.

    2443.   i. ANNIE F., b. May 4, 1860; died April 13, 1878, aged 18 years.
    2444.   ii. HARRIET E., b. Feb. 21, 1863.
    2445.   iii. JOSEPHINE B., b. April 28, 1865; died Aug. 6, 1865.
    2446.   iv. JENNIE B., b. Aug. 26, 1867.

(1753.) v. ELBRIDGE LEWIS, b. about 1822; m. April 1855, Sarah D. Felton, b. March 26, 1836, daughter of Aaron H. Felton, (No. 906.) Many years a shoe-maker; foreman in finishing room of George Houghton's shoe factory in Hudson, Mass., 19 years. In 1877, became proprietor of the Mansion House in Hudson and proved a popular landlord. He died of paralysis after an illness of a few days, Nov. 22, 1885, aged 54 years; buried in Marlboro.

About one year before Mr. Lewis' death, on Thanksgiving day, Nov. 27, 1884, there was a Felton family gathering at the Mansion House. Mrs. Felton, the mother, and ten of her children were present. In 1886, Mrs. Felton is living and all of her twelve children, between the ages of 56 and 34 years.

(1755.) vii. JOHN SULLIVAN FELTON[8], (*Aaron H.*[7],

Aaron[6], Stephen[5], Jacob[4], Samuel[3], John[2], Nathaniel[1],) b. March 11, 1841; m. Jan. 25, 1866, Lucia A. Gibbs of Lowville, N. Y. He is a shoe manufacturer in Marlboro; for several years has been superintendent of one of S. H. Howe's large shoe factories in town.

   2447.   i. FREDERICK, b. March 18, 1869; died in Guilford, N. Y., Oct. 7, 1882, aged 13 years; buried in Marlboro, Mass.
   2448.   ii. HERBERT R., b. in Marlboro, May 23, 1883.

(1756.) viii. HENRY FRANKLIN FELTON[8], (Aaron H.[7], Aaron[6], Stephen[5], Jacob[4], Samuel[3], John[2], Nathaniel[1],) b. June 25, 1843; he is a musician, a good organist; has been employed several years by the Universalist society in Lowell, Mass. Mr. Felton m. June 1876, Jennie Webb; she was a vocalist, also organist. Mrs. Felton died in Lowell, Jan. 15, 1884.

(1761.) i. JOHN ADDISON FRYE, b. Nov. 27, 1839, son of Lewis T. and Lovinah S. (Felton) Frye, (No. 909.) He m. Sept. 26, 1861, (Fast Day,) Elvira F. Russell, b. April 1, 1839, daughter of Otis and Lovinah Russell of Marlboro. Mr. Frye is one of the prominent shoe manufacturers of Marlboro. Has one of the largest shoe factories in town. He also has one of the largest dairies in the place.

   2449.   i. WALTER P., b. Feb. 7, 1863; graduated at Marlboro High School in 1879; m. March 31, 1885, Adaline L. Holyoke, daughter of the late Freeman Holyoke of Marlboro.
   2450.   ii. CARRIE L., b. Sept. 10, 1864.
   2451.   iii. BERTHA R., b. Nov. 9, 1865; died Aug. 14, 1866.
   2452.   iv. LILLIAN H., b. May 31, 1869; died same year.
   2453.   v. DELLA M., b. Aug. 28, 1876.

(1762.) ii. CHARLES LEWIS FRYE, b. April 4, 1842, son of Lewis T. and Lovinah S. Frye, (No. 909.) He m. April 3, 1861, Lucinda E. Howe, daughter of Winthrop Howe, a native of Marlboro. Mr. Frye is a shoe manufacturer in Marlboro.

   2454.   i. LEWIS T., b. Oct. 15, 1861; in 1880 to 1882, was called the champion amateur bicycler of America. He is a shoe manufacturer of the firm of C, L. & L. T. Frye in Marlboro.
   2455.   ii. LAURA M., b. Aug. 13, 1863; m. Jan. 1866, Jesse W. Shaw, proprietor of Marlboro and Boston Express.
   2456.   iii. WINNIE H., b. July 9, 1864; died Sept. 11, 1864.

2457. iv. ARTHUR W., b. Sept. 16, 1865.
2458. v. EUGENE, b. Jan. 25, or 28, 1868; died April 7, 1868.
2459. vi. HERVEY b. Jan. 23, 1869; died young.
2460. vii. ETTA G., b. June 1871; died Sept. 10, 1872.
2461. viii. ROY H., b. Nov. 13, 1873.
2462. ix. BENJAMIN, b. March 24, 1875; died Aug. 20, 1875.
2463. x. ERNEST C., b. Oct. 23, 1876; died Nov. 2, 1885, aged 9 years.

(1763.) iii. CHARLES COTTING, b. about 1842, (son of Willard and Maria Cutting of Framingham;) m. Sept. 1, 1867, Lucy Frye, b. Dec. 1, 1844, daughter of Lewis T. and Lovinah S. Frye, (No. 909.) He was a shoe-maker several years in Marlboro; he is now a farmer in the northwest part of Framingham. Have one son.

2464. i. CHESTER F., b. in Marlboro, June 7, 1868.

(1793.) i. LUCIUS ELY FELTON[8], (*Silas A.*[7], *Stephen*[6], *Stephen*[5], *Jacob*[4], *Samuel*[3], *John*[2], *Nathaniel*[1],) b. about 1849, in Massena, N. Y.; he attended Burlington College in 1868 and 1869; in Nov. 1869, at the Medical College, N. Y. Dr. Felton settled at Potsdam, St. Lawrence County, N. Y., in 1871. March 26, 1878, he procured a patent for an inhaler, No. 201,659. In the winter or spring of 1883, Dr. L. E. Felton delivered a lecture before the St. Lawrence University at Canton, on Modern Application of Electricity. Dr. Felton m. and had two or more children.

2465. i. A son, b. Feb. 1875; died Sept. 9, 1876, aged 17 months.
2466. ii. A daughter, b. about Sept. 1876.

(1815.) i. JOSEPH V. JACKMAN, b. in Newburyport in 1837, (son of William Jackman, a relative of ex-Mayor George W. Jackman, who was appointed, May 1886, collector of customs at Newburyport by Pres. Cleveland.) Mr. J. V. Jackman is a school teacher, and commenced teaching in Marlboro in Sept. 1868, and continued 18 years. He m. Dec. 25, 1872, Sarah M. Maynard, b. June 23, 1842, daughter of Dea. Samuel B. Maynard of Marlboro. Mrs. Jackman taught school several years in this town.

2467. i. MARION M., b. Aug. 13, 1877.
2468. ii. ALICE M., b. Nov. 19, 1878.
2469. iii. CLARENCE P., b. June 5, 1886; died same month aged 12 days.

FELTON FAMILY.

(1834.) iii. IRA EZEKIEL PARMENTER, b. Dec. 19, 1848, son of Elbridge G. Parmenter of Marlboro, (No. 1523;) m. Nov. 6, 1873, Emma Susanna Huntington, b. Oct. 4, 1851, daughter of Ozias and Mary Huntington of Marlboro. They lived a few years in Wilkinsville, Hudson, Mass.; now reside in the city of Brockton, Mass.

2470. i. FREDERICK A., b. in Hudson, Aug. 22, 1874.
2471. ii. EDNA B., b. April 2, 1876.
2472. iii. ALLYN E., b. April 19, 1878.
2473. iv. MARY E., b. Oct. 28, 1880.
2474. v. CHESTER A., b. in 1882.
2475. vi. A daughter, b. in 1885.

(1847.) ii. FREDERICK LUTHER FELTON^8, (*Luther H.^{7}, Luther^6, Joel^5, Jacob^4, Samuel^3, John^2, Nathaniel^1,*) b. Sept. 9, 1849; m. Sept. 14, 1870, Laura B. Woodworth, b. in Roxbury, Oct. 30, 1848, daughter of Ebenezer Woodworth of West Newton, Mass. Mr. Felton is a distiller in Boston, of the firm of Luther H. Felton & Son.

2476. i. HERBERT L., b. in West Newton, July 1871.
2477. ii. WALTER E., b. March 27, 1874, in West Newton.
2478. iii. GRACE, b. in Boston, July 1, 1877.

Mr. Felton's great uncle, Joel Felton of Bolton, Mass., (No. 423 on page 92,) deceased, (about the time his family record was passing through the press,) May 12, 1886, aged 94 years, 25 days. His sister, Mrs. Susanna (Felton) Rice of Marlboro, lived 94 years, 7 months and 21 days.

(1861.) i. FRANKLIN PIERCE RICE, b. in Marlboro, July 29, 1852, son of Minot and Mary B. (Felton) Rice, (No. 948.) He resides at Worcester. Since 1880, he has edited and published several pamphlets and books for the Worcester Society of Antiquity, of the early records of the town of Worcester and Worcester County, Mass.

(1951.) i. HENRY L. RICHARDS, b. in 1814, son of Dr. William S. Richards of Granville, Ohio, (No. 1259;) he m. May 1, 1842, Cynthia Cowles; he was a preacher until 1852, when he became a Catholic and abandoned the ministry. He is now a merchant in Boston; his home is in Winchester, Mass.

2479. i. LAURA I.
2480. ii. HENRY L.
2481. iii. WILLIAM D.

2482. iv. HAVENS C.
2483. v. MARY.

(1953.) iii. WILLIAM RICHARDS, b. in 1819, son of Dr. William S. Richards of Granville, Ohio. Mr. Richards, A. M., is a lawyer in Washington, D. C. He m. Oct. 16, 1844, Helen Ralston. William Richards, Esq., delivered an address June, 1882, at Carroll institute.

2484. i. HELEN F.
2485. ii. MARY A.
2486. iii. JANET.

William Richards' sister, Mrs. Hillyer, had 3 sons, and his sister, Mrs. Howell, 3 daughters.

(1964.) vi. ALLYN ALFRED AVERY, b. Dec. 19, 1835, (son of Alfred and Jane (Mower) Avery and grandson of Samuel P. and Jane (Felton) Mower;) m. in 1868, H. Louisa Billings, and settled at Beaver Dam, Wis., where they were living in 1879. In 1878, he visited his native place, and friends in Ohio and New York State.

(1972.) v. GEORGE O. FESSENDEN, m. March 8, 1851, Laurett Chamberlin, b. March 25, 1832, daughter of Dr. Moses and Eliza F. (Felton) Chamberlin of Jamaica, Vt. They had 4 children.

2487. i. EDWIN O., b. Nov. 14, 1852.
2488. ii. WILLIE B., b. June 2, 1855; died Sept., 1856.
2489. iii. FRANKLIN H., b. Oct. 8, 1859.
2490. iv. WILMA J., b. June 5, 1863.

(1973.) vi. JOHN QUINCY FESSENDEN, m. Dec. 3, 1854, Jane Chamberlin, b. Jan. 18, 1834, daughter of Dr. Moses Chamberlin, (No. 1269.) Had four children die in infancy. Mrs. Jane Fessenden died March 29, 1866, aged 32 years.

2491. v. HATTIE T., b. Dec. 2, 1865; she is called Hattie T. Felton, and lives in Henry H. Felton's family in Jamaica, Vt.

Mrs. Jane Fessenden's aunt, Mrs. Lucy D. Twitchell, married Col. Jonas Twitchell, and not Col. James Twitchell, as printed on page 188.

(1985.) i. JAY FELTON^8, (*Joseph C.^{7}, Joseph^6, Benjamin^5, Joseph^4, Skelton^3, Nathaniel^2, Nathaniel^1,*) b. about 1819; m.

Chloe Sherman. Jay Felton died before 1876. They had one son and one daughter.

2492. i. JAY, JR.. m. before 1876.
2493. ii. The daughter, b. about 1856.

(1986.) ii. JOSEPH CHENEY FELTON[8], (*Joseph C.*[7], *Joseph*[6], *Benjamin*[5], *Joseph*[4], *Skelton*[3], *Nathaniel*[2], *Nathaniel*[1],) b. about 1821; m. and had one daughter and three sons. Mr. Felton was a soldier and lost his life in the late civil war.

2494. i. A daughter, m. and had 2 children before 1876.
2495. ii. JOSEPH C., JR.; was living in 1876.

(1990.) ii NORVELL D. WAITE, m. Marion Willson, daughter of Loten and Lodisa (Felton) Willson, (No. 1279.) They have 3 children. Mrs. Waite aided me by giving information of the descendants of her grandfather, Joseph Felton, (No. 601.)

2496. i. LUCIAN; Prof. of mathematics at Ithaca, N. Y., in 1876.
2497. ii. HORACE; graduated at Yale College, June, 1876.
2498. iii. FRANCES L.; m. Charles Comstock; residence in 1876, Decorah, Iowa.

(2003.) viii. BENJAMIN WELLINGTON FELTON[8], (*Benjamin S.*[7], *Joseph*[6], *Benjamin*[5], *Joseph*[4], *Skelton*[3], *Nathaniel*[2], *Nathaniel*[1],) b. in Fairfax, Vt., in 1833; m. Sept. 12, 1866, Angeline E. Moore, b. about 1846, daughter of Henry C. and Emma Moore. Mr. Felton is a stove merchant at Boston Highlands. In 1880, received a patent for Felton's Furnace and Ventilators. Many of his furnaces are in use in Boston Highlands and vicinity.

(2006.) i. REV. WILLARD W. AMES, b. about 1829, (son of Franklin Ames of West Bridgewater, Mass.;) m. in Greenfield, Mass., May 7, 1856, Marcia M. Felton of Lowell, Mass., b. in Fairfax, Vt., about 1831, daughter of Montgomery B. Felton, (1281.)

(2012.) i. WILLARD BARNES FELTON[8], (*William H.*[7], *Nathan*[6], *Benjamin*[5], *Joseph*[4], *Skelton*[3], *Nathaniel*[2], *Nathaniel*[1],) b. in Prescott, Mass., Nov. 26, 1837; he went to Boston in 1854, and lived there until the spring of 1862; he m. in 1858, in Roxbury, Frances Ann Burbank, daughter of Isaac and Betsey Burbank of Millbury, Mass. Mrs. Felton followed lecturing upon Spiritualism in Mass., R. I., Conn., N. Y., and Pa. Mrs. Fannie B. Felton died in 1872, aged 43 years. Mr. Felton moved to Colorado in 1862; he was a miner several years; followed farming and stock raising four years; was publisher and editor of a newspaper about six years; he has been superintendent of schools; a county judge; a delegate to two constitutional conventions; was chief clerk of the two first sessions of the State Legislature in 1876-77, and '79. In 1880, was clerk of the District Court for Saguache County. In Dec., 1880, was appointed by the Governor, warden of Col. State Penitentiary, and moved to Canon City.

(2129.) i. WILLIAM AMORY FELTON[8], (*Amory*[7], *Skelton*[6], *Benjamin*[5], *Joseph*[4], *Skelton*[3], *Nathaniel*[2], *Nathaniel*[1],) b. Dec. 27, 1836; m. Oct., 1859, Mary Ann Faxon, b. Oct. 13, 1837, daughter of Samuel Dexter Faxon of Hoosac Falls, N. Y. Mr. Felton is an accountant in Troy, N. Y. He was employed many years by the firm of Sweet, Quimby & Co., of the city. Mrs. Felton died several years ago.

2499. i. MINNIE, b. May 6, 1861; died April 16, 1862.
2500. ii. ANNIE S., b. Jan. 20, 1866; died Oct. 22, 1870, aged 4 years, 9 months.

(2130.) ii. CHARLES HENRY FELTON[8], (*Amory*[7], *Skelton*[6], *Benjamin*[5], *Joseph*[4], *Skelton*[3], *Nathaniel*[2], *Nathaniel*[1],) b. Feb. 18, 1840; m. Sept. 25, 1865, Lizzie R. Barthwick; had one son. Mr. Felton enlisted as private in a battery of artillery at the beginning of the civil war; was promoted corporal, quarter-master, sergeant, orderly sergeant, second lieutenant, first lieutenant, and adjutant of artillery; he served under several generals. Soon after the close of the war, was in railroad business at Chicago, Ill. Has been a traveling agent. In 1885, doing business in London, England.

2501. i. One son, died young.

(2131.) iii. HERBERT CLARK FELTON[8], (*Amory*[7], *Skelton*[6], *Benjamin*[5], *Joseph*[4], *Skelton*[3], *Nathaniel*[2], *Nathaniel*[1],) b. Nov. 3, 1846; m. April 10, 1872, Harriet Louisa Job, eldest daughter of Thomas and Mary Job of Troy, N. Y. Mr. Felton is secretary, treasurer and superintendent of a ferry company between Camden and Philadelphia; his residence, Camden, N. J.

(2132.) iv. FREDERICK KENT LYON, b. June 21, 1850, in Uniondale, Susquehanna County, Pa.; m., March 31, 1880, Emma Louisa Felton, b. in Troy, N. Y., Dec. 27, 1852, daughter of Amory Felton, (No. 1307.) In 1885, were living at Dunkirk, N. Y.

2502. i. RAYMOND F., b. Jan. 25, 1881, in Montrose, Pa.
2503. ii. HERBERT K., b. Aug. 31, 1882, in Montrose, Pa.

(2163.) i. FREDERICK BALCH DEANE, (son of Francis Deane, Esq., a lawyer who died in Aug., 1885, aged 80 years;) m Dec. 24, 1866, Cordelia C. Chamberlain, b. July 15, 1838, daughter of Charles C. and Cordelia M. (Felton) Chamberlain, (No. 1342.) Have lived in Worcester, Marlboro, and a few other towns in Mass.

2504. i. EMMA C., b. Nov. 17, 1867.
2505. ii. ARTHUR F., b. May 4, 1870.
2506. iii. FANNY C., b. May 19, 1873.
2507. iv. MARY C., b. May 27, 1875; died Dec. 5, 1875.
2508. v. FRANCIS C., b. Feb. 1, 1877; died Sept. 9, 1877.

(2164.) ii. JAMES CALVIN CHITTENDEN, m. May 15, 1860, Mary Caroline Chamberlin, b. Sept. 23, 1840, dau. of C. C. and C. M. (Felton) Chamberlin.

2509. i. CHARLOTTE C., b. Oct. 8, 1862.
2510. ii. MARY A., b. Nov. 1, 1865.

Mrs. Mary C. Chittenden m. second Dr. Crane; reside in Boston.

(2165.) iii. DAVID HENRY McIVOR, m. Oct. 1864, Sophia Hinckly Chamberlin, b. Sept, 23, 1843, daughter of C. C. and C. M. Chamberlin, (No. 1342.) Mr. McIvor died in 1871. Had one son.

2511. i. CHARLES HENRY, b. Dec. 15, 1866; died Oct. 8, 1873, aged 7 years.

Mrs. Sophia H. McIvor m. second, May 21, 1873, George S. Boutwell. They reside in Worcester, Mass.; his business, iron and heavy hardware.

(2168.) i. VERNON LONG of Rutland, Vt., m. Sept. 10, 1867, Adaline S. Hammond, b. Jan. 17, 1845, daughter of Elijah and Caroline N. (Felton) Hammond of Worcester, Mass. Mr. Long is a confectioner at Buffalo, N. Y.

2512. i. VERNON H., b. June 25, 1869; died Aug. 26, 1869.
2513. ii. BLANCHE S., b. Nov. 17, 1870.
2514. iii. ALBERT E., b. Sept. 24, 1872.
2515. iv. FRANK E., b. Nov. 13, 1874.
2516. v. ALICE, b. Feb. 25, 1877.

(2389.) v. SAMUEL MORSE FELTON[8], (Samuel M.[7], Cornelius C.[6], Thomas[5], Thomas[4], Daniel[3], Nathaniel[2], Nathaniel,[1]) b. Feb. 3, 1853; he graduated at the Massachusetts Institute of Technology in civil and-mechanical engineering. It is said been practically engaged in railroading since he was 16 years old; first as a civil engineer on the Reading railroad in Pa.; secondly as general superintendent of 'the Pittsburg, Cincinnati and St. Louis railroad for about 8 years; was general manager of the New York and New England railroad, 1882 to 1884, and resided at Boston. In 1884, took charge as general manager of the New York, Pennsylvania and Ohio railroad, with headquarters at Cleveland, Ohio. Mr. Felton m. Oct. 21, 1880, Dora Hamilton, b. Oct. 25, 1856, daughter of George and Hadanah Hamilton.

 2517. i. HADANAH H., b. July 14, 1881.
 2518. ii. RUTH, b. Nov. 19, 1882.
 2519. iii. DOROTHY L., b. April 16, 1884.

(2390.) vi. EDGAR CONWAY FELTON[8],(*Samuel M.*[7], *Cornelius C.*[6], *Thomas*[5], *Thomas*[4], *Daniel*[3], *Nathaniel*[2], *Nathaniel*[1],) b. April 13, 1858; graduated at Harvard College in 1879; he has been for several years in the employ of the Pennsylvania Steel Company, and resides at Steelton, near Harrisburg, Pa. Mr. Felton m. June 2, 1884, Abbie Bent, b. June 2, 1862, dau. of Winslow B. and Jane Elizabeth (Tomlinson) Bent.

 2520. i. MARGARET, b. July 15, 1885.

In 1876, Mr. Felton's brother-in-law, Capt. Eben F. Barker, was secretary of the Penn. Steel Co., and their brother-in-law, Maj. Luther S. Bent, was superintendent of the works in Steelton, Pa.

SUPPLEMENTARY NOTES.

SUPPLEMENT NO. 1.

JOHN A. FELTON was b. in Spain, in or near Gibraltar, Aug. 16, 1799; came to America, when 9 years of age, in a vessel commanded by Capt. Atkins Adams and settled in Marblehead, Mass. Mr. Felton was a coffin maker and many years a sexton and undertaker. He m. Dec. 31, 1820, Mary Stacy, daughter of Edward Stacy of Marblehead; she died Feb. 17, 1822, aged 32 years; also their child died the same day. He m. second, April 13, 1823, Mrs. Elizabeth Grant, daughter of Stephen Chapman of Marblehead. Had 10 children. Mrs. E. C. Felton died March 14, 1858, aged 59 years, 6 months. Mr. Felton died Oct. 24, 1867, aged 68 years, 2 months and 8 days.

   i. A child, died Feb. 17, 1822.
   ii. JOHN, b. about 1823–24; was lost at sea on Grand Bank in Nov. 1844, aged 21 years.
   iii. ATKINS A., b. about May 1825; died of hooping cough, March 25, 1826, aged 10 months.
   iv. ATKINS A., b. about 1827; m. July 1857, aged 29 years, to Hannah D. Butman, aged 26 years. They had several children. He was a shoe cutter. In 1872, Mr. Felton with Frederick C. Floyd of Boston, procured a patent on a boot, No. 133,767.
   v. WILLIAM H., b. July 4, 1829; was drowned in Salem Harbor, Dec. 9, 1857, aged 28 years.
   vi. ELIZABETH C., b. Sept., 1831; m. Jan. 3, 1854, Ebenezer R. Mitchell, aged 22 years.
   vii. ROBERT P., b. Dec. 22, 1833; m. in 1858, Jane (Bartlett) Rhodes; she died July 18, 1873, aged 36 years, 9 months; he m. second, Feb. 16, 1882, Mrs. Mary Elizabeth West. He was a sergeant and lieutenant in the late civil war.
   viii. STEPHEN C., b. Sept. 4, 1835; was a soldier 1861 to 1865; a sergeant in Dec. 1863; a representative of Marblehead in 1868; chosen moderator in 1876; was elected town clerk in 1881, and re-elected five times.

ix. FRANCIS S., b. July 19, 1837; m. June 1858, Rebecca A. Symonds. Have had several children; one son, George F., died July 26, 1880, aged 16 years, 6 months. Mr. Felton was also a soldier in the Union army. He is a bill poster and distributer in Marblehead.
x. HANNAH B., b. Nov., 1839; m. March 20, 1862, George H. Martin.
xi. REBECCA B., b. about 1841; m. Aug. 1861, Edward Crowninshield, 2d.

SUPPLEMENT NO. 2.

In Oct., 1876, we received an interesting letter from REV. CYRUS ERASTUS FELTON of Pittsburg, Pa., but before this date of Chicago, Ill. His grandfather, Erastus Felton, moved West from one of the New England States. It was all the information he had in regard to his origin. He had four sons, Erastus, Jr., Thomas, Levi and one more, the name he had forgotten. Erastus Felton, Sen., lived near 70 years. Erastus Felton, Jr., also had four sons, Rev. Cyrus Erastus, b. about 1830, Josiah, who was lost in the late civil war, John and William, both living in 1876. Erastus Felton, Jr., died at the early age of 37 years.

Rev. C. E. Felton was preaching in Chillicothe, Ohio, in 1860. He preached several years in St. Louis, Mo., and Chicago, Ill. In March, 1883, moved to Baltimore, Md., and became pastor of the Methodist Episcopal church, Mt. Vernon Place, in that city. Rev. Dr. Felton had two sons living in 1876, George and Jae Felton.

SUPPLEMENT NO. 3.

When Rev. C. F. LeFebre settled in Sherbrook, Canada, about 1828, he found among his parishioners a widow Felton, and her three sons and three daughters; the family being the first in wealth and station in that part of the country. The sons were:— Hon. Wm. B., Lieut. John and Charles B. Felton. One daughter was a school teacher, one married a purser in the navy, and one married a merchant.

HON. WILLIAM B. FELTON had amassed a considerable fortune as naval store keeper at Port Mahon, in the island of Minorca. He came to Canada about 1816, and a large tract of land was given him by the government as a settler. He was a member of the Governor or Legislative Council ten or more years from 1823. It is said he expended his large fortune, about $150,000, in the purchase and improvement of land which never brought him anything, so that when he died his widow was left with a bare competency. The interests of his brothers were embarked with him in his land operations.

Hon. William Bowman Felton married a Spanish lady and had 3 sons and 8 daughters. His widow and two sons were living in Sherbrook in 1856: W. L. Felton, Esq., the advocate and publisher of the *St. Francis Telegraph*; E. P. Felton, Esq., a notary in the Square of Sherbrook. The third son, many years before 1858, went to Australia. Hon. Wm. B. Felton's daughters all married; the oldest one married the Chief Justice of Quebec.

Lt. JOHN FELTON in 1852, was Crown Land Agent, Main St., Sherbrook. He was a signal midshipman on board of the Victory, Lord Nelson's flag-ship at Trafalgar, and was promoted to the rank of lieutenant; but having lost a ship, sloop of war Cassia, in the West Indies afterwards, he was deprived of his rank. The case being one of hardship, and Mr. Felton being an aged and respected citizen, when the Prince of Wales was on a visit to Sherbrook, Aug. 30, 1860, on being informed of the particulars, he restored Mr. Felton his rank together with pay. The act gave great satisfaction, and was loudly applauded. It was a fortunate thing for him, for his affairs, after the death of his brother William, were at a very low ebb. Lt. John Felton married a Spanish lady, but had no issue.

CHARLES B. FELTON, brother of Lt. John Felton, had a grant of land of 200 acres. He married and had several children. He moved to New York, and suppose was living, in 1858, with some of his children.

SUPPLEMENT NO. 4.

In 1856, ELI F. FELTON of Andes, Delaware County, N. Y., wrote that he came to America in 1820, from Birmingham, Warwickshire, England. His grandfather, George Felton, was a clock-maker in Buford, Shropshire, and moved to Birmingham about 1786, with five sons and four daughters. George Felton's ancestors were brought up in Shropshire, one of the four western counties of England. Thomas Felton, (an uncle of Eli named above,) was a silversmith in Hinckley, Leicestershire, when Mr. Felton left England in 1820. His uncle had a record of the Feltons back to Oliver Cromwell's time. John Felton, another uncle, lived in Australia and had a large family. One of Mr. Felton's uncles came to America before 1790. Eli, George and Thomas were common among his grandfather's descendants. An Eli Felton died in N. Y.

city in 1845, who was his relative; there were two Eli Feltons in the same city in 1856, his relatives. Mr. Felton's brother, Frederick Felton, died at Gibraltar about 1849. There was one Mr. Felton in Birmingham, when he left England, in 1820, a baker by trade, who did not belong to their family.

SUPPLEMENT NO. 5.

A few Feltons of North Carolina, Georgia and Alabama. In Nov. 1855, we received a letter from THADDEUS W. FELTON, postmaster at La Grange, Ala. His father was William Felton from N. C., where he had brothers, Bolin and Boon Felton, who lived and died in that state. Their father was Elisha Felton and had brothers; John, William, Cater and Noah Felton. The five brothers resided in Halifax Co., N. C.

Dr. WILLIAM H. FELTON, a member of Congress 6 years from Ga., 1875 to 1881, says his grandfather, Job Felton, removed from North Carolina to Georgia about 1785, and died an aged man. Dr. Felton's father, John Felton, was born in 1790, and lived 80 years. Hon. Wm. H. Felton was born June 19, 1823; graduated at Georgia Medical College. Dr. Felton also wrote. "There was one of the old brothers, (sup. of his grandfather,) who lived in the lower counties of North Carolina, and some members of that family are in Macon Co., Georgia."

SUPPLEMENT NO. 6.

Most of the Feltons in Pennsylvania are of German lineage; their ancestors were from Germany. We called upon a few in 1876, Centennial year.

In 1834, JACOB FELTON of Nicholson, Pa., was agent for newspapers.

From 1843 to 1846, ANTHONY and A. C. FELTON, gardeners, were connected with horticultural exhibitions in Phila., receiving several premiums.

In 1856, ANTHONY WAYNE FELTON of Sterlingville, Wyoming County, says, that his great-grandfather, Henry Felton came to Phila. from Germany. His grandfather, Henry Felton, Jr., who was born in Philadelphia, had five sons, viz.: Henry, Jr., George, Christiana, Jacob and William.

THOMAS FELTON of Northern Liberties, Phila., whose estate was settled in 1794, had sons, Thomas, Jr., James and George Washington Felton.

PHILIP FELTON of Phila., whose will was set up in 1825, had sons, Philip, Jr., and John Felton; the last named, John Felton, was a representative in 1842; his son, Samuel K. Felton, was living in Philadelphia in 1876.

WILLIAM FELTON of Borough of Frankfort, Philadelphia County, in 1826, had brothers, Michael and George Felton; George had a son, William Felton.

In 1856, there were 10 names of Feltons in the Philadelphia Directory, (besides Samuel M. Felton, who was from Mass.) In 1876, there were 18 names; two of these from Mass., Samuel M. and Matthias Felton. A few of the remaining 16 were printed Felten, "ten" instead of "ton."

In 1854, GEORGE W. FELTON was postmaster at Feltonville in Philadelphia County, Pa.

In 1876, A. L. FELTEN, Corner of Park Avenue and 31st St., Phila., had in Agricultural Hall, on the Centennial grounds, a table 60 feet in length, containing 500 varieties of fruits and vegetables; was awarded a prize medal and diploma.

SUPPLEMENT NO. 7.

JOHN FELTON, who was born in Newburyport, Mass., about 1810, says he is a genuine Felton. His reputed father was living in 1855. In 1830 and 1833, John Felton was living in Rowley, Mass.; the former year he had his name changed to John Grayham Milgrove, and the latter year changed back to John Felton. He married Miss Judith Morse Sargent of Dunbarton, N. H. Mrs. Felton died May 22, 1851, aged 34 years. They had two daughters, both born in Bradford, Mass.

    i. SARAH G., b. in 1842; m. Julius C. Johnson of Enfield, Conn.
    ii. MARY A., b. Aug. 8, 1845; died in Georgetown, Mass., Aug. 17, 1846, aged 1 year.

In 1855, Mr. Felton and Mr. and Mrs. Johnson resided at Springfield, Mass. In 1868 to 1872, Mr. Felton was a shoe-cutter in Marlboro, Mass. In 1880, he lived in Lowell, Mass. Mr. and Mrs. Johnson have two daughters. Residence, Lowell, 1880.

    i. MARGARET B., b. Oct. 11, 1864.
    ii. SARAH E., b. Jan., 1867.

There are Felton families in Mass. we have not traced; some of them have lived in several towns. One family, Robert Felton and wife, born in St. John, N. B.

APPENDICES.

APPENDIX A.—TOMPKINS.

In Sept. 1635, RALPH TOMPKINS, aged 50 years, arrived in Mass., with wife Katherine, aged 58 years, and 4 children; the same year, 1635, had a grant of land in Salem, at the head of Cow-house river, afterwards called Endicott river and Waters river. He was made freeman, May, 1638. His wife was sister of Samuel Aborne. He died at Salem in Nov., 1666. His son John Tompkins settled the estate and had his father's farm. Nathaniel Felton was one of the appraisers.

    i. JOHN, b. about 1610; m. Margaret ———; had 10 or more children.
    ii. SAMUEL, b. about 1613; m. Oct., 1639, Lestice Foster of Scituate, and lived in Duxbury, afterwards in Bridgewater, Mass.
    iii. ELIZABETH, b. about 1617.
    iv. MARY, b. about 1621; m. ——— Foster.

In May 1642, JOHN TOMPKINS, SR. and JR., (supposed junior only in years,) took the oath of freemen. One of them settled at Salem; the other one, supposed lived a few years at Concord, and afterwards at Bridgewater, and was sometimes called, "John Tompkins from Salem."

JOHN[2] TOMPKINS, (son of Ralph,) m. Margaret ———; she died July 18, 1672. He m. second, Sept. 1673, Mary Read. Mr. Tompkins died June 23, 1681, aged 71 years. Nathaniel Felton and Edward Batter were the appraisers of his estate.

    i. NATHANIEL, the oldest, was living in 1681.
    ii. HANNAH, bapt. Feb., 1638; died young.
    iii. ELIZABETH, bapt. 19th of third month, 1639; died young.
    iv. HANNAH, bapt. 21st of twelfth month, 1640; not named in the will, 1681.
    v. SARAH, bapt. Jan. 1, 1642; m. in 1663, John Waters.

vi. JOHN, JR., bapt. 16th of twelfth month, 1644; m. in June, 1671, Rebecca Knights; had 5 or more children at Salem, Mass.
vii. ELIZABETH, b. Nov. 29, bapt. in Jan. 1646–47; was living in 1681.
viii. MARY, bapt. 29th of second month, (April,) 1649; m. John Felton in 1670, (No. 2,) page 11.
ix. DEBORAH, bapt. 8th of fourth month, 1651; named in 1681.
x. PRISCILLA, sup. b. about 1653; m. 1679, Samuel Marsh.

APPENDIX B.—HOULTON OR HOLTON.

JOSEPH HOULTON in 1641, was a "servant to Richard Ingersoll." About 1651, Mr. Houlton m. Sarah Haynes, a widow of William Haynes and daughter of Richard Ingersoll above named. They lived in Salem and had 5 sons, and 2 daughters. Mr. Houlton died May 30, 1705.

i. JOSEPH, JR., b. in 1652; bapt. Jan., 1652–3; m. Hannah ———, and had 3 or more children; son Joseph, Jr., b. Aug., 1673.
ii. BENJAMIN, bapt. Feb. 14, 1657; m. Sarah ———, and had Benjamin, Jr., b. in 1689. Mr. Houlton died June 13, 1689, aged 32 years. Mrs. Sarah Houlton m. second, Dea. Benjamin Putnam; his second marriage.
iii. ELIZABETH, b. in 1660.
iv. HENRY, b. in 1662; m. about 1688, Abigail Flint, and had, at Salem, 7 children; son Samuel, b. in 1707, was father of Hon. Samuel Holton, b. in 1738; d. in Danvers, Jan. 2, 1816, aged 77 yrs.
v. JAMES, b. in or about 1664; m. Ruth Felton, (No. 3,) page 12. He was a selectman of Salem several years.
vi. JOHN, b. in 1667.
vii. SARAH, b. in 1669.

APPENDIX C.—HORN OR ORNE.

JOHN HORN was made freeman in 1631; he was a deacon in Salem 50 years. He m. Ann ———, and had 8 or more children. Dea. Horn's will dated Oct. 8, 1679; proved Nov. 1684; he died that month aged 82 years. Part if not all of Dea. John Horn's descendants dropped the H from Horn, which left their surname, Orne. Several of his descendants have been men of note. The first baptism recorded at Salem was Recompence Orne in 1636. Dea. Horn's children—probably not in this order.

i. JOHN, JR., m. Oct., 1667, Mary Clarke; had 8 children.
ii. SYMOND, m. Feb. 1675, Widow Rebecca Stevens; had 2 or more children.
iii. JOSEPH, m. July 1677, Ann Thompson; had one or more children.
iv. BENJAMIN, m. before 1684, and had 3 or more children.
v. ELIZABETH, the oldest daughter, m. —— Gardner.
vi. MARY, m. —— Smith.
vii. JEHOADAN, m. —— Hervey, sup. before 1670.
viii. ANN, JR., m. Nathaniel Felton, Jr., (No. 7,) page 13.

APPENDIX D,—PROCTOR.

About 1635, came to New England, JOHN PROCTOR, aged 46 years; Martha Proctor, aged 28 years, with 2 children; John, Jr., aged 3 years; Marie, aged 1 year. They settled in Ipswich, Mass. John Proctor of Ipswich, (son of John and Martha, m. Elizabeth Thorndike (daughter of John and Elizabeth Thorndike,) and moved from Ipswich to Salem about 1666. Mrs. Elizabeth Proctor died Aug. 30, 1672. Mr. Proctor m. second, April 1, 1674, Elizabeth Bassett. Mr. Proctor had 14 or 15 children. He was executed for witchcraft Aug. 19, 1692, aged supposed about 60 years. Mr. Proctor wrote a letter July 23, 1692, in Salem prison to 5 ministers. Mrs. Proctor was arrested, but not executed; she m. about 3 years afterwards, —— Richards.

i. ELIZABETH, probably the oldest; m. in 1681, Thomas Very.
ii. MARTHA, b. in Salem, June 4, 1666.
iii. MARY, b. Oct. 20, 1667; died Feb. 15, 1667-8.
iv. JOHN, JR., b. Oct. 28, 1668.
v. MARY, again, b. Jan. 30, 1669-70; was living in 1712.
vi. THORNDIKE, b. July 15, 1672; m. Mrs. Hannah (Felton) Endicott, widow of Samuel Endicott, and dau. of Nathaniel Felton, Sr., of Salem.
vii. BENJAMIN, sup. b. in 1674; m. Dec., 1694, Mary Withridge, and had 4 children. He was arrested for witchcraft in 1692.
viii. WILLIAM, b. Feb. 16, 1674-5; was arrested with Benjamin in 1692.
ix. SARAH, b. June 28, 1676; sup. m. Isaac Williams.
x. JOSEPH, sup. b. about 1680; was living in 1712.
xi. THOMAS, sup. b. about 1683.
xii. SAMUEL, b. Jan. 11, 1685; sup. m. and had 6 children; died in 1765, aged 80.
xiii. ELISHA, b. April 28, 1687; died Nov. 11, 1688.
xiv. ABIGAIL, b. in Jan., or June, 1689; living in 1712.

xv. One child, it is said, was born a few weeks after the father was executed.

It is also reported that some of the children of John Proctor, viz: Mrs. Elizabeth Very, Abigail Proctor and Mary Proctor received from the General Court about 1712, the sum of £11, 5s. apiece as compensation for damages for the imprisonment and death of their father in 1692.

After 19 persons had been executed and one pressed to death in 1692, the awful delusion vanished.

APPENDIX E.—FOOT.

PASCO FOOT was in Salem in 1637. Feb. 6, 1653, had 8 children baptised, viz: John, Malachi, Samuel, Elizabeth, Mary, Isaac, Pasco, Jr., and Abigail. Mr. Foot died in 1670. The two first children not named in his will. Abigail Foot, m. in 1670, George Early. Isaac Foot, m. Dec., 1668, Abigail Ingalls, (perhaps is the name) and had 6 or more children, viz:

 i. ISAAC, JR., b. in 1670.
 ii. ABIGAIL, b. in 1671.
 iii. SAMUEL, b. in 1673.
 iv. ELIZABETH, b. April, 1675; m. June, 1698, Nathaniel Felton[3], (No. 11,) page 14.
 v. MALACHI, b. in 1680; m. Dec., 1710, Elizabeth Masters, b. July, 1684.
 vi. SARAH, b. in 1685, (probably a daughter or a relative;) m. Nov. 1719, John Felton of Marblehead, (No. 22,) page 17.
 vii. MARY, b. in 1691.

APPENDIX F.—GOODALE.

In 1634, ROBERT GOODALE, aged 30 years, and Katherine, his wife, aged 28 years, and 3 children, came to America and settled in Salem, Mass., where he had 480 acres between Ipswich river, Reading road and Newburyport turnpike.

 i. MARY, b. in 1630.
 ii. ABRAHAM, b. in 1632.
 iii. ISAAC, b. in 1633; m. Jan., 1668, Patience Cook, and had 6 or more children at Salem.
 iv. ZACHARIAH, b. in 1639; m. in 1666, Elizabeth Beacham, daughter of Edward Beacham of Salem, and had 11 children.
 v. JACOB, bapt. Jan. 9, 1641.
 vi. SARAH.
 vii. ELIZABETH.
 viii. HANNAH.

ZACHARIAH GOODALE was living in 1708. Zachariah and Elizabeth Goodale's children were born at Salem.

    i. ZACHARIAH, JR., b. Feb. 9, 1667; m. Sarah ———, and had 6 children at Salem.
    ii. SAMUEL, b. Dec., 1669; m. Dec. 3, 1696, Mary Buxton, and had 7 children.
    iii. JOSEPH, b. Sept. 23, 1672; m. Mary ———, about 1695; had 7 or more children.
    iv. MARY, b. Nov. 27, 1674; m. Dea. Joseph Whipple; had 8 or 9 children.
    v. THOMAS, b. Dec. 30, 1676.
    vi. ABRAHAM, b. Nov. 7, 1678; m. April 1704, Hannah Rhodes of Lynn; had 9 children.
    vii. JOHN, b. Aug. 10, 1681; m. Sept. 1703, Elizabeth Witt, and settled in Marlborough; had 3 or more children. Mrs. Goodale died in 1738. Mr. Goodale died May 11, 1752, aged 71 years. Mrs. Elizabeth Goodale, his second wife, died the same month, May, 1752.
    viii. ELIZABETH, b. about 1683; sup. m. in 1704, Samuel Howe, Jr., of Sudbury.
    ix. SARAH, b. about 1685; m. in 1709, Samuel Felton of Salem, (No. 16.)
    x. BENJAMIN, b. July 4, 1687: m. Hannah ———, and settled in Marlborough. They had 9 children. Mrs. Goodale died Feb. 20, 1754, Mr. Goodale, a week afterwards, aged 66 years, 8 months.
    xi. DAVID, b. March, 1688-9; m. Jan., 1712-13, Abigail Elliot. They had 2 or more children. The David Goodale farm was in Salem-Danvers, now in Danvers, near West Peabody line. It is now, (1886,) owned and occupied by Jasper Pope, an octogenarian.

Zachariah and Elizabeth Goodale's seven last named children were baptised in Salem Village, (now Danvers,) March 23, 1690. We may expect a good genealogy of the Goodale and Goodell families within a few years, by Abner C. Goodell, Jr., Esq., of Salem, Mass.

APPENDIX G.—WATERS.

In 1637, RICHARD WATERS, the emigrant, had ten acres granted him in Salem, near Cow-house river, sometimes called Endicott river, now Waters river. Before the erection of a bridge the ferry was known as Waters' ferry. Waters river is in Danvers and Peabody. Richard Waters m. Joyce, dau. of William Plaise, who died in Salem about 1646. Mr. Plaise and Mr. Waters were gunsmiths. Mr. Waters had 10 children; 4 sons, John, James, Ezekiel and William; 6 daughters,

JOHN WATERS, bapt. in 1640, (son of Richard, Sr.;) m. Aug., 1663, Sarah Tompkins, a sister of Mrs. Mary (Tompkins) Felton, wife of John Felton, No. 2. They had 10 children. John Waters' estate settled in 1714. The sons were: John, Jr., b. July, 1665; Richard in 1669; Nathaniel in 1671; Samuel, b. in 1675. The youngest daughter, Abigail, b. in 1683; m. in 1704, John Jacobs.

JOHN WATERS, JR., b. July, 1665; m. Mary ———, and had 6 children. His estate was settled in 1742; had one son, John, Jr., who m. and had 7 children.

John and Mary Waters' daughter, Mary Waters, m. April, 1721, John Felton, No. 17.

APPENDIX M.—DEALAND.

The Beverly town records have it, BENJAMIN DEALAND, m. Katherine Hodge in Boston, Dec., 1681. They had 4 children recorded at Beverly, Mass. In June, 1696, Mrs. Katherine Dealand, then a widow, was baptised with her children, viz: Benjamin, George and Mary. In 1708, 1709, and 1710, Mrs. Dealand kept school in James Houlton's house in Salem, the part now Peabody. She probably taught afterwards in the first school house built in Salem Village, now Danvers, for Widow Dealand received five pounds for keeping school in ye village. Mrs. Catherine Dealand died Jan. 2, 1712–13. Mr. and Mrs. Dealand's children were:

  i. MARY, b. Nov. 27, 1683.
 ii. BENJAMIN, JR., b. May 31, 1686; m. Mary ——— before 1711–12.
iii. JOHN, b. Sept. 14, 1688.
 iv. GEORGE, b. Feb. 1690–91; m. May, 1711, Bethiah Peters.

BENJAMIN and GEORGE DEALAND settled in Salem. Jan. 6, 1711–12, Mrs. Mary Dealand, wife of Benjamin Dealand, was baptised at Salem Village. They had one or more children.

  i. BENJAMIN, JR., m. Sept. 27, 1744, Elizabeth Felton, No. 58.

George and Bethiah Dealand had 9 children; three of them were sons.

i. GEORGE, JR., b. June 18, 1721; m. Abigail Proctor, b. Aug. 27, 1727, daughter of Thorndike Proctor, Jr., No. 34 in the Felton book. They had several children; their daughter, Sarah, b. May, 1762, m. Stephen Felton of New Salem, No. 263.

NOTE.—On account of the fulness of the volume, we must omit many appendices we had partly prepared for this work.

ERRATA.

Page 22.—The fourth generation commences near the bottom, with Dea. Malachi Felton's family.
Page 28.—21st line from the top, for Beaves, read Reeves.
Page 40.—14th line from bottom, for Creuzy, read Creasey.
Page 112.—2d line from top, for Tamison, read Elizabeth.
Page 112.—20th line from top, for (554,) read (551.) The next six families read, (552,) (553,) (555,) (556,) (557,) (558.)
Page 202.—6th line from bottom, for Alvin, read Alvan.

Information of errors in names, dates and other inaccuraracies herein, and also further information respecting the FELTON FAMILY will be cheerfully received by,

CYRUS FELTON,
Marlboro, Mass., August, 1886.

INDEX TO FELTON FAMILIES.

A
Aaron, 88
Aaron H., 164
Abijah, 108
Abraham, 69
Albert H., 226
Albert Q., 198
Alexander, 105
Alexander C., 136
Alexander W., 151
Almon D., 192
Alonzo, 156
Alonzo L., 217
Alvan, 202
Amory 121, 194
Amos, 35, 55, 68, 107
Anthony, 37, 242
Anthony W., 242
Archelaus, 37
Artemas, 90
Asa, 51
Asa E., 187
Asa Y., 177
Aurelia S., 103
Austin, 216

B
Benjamin, 6, 23, 35, 63, 69, 117, 125
Benjamin F., 199
Benjamin K., 159
Benjamin R., 136
Benjamin W., 235

C
Charles, 82, 155, 157
Charles A., 204, 213
Charles B., 241
Charles C., 147
Charles E., 199
Charles H., 236
Charles N., 227
Cornelius C., 153, 218, 226
Cyrus, 162
Cyrus E., 240
Cyrus W., 137

D
Daniel, 38, 53, 75, 99, 131, 139, 140, 143, 150
Daniel B., 135
Daniel C., 216
Daniel H., 208
Darling, 152
David, 27, 34, 51, 108, 150, 201
David H., 104, 129

E
Ebenezer, 18, 35, 61, 67, 70, 132
Edgar C., 238
Edward, 145
Edward J., 46
Edwin, 155
Elbridge G., 191
Eli F., 241
Elijah W., 82
Elisha, 29, 59
Erastus, 240
Ezra, 150
Ezra B., 180

F
Francis, 33, 127
Francis A., 200
Frank A., 182
Franklin E., 225
Frederick A., 182
Frederick L., 233

G
George, 92
George D., 133
George H., 174
George L., 174
George M., 180
George N., 173
George W., 54, 103, 141, 208, 243.

H
Henry, 242
Henry F., 231
Henry H., 188
Henry O., 166
Herbert C., 236
Hiram G., 113
Horace, 148, 149
Horatio L., 188

I
Isaac, 74

J
Jacob, 25, 89, 90, 242
James, 66, 67, 74, 76, 96, 127, 129, 149, 216
James M., 192
James P., 176
James S., 137, 149, 217
Jay, 234
Jedediah, 71, 85
Joel, 49, 92
John, 11, 16, 17, 29, 33, 47, 58, 61, 66, 73, 85, 93, 113, 119, 135, 146, 199, 241, 243
John A., 239
John B., 224
John R., 158
John S., 95, 128, 230
John W., 157
Jonathan, 19, 71, 141
Jonathan N., 142
Jonathan W., 125
Joseph, 31, 118, 126, 218
Joseph C., 188, 235
Joseph O., 195
Joseph P., 203
Joshua, 44, 83
Joshua M., 226
Josiah D., 124

L
Lambert A., 166
Lansford B., 203.
Leonard A., 181
Levi, 85, 93, 160
Levi L., 213
Levi P., 206
Lewis, 166
Lewis E., 176
Lloyd, 98
Lucius E., 232
Luther, 91
Luther H., 173
Lyman, 91, 98, 147
Lyman B., 165
Lyman S., 169

M
Malachi, 22
Martin, 75
Matthias, 48, 90, 93
Matthias B., 169
Merrick, 167
Montgomery B., 189
Moses H., 119, 192
Moses O., 104

N
Nathan, 59, 118
Nathan B., 186
Nathan H., 193
Nathaniel, 11, 13, 14, 24, 36, 43, 70, 71, 136, 138
Nathaniel W., 207.

Nehemiah H., 190
Nelson, 152
Nymphus P., 194

O
Oliver C., 122

P
Philip. 243
Proctor, 132

Robert, 75, 129, 152

S
Sampson, 149
Samuel, 15, 27, 52, 66, 155, 227
Samuel M., 221, 237

Silas, 86
Silas A., 166, 230
Simeon Y., 177
Skelton, 17, 65, 120, 123
Stephen, 24, 46, 48, 68, 83, 89, 130, 158, 204
Stephen O., 182
Sylvanus, 86

T
Thaddeus W., 242
Thomas, 39, 76, 154, 242
Thomas K., 127
Thomas S., 190
Thorndike, 131
Timothy, 30, 59
Timothy P., 115

W
Welcome, 205
Willard B., 235
William, 29, 45, 72, 81, 87, 97, 144, 243
William A., 195, 236,
William B., 240
William C., 156
William F., 177
William H., 190, 206, 242
William L., 190
William N., 158, 173
William P., 108
William S., 115
William T., 115

Z
Zachariah, 28, 97

INDEX OF OTHER FAMILIES.

A
Adams Samuel, 128
Adams William H., 113
Ames Willard W., 235
Amsden Jacob, 128
Amsden Lee, 109
Atkins Joseph H., 200
Atwood George W. B., 156
Avery Alfred, 185
Avery Allyn A., 234
Ayres Joseph, 65

B
Barber Joseph, 173
Bartlett Henry, 214
Bartlett Montgomery, 66
Batchelder Andrew, 120
Batchelder Jonathan, 80
Batchelder Oliver F., 195
Bates Sylvanus W., 204
Benjamin Daniel, 54, 100
Bennett Jonathan, 98
Bent George E., 223
Bent James M., 178
Bigelow Granville, 208
Bigelow Julian F., 229
Bigelow Leander, 161
Bigelow Lyman M., 143
Bigelow William, 208
Bill Wells, 197
Bispham Thomas W., 211
Blake Elias, 94
Blake Joel, 95
Boardman Hiram, 185
Boutwell George S., 237
Bowers Luke, 213
Bowker Josiah C., 199
Bowls John R., 95

Boyd Roger, 230
Brigham Abel, 161
Brigham Charles H., 162
Brigham Eli, 109
Brigham Eugene O., 229
Brigham Jonas E., 184
Brigham Silas E., 184
Brooks Joel, 110
Brown Howard, 128
Burnett David, 134
Burnham John, 141

C
Camp George, 107
Case Henry, 170
Chamberlain Charles C., 197
Chamberlain Cyrus N., 205
Chamberlain George F., 204
Chamberlain Levi, 133
Chamberlain Moses, 186
Chamberlain William H., 212
Chamnese Arthur, 15
Chittendon, James C., 237
Clarke Asa B., 194
Clarke Ezra D., 113
Clarke, Russell, 177
Clifford Pliny, 201
Cone Samuel, 126
Cook George W., 161
Cramm John, 101
Culver William C., 196
Currier Daniel, 114
Curtis Mrs. Sarah, 64
Cutting Charles, 232

D
Dealand Benjamin, 28, 57, 249
Dealand George, 41, 249

Dealand Joseph. 110
Damon Charles. 101
Damon Charles R., 179
Davis Christopher W., 227
Davis John C., 106
Derby John. 84
Derrick Bybie L., 159
Deane Frederick B., 237
Dodge Thomas, 52

E
Elliot Amos, 140
Endicott Elias, 40
Endicott John. 40, 77
Endicott Samuel, 13, 20
Eppes John, 70

F
Farlow Mrs. Lauretta A., 217
Farnham Osman P., 108
Farrar Nathaniel, 103
Fessenden George O., 234
Fessenden John Q., 234
Filkins William, 176
Fisher Mark, 147
Fiske Joel B., 112
Fiske Welcome V., 228
Foot David A., 203
Foot Isaac, 247
Foot Pasco, 247
Foster Ebenezer, 30, 62
Foster Samuel, 130
French Tobin, 178
Frost Oren, 206
Frye Charles L., 231
Frye John A., 231
Frye Lewis T., 165
Frye William, 137

G
Gale Thomas, 75
Gassett John, 51
Giles William, 145
Goodale Austin W., 174
Goodale Robert, 247
Goodale Zachariah, 248
Goodnough Sylvanus, 151
Gray John H., 196
Green Bartholomew, 123
Grout Eli, 134
Grout John, 33
Guild Joseph, 74

H
Hadley Ira, 140
Hager Charles, 202
Hamilton Moses, 63
Hammond Elijah, 198
Hardy Dudley, 47
Hardy Theophilus, 49
Harwood Jacob, 68
Haskell Daniel, 175
Haskell Levi, 169
Haywood Samuel, 32

Herrick Martin, 20
Holyoke Henry A., 211
Hooper Ebenezer, 131
Houlton James, 12, 63
Houlton Joseph, 31, 116, 245
Howe Benjamin, 112
Howe Ebenezer, 57
Howe Ezekiel, 111
Howe Gershom, 51
Howe Jedediah, 56
Howe Jonathan, 50
Howe Moses, 26
Howe Perley, 111
Howe Rewell, 110
Howe Samuel, 50, 94
Hoyt John F., 123
Hoyt Wyman, 64
Hunt John, 100
Huntington Ozias, 172
Hyde Lucius L., 182

I
Ide Daniel, 184
Ingersoll John, 8
Irish Jonathan, 197

J
Jackman Joseph V., 232
Jackson Artemus, 105
Jacobs David H., 180
Jacobs James M., 179
Jacobs Thomas M., 102
Jacobs Thomas R., 180
Jewett Frederick, 229
Johnson Aaron, 99
Johnson Amos, 99
Johnson Bartholomew, 85
Johnson Henry, 99
Johnson Jonathan, 53, 177

K
Kendrick George P., 196
Kendrick Jacil, 121
Kemp Aaron, 100
Kent Benjamin, 43, 80
Keyes Isaac, 106
Keyes Samuel, 100

L
LaCroix Edward, 196
Lander Jonathan, 52
Leonard Ezekiel, 130
Leonard Thorndike, 202
Lewis Elbridge, 230
Lincoln David, 81, 154
Lincoln Nathan, 226
Lloyd William A., 205
Long Daniel F., 169
Long Vernon, 237
Lord George C., 168
Lyon Frederick H., 236

M
Macomber Samuel, 131

McClelland James, 218
Mackintire Archelaus, 29
Mackintire John, 58
Mackintire Samuel, 97
McIntosh Francis, 147
McIvor David H. 237
Manson George E. 160
Manson George L., 228
Manson Silas F., 228
Marsh James, 139
Mason Ambrose A., 181
Martin L., 195
Maxon Jonathan, 151
Maynard John P., 142
Maynard Samuel B., 170
Mead Joseph W., 176
Merrill Joseph, 115
Miles Joseph, 7
Miller Charles, 194
Moody Edward, 181
Morse Aaron, 73
Morse James O., 146, 215
Morse Oliver A., 215
Morse Stewart, 215
Mower Benjamin F., 186
Mower Lucius D., 185
Mower Samuel P., 117

N

Newell Amos, 94
Nickerson Daniel, 96
Nobles Mrs. Hannah A., 217
Nutt John, 39

O

Oakes Ebenezer, 212
Orne (Horn) John, 245

P

Page Isaac, 70
Paine Joshua, 147
Parker George A., 223
Parmenter Elbridge G., 208
Parmenter Ira E., 233
Penfield William, 177
Perley Amos P., 195
Perry Calvin, 119
Perry William, 116
Peverly Horace L., 214
Phelps Andrew J., 229
Phillips Jared L., 191
Pidgin Benjamin G., 158
Pierce Caleb, 56
Pocorney Joseph, 102, 179
Pope Jasper, 140
Porter Benjamin, 21
Potter Charles, 214
Potter Cyrus, 214
Potter James, 145
Potter John, 168
Potter Merrick, 214
Pousland George W., 115
Powers Asa, 129
Powers John, 130

Pratt John B., 192
Pratt Joseph, 76
Pratt Jotham B., 193
Preston Levi, 138
Preston Moses, 62
Price William, 114
Prince Daniel, 70
Proctor Ebenezer, 22
Proctor Elizabeth, 42
Proctor John, 246
Proctor Jonathan, 22, 41, 79
Proctor Nathan, 21, 41
Proctor Nathan S., 78
Proctor Stephen, 40, 61
Proctor Thorndike, 13, 22, 79
Putnam Amos, 60
Putnam Herrick, 175
Putnam Israel, 78
Putnam Martin, 175
Putnam Rufus, 95, 176
Putnam Samuel, 136
Putnam Willard, 205

R

Randall William, 201
Reeves Freeborn, 15
Reeves Samuel, 58
Rhodes Charles B., 206
Rice Edward, 91
Rice Edward G., 171
Rice Franklin P., 233
Rice George E., 172
Rice Minot, 174
Richards Henry L., 233
Richards William, 234
Richards William S., 185
Richardson Abijah, 79
Richardson Joseph, 42, 45
Richardson Malachi, 154
Richardson Willard, 135
Richardson Zaccheus, 69
Robertson Gilman, 113
Robertson Joseph, 58
Robinson Jeremiah, 123
Robinson Nye, 188
Rollins Edward F., 183
Ross Joseph, 46, 84
Rowland George A., 228

S

Samon George, 7
Shaw Jacob, 32
Sheldon Warren, 114
Shules Russell, 98
Shumway Emory, 180
Skelton Samuel, 5
Skidmore Richard, 83
Skidmore Stephen F., 159
Slayton Joshua, 64
Sleeper James, 95
Smead John, 123
Smith Caleb, 176
Smith Heman, 167
Smith Marcellus, 198

Southwick Isaac, 34
Southwick Simeon, 129
Spaulding Abel 147
Sperry James L. 207
Stanton Stephen, 178
Stevens Abraham G., 211
Stevens Daniel W., 209
Stevens Isaac E., 209
Stevens Isaac T., 143
Stevens Levi L., 210
Stevens John S., 209
Stevens William R., 211
Stiles Joseph H., 205
Stimson Charles, 106
Stimson Edward, 106
Stimson Elbridge. 106
Stimson Fordyce M., 183
Stimson Lemuel, 55
Stimson Mirick, 107
Stimson Royal. 106
Stone David, 52
Story Albert G., 215
Stowe Ebenezer V., 212
Stratton William, 171
Stuart Silas, 161

T
Tarbell Charles D., 183
Tarbell Jonathan, 36
Tolman James P., 148
Tompkins John, 244
Tompkins Ralph. 244
Townsend Samuel S., 210
Tuttle Ebenezer H., 112
Twitchell Jonas, 188

U
Upton Franklin, 175
Upton William, 29

V
Vaughan Henry M., 228
Vaughan Jacob, 137

W
Wadsworth Paul, 193
Waite Norvell D., 235
Walcutt Jabez S., 142
Waller Christopher, 8
Ward Francis J., 200
Ward Pemberton, 126
Wardell, Nathaniel, 46
Warner Otis, 155
Wastcoat David W., 156
Waters John, 249
Waters Richard, 248
Watkins Thomas, 12
Weatherwax Andrew, 149
Webber William, 15
Weeks John, 72, 142
Wetherell Sampson, 65, 126
Weymouth Daniel, 159
Whall Joseph B, 169
Wheeler Ager, 163
Wheeler William R., 143
Whitmore Charles S., 183
Whitmore James, 105
Whitmore James H., 182
Whitney Benjamin, 107
Whittemore Stephen, 37
Wiggin Levi, 201
Willard Emory, 101
Williams Isaac, 83
Willis John H., 198
Willson Loten, 189
Wilson John, 80
Wilson Malachi, 81
Wilson Moses W., 97
Wilson Newhall, 81
Wilson Robert, 43, 80
Winter Jonas H., 181
Wood Alonzo, 184
Wood Alonzo F., 164
Wood Frederick W., 163
Wood Luther, 88
Wood Luther H., 229
Wyeth Andrew N., 183
Wyman Levi, 201

INDEX OF OTHER NAMES THAN FELTON.

A
Abbott, 84, 93, 102, 138
Aborne, 22, 244
Adams, 113, 120, 128, 191, 239
Albee, 204
Alexander, 179
Allen, 67, 107, 128, 172, 180, 214
Allerton, 74
Allyn, 141
Ames, 235

Amsden, 109, 128
Andrew, 20
Andrews, 40, 145
Arnold, 119
Ashley, 229
Ashton, 33
Atkins, 200
Atwood, 156, 165
Austick, 126
Austin, 113
Avery, 185, 234
Ayres, 65, 130, 180

B
Babb, 4
Babcock, 167
Bacon, 4
Bailey, 41, 176
Baker, 46, 87, 103, 164, 165
Balch, 14
Baldwin, 108, 140, 224, 225
Ballard, 31, 193
Ballou, 172
Bancroft, 75

FELTON FAMILY.

Banister, 123
Banks, 136
Barber, 173
Barker, 210, 223, 238
Barnes, 25, 87, 118, 190
Barrett, 25, 45, 107, 178
Barthwick, 236
Bartlett, 51, 59, 66, 76, 87, 96, 118, 165, 214, 222
Bartley, 137
Bartol, 224
Barton, 8
Bassett, 246
Batchelder, 80, 120, 121, 195.
Bates, 194, 203, 204
Batter, 244
Beacham, 4, 247
Beal, 4
Beals, 141
Beard, 163
Beebe, 104
Belcher, 111
Bell, 84, 222
Bellows, 190
Benjamin, 54, 100, 101
Bennett, 98
Bent, 169, 178, 198, 223, 238
Berry, 80, 209
Bethune, 91
Bigelow, 88, 100, 142, 143, 161, 181, 208, 229
Bill, 197
Billings, 130, 156, 234
Bingham, 204
Bird, 198
Bishop, 4
Bispham, 210, 211
Blair, 133
Blake, 94, 95
Bliss, 166
Blodgett, 163
Blood, 173
Bly, 7, 111
Boardman, 185
Bond, 178
Bonesteel, 217
Boutwell, 237
Bowden, 4, 33, 127
Bowers, 137, 195, 213
Bowker, 50, 112, 136, 199, 200
Bowles, 133
Bowls, 95
Bowman, 123
Boyd, 230
Boynton, 94, 153, 194
Bradley, 186
Brandt, 195
Brattle, 17
Brentnall, 226
Brewer, 202
Briant, 131

Bridges, 4, 203
Brierly, 122
Briggs, 156
Brigham, 48, 49, 109, 160, 161, 162, 163, 172, 184, 214, 222, 229
Brock, 100
Bromley, 119, 191, 192
Brooks, 76, 110, 165
Brown, 4, 15, 42, 79, 84, 109, 128, 138, 140
Brownell 150
Bruce, 169, 171
Bryant, 157
Buck, 190
Bucklin, 214
Buckman, 42
Bugbee, 65
Bullard, 123, 124, 125
Bullock, 4
Bumpus, 154
Burbank, 235
Burdett, 214
Burditt, 209
Burgess, 111
Burke, 34, 186
Burnap, 50
Burnett, 134, 136, 205
Burnham, 141, 142, 198
Burrows, 157
Burt, 175
Butler, 175, 222
Butman, 239
Buxton, 248

C

Caldwell, 107
Calhoun, 112
Camp, 107
Canfield, 53, 137
Cantlebury, 4
Card, 83
Carpenter, 134
Carter, 121
Cary, 219
Case, 170
Casebeer, 150
Cassidy, 143
Chamberlain, 105, 106, 131, 133, 182, 186, 194, 197, 204, 205, 212, 234, 237
Chamnese, 15
Chandler, 53
Chapman, 199, 239
Chase, 204
Chatfield, 163
Cheever, 70
Childs, 165
Chilson, 104
Chipman, 166
Chittenden, 237
Choate, 136, 174, 222
Church, 25
Churchill, 200

Claffin, 202
Clapp, 179
Clarke, 20, 90, 113, 176, 177, 178, 194, 195, 215
Clement, 99
Cleveland, 77, 232
Clifford, 201, 202
Clough, 95, 159, 212
Coats, 135
Cobleigh, 102
Cobley, 142
Coffeen, 172
Cogswell, 135
Colby, 79
Cole, 47
Colehorne, 4
Collins, 96
Compton, 199
Comstock, 235
Conant, 111
Cone, 126
Coukey, 36
Connable, 82
Conway, 76, 153
Cook, 38, 116, 161
Coolidge, 23, 69, 101
Cooms, 8
Cooper, 100, 110
Corneins, 115
Cotlee, 189
Cotting, 229
Covell, 137
Cowles, 217, 233
Cox, 158
Crafts, 104
Cragin, 31
Cramm, 101
Crandall, 72, 128
Crane, 46, 237
Cranston, 86
Crawford, 124
Crensey, 40
Cressey, 12
Crissey, 188
Crocker, 201
Crosby, 122
Crossit, 99
Crowninshield, 240
Culver, 196
Cummings, 104, 148
Currier, 114, 221
Curtis, 32, 64, 192
Cutter, 180
Cutting, 164, 232

D

Daggett, 24
Dailey, 163, 176, 210
Daland, 15, 28, 41, 57, 58, 68, 81, 116, 249
Dame, 170
Damon, 111, 178, 179
Dane, 158
Danforth, 103

Darling, 75, 110, 157
Davenport. 184
Davis,80, 94. 104, 106. 166, 175. 182. 183. 193, 227
Day, 168. 176. 183
Deane, 126. 179, 180, 237
De Camp, 197
Decartes. 198
Dennis, 8
Derby. 84. 111, 222
Derrick, 159
Dexter, 25, 196
Dickinson. 63, 82
Doak, 52. 76
Dodd, 127
Dodge, 28, 52, 128
Dole, 20
Dorchin, 191
Dorrity, 63
Douglas, 177
Drake, 142
Draper, 87
Drown, 185
Drury, 66. 132
Dudley, 135, 178, 230
Duncan, 187
Dunham, 125
Dunton, 181
Durfield, 196
Dyer, 167

E

Eames, 204
Earle, 79
Early, 247
Eastman. 175
Eaton, 100. 202
Edwards. 222
Ellery, 82
Elliot, 71, 82, 140
Ellis, 75, 117, 184, 187
Emerson, 122, 143
Emery, 126
Endicott, 4, 5, 13, 17, 20, 21, 40, 77. 78, 168
English, 8
Eppes, 17, 51, 57,70, 71
Estabrook. 179
Everett, 219, 221
Ewell, 103

F

Fairbanks,63, 112,178, 197, 209
Farley, 221
Farlow, 217
Farnham, 108
Farnum, 58, 101
Farr, 187
Farrar, 103, 181, 222
Farrell, 132
Farrow, 103
Farwell. 221
Fay, 86, 162, 166, 211

Felt, 4, 29
Ferrin, 53, 207
Fessenden, 234
Field, 186
Filkins, 176
Fish, 104. 159
Fisher, 45, 65, 147
Fiske, 112, 228
Fitts, 31
Flagg, 95
Flint, 21. 245
Floyd, 140, 239
Foot, 14. 17, 203, 247
Forbes, 148
Foster, 17, 20, 23, 30, 31, 62, 63, 106, 126, 130, 244
Fowle, 21
Fowler, 53
Frayll, 5
Freeman, 168, 202
French, 178, 179
Frost, 47, 206
Frye,70, 129. 137, 165,231 232
Fuller,4,9, 53, 80, 105,106 222

G

Gaffin, 129
Gale, 39, 75, 76, 199
Ganson, 63
Gardner, 158, 246
Gary, 97
Gaskill, 5
Gassett, 51
Gates, 72, 157
Gay, 160, 229
Gerrill, 66
Gerry, 40
Gibbs, 231
Gibson, 202
Giddings, 77
Gilbert, 214
Giles, 145. 200
Gill, 111
Gilman, 140, 222
Given, 216
Gleason, 211
Glidden, 121
Glover, 33
Godfrey, 132
Goldsmith. 80
Goldthwaite. 4
Good, 191
Goodale, 4, 15, 25, 29, 55, 61, 174, 247, 248
Goodell, 248
Goodhue, 58
Goodnough, 75, 151, 218
Goss, 176
Gott, 6, 7
Gould, 4, 51, 66, 78, 134, 138

Goulding, 200
Gratton. 7
Grant, 142, 163
Graves. 127
Gray, 77. 84, 124, 196
Green, 123, 124, 152, 198
Greenleaf, 221
Greenwood, 80, 154
Grey. 188
Grout, 17, 33, 134
Guild, 38, 74, 147
Guilford, 110

H

Hadley, 140
Hager, 143
Hale, 65
Halfpenny, 39
Hall, 93, 108, 113, 150, 190
Hamilton, 63, 64, 119, 238
Hamlin, 24
Hammond, 198, 237
Handley, 179
Hapgood, 212, 213
Hardy, 47, 48, 49, 78, 114
Harris, 107, 111, 157
Harwood, 68
Haskell, 115, 116, 169, 175, 228
Haskins, 104, 182
Hastings, 171
Hawes, 137, 144
Hawkes, 77, 203
Hawthorne, 7, 20
Haynes, 47, 245
Hayward, 57
Haywood, 32, 33
Hay, 79
Healey, 193
Heath, 24
Henderson, 121
Henry. 193
Herrick, 13, 20, 21, 80
Hervey, 246
Hickock, 53
Higgins, 157
Higginson, 5
High, 127
Hill, 57, 112, 164
Hillyer, 185, 234
Hinckley, 148
Hinds, 31, 118
Hinsdale, 228
Hoar, 157
Hobart, 189
Hodge, 190, 249
Hodges, 164, 173
Hodskin, 129
Hogan, 100
Holbrook, 101, 188
Holden, 69, 131, 170, 203
Hallowell, 121
Holman, 89, 196
Holt, 29, 40, 52

FELTON FAMILY.

Holyoke, 89, 211, 212, 214, 231
Honey, 209
Hooker, 190
Hooper, 39, 131
Horton, 216
Houghton, 126
Houlton, 5, 8, 10, 12, 14, 17, 22, 28, 31, 34, 63, 67, 68, 116, 245, 249
Houston, 197
Howard, 83, 134, 181
Howe, 15, 25, 26, 27, 48, 50, 51, 56, 57, 63, 73, 89, 94, 95, 109, 110, 111, 112, 161, 184, 206, 210, 231, 248
Howell, 185, 234
Hoyt, 64, 123, 196
Hudson, 67
Hunt, 50, 72, 82, 100, 103, 127, 142, 180, 186
Hunter, 37
Hunting, 92
Huntington, 171, 172, 209, 233
Hurlburt, 133
Hutchins, 185
Hutchinson, 198
Hyde, 182, 183

I
Ide, 184
Ingalls, 247
Ingersoll, 8, 245
Irish, 193

J
Jackman, 232
Jackson, 55, 105
Jacobs, 14, 20, 22, 23, 24, 40, 102, 179, 180
James, 4
Jenkins, 93, 126
Jennison, 101
Jewell, 154, 226
Jewett, 229
Job, 236
Johnson, 12, 53, 54, 56, 85, 86, 99, 100, 119, 125, 163, 166, 174, 175, 177, 178, 179, 243
Jones, 20, 21, 33
Joslyn, 160

K
Kafity, 128
Keeleo, 180
Keger, 176
Keith, 193
Kellogg, 31, 67, 135, 181
Kelley, 211
Kemfield, 39
Kemp, 100

Kendall, 18, 47, 49, 68, 112, 116, 127, 140
Kendrick, 121, 196
Kennedy, 154
Kenney, 41
Kent, 43, 46, 80
Keyes, 100, 106
Kidder, 107
Kimball, 33
King, 68, 178
Kirk, 165
Knapp, 54, 99
Knight, 94, 117
Knights, 42
Knowlton, 82, 122, 155
Knox, 130

L
LaCroix, 196
Ladd, 143
LaFayette, 161
Lamb, 33, 130
Lamson, 211
Lander, 52, 97
Langley, 127
Larkin, 66
Lawrence, 45
Leak, 69
Learned, 167
Leatherbee, 173
Leavens, 181
Lee, 104, 121
LeFevre, 240
Leighton, 162
Leland, 160
Leonard, 130, 156, 180, 201, 202
Lewis, 116, 148, 210
Libbey, 198
Lick, 225
Liffitt, 223
Lilley, 66
Lincoln, 44, 62, 81, 154, 155, 203, 214, 222, 226
Littlefield, 93, 138
Livermore, 23, 24
Lloyd, 133
Locker, 5
Lockwood, 117, 186
Logan, 104
Loker, 178
Long, 169, 170, 237
Longee, 168
Longfellow, 219
Longley, 129
Lord, 7, 105, 168
Loring, 179
Lorlett, 191
Lovell, 102
Lowell, 219, 221
Lovejoy, 109, 178
Lyman, 174
Lynch, 214
Lyon, 194

Lyons, 158

M
McCabe, 177
McClelland, 218
McClenning, 80
McCully, 200
McDonnell, 92
McIntosh, 147
McIvor, 237
McLyman, 217
Macomber, 131
Mackey, 167
Mackintire, 16, 28, 29, 52, 58, 97, 124
Mahan, 166
Mann, 228
Manning, 8
Mansfield, 175
Manson, 160, 185, 228
Marble, 20
Marsh, 4, 5, 6, 13, 139, 178, 192, 245
Marston, 6, 9
Martin, 38, 78, 128, 195, 240
Mason, 181
Masters, 247
Maxon, 151
May, 152
Maynard, 49, 142, 170, 171, 208, 232
Meacham, 9
Mead, 176
Melvin, 33
Mendum, 179
Merell, 136
Merley, 204
Merrill, 61, 115
Miller, 57, 194
Miles, 7
Millet, 76
Millington, 177
Miner, 179
Mitchell, 239
Mock, 162
Montague, 213
Moody, 104, 169, 181, 182
Moor, 157
Moore, 101, 143
More, 85
Morey, 126
Morgram, 84
Morse, 73, 76, 90, 146, 153, 154, 185, 215
Moulton, 100
Mower, 117, 185, 186
Mudge, 127, 139
Mussey, 58
Myers, 126

N
Neal, 35, 138
Needham, 13, 19
Newell, 94, 129

Newhall, 103
Newton, 37, 122, 165
Nichols, 37, 60, 63
Nickerson, 96, 155
Nobles, 217
Norton, 219, 226
Nourse, 20, 80
Nutt, 39, 40
Nye, 65, 125

O

Oakes, 140, 212
Olds, 82
Oliver, 55, 146
Olmstead, 217
Orcutt, 69, 193
Orne, 13, 17, 40, 245
Osborne, 40, 60, 121, 190, 195
Osgood, 82

P

Paddock, 94
Page 67, 70, 77, 167
Paine, 147
Palfrey, 219
Palmer, 155, 206
Park, 171
Parker, 43, 77, 94, 181, 189, 203, 220, 223, 224
Parks, 178
Parmenter, 72, 142, 208, 233
Parnell, 84
Partridge, 209
Patch, 72
Pattee, 44
Patterson, 142
Payson, 111, 208
Peabody, 51
Penfield, 177
Percival, 182
Perkins, 48, 76, 92, 163
Perley, 121, 195
Perry, 116, 119, 210
Peters, 6, 223, 249
Peverly, 214
Phelps, 160, 166
Phillips, 132, 146, 169, 191
Pidgin, 158
Pierce, 56, 58, 69, 177, 188
Pike, 139
Piper, 73
Pitman, 13, 17
Plaise, 248
Pocorney, 102, 179
Pond, 24, 45, 46
Poor 84
Pope, 121, 140, 248
Porter, 6, 13, 15, 21, 40, 44, 52, 62, 66, 92, 121
Potter, 21, 115, 145, 168, 213, 214, 215
Pousland, 115

Powell, 105
Powers, 76, 85, 104, 129, 130
Pratt, 20, 65, 76, 93, 119, 135, 158, 192, 193
Prentiss, 33
Prescott, 32, 132
Preston, 8, 39, 52, 62, 138
Prey, 114
Price, 114, 200
Prichard, 37
Priest, 167, 228
Prince, 7, 70, 71
Proctor, 4, 12, 13, 14, 15, 20, 21, 22, 30, 40, 41, 42, 43, 59, 61, 62, 68, 71, 78, 79, 97, 246, 247
Puffer, 54
Putnam, 8, 20, 52, 59, 60, 63, 69, 77, 78, 95, 96, 116, 120, 136, 166, 173, 175, 176, 205, 245
Pynchon, 45

Q

Quimby, 236

R

Ralston, 232
Ramsdell, 74
Ramswell, 45
Randall, 128, 201
Ranney, 140
Rawson, 137
Ray, 40, 70, 116
Raymond, 103, 151, 191
Redding, 187
Redington, 182
Read, 244
Reed, 14, 21, 54, 97, 121
Reeves, 15, 58
Reynolds, 67, 70
Rhoades, 206, 239, 248
Rice, 25, 26, 87, 91, 110, 122, 143, 170, 171, 172, 174, 239
Rich, 35
Richards, 74, 185, 231, 234, 246
Richardson, 24, 31, 42, 45, 69, 79, 135, 136, 154, 201, 227
Ridout, 126
Riley, 145
Ritchie, 217
Rix, 4, 6
Robbins, 198
Roberts, 107
Robertson, 58, 113
Robinson, 50, 122, 123, 158, 188, 189
Rogers, 47, 54
Rollins, 106, 183
Root, 156
Ropes, 8
Ross, 46, 47, 84
Rowland, 228
Ruggles, 23

Russell, 79, 91, 162, 189, 197
Ryder, 191

S

Saben, 188
St. John, 159
Salisbury, 210
Salmon, 9
Samon, 7, 9
Sampson, 74, 147
Sanderson, 48, 170
Sanford, 6
Sargent, 217, 243
Saulsbury, 107
Savage, 7, 193
Sawyer, 158, 166
Scammon, 159
Scarlett, 6
Scofield, 150
Scott, 91, 189
Sears, 130
Seaver, 105
Sedge, 146
Senter, 168
Severy, 111
Shafer, 109
Shattuck, 113
Shaw, 32, 67, 128, 129, 137, 231
Shedd, 155
Sheldon, 13, 17, 114
Shepard, 124
Sherman, 142, 150
Shules, 98
Shumway, 180
Sias, 85
Simmons, 102
Simpson, 212
Skelton, 5, 11, 21, 78
Skidmore, 83, 84, 159
Skinner, 33, 83, 157
Slade, 147
Slayton, 64, 65
Sleeper, 95
Sloan, 172
Smead, 123
Smith, 5, 27, 29, 31, 46, 50, 56, 66, 91, 92, 116, 124, 129, 147, 148, 167, 176, 177, 198, 204, 216, 222, 246
Snyder, 158
Southack, 132
Souther, 81, 154
Southwick, 19, 34, 35, 80, 129
Sparks, 218
Sparrow, 105
Spaulding, 146
Speller, 229
Spelman, 134
Spencer, 66
Sperry, 206, 207
Sprague, 28, 51
Spring, 92
Stackpole, 119
Stacy, 35
Stanton, 178
Stedry, 216

Stephens, 181
Stetson, 23
Stevens, 115, 124, 143, 144, 152, 158, 209, 210, 211, 227, 246
Stickney, 140
Stiles, 205
Stimson, 55, 105, 106, 107, 183
Stinson, 168
Stone, 5, 52, 53, 54, 115, 145, 166
Story, 114, 146, 215
Stowe, 48, 144, 166, 182, 212
Stratton, 111, 170, 171, 172
Strong, 177
Strope, 75
Stuart, 161
Sumner, 165
Swain, 108
Swan, 199
Swinton, 51
Sweet, 236
Symmons, 42
Symonds, 240

T

Tabor, 44
Tarbell, 36, 37, 107, 183
Tappan, 80
Tate, 81
Taylor, 14, 182
Temple, 94, 142, 202, 208
Tenney, 82, 156
Thayer, 205, 224
Thomas, 68
Thompson, 116, 119, 170, 246
Thorndike, 246
Thurston, 43, 71, 202
Tillotson, 137
Tisdale, 135
Todd, 82, 156
Tolman, 148
Tompkins, 4, 11, 244
Topliff, 132
Torrey, 195
Towne, 77, 97
Townsend, 210, 229
Tracy, 74, 82, 155
Trask, 31, 70
Trumbull, 45

Tubbs, 171
Tucker, 119, 127, 192, 197
Tupper, 122
Turner, 33, 193
Tuttle, 112
Twitchell, 165, 188, 213, 234
Tyler, 121, 195

U

Usher, 198
Upham, 5
Upton, 16, 24, 28, 29, 70, 122, 175

V

Valentine, 228
Van Doom, 90
Vaughan, 137, 228
Very, 246, 247
Vose, 143

W

Wadsworth, 193
Waite, 44, 235
Walcutt, 142, 143
Waldo, 80
Walker, 105, 179
Wallace, 145
Waller, 4, 8, 9
Walls, 67
Walsh, 140
Ward, 18, 25, 50, 73, 126, 129, 146, 200
Wardell, 44, 46
Warner, 82, 116, 155
Warren, 136
Wason, 168
Wastcoat, 82, 156
Waterman, 186
Waters, 16, 41, 244, 248
Watkins, 12, 13
Watson, 95
Weatherwax, 75, 149
Webb, 96, 231
Webber, 15
Webster, 136
Weeks, 38, 54, 72, 89, 115, 142, 143
Wells, 105
Wesson, 46
West, 239
Wetherell, 65, 66, 100, 126, 127

Weymouth, 159, 227
Whall, 169
Wheeler, 54, 67, 129, 135, 143, 157, 163
Whelan, 7
Whipple, 21, 74, 248
White, 100, 121
Whiting, 36
Whitlock, 97
Whitmore, 105, 106, 182, 183
Whitney, 107, 111, 166, 183, 202, 213, 219
Whiton, 155
Whittaker, 157
Whittemore, 37, 101, 141
Whittredge, 141
Whitwell, 215
Wiggin, 206
Wilder, 27, 53, 148
Wilkins, 59, 84, 89, 210
Willard, 101, 102, 199
Williams, 6, 17, 18, 25, 31, 33, 35, 37, 43, 44, 45, 193
Willis, 198
Willson, 31, 189, 235
Wilson, 6, 14, 22, 43, 79, 80, 81, 97, 171, 175
Winchester, 150, 152
Wing, 174
Winslow, 191
Winter, 181, 182
Withington, 173
Withridge, 246
Witt, 248
Wood, 57, 71, 88, 95, 111, 141, 163, 164, 184, 210, 229
Woodard, 99
Woodman, 159
Woodrow, 9
Woods, 135
Woodworth, 233
Wright, 17, 96, 116
Wyatt, 67
Wyeth, 105, 183
Wyman, 113

Y

Young, 98, 115, 204, 209

Z

Zimgiebel, 183